T0305179

Asset Pricing Theory

Asset Pricing Theory
IS PART OF THE
PRINCETON SERIES IN FINANCE

SERIES EDITORS

Darrell Duffie   Stephen Schaefer
Stanford University   *London Business School*

Finance as a discipline has been growing rapidly. The numbers of researchers in academy and industry, of students, of methods and models have all proliferated in the past decade or so. This growth and diversity manifests itself in the emerging cross-disciplinary as well as cross-national mix of scholarship now driving the field of finance forward. The intellectual roots of modern finance, as well as its branches, are represented in the Princeton Series in Finance.

Titles in this series are scholarly and professional books, intended to be read by a mixed audience of economists, mathematicians, operations research scientists, financial engineers, and other investment professionals. The goal is to provide the finest cross-disciplinary work in all areas of finance by widely recognized researchers in the prime of their creative careers.

OTHER BOOKS IN THIS SERIES

Financial Econometrics: Problems, Models, and Methods by Christian Gourieroux and Joann Jasiak

Credit Risk: Pricing, Measurement, and Management by Darrell Duffie and Kenneth J. Singleton

Microfoundations of Financial Economics: An Introduction to General Equilibrium Asset Pricing by Yvan Lengwiler

Credit Risk Modeling: Theory and Applications by David Lando

Quantitative Risk Management: Concepts, Techniques, and Tools by Alexander J. McNeil, Rudiger Frey, and Paul Embrechts

Asset Pricing Theory

Costis Skiadas

PRINCETON UNIVERSITY PRESS

PRINCETON AND OXFORD

Copyright © 2009 by Princeton University Press
Published by Princeton University Press, 41 William Street,
Princeton, New Jersey 08540
In the United Kingdom: Princeton University Press,
6 Oxford Street, Woodstock, Oxfordshire OX20 1TW

Library of Congress Cataloging-in-Publication Data

Skiadas, Costis, 1965–
Asset pricing theory / Costis Skiadas.
p. cm.—(Princeton series in finance)
Includes bibliographical references and index.
ISBN 978-0-691-13985-2 (hardcover : alk. paper)   1. Capital assets
pricing model.   2. Finance—Mathematical models.   I. Title.
HG4636.S55 2009
338.4'30001—dc22   2008039426

British Library Cataloging-in-Publication Data is available

This book has been composed in Times New Roman MT Std

Printed on acid-free paper. ∞

press.princeton.edu

Printed in the United States of America

1   2   3   4   5   6   7   8   9   10

As this is a book about time and uncertainty,
it is dedicated to
my parents, *Βάνα* and *Νίκο*,
and my children, *Alison* and *Elaine*.

Contents

Preface

THIS BOOK IS an advanced introduction to the theory of competitive asset pricing and optimal consumption/portfolio choice, intended mainly for doctoral students and academic researchers in the area. As a theory text, it organizes classic arguments, with some new twists and even original results, without taking a stand on their empirical validity. Far from being comprehensive, the choice of material is guided by a focused view of the subject that minimizes essential economic assumptions, while maintaining simplicity through mathematical restrictions that do no harm to the economics. The expositional style is spartan and should appeal to readers with a taste for mathematical rigor. At the same time great emphasis is placed on the economic soundness of arguments throughout. As such the book is addressed to economists with an interest in mathematical methods in finance, as well as mathematically minded readers with an interest in the economics of finance. The material is limited to the case of finitely many states and time periods, yet it is presented from an advanced perspective that should ease the transition to models with infinitely many states and continuous time. The exposition is largely self-contained, although prior knowledge of basic linear algebra and probability theory is helpful if not essential.

The book is organized in two parts and two appendices. In Part I, the uncertainty model consists of only a single time period and finitely many states, while Part II deals with the extension of the theory to a finite information tree. By adopting a geometric viewpoint, and sufficiently abstract language, the material of Part I applies with little or no change in notation to the multiperiod setting. Part II introduces tools that pave the way for understanding continuous-time models, which are typically covered in a second course on asset pricing. Appendix A is an introduction to convex optimization theory and should be read concurrently with Part I. Appendix B is an introduction to stochastic analysis and should be read concurrently with Part II. As with the main text, the formal development of the appendices anticipates the needs of the more advanced theory. For example, the finite-tree treatment of martingale representation and Girsanov's theorem in Appendix B should help demystify topics that are typically introduced in the context of Brownian motion.

I have used Part I, with Appendix A, to teach a ten-week first Ph.D. course on asset pricing theory. I have used Part II, with Appendix B, to teach the first five weeks of a second Ph.D. course on asset pricing theory, followed with the continuous-time theory, using Duffie (2001) and my handbook chapter (Skiadas (2008)) on continuous-time recursive utility and its use in optimal consumption/portfolio choice. The audience in my classes consisted of Ph.D. students in finance, economics, engineering and mathematics.

Advanced readers will recognize that the expositional approach is largely novel and that several results go beyond the existing literature. A main example of this is Chapter 6, which presents a finite-information-tree theory of equilibrium pricing and optimal consumption/portfolio choice under recursive utility. For instance, in the homothetic case, it is invariably assumed in the literature that recursive utility takes the so-called Epstein-Zin-Weil parametric form. This form belongs to a larger class of homothetic, or "scale-invariant," recursive utilities, whose use in Chapter 6 simplifies and clarifies the structure of the theory and reveals the implications of ad hoc aspects of the common parameterization. A theory of "translation-invariant" recursive utility, a generalization of expected discounted exponential utility, is also presented. As explained in the chapter's endnotes, these results are finite-information versions of analogous continuous-time results that appear in my joint research papers with Mark Schroder.

To further whet the advanced reader's appetite, here is a short sample of other novelties. Chapter 2 proves an apparently new bound on the error in the calculation of Sharpe ratios through beta pricing, as a result of using a proxy rather than a true beta-pricing portfolio return. Chapter 3 gives a new definition of an "effectively complete market," loosely speaking, as a market in which a financial innovator cannot offer desirable trades for a fee and then unload all positions in the existing market. Allocations of effectively complete market equilibria are shown to be allocations of Arrow-Debreu equilibria, essentially providing a variant of the usual competitive-equilibrium welfare analysis. Chapter 4 gives a new definition of a risk-averse agent as one who rejects, incrementally to a deterministic payoff, any scaled-up version of a rejected trade. This definition is less restrictive than more standard ones yet reduces to the same concavity condition in the context of expected utility. Chapter 5 offers an arbitrage-pricing theory of a generalized notion of American option, where the option holder can select, without commitment, an entire cash flow out of a given opportunity set, rather than just an exercise time. The associated arbitrage-pricing argument weakens the usual market completeness assumption and deals formally with the potentially suboptimal choice of the option buyer in the scenario in which the arbitrageur has to write the option.

Every chapter is concluded with bibliographical notes, which are not, and are not intended to be, comprehensive. While I have tried to find some of the earliest references, including a few I think the literature has not attributed proper credit to, I did not attempt to provide a proper history of the ideas; the choice of references is clearly biased by my personal path through the subject.

Acknowledgments: This book owes its existence to all the Ph.D. students who have suffered in my classes over the years. Among them, Costel Andonie, Evren Baysal, Kevin Crotty, Flavio de Andrade, Vadim de Pietro, David Dicks, Joey Engelberg, Zhiguo He, Andrei Jirnyi, Soohun Kim, Srikant Marakani, Sorin Maruster, Ioan Mirciov, Mallesh Pai, George Skoulakis, Kane Sweeney, Jared Williams and Kostas Zachariadis caught an embarrassing number of mistakes, or made good suggestions. The feedback of Maruster, Mirciov and Skoulakis was particularly useful in making substantial improvements. In various stages of this project, I have benefited from general discussions with Peter DeMarzo, Darrell Duffie, Mark Loewenstein, Marco Scarcini and Dimitri Vayanos, who as a result have had some indirect impact on the outcome. I appreciate the encouragement I received from George Constantinides. I am grateful to Mark Schroder for reading the manuscript and providing useful feedback, as well as all the great fun we've been having cooperating on research. I thank Jonathan Parker for testing this text in his class and for providing constructive feedback. I am deeply indebted to Darrell Duffie for introducing me to the subject as a graduate student and his continued encouragement and inspiration ever since.

Notation and Conventions

To the extent possible, mathematical notation and conventions follow common practice, as reflected in mainstream texts on real analysis, linear algebra, and probability theory. Some clarifications are listed below.

"$\Longrightarrow$" means "implies."

"$\Longleftrightarrow$" means "is equivalent to."

$\cup$ denotes set union.

$\cap$ denotes set intersection.

$\mathbb{R} = (-\infty, \infty)$ = set of real numbers.

$\mathbb{R}_+ = [0, \infty)$ = set of **nonnegative** reals.

$\mathbb{R}_{++} = (0, \infty)$ = set of **positive** reals.

$A \times B = \{(a, b) : a \in A, \ b \in B\}$, for any sets A and B.

$S_1 \times \cdots \times S_n = \{(s_1, \ldots, s_n) : s_i \in S_i \text{ all } i\}$, for any sets $S_1, \ldots, S_n$.

$S^n = \{(s_1, \ldots, s_n) : s_i \in S \text{ all } i\}$, for any set S; for example,

$$\mathbb{R}^n_+ = \{x \in \mathbb{R}^n : x_i \geq 0 \text{ all } i\} \quad \text{and} \quad \mathbb{R}^n_{++} = \{x \in \mathbb{R}^n : x_i > 0 \text{ all } i\}.$$

Elements of S^n are treated as row vectors, unless otherwise indicated.

For $x, y \in \mathbb{R}^n$, $x \geq y \Longleftrightarrow x_i \geq y_i$ all i.

A function f is **nondecreasing** if $x \geq y$ implies $f(x) \geq f(y)$.

A function f is **increasing** if $x \geq y \neq x$ implies $f(x) > f(y)$.

Either superscripts or subscripts are used to index rows and columns.

x' denotes the transpose or the derivative of x, depending on the context.

For any $x, y \in \mathbb{R}^n$, $x \cdot y = \sum_{i=1}^n x_i y_i$.

$\mathbf{1}$ is a vector of ones whose dimensionality is implied by the context.

If $x \in \mathbb{R}^n$ and $\alpha \in \mathbb{R}$, then $x + \alpha = x + \alpha\mathbf{1} = (x_1 + \alpha, \ldots, x_n + \alpha)$.

If x and y are scalars or random variables,

$$x \vee y = \max\{x, y\}, \quad x \wedge y = \min\{x, y\},$$
$$x^+ = x \vee 0, \quad x^- = -(x \wedge 0), \quad |x| = x^+ + x^-.$$

For random variables, these expressions are interpreted state by state; for example, $(x \wedge y)(\omega) = x(\omega) \wedge y(\omega)$ for every state ω.

PART ONE

SINGLE-PERIOD ANALYSIS

CHAPTER ONE

Financial Market and Arbitrage

AGENTS TRADE in financial markets in order to transfer funds across time and states of nature. Transfers across time correspond to saving or borrowing. Transfers across states of nature correspond to hedging or speculation. This chapter introduces a simple and highly idealized model that captures this basic function of financial markets and will also serve as a building block in the dynamic extension of Part II. Within this simple model, we develop the foundations of arbitrage-pricing theory. The mathematical background for Chapters 1 and 2 is contained in the first seven sections of Appendix A.

1.1 MARKET AND ARBITRAGE

There are two times, labeled zero and one. At time zero there is no uncertainty, while at time one there are K possible **states** that can prevail, labeled $1, 2, \ldots, K$. We treat time zero and each of the K states in an integrated fashion and we refer to them as **spots**. There are therefore $1 + K$ spots, labeled $0, 1, \ldots, K$.

A **cash flow** is a vector of the form $c = (c_0, c_1, \ldots, c_K) \in \mathbb{R}^{1+K}$. Alternatively, a cash flow c can be thought of as the **stochastic process** $(c(0), c(1))$, where $c(0) = c_0$ and $c(1) \in \mathbb{R}^K$ is a **random variable** taking the value $c(1)_k = c_k$ at state k. We assume that each c_k is real-valued, representing a spot-contingent payment in some unit of account. We regard the set of cash flows as an inner-product space with the usual Euclidean inner product:

$$x \cdot y = \sum_{k=0}^{K} x_k y_k.$$

The **Arrow cash flow** corresponding to spot k is denoted $\mathbf{1}^k$ and is defined by

$$\mathbf{1}_l^k = \begin{cases} 1, & \text{if } l = k; \\ 0, & \text{if } l \neq k. \end{cases}$$

In particular, $\mathbf{1}^0 = (1, 0, \ldots, 0)$. The Arrow cash flows correspond to the usual Euclidean basis of $\mathbb{R}^{1+K}$ and therefore every cash flow is a linear combination of Arrow cash flows.

A financial market can be thought of as a set X of net incremental cash flows that can be obtained by trading financial contracts such as bonds, stocks, futures, options and swaps. In this text, we consider perfectly competitive markets, that is, markets in which every trader has negligible market power and therefore takes the terms and prices of contracts as given. Unless otherwise indicated, we also assume that there are no position limits or short sale constraints, there are no transaction costs such as bid-ask spreads and no indivisibilities such as minimum amounts that one can trade in any one contract.

The above informal assumptions motivate the following formal properties of the set of traded cash flows X:

1. $x, y \in X$ implies $x + y \in X$.
2. $x \in X$ and $\alpha \in \mathbb{R}_+$ implies $\alpha x \in X$.
3. $x \in X$ implies $-x \in X$.

Conditions 1 and 2 mean that trades can be combined and arbitrarily scaled. They both hold if and only if X is a convex cone. Condition 3 means that the reverse to every trade is also a possible trade. Conditions 2 and 3 combined imply the possibility of short-selling. A convex cone X satisfies condition 3 if and only if X is a linear subspace, motivating the following formal definition of a market.

Definition 1.1. *A **market** is a linear subspace X of the set of cash flows* $\mathbb{R}^{1+K}$.

A market X is taken as given throughout this chapter. We call its elements the **traded cash flows** or just **trades**. We are interested in the implications of the assumption that the market X contains no arbitrage opportunities. An arbitrage is a trade that results in an inflow at some spot and an outflow at no spot. For example, if two securities trade at different prices but generate identical future cash flows, a trader can short the relatively more expensive security and buy the relatively cheaper one, generating cash at time zero with no subsequent net cash flow. (The impossibility of this special type of arbitrage is known as the "law of one price" and is further discussed in the exercises.) In a perfectly competitive market there are no impediments to immediately exploiting arbitrage opportunities, which consequently cannot exist in equilibrium. Equilibrium will be formalized in Chapter 3. In this chapter we directly impose the no-arbitrage assumption and explore its consequences.

Definition 1.2. *A cash flow c is an **arbitrage** if $0 \neq c \geq 0$. The market X is **arbitrage-free** if it contains no arbitrage.*

We note that the market X is arbitrage-free if and only if it intersects the positive orthant of $\mathbb{R}^{1+K}$ only at zero, that is, $X \cap \mathbb{R}_+^{1+K} = \{0\}$.

Trades are often implemented by spot or forward trading of some asset. Formally, we model an **asset** as a random variable $D \in \mathbb{R}^K$, representing a time-one payoff. The scalar S is a **spot price** of the asset D if $(-S, D) \in X$. The scalar F is a **forward price** of the asset D if $(0, D - F\mathbf{1}) \in X$. A **unit discount bond** is the asset $\mathbf{1}$, that is, the asset that pays one at every state. A **risk-free discount factor** is a spot price of the unit discount bond, that is, any scalar ρ such that $(-\rho, \mathbf{1}) \in X$. In an arbitrage-free market an asset has at most one spot price and at most one forward price. In particular, there can be at most one risk-free discount factor, which is necessarily strictly positive.

Proposition 1.3. *Suppose the market is arbitrage-free and ρ is a (necessarily unique) risk-free discount factor. If S is the spot price of an asset D and F is the forward price of D, then $S = F\rho$.*

Proof. Adding up the trades $(-S, D), (0, F\mathbf{1} - D), (F\rho, -F\mathbf{1}) \in X$ implies $(F\rho - S)\mathbf{1}^0 \in X$. Since $\mathbf{1}^0 \notin X$, it follows that $S = F\rho$. ∎

Proposition 1.3 exemplifies a typical arbitrage argument. The three trades of the proof represent what is known as a **cash-and-carry arbitrage**: buy the asset in the spot market, sell it forward and borrow the present value of the forward payment. If $S < F\rho$, then the result is the positive inflow $F\rho - S$ at time zero, with no subsequent cash flow. If $S > F\rho$, a **reverse cash-and-carry arbitrage** is achieved by reversing the above trades. Trading constraints limit the arbitrage argument. For example, if the potential arbitrageur has no current inventory of the asset and cannot sell the asset short in the spot market, then reverse cash-and-carry arbitrage is not possible and therefore the possibility that $S > F\rho$ cannot be excluded. We return to this issue in Section 1.7.

5

1.2 PRESENT VALUE AND STATE PRICES

A dual approach to arbitrage pricing is based on the following notion of present value.

Definition 1.4. *A **present-value function** is a linear function of the form* $\Pi : \mathbb{R}^{1+K} \to \mathbb{R}$ *with the following three properties:*

1. $\Pi(x) \leq 0$ *for every* $x \in X$.
2. $\Pi(c) > 0$ *for every arbitrage cash flow* c.
3. $\Pi(\mathbf{1}^0) = 1$.

The first restriction on Π can be thought of as an expression of the perfect competition assumption, which implies that there cannot be a net trade of strictly positive value. Since X is a linear subspace, condition 1 is equivalent to $\Pi(x) = 0$ for all $x \in X$. In Section 1.7 we relax the assumption that X is a linear subspace to allow for trading constraints, in which case the present value of a traded cash flow can be strictly negative. The second restriction on Π expresses the assumption that an arbitrage is valuable to every agent and therefore must be assigned a positive value by any present-value rule. The first two restrictions on Π together rule out arbitrage trades. The last restriction on Π is merely a normalization.

A simple example of the use of a present-value function in deriving arbitrage restrictions follows.

Example 1.5. *Suppose* Π *is a present-value function and* S *is the spot price of an asset* D. *Applying the restriction* $\Pi(x) = 0$ *to the trade* $x = (-S, D) = -S\mathbf{1}^0 + (0, D)$ *and using the linearity of* Π *and the fact that* $\Pi(\mathbf{1}^0) = 1$, *we find* $S = \Pi(0, D)$. *In particular, if* ρ *is a risk-free discount factor, then* $\rho = \Pi(0, 1) > 0$. *If* F *is the forward price of the asset* D, *setting the present value of the trade* $(0, F\mathbf{1} - D)$ *to zero results in* $F\Pi(0, 1) = \Pi(0, D)$. *Combining the equations for* S, ρ *and* F, *we recover the restriction* $S = \rho F$ *of Proposition 1.3.*

The above example proves Proposition 1.3 under the additional assumption that a present-value function exists. We will see shortly, however, that this assumption is a consequence of the no-arbitrage condition.

Present-value functions are conveniently represented in terms of state prices.

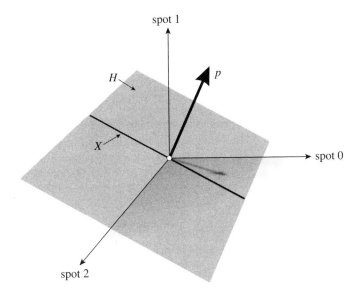

Figure 1.1 A state-price vector.

Definition 1.6. *A **state-price vector** is any vector of the form*

$$p = (p_0, p_1, \ldots, p_K) \in \mathbb{R}_{++}^{1+K}$$

*such that $p \cdot x \leq 0$ for all $x \in X$. A state-price vector p **represents** the present-value function*

$$\Pi(c) = \frac{p \cdot c}{p_0} = c_0 + \sum_{k=1}^{K} \frac{p_k}{p_0} c_k, \quad c \in \mathbb{R}^{1+K}. \tag{1.1}$$

While this definition will apply more generally in Section 1.7, in the current context X is a linear subspace and therefore a state-price vector p is necessarily orthogonal to X (see Figure 1.1).

Any given present-value function Π is represented by the state-price vector $\bar{p}$, where $\bar{p}_k = \Pi(\mathbf{1}^k)$. Mathematically, $\bar{p}$ is the Riesz representation of Π (see Proposition A.8). Any other state-price vector p representing Π satisfies $p = p_0 \bar{p}$ and therefore

$$\frac{p_k}{p_l} = \frac{\Pi(\mathbf{1}^k)}{\Pi(\mathbf{1}^l)}, \quad k, l \in \{0, 1, \ldots, K\}.$$

In words, state prices represent the relative present value of Arrow cash flows.

7

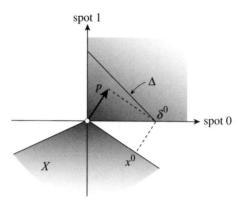

Figure 1.2 Proof of the first fundamental theorem of asset pricing.

To visualize the duality between the no-arbitrage condition and state pricing, consider any nonzero vector p in $\mathbb{R}^{1+K}$ and the orthogonal hyperplane H it defines (see Figure 1.1). Let $H_{++} = \{y : p \cdot y > 0\}$ be the open half-space on the side of H containing p, and let $H_- = \{x : p \cdot x \leq 0\}$ be the closed half-space on the other side of H. The nonzero vector p is a state-price vector if and only if the market X is included in H_- and the set of all arbitrage cash flows is included in H_{++}. Intuitively, the existence of such a strictly separating hyperplane is equivalent to the nonintersection of the two convex sets being separated, which is exactly the no-arbitrage condition. This is formally proved below using the projection theorem.[1]

Theorem 1.7 (First Fundamental Theorem of Asset Pricing). *A present-value function exists if and only if X is arbitrage-free.*

Proof. Although we assumed that X is a linear subspace, the proof uses only the assumption that X is a closed convex cone. (This generality will be utilized in Proposition 1.14 and Section 1.7.) If Π is a present-value function, then $\Pi(c) > 0$ for every arbitrage c, while

---

[1] The separating hyperplane theorem (Corollary A.30), whose proof is also based on the projection theorem, implies only the weak separation of an arbitrage-free market X and the positive orthant. The fact that the positive orthant contains no lines is important for strict separation, since two intersecting lines cannot be strictly separated.

$\Pi(x) \le 0$ for every $x \in X$. Therefore, X must be arbitrage-free. Conversely, suppose X is arbitrage-free and let

$$\Delta = \left\{ x \in \mathbb{R}_+^{1+K} : \sum_{k=0}^{K} x_k = 1 \right\}.$$

Since X is arbitrage-free, $X \cap \Delta = \emptyset$. By Proposition A.19, there exists a $(x^0, \delta^0) \in X \times \Delta$ that minimizes the Euclidean distance $\|x - \delta\|$ over all $(x, \delta) \in X \times \Delta$. Note that x^0 is the projection of δ^0 on X and δ^0 is the projection of x^0 on Δ. By Theorem A.21, $-p = x^0 - \delta^0$ supports X at x^0 and therefore $p \cdot x \le p \cdot x^0$ for all $x \in X$. Since X is a cone, it follows that $p \cdot x^0 = 0$ and $p \cdot x \le 0$ for all $x \in X$. Similarly, $p = \delta^0 - x^0$ supports Δ at δ^0, implying that $p \cdot \delta \ge p \cdot \delta^0$ for all $\delta \in \Delta$. Since $p \cdot x^0 = 0$, $p \cdot \delta^0 = p \cdot p > 0$. Therefore, $p \cdot \delta > 0$ for all $\delta \in \Delta$, which implies that p is strictly positive. A corresponding present-value function is defined by (1.1). ∎

1.3 MARKET COMPLETENESS AND DOMINANT CHOICE

A present-value function need not be unique. For example, in Figure 1.1 the shaded plane H is orthogonal to the state-price vector p and is associated with a present-value function relative to the market X. The plane H can be rotated around the line X and as long as it does not cut into the positive orthant, it defines a whole range of present-value functions. On the other hand, if X were the whole plane H, a present-value function would be unique.

To characterize uniqueness of a present-value function more generally, we introduce the notion of market completeness.

Definition 1.8. *A cash flow m is **marketed** if there exists some $w \in \mathbb{R}$ such that $m - w\mathbf{1}^0 \in X$. The market X is **complete** if every cash flow is marketed, and **incomplete** otherwise.*

Recall that a cash flow x is traded if and only if $x \in X$. A traded cash flow is therefore marketed, but the converse need not be true. We let M denote the set of marketed cash flows associated with the market X. Geometrically, M is the linear subspace spanned by X and $\mathbf{1}^0$. The market X is complete

9

if and only if $M = \mathbb{R}^{1+K}$. Assuming X is arbitrage-free, it follows that the market X is complete if and only if it is a hyperplane, meaning that its orthogonal subspace is one-dimensional, a condition that clearly implies the uniqueness of a present-value function. More generally, the present value of any marketed cash flow is uniquely defined, even if the market is incomplete.

Proposition 1.9. *If Π is a present-value function and m is a marketed cash flow, then $\Pi(m)$ is the unique value of w such that $m - w\mathbf{1}^0 \in X$.*

Proof. If $m - w\mathbf{1}^0 \in X$, then $\Pi(m - w\mathbf{1}^0) = 0$ and therefore $w = w\Pi(\mathbf{1}^0) = \Pi(m)$. ∎

Theorem 1.10 (Second Fundamental Theorem of Asset Pricing). *A present-value function is unique if and only if the market is complete.*

Proof. If the market is complete, then every cash flow is marketed, and the uniqueness of present values follows from the last proposition (or the above geometric argument). Conversely, suppose the market is incomplete and $\Pi^0(x) = p^0 \cdot x$ is a present-value function, where $p^0 \in \mathbb{R}^{1+K}_{++}$. Fix any nonmarketed cash flow c. By Corollary A.25, $c = m + n$, where $m \in M$ and n is nonzero and orthogonal to $M = \operatorname{span}(X, \mathbf{1}^0)$. Let $\beta \in \mathbb{R}$ be small enough so that $p^\beta = p^0 + \beta n \in \mathbb{R}^{1+K}_{++}$. Since n is orthogonal to X, $p^\beta \cdot x = 0$ for all $x \in X$, and since n is orthogonal to $\mathbf{1}^0$, $p^\beta \cdot \mathbf{1}^0 = p^0 \cdot \mathbf{1}^0 = 1$. Therefore, $\Pi^\beta(x) = p^\beta \cdot x$ is a present-value function and $\Pi^\beta(c) = \Pi^0(c) + \beta n \cdot n \neq \Pi^0(c)$. ∎

A complete arbitrage-free market has the remarkable property that it removes the subjectivity of the optimality of a cash flow choice within any given set. To elaborate, consider the problem of selecting a cash flow δ out of a given set $\mathcal{D}$ of cash flows. In the absence of a market, the optimal choice generally depends on the preferences and endowment of the agent making the choice, as will be discussed in Chapter 3. Suppose now that the market X is also available.

Definition 1.11. *A cash flow $\delta^* \in \mathcal{D}$ is **dominant** (in $\mathcal{D}$ given X) if for any $\delta \in \mathcal{D}$, there exists some $x \in X$ such that $\delta^* + x \geq \delta$.*

A dominant choice is optimal for any two agents who do not dislike additional income at any spot. For $i \in \{1, 2\}$, suppose agent i finds δ^i optimal in $\mathcal{D}$. If $\delta^* \in \mathcal{D}$ is dominant, then there exist trades $x^1, x^2 \in X$ such that $\delta^* + x^i \geq \delta^i$. Agent i is therefore at least as well off selecting δ^* instead of δ^i and at the same time entering the trade x^i. In this sense, both agents agree on the optimality of δ^*, even though the way they use the market to transform δ^* can differ. Given a complete arbitrage-free market, a dominant choice is one that maximizes present value.

Proposition 1.12. *Suppose the market X is complete and Π is a present-value function. For any set of cash flows $\mathcal{D}$, the cash flow $\delta^* \in \mathcal{D}$ is dominant in $\mathcal{D}$ if and only if $\Pi(\delta^*) = \max\{\Pi(\delta) : \delta \in \mathcal{D}\}$.*

Proof. Suppose δ^* is dominant. For any $\delta \in \mathcal{D}$, we can write $\delta^* \geq \delta + x$ for some $x \in X$. Taking present values, $\Pi(\delta^*) \geq \Pi(\delta + x) = \Pi(\delta)$. Conversely, suppose δ^* maximizes present value in $\mathcal{D}$ and $\delta \in \mathcal{D}$. Since X is complete, we can write $\delta^* = \Pi(\delta^*)\mathbf{1}^0 + y^*$ and $\delta = \Pi(\delta)\mathbf{1}^0 + y$ for some $y^*, y \in X$. Therefore, $\delta^* \geq \Pi(\delta)\mathbf{1}^0 + y^* = \delta + x$, where $x = y^* - y \in X$, confirming the dominance of δ^*. ∎

Corollary 1.13. *Suppose the set of cash flows $\mathcal{D}$ is compact and the market X is complete and arbitrage-free. Then a dominant choice in $\mathcal{D}$ exists.*

A generalization of the last proposition that does not require the market X to be complete follows.

Proposition 1.14. *Suppose the market X is arbitrage-free. For any set of cash flows $\mathcal{D}$, the cash flow $\delta^* \in \mathcal{D}$ is dominant in $\mathcal{D}$ if and only if $\Pi(\delta^*) = \max\{\Pi(\delta) : \delta \in \mathcal{D}\}$ for every present-value function Π.*

Proof. The "only if" part follows exactly as for Proposition 1.12. Conversely, suppose $\delta^* \in \mathcal{D}$ is not dominant in $\mathcal{D}$ and therefore there exists some $\delta \in \mathcal{D}$ such that $\delta^* - \delta + x \notin \mathbb{R}_+^{1+K}$ for all $x \in X$. Let $x^* = \delta^* - \delta$. The set

$$X^* = \{x + \alpha x^* : x \in X, \ \alpha \in \mathbb{R}_+\}$$

is a closed convex cone that contains no arbitrage. The proof of the first fundamental theorem of asset pricing implies the existence of a vector $p \in \mathbb{R}_{++}^{1+K}$ such that $p \cdot x \leq 0$ for every $x \in X^*$. Such a vector p is a state-price vector that satisfies $p \cdot x^* \leq 0$. If $p \cdot x^* = 0$, we can construct a new state-price vector p^ε such that $p^\varepsilon \cdot x^* < 0$. To see how, we project x^* onto X to write $x^* = \bar{x} + n$, where $\bar{x} \in X$ and n is nonzero and orthogonal to X. For any small enough scalar $\varepsilon > 0$, $p^\varepsilon = p - \varepsilon n$ is a state-price vector. If $p \cdot x^* = 0$, then $p^\varepsilon \cdot x^* = -\varepsilon n \cdot n < 0$. We conclude that for some $\varepsilon \geq 0$, the present-value function Π defined by p^ε is such that $\Pi(x^*) < 0$ and therefore $\Pi(\delta^*) < \Pi(\delta)$. ∎

1.4 PROBABILISTIC REPRESENTATIONS OF VALUE

Arbitrage arguments rely on an assumed set of possible states but not the likelihood that one assigns to these states. Nevertheless, probabilistic representations of present value, introduced below, are methodologically useful, because they relate the valuation problem to a powerful set of available probabilistic tools. The benefit of these tools becomes clearer in dynamic extensions of the theory.

For the remainder of this chapter, we take as given a **strictly positive probability** P, defined as any vector $P \in \mathbb{R}_{++}^K$ whose elements add up to one. While in applications P_k typically represents an economic agent's or an econometrician's prior belief that state k will occur, the manipulations that follow apply for any choice of a reference strictly positive probability P. Given any random variables $x, y \in \mathbb{R}^K$, we denote their usual probabilistic averages relative to P as follows:

- (expectation) $\mathbb{E}[x] = \mathbb{E}x = \sum_{k=1}^K x_k P_k$.
- (covariance) $\mathrm{cov}[x, y] = \mathbb{E}[(x - \mathbb{E}x)(y - \mathbb{E}y)] = \mathbb{E}[xy] - \mathbb{E}x\mathbb{E}y$.
- (variance) $\mathrm{var}[x] = \mathrm{cov}[x, x]$.
- (standard deviation) $\mathrm{stdev}[x] = \sqrt{\mathrm{var}[x]}$.
- (correlation coefficient) $\mathrm{corr}[x, y] = \mathrm{cov}[x, y]/(\mathrm{stdev}[x]\mathrm{stdev}[y])$.

We continue with the reference market X taken as given.

Definition 1.15. *A **state-price density (SPD)** is a vector of the form $\pi = (\pi_0, \pi_1, \ldots, \pi_K)$ such that $p = (\pi_0, \pi_1 P_1, \ldots, \pi_K P_K)$ is a state-price vector.*

*The present-value function **represented** by π is the present-value function represented by p.*

Like any vector in $\mathbb{R}^{1+K}$, we can equivalently regard an SPD π as a stochastic process $\pi = (\pi(0), \pi(1))$, where $\pi(0) = \pi_0$ and $\pi(1)_k = \pi_k$ for $k = 1, \ldots, K$. The present-value function Π represented by an SPD π can therefore be written as

$$\Pi(c) = c(0) + \mathbb{E}\left[\frac{\pi(1)}{\pi(0)}c(1)\right]. \tag{1.2}$$

Our earlier discussion of the relationship between state-price vectors and present-value functions implies that a present-value function can be represented by an SPD that is unique up to positive scaling.

The **risk-free discount factor implied** by the SPD π is

$$\rho = \mathbb{E}\left[\frac{\pi(1)}{\pi(0)}\right], \tag{1.3}$$

which is the price of a unit discount bond if one is traded. In terms of ρ, the present-value equation (1.2) can be expressed as

$$\Pi(c) = c(0) + \rho\mathbb{E}[c(1)] + \text{cov}\left[\frac{\pi(1)}{\pi(0)}, c(1)\right]. \tag{1.4}$$

Note that risks are not priced based on their variance. For example, suppose $\bar{c} = (c(0), \mathbb{E}c(1))$ and $\text{cov}[\pi(1), c(1)] > 0$. Then $\Pi(c) > \Pi(\bar{c})$, even though c is riskier than $\bar{c}$ in the sense of higher variance. Intuitively, while c is variable, it tends to pay more at spots where one unit of account is more highly valued.

Another common way of representing present-value functions is in terms of equivalent martingale measures.

Definition 1.16. *An **equivalent martingale measure (EMM)** is a probability Q such that $p = (1, \rho Q_1, \rho Q_2, \ldots, \rho Q_K)$ is a state-price vector for some scalar ρ, in which case (Q, ρ) is an **EMM-discount pair**. The present-value function **represented** by (Q, ρ) is the present-value function represented by p.*

By letting $\mathbb{E}^Q$ denote the expectation operator relative to the probability Q, the present-value function Π represented by an EMM-discount pair (Q, ρ) can be written as

$$\Pi(c) = c(0) + \rho\mathbb{E}^Q[c(1)]. \tag{1.5}$$

13

Any present-value function is represented by a unique EMM-discount pair. The fundamental theorems of asset pricing can therefore be restated as: *The market is arbitrage-free if and only if an EMM exists. An EMM-discount pair is unique if and only if the market is complete.*

State-price densities and EMM-discount pairs are matched by equations (1.3) and

$$\frac{\pi(1)}{\pi(0)} = \rho\frac{dQ}{dP},\tag{1.6}$$

where dQ/dP is the **density** of Q with respect to P, defined as the random variable taking the value Q_k/P_k at state k. If (Q,ρ) is an EMM-discount pair representing the present-value function Π, then equation (1.6) defines the unique SPD representation of Π given any positive value of $\pi(0)$. Conversely, suppose π is an SPD representing Π and let ρ be its implied risk-free discount factor. Then (Q,ρ), where Q is defined by (1.6), is the unique EMM-discount pair that represents Π.

The forward price of a traded asset D is given in terms of an EMM Q by

$$F = \mathbb{E}^Q[D] = \mathbb{E}D + \text{cov}\left[\frac{dQ}{dP},D\right].\tag{1.7}$$

The expectation operator $\mathbb{E}^Q$ relative to an EMM Q can therefore be interpreted as a forward-pricing operator. For instance, suppose D is an **Arrow security**, meaning that there exists some state k such that $D_k = 1$ and $D_l = 0$ for $l \neq k$. If (Q,ρ) is an EMM-discount pair, then the forward price of D is Q_k. The Arrow security can be thought of as an insurance contract against the occurrence of state k. The probability Q_k is the forward premium of this insurance contract.

The term equivalent martingale measure comes from probability theory. Two probabilities are **equivalent** if they assign zero probability to the same events. In our simple context, an EMM Q is equivalent to P since both are assumed to be strictly positive. The term **martingale measure** reflects the fact that given an EMM-discount pair (Q,ρ) and an asset D with spot price S, the discounted price process $(S,\rho D)$ is a **martingale** relative to the probability Q, which in our simple context means that $S = \mathbb{E}^Q[\rho D]$. The role of martingales will become clearer in Part II.

Pricing in terms of an EMM Q is also known as **risk-neutral pricing**, the probability Q is known as a **risk-neutral probability**, and the expectation $\mathbb{E}^Q$ as a **risk-neutral expectation**. The basic idea is that in a fictitious world in which beliefs coincide with Q, the present value of a time-one payoff is its expected value discounted as if it were a sure payment, as in equation (1.5). The economic interpretation of Q is, however, as a list of forward premia, not beliefs.

1.5 FINANCIAL CONTRACTS AND PORTFOLIOS

In a financial market in which every traded cash flow is customized to fit a particular trader's individual needs, finding a suitable counterparty and enforcing the resulting contract can be expensive. This consideration has led to the creation of standardized contracts that are traded in highly competitive and liquid markets. Traders can combine standardized contracts in ways that best approximate their individual cash flow needs. In this section we model the implementation of an ideal competitive financial market through the trading of (financial) contracts.

Formally, a **contract** is any stochastic process $v = (v(0), v(1)) \in \mathbb{R} \times \mathbb{R}^K$, with $v(t)$ interpreted as the time-t market value of the contract. For any $\alpha \in \mathbb{R}$, a trader can enter into α contracts resulting in an incremental cash flow $\alpha(-v(0), v(1))$. A positive value of α corresponds to a **long position** in the contract, while a negative value of α corresponds to a **short position**. We say that a contract v is **traded** in the market X if $(-v(0), v(1)) \in X$.

Throughout this section, we fix the reference contracts $V_1, \ldots, V_J$ and we define the matrix

$$V = \begin{pmatrix} V_1 \\ \vdots \\ V_J \end{pmatrix} = \begin{pmatrix} V_1(0) & V_1(1) \\ \vdots & \vdots \\ V_J(0) & V_J(1) \end{pmatrix} = (V(0), V(1)). \quad (1.8)$$

V can equivalently be viewed as a column vector of stochastic processes or as a $J \times (1+K)$ matrix with V_j as its jth row. A **portfolio** is a column vector $\theta = (\theta_1, \ldots, \theta_J)' \in \mathbb{R}^J$, where θ_j represents a position in contract V_j. A portfolio θ **generates** the cash flow x defined by

$$x(0) = -\theta' V(0) \quad \text{and} \quad x(1) = \theta' V(1). \quad (1.9)$$

The market **implemented** by the contracts $V_1, \ldots, V_J$ is denoted and defined by

$$X(V_1, \ldots, V_J) = X(V) = \{x : x \text{ is generated by some } \theta \in \mathbb{R}^J\}. \quad (1.10)$$

The **synthetic contract generated** by the portfolio θ is the contract

$$V^\theta = \theta' V.$$

15

Introducing a synthetic contract does not change the implemented market:

$$X(V^\theta, V_1, \ldots, V_J) = X(V_1, \ldots, V_J), \quad \text{for all } \theta \in \mathbb{R}^J. \qquad (1.11)$$

The portfolio θ **replicates** the contract v if $v(1) = V^\theta(1)$. If the market $X(v, V_1, \ldots, V_J)$ is arbitrage-free[2] and θ replicates v, then $v(0) = V^\theta(0)$, in which case v is said to have been priced by arbitrage.

Example 1.17. *Suppose that $J = 3$ and*

$$V_1 = (\rho, 1), \quad V_2 = (S, D), \quad V_3 = (0, D - F1).$$

The three contracts implement, respectively, default-free borrowing and lending, spot trading of asset D and forward trading of asset D. Each of these contracts can be replicated by a portfolio in the other two. If $X(V)$ is arbitrage-free, any of these replication relationships leads to equation $S = F\rho$ of Proposition 1.3. If $S = F\rho$, then each one of the three contracts is a synthetic contract in the other two.

Example 1.18. *Suppose the arbitrage-free market X is implemented by spot trading in the J assets forming the rows of the $J \times K$ matrix $D = (D'_1, \ldots, D'_J)'$. That means $X = X(V)$, where $V(1) = D$ and $V(0) = S$ for a column vector $S \in \mathbb{R}^J$ whose jth entry is the spot price of asset D_j. If $D_k = \theta' D$ for some replicating portfolio θ with $\theta_k = 0$, then $S_k = \theta' S$. The analogous discussion applies to a forward market in the J assets.*

The contracts $V_1, \ldots, V_J$ are **independent** if they are linearly independent as vectors in $\mathbb{R}^{1+K}$. (This notion of independence is therefore unrelated to any underlying probability and should not be confused with stochastic independence.) If $X = X(V)$, the corresponding set of marketed cash flows is given by

$$M = \{(w, \theta' V(1)) : w \in \mathbb{R}, \ \theta \in \mathbb{R}^J\}.$$

Viewing $V(1)$ as a $J \times K$ matrix, we note that the dimensionality of M is $1 + \text{rank}(V(1))$. The market X is complete if and only if $M = \mathbb{R}^{1+K}$. This shows that X is complete if and only if $J \geq K$ and $V(1)$ is full rank. We conclude the section with some related observations.

---

[2] As verified in Exercise 9, here and throughout this section the no-arbitrage assumption can be weakened to the law of one price.

Proposition 1.19. *Suppose $X(V)$ is arbitrage-free. Then the rank of $V \in \mathbb{R}^{J \times (1+K)}$ is the same as the rank of $V(1) \in \mathbb{R}^{J \times K}$. In particular, the contracts $V_1, \ldots, V_J$ are independent if and only if $V_1(1), \ldots, V_J(1)$ are linearly independent as vectors in $\mathbb{R}^K$.*

Proof. Suppose V_* is a submatrix of V obtained by isolating a set of independent contracts. If θ_* is a portfolio in those contracts and $\theta_*' V_*(1) = 0$, then $\theta_*' V_*(0) = 0$ and therefore $\theta_*' V_* = 0$. Since V_* has independent rows, it follows that $\theta_* = 0$, proving that $V_*(1)$ also has independent rows. This proves that $\operatorname{rank}(V(1)) \geq \operatorname{rank}(V)$. The remaining claims are immediate. ∎

Corollary 1.20. *An arbitrage-free market is complete if and only if it can be implemented by K independent contracts.*

1.6 RETURNS

Empirical and theoretical results in the asset pricing literature are often reported in terms of returns rather than prices and payoffs. Returns have the advantage of being independent of the unit of account and the size of the initial investment, allowing easy comparison across different contracts. On the other hand, returns are not defined for contracts with zero initial cash flow such as forward contracts. In this section we extend our discussion of arbitrage pricing focusing on returns rather than cash flows.

We use the term "return" to mean cumulative return throughout; that is, a return is a payoff divided by the corresponding initial investment. Formally, the **return** of a cash flow x such that $x(0) \neq 0$ is defined to be the ratio $-x(1)/x(0)$. Fixing the reference market X, we denote the corresponding set of all **traded returns** by

$$\mathcal{R} = \left\{ -\frac{x(1)}{x(0)} : x \in X, \ x(0) \neq 0 \right\}.$$

An exercise shows that $\mathcal{R}$ is a linear manifold.

Example 1.21. *Suppose X is implemented by spot trading in the assets $D = (D_1', \ldots, D_J')'$, with corresponding spot-price vector $S = (S_1, \ldots, S_J)'$, where $S_j \neq 0$ for all j. We let $R_j = D_j/S_j$ denote the **return of asset** j and we define the $J \times K$ matrix $R = (R_1', \ldots, R_J')'$. Portfolio return calculations can* *be carried out in terms of asset returns alone. Given any portfolio θ such that $\theta'S \neq 0$, we define the column vector of **portfolio weights** $\psi = (\psi_1, \ldots, \psi_J)'$, where $\psi_j = \theta_j S_j / \theta'S$. The corresponding portfolio return is $\psi'R = \theta'D/\theta'S$. The set of traded returns is therefore*

$$\mathcal{R} = \{\psi'R : \psi_1 + \cdots + \psi_J = 1, \psi \in \mathbb{R}^{J \times 1}\},$$

which can be visualized as the linear manifold through the points $R_1, \ldots, R_J$.

Proposition 1.22. *Suppose $\mathcal{R} \neq \emptyset$. A strictly positive stochastic process π is an SPD if and only if*

$$\mathbb{E}\left[\frac{\pi(1)}{\pi(0)} R\right] = 1 \quad \text{for all } R \in \mathcal{R}. \tag{1.12}$$

Similarly, a pair of a strictly positive probability Q and a positive scalar ρ is an EMM-discount pair if and only if

$$\mathbb{E}^Q[R] = \frac{1}{\rho} \quad \text{for all } R \in \mathcal{R}. \tag{1.13}$$

Proof. Suppose (1.12) holds. Given any $x \in X$, we wish to verify that

$$\pi(0)x(0) + \mathbb{E}[\pi(1)x(1)] = 0. \tag{1.14}$$

If $x(0) \neq 0$, equation (1.14) follows by rearranging (1.12) for $R = -x(1)/x(0)$. Suppose now that $x(0) = 0$. Since $\mathcal{R} \neq \emptyset$, there exists some $x^0 \in X$ such that $x^0(0) \neq 0$, which implies that $y = x + x^0 \in X$ and $y(0) \neq 0$. Subtracting equation (1.14) with x^0 in place of x from equation (1.14) with y in place of x, we obtain (1.14). This proves that π is an SPD. The converse is immediate. The proposition's last part is obtained from the first one with Q in place of P and the process $(1, \rho)$ in place of π. ∎

Equation (1.13) states that the expectation of every traded return under the EMM is the risk-free return, a fact that motivates the alternative term "risk-neutral probability" for an EMM.

Given a reference risk-free discount factor ρ, the **risk premium** of a traded return R is the difference $\mathbb{E}R - (1/\rho)$. The following proposition relates the risk premium of a traded return to its covariance with a state-price density, or an EMM density, in a way that is consistent with our earlier interpretation of these covariances as a measure of the market price of risk. The proposition also shows that although the standard deviation of a traded return does not explain its risk premium, the ratio of absolute risk premium to standard deviation is bounded above by the standard deviation of an EMM density.

Proposition 1.23. *Suppose π is an SPD with implied risk-free discount factor ρ and corresponding EMM Q. Then for every $R \in \mathcal{R}$,*

$$\mathbb{E}R - \frac{1}{\rho} = -\frac{1}{\rho} \operatorname{cov}\left[\frac{\pi(1)}{\pi(0)}, R\right] = -\operatorname{cov}\left[\frac{dQ}{dP}, R\right], \qquad (1.15)$$

and provided R has positive variance,

$$\frac{|\mathbb{E}R - (1/\rho)|}{\operatorname{stdev}[R]} \leq \frac{1}{\rho} \operatorname{stdev}\left[\frac{\pi(1)}{\pi(0)}\right] = \operatorname{stdev}\left[\frac{dQ}{dP}\right].$$

Proof. The definition of a covariance implies

$$\operatorname{cov}\left[\frac{\pi(1)}{\pi(0)}, R\right] = \mathbb{E}\left[\frac{\pi(1)}{\pi(0)}R\right] - \mathbb{E}\left[\frac{\pi(1)}{\pi(0)}\right]\mathbb{E}[R] = 1 - \rho\mathbb{E}[R].$$

Rearranging gives the first claimed equation in (1.15), while the second one follows from equation (1.6). To show the claimed inequality, let

$$\varrho = \operatorname{corr}\left[\frac{\pi(1)}{\pi(0)}, R\right].$$

Then (1.15) can be restated as

$$\frac{\mathbb{E}R - (1/\rho)}{\operatorname{stdev}[R]} = -\frac{\varrho}{\rho} \operatorname{stdev}\left[\frac{\pi(1)}{\pi(0)}\right] = -\varrho \operatorname{stdev}\left[\frac{dQ}{dP}\right].$$

By the Cauchy-Schwarz inequality, $|\varrho| \leq 1$, and the result follows. ∎

1.7 TRADING CONSTRAINTS

Trading constraints generally weaken the pricing implications of the no-arbitrage assumption. This section introduces the role of trading constraints with a simple generalization of this chapter's main market model for which the first fundamental theorem of asset pricing remains valid.

We analyze the arbitrage opportunities of a reference trader in the market implemented by the contracts $V_1, \ldots, V_J$ under the constraint that the trader's portfolio must lie in the set $\Theta \subseteq \mathbb{R}^J$. The trader's current positions are given by the portfolio $\theta^0 \in \Theta$. For any incremental portfolio θ, we define the corresponding generated cash flow x as before by (1.9). The set of feasible incremental cash flows for this trader is

$$X = \{x : x \text{ is generated by some } \theta \text{ such that } \theta^0 + \theta \in \Theta\}. \quad (1.16)$$

From the trader's perspective, X is the market in the informal sense we have used the term, but clearly X need not be a linear subspace and can depend on the trader's initial positions θ^0. Some examples of the constraint set Θ follow. Examples involving margin requirements and bid-ask spreads are given in Exercises 17 and 18, respectively.

Example 1.24 (Missing Markets). *Suppose that contracts indexed in the nonempty set $A \subseteq \{1, \ldots, J\}$ cannot be traded. The corresponding portfolio constraint set is*

$$\Theta = \{\theta \in \mathbb{R}^J : \theta_j = 0 \text{ for all } j \in A\}.$$

In this case no modification of our earlier theory is required, since X is a linear subspace. Assuming the contracts $V_1, \ldots, V_J$ are independent, X is an incomplete market. Market incompleteness is a form of trading constraint.

Example 1.25 (Short-Sale Constraints). *Suppose that contracts indexed in the set $A \subseteq \{1, \ldots, J\}$ cannot be sold short. The corresponding portfolio constraint set is*

$$\Theta = \{\theta \in \mathbb{R}^J : \theta_j \geq 0 \text{ for all } j \in A\}.$$

In this case the market X is a function of the reference trader's initial portfolio θ^0. For a simple illustration of a short-sale constraint, consider the setting of Example 1.17 with the assumption that the asset cannot be sold short in the spot market ($A = \{2\}$). As explained at the end of Section 1.1, reverse cash-and-carry arbitrage requires the selling of the asset in the spot market. Given the short-sale constraint, an arbitrage-free market X implies that $S = F\rho$ if $\theta_2^0 > 0$, but the strict inequality $S > F\rho$ cannot be ruled out by an arbitrage argument if $\theta_2^0 = 0$. Even if $\theta_2^0 > 0$, the scale of reverse cash-and-carry arbitrage is limited by the trader's initial position θ_2^0, in contrast to an unconstrained market where any arbitrage can be scaled arbitrarily.

We will formulate a generalized version of the first fundamental theorem of asset pricing that applies with the type of constraints discussed above and in the exercises. For this purpose, we extend the definition of a market.

Definition 1.26. *A **constrained market** is a closed convex set of cash flows* $X \subseteq \mathbb{R}^{1+K}$ *such that* $0 \in X$ *and for some* $\varepsilon > 0$,

$$x \in X \text{ and } 0 < \|x\| < \varepsilon \quad \text{implies} \quad \frac{\varepsilon}{\|x\|} \, x \in X. \tag{1.17}$$

Here $\|x\|$ can be taken to be the Euclidean norm of x, although, for reasons that are explained in Section A.5, Definition 1.26 does not depend on the norm choice. Condition (1.17) states that every nonzero trade whose norm is less than ε can be scaled up so that its norm equals ε.

The preceding examples are all instances of a constrained market specification, as a consequence of the following observation.

Proposition 1.27. *Suppose* $\Theta \subseteq \mathbb{R}^J$ *is a finite intersection of closed half-spaces and* $\theta^0 \in \Theta$. *Then equation* (1.16) *defines a constrained market* X.

As before, X is arbitrage-free if and only if $X \cap \mathbb{R}_+^{1+K} = \{0\}$. Definition 1.4 of a present-value function and its various representations in Section 1.4 also apply relative to a constrained market X. Whereas in the unconstrained case the present value of any traded cash flow is zero, the present value of a traded cash flow in a constrained market can be strictly negative. The first fundamental theorem of asset pricing remains valid.

Theorem 1.28. *For a constrained market* X, *a present-value function exists if and only if* X *is arbitrage-free.*

Proof. Let $C = \{kx : x \in X, \ k \in \mathbb{R}_+\}$ be the cone generated by X. One can easily check that X is arbitrage-free if and only if $C \cap \mathbb{R}_+^{1+K} = \{0\}$. Clearly, C is convex. If it is also closed, then the result follows from the proof of Theorem 1.7 (where X was assumed to be a closed convex cone). Given the $\varepsilon > 0$ of condition (1.17), let $B = \{x \in \mathbb{R}^{1+K} : \|x\| \leq \varepsilon\}$. The cone C is closed if and only if $C \cap B$ is closed (why?). Since X and B are closed, we prove the closure of C by showing that $C \cap B = X \cap B$. Clearly, $X \cap B \subseteq C \cap B$. Conversely, suppose $y \in C \cap B$ and therefore $y = kx$ for some $x \in X$ and $k \in \mathbb{R}_+$. If $k \leq 1$, then y is a convex combination of 0 and x. If $k > 1$, then y is a convex combination of x and $\varepsilon x / \|x\|$, which is an element of X by condition (1.17). In either case, y is a convex combination of elements of X and therefore $y \in X \cap B$. ∎

21

1.8 Exercises

1. In the discussion leading to the definition of the market X as a linear subspace, conditions 2 and 3 combined are said to imply the possibility of short selling. Does condition 3 ($x \in X \implies -x \in X$) alone imply the possibility of short selling? Explain.

2. (a) Verify the claims of Example 1.17.

   (b) Show that every complete arbitrage-free market can be implemented by trading in a unit discount bond and a set of forward markets in Arrow securities. How many such contracts are needed?

3. A **call option** (resp. **put option**) on asset $D \in \mathbb{R}^K$ with strike $L \in \mathbb{R}$ is the asset $(D - L\mathbf{1})^+$ (resp. $(L\mathbf{1} - D)^+$). Consider an arbitrage-free market X that allows unrestricted spot trading of a unit discount bond, the asset D as well as a call and a put on D, both with strike L. The respective spot prices are denoted ρ, S, S_c and S_p. Express the difference $S_c - S_p$ in terms of ρ, S and L. (The resulting identity is known as put-call parity.) Show your result in two ways: (a) by constructing a suitable arbitrage as a consequence of the violation of the claimed relationship, and (b) by using the existence of a present-value function.

4. Suppose there are only two states ($K = 2$) and consider a market that is implemented by spot trading of an asset $D \in \mathbb{R}^2$ with spot price $S > 0$, a unit discount bond with corresponding discount factor $\rho > 0$, and a call option on the asset D with strike L, which is the asset $(D - L\mathbf{1})^+$. The option's spot price, known as its premium, is S_c. The possible values of D are $D_1 = (1 + u)S$ in state one and $D_2 = (1 + d)S$ in state two, where $u > d > -1$.

   (a) Derive necessary and sufficient conditions on the parameters for the market implemented by spot trading on the stock and the bond to be arbitrage-free. Assume these conditions are satisfied for the remainder of this question.

   (b) Show that the market implemented by spot trading in the stock and the bond is complete and compute the corresponding state-price vectors.

   (c) Compute the arbitrage price S_c of the call using a state-price vector.

(d) Rederive the arbitrage price of the call by pricing a portfolio in the stock and the bond that replicates the call option.

5. Show that if the market is arbitrage-free and the cash flow $(0, 1)$ is not marketed, then there are two state-price densities implying different risk-free discount factors.

6. Suppose the market X is arbitrage-free.

(a) Show that a cash flow c is marketed if and only if there exists a scalar w such that $\Pi(c) = w$ for every present-value function Π.

(b) Show that $x \in X$ if and only if $\Pi(x) = 0$ for every present-value function Π.

7. This exercise shows that for a complete market, the proof of the first fundamental theorem of asset pricing simplifies significantly. Suppose X is a complete arbitrage-free market and let $p = \mathbf{1}^0 - x^0$, where x^0 is the projection of $\mathbf{1}^0$ on X. Show that $p_0 > 0$ and verify that the linear functional $\Pi(c) = p_0^{-1}(p \cdot c)$ is a present-value function. Finally, give a second proof by showing the converse to Proposition 1.9 for an arbitrage-free complete market.

8. Consider an "option," defined as a set $\mathcal{D}$ of cash flows, out of which the option owner must choose exactly one cash flow. Given an arbitrage-free reference market X, suppose that the option $\mathcal{D}$ contains a dominant choice δ^*. Suppose further that δ^* is marketed and therefore δ^* has a uniquely defined present value p^*.

(a) Suppose the option $\mathcal{D}$ can be bought for a premium p, meaning that any cash flow of the form $-p\mathbf{1}^0 + \delta$, where $\delta \in \mathcal{D}$, is available and can be combined with any trade in X. Show that no arbitrage can be created in this manner if and only if $p \geq p^*$.

(b) Suppose the option $\mathcal{D}$ can be sold (or written) for a premium p, meaning that some cash flow of the form $p\mathbf{1}^0 - \delta$, where $\delta \in \mathcal{D}$, is available and can be combined with any trade in X. Note that δ is selected by the option buyer and it need not be the dominant choice. Show that a seller of the option $\mathcal{D}$ has no arbitrage available for any choice by the option buyer if and only if $p \leq p^*$.

9. The market X satisfies the **law of one price** if $x(1) = y(1)$ implies $x(0) = y(0)$, for all $x, y \in X$.

(a) Show that the law of one price is equivalent to the condition $\mathbf{1}^0 \notin X$ and is therefore a consequence of the no-arbitrage assumption. Is a market that satisfies the law of one price necessarily arbitrage-free?

(b) Verify that Proposition 1.3, Example 1.17, Proposition 1.19 and Corollary 1.20 remain valid if the arbitrage-free assumption is replaced by the law-of-one-price assumption.

(c) Let us call a **linear valuation rule** any linear functional Π : $\mathbb{R}^{1+K} \to \mathbb{R}$ such that $\Pi(x) \leq 0$ for all $x \in X$ and $\Pi(\mathbf{1}^0) = 1$; that is, a linear valuation rule is a present-value function without the strict positivity requirement. Show that the market satisfies the law of one price if and only if there exists a linear valuation rule.

For the remainder of this exercise, assume that the market satisfies the law of one price.

(d) Show that if the market is complete, there exists a unique linear valuation rule.

(e) Suppose the market X is incomplete. Show that given any non-marketed cash flow c and any scalar α, there exists some linear valuation rule that assigns the value α to c.

10. Given a market X, prove that $\mathbf{1}^0 \notin X$ and $(0, \mathbf{1}) \notin X$ if and only if there exists a vector p such that $p_0 > 0$, $\sum_{k=1}^{K} p_k > 0$ and $p \cdot x \leq 0$ for all $x \in X$.

11. Let H be a finite-dimensional vector space with the inner product $(\cdot \mid \cdot)$. Suppose $C \subseteq H$ is a closed convex cone such that $C \cap (-C) = \{0\}$, where $-C = \{-x : x \in C\}$. Then there exists a nonzero vector p such that $(p \mid x) > 0$ for all nonzero $x \in C$. Prove this claim by generalizing the argument used to show the first fundamental theorem of asset pricing. Show that the latter is a special case. *Hint:* The role of the set Δ can be played by the convex hull of the set $C \cap \{x : \|x\| = 1\}$.

12. Define an inner product under which an SPD π such that $\pi(0) = 1$ is the Riesz representation of the present-value function it represents. Appendix A shows that in a finite-dimensional inner product space every linear functional has a unique Riesz representation. Use this fact to conclude that every present-value function can be represented by a unique, up to positive scaling, SPD. Finally, express your inner product as a quadratic form; that is, define a positive definite symmetric matrix Q such that $(x \mid y) = xQy'$, where the cash flows x and y are viewed as row vectors.

13. (a) Show that any present-value function is represented by a unique EMM-discount pair.

(b) Show that the second equation in (1.7) holds for any probability Q (not necessarily an EMM). Use this fact to show the equivalence of the present-value representations (1.4) and (1.5).

14. Show that the set of traded returns $\mathcal{R}$ is a linear manifold.

15. In the context of Section 1.5, show the following:

(a) The contracts $V_1, \ldots, V_J$ are traded in a market X if and only if $X(V) \subseteq X$.

(b) $X(V)$ is equal to the intersection of all markets in which all of the contracts $V_1, \ldots, V_J$ are traded.

(c) Equality (1.11) and Corollary 1.20.

16. Does Theorem 1.28 remain valid if condition (1.17) is omitted from the definition of a constrained market? If yes, prove the stronger result. If not, give a counterexample and explain what step of the proof of Theorem 1.28 is no longer valid.

17. (Margin Requirements) This exercise models a simple example of a margin requirement, which is a type of collateral constraint. For each $j \in \{1, \ldots, J\}$, let $V_j = (S_j, D_j)$ for some asset D_j and spot price $S_j > 0$. The first asset is a unit discount bond ($D_1 = 1$), while the remaining assets are risky. The margin requirement is that the combined value of all long risky-asset positions plus the (possibly negative) value of the discount-bond position must be at least equal to half the total value of long risky-asset positions plus one and a half times the amount raised by short selling risky assets.

(a) Show that corresponding portfolio constraint set can be written as

$$\Theta = \left\{ \alpha \in \mathbb{R}^J : \sum_{j=1}^{J} \alpha_j S_j \geq \frac{1}{2} \sum_{j=2}^{J} |\alpha_j| S_j \right\},$$

and verify that Theorem 1.28 applies in this context.

(b) For a simple illustration of how the margin constraint weakens the arbitrage-pricing argument, suppose that $J = 3$, $S_1 = S_2 = 1$, $S_3 = 1 + \delta > 1$ and $D_2 = D_3$. Suppose a trader with no initial

25

holdings of assets two or three ($\theta_2^0 = \theta_3^0 = 0$) attempts to arbitrage the difference in price of the two identical assets by purchasing a port-folio $\theta = (\theta_1, \theta_2, \theta_3)$, where $\theta_2 = \beta > 0$ and $\theta_3 = -\beta$. Show that θ generates an arbitrage and satisfies the margin requirement if and only if

$$\beta\delta \geq \theta_1 \geq 0 \quad \text{and} \quad \theta_1^0 + \theta_1 \geq \beta\left(1 + \frac{3\delta}{2}\right).$$

The arbitrage is possible if and only if the trader has some initial capital $\theta_1^0 > 0$, in which case the size of the arbitrage is limited by the initial capital.

18. (Bid-Ask Spreads) This exercise models bid-ask spreads by regarding the purchase and the sale of an asset as separate contracts on which short positions are not possible. (The approach is limited to the single-period case.) A **long spot position** in asset D is the contract $(-S_a, D)$, the scalar S_a representing the **ask spot price** of the asset. A **short spot position** in asset D is the contract $(S_b, -D)$, the scalar S_b representing the **bid spot price** of the asset. In particular, a long spot position in a unit discount bond $(-\rho_a, 1)$ implements default-free lending with interest rate $r_l = (1/\rho_a) - 1$, and a short position in a unit discount bond $(\rho_b, -1)$ implements default-free borrowing with interest rate $r_b = (1/\rho_b) - 1$. Bid-ask spreads in the forward market for an asset D are modeled analogously through the contracts $(0, D - F_a 1)$ and $(0, F_b 1 - D)$, representing **long** and **short forward positions**, respectively. The prices F_a and F_b are the **ask** and **bid forward prices** of the asset, respectively.

(a) Show that in an arbitrage-free market the following restrictions must hold:

$$r_l \leq r_b, \quad \rho_b \leq \rho_a, \quad S_b \leq F_a \rho_a \quad \text{and} \quad \rho_b F_b \leq S_a. \qquad (1.18)$$

Can the size of the spreads $r_b - r_l$, $\rho_a - \rho_b$, $S_a - S_b$ and $F_a - F_b$ be limited by an arbitrage argument? (In actual dealership markets, bid-ask spreads are limited by dealer competition. Even in a perfectly competitive dealership market, however, bid-ask spreads are positive to compensate dealers for carrying an inventory and for trading with potentially better informed traders.)

(b) Show that if (Q, ρ) is an EMM-discount pair, then

$$\rho_b \leq \rho \leq \rho_a, \quad S_b \leq \rho\mathbb{E}^Q[D] \leq S_a \quad \text{and} \quad F_b \leq \mathbb{E}^Q[D] \leq F_a.$$

Use these inequalities to recover the pricing restrictions (1.18). Does Theorem 1.28 apply here and how?

(c) Explain how restrictions (1.18) can be improved under various assumptions on the initial positions of a potential arbitrageur.

1.9 NOTES

The simple but powerful idea that a contingent payoff can be thought of as a basket of what we called "Arrow securities" is due to Arrow ((1953); translated in English in Arrow (1963)). Identifying an Arrow security with a commodity, also known as an Arrow-Debreu commodity in this context, was the key step in extending classical competitive analysis to financial markets, as further explained in Chapter 3. Pricing through arbitrage arguments first achieved prominence in financial theory in the seminal arguments of Modigliani and Miller (1958), Merton (1973b) and Black and Scholes (1973).

The equivalence of the no-arbitrage condition and the existence of a present-value function, commonly referred to as the first fundamental theorem of asset pricing, is due to Ross (1978b) for the case of a finite uncertainty model. As we saw, mathematically the result amounts to the strict separation of convex cones. Assuming the market is implemented by some finite set of contracts (possibly under constraints), the finite-dimensional fundamental theorem of asset pricing is an example of the so-called theorems of the alternative in convex analysis, a textbook account of which can be found, for example, in Chapter 1 of Stoer and Witzgall (1970). The idea of risk-neutral pricing already appears in Arrow (1970) and Drèze (1971), and it is exploited in option pricing by Cox and Ross (1976). Harrison and Kreps (1979), who coined the term equivalent martingale measure, established clearly the relationship between positive linear pricing and the martingale property of properly discounted prices, as explained in Part II. An extension with bid-ask spreads was given in Jouini and Kallal (1995).

The fundamental theorem of asset pricing was extended to infinite-dimensional spaces by Kreps (1981) in a strict-separation result that was independently shown in the mathematics literature by Yan (1980) and is known as the Kreps-Yan theorem. A remarkably simple to state result for the case of a market generated by finitely many assets (in discrete time) and infinitely many states is due to Dalang, Morton, and Willinger (1990), with simplified proofs given by Schachermayer (1992) and Kabanov and

27

Kramkov (1994). This line of research continued in mathematics, with notable contributions by Delbaen and Schachermayer (1994, 1998, 2006).

Exercise 1.4 is the single-period case of the binomial option pricing model first proposed by Cox, Ross and Rubinstein (1979), Rendleman and Bartter (1979) and Sharpe (1978). The model will be revisited in Chapter 5.

CHAPTER TWO

Mean-Variance Analysis

CONTINUING THE STUDY of an arbitrage-free market, in this chapter we introduce the basics of the mean-variance analysis of traded returns. A main problem we study is that of finding a traded return that minimizes variance given its expected value. From a dual pricing perspective, we show that risk premia in the market are proportional to the beta of a simple regression against a minimum-variance return and we compute the maximum absolute Sharpe ratio in the market. A final section introduces factor pricing. The chapter's mathematical prerequisites are contained in Appendix A, with special emphasis on projections.

2.1 MARKET AND INNER PRODUCT STRUCTURE

This section introduces primitives and notation that apply to the entire chapter. As in the last chapter, the uncertainty model consists of $1 + K$ spots: time zero and K time-one states. A cash flow c can be thought of either as an element of $\mathbb{R}^{1+K}$ or as a stochastic process $(c(0), c(1))$. All probabilistic averages (expectations, covariances and so on) are defined relative to an underlying strictly positive probability $P = (P_1, \ldots, P_K)$.

We take as given an arbitrage-free[1] market X, that is, a linear subspace $X \subseteq \mathbb{R}^{1+K}$ such that $X \cap \mathbb{R}_+^{1+K} = \{0\}$. The set of **traded payoffs** is denoted

$$X(1) = \{x(1) : x = (x(0), x(1)) \in X\}.$$

Since the market is assumed to be arbitrage-free, the **present value** of a traded payoff $x(1) \in X(1)$ is well-defined as the unique value $-x(0)$ such that $x = (x(0), x(1)) \in X$. The market may or may not allow default-free borrowing and lending, meaning that $X(1)$ may or may not include the

---

[1] The chapter's results go through if the assumption of an arbitrage-free market is weakened to $1^0, (0, 1) \notin X$. A version of the first fundamental theorem of asset pricing for this case is given in Exercise 10 of Chapter 1.

unit discount bond payoff **1**. If **1** $\in X(1)$, then the corresponding risk-free discount factor, denoted ρ, is the present value of **1** and is positive since X is arbitrage-free.

On the linear space $X(1)$, we define the inner product

$$(x(1) \mid y(1)) = \begin{cases} \mathbb{E}[x(1)y(1)], & \text{if } \mathbf{1} \in X(1); \\ \text{cov}[x(1), y(1)], & \text{if } \mathbf{1} \notin X(1). \end{cases}$$

The demeaned version of a random variable z is denoted $\hat{z} = z - \mathbb{E}z$. More precisely, this means $\hat{z} = z - \mathbf{1}\mathbb{E}z$, but as is common in probability theory, we identify a scalar α with the random variable that is identically equal to α.

On occasion, we work with the space of zero-mean random variables

$$\hat{L} = \{z \in \mathbb{R}^K : \mathbb{E}z = 0\} = \{\hat{z} : z \in \mathbb{R}^K\}$$

with the inner product

$$(z_1 \mid z_2) = \mathbb{E}[z_1 z_2] = \text{cov}[z_1, z_2], \quad z_1, z_2 \in \hat{L}.$$

The set of demeaned traded payoffs

$$\hat{X}(1) = \{\hat{x}(1) : x \in X\}$$

is a linear subspace of $\hat{L}$ and inherits the same inner product.

The following two cash flows play a central role throughout the chapter.

Definition 2.1. *The cash flows x^Π and $x^\mathbb{E}$ are the unique elements of X satisfying, for all $x \in X$,*

$$(x^\Pi(1) \mid x(1)) = -x(0) \quad and \quad (x^\mathbb{E}(1) \mid x(1)) = \mathbb{E}x(1). \tag{2.1}$$

The random variable $x^\Pi(1) \in X(1)$ is the Riesz representation of the present-value functional on $X(1)$, and $x^\Pi(0)$ is the present value of $-x^\Pi(1)$. Similarly, $x^\mathbb{E}(1) \in X(1)$ is the Riesz representation of the expectation functional on $X(1)$, and $x^\mathbb{E}(0)$ is the present value of $-x^\mathbb{E}(1)$. Setting $x = x^\Pi$ in (2.1), we obtain

$$x^\Pi(0) = -(x^\Pi(1) \mid x^\Pi(1)) \quad \text{and} \quad x^\mathbb{E}(0) = -\mathbb{E}[x^\Pi(1)].$$

If $\mathbf{1} \in X(1)$, then $x^\mathbb{E} = (-\rho, \mathbf{1})$ and $\mathbb{E}x^\Pi(1) = \rho$. Also, if $\mathbf{1} \notin X(1)$, then $\mathbb{E}x^\mathbb{E}(1) = \text{var}[x^\mathbb{E}(1)]$.

Example 2.2. *Suppose the market* X *is implemented by spot trading in* J *linearly independent assets, forming the rows of the* $J \times K$ *matrix* $D = (D'_1, \ldots, D'_J)'$. *The corresponding spot prices are given by the column matrix* $S = (S_1, \ldots, S_J)'$. *Let* $(D \mid D')$, *with typical element* $(D \mid D')_{ij} = (D_i \mid D_j)$, *denote the Gram matrix of* D *and define the column vector of expected asset payoffs*

$$\mu = (\mathbb{E}D_1, \ldots, \mathbb{E}D_J)'.$$

By Proposition A.8, the portfolios θ^Π *and* $\theta^\mathbb{E}$ *such that*

$$x^\Pi(1) = \theta^{\Pi\prime} D \quad and \quad x^\mathbb{E}(1) = \theta^{\mathbb{E}\prime} D$$

are given by

$$\theta^\Pi = (D \mid D')^{-1} S \quad and \quad \theta^\mathbb{E} = (D \mid D')^{-1} \mu.$$

By Proposition A.7, $(\theta^{1\prime} D \mid \theta^{2\prime} D) = \theta^{1\prime}(D \mid D')\theta^2$ *for any portfolios* θ^1 *and* θ^2. *In particular,*

if $\mathbf{1} \notin X(1)$, *then* $\mathrm{var}[x^\Pi(1)] = \theta^{\Pi\prime}(D \mid D')\theta^\Pi = S'(D \mid D')^{-1} S.$

Example 2.3, a special case of the last example, elaborates on the case in which the market allows default-free borrowing and lending. Exercise 3 shows the consistency of the two examples with a calculation that highlights the advantages of a well-chosen inner product definition.

Example 2.3. *We assume that the market* X *is implemented by spot trading in the* $1 + J$ *linearly independent assets* $\mathbf{1}, D_1, \ldots, D_J$. *As usual,* ρ *is the risk-free discount factor, while the risky-asset spot prices form the column matrix* $S = (S_1, \ldots, S_J)'$. *We write* $D = (D'_1, \ldots, D'_J)'$ *for the* $J \times K$ *matrix whose rows are the* J **risky assets**, *with the decomposition*

$$D = \mu + \hat{D}, \quad where \quad \mu = (\mathbb{E}D_1, \ldots, \mathbb{E}D_J)' \quad and \quad \hat{D} = (\hat{D}'_1, \ldots, \hat{D}'_J)'.$$

The **variance-covariance matrix** *of* D, *denoted* Σ, *is defined by*

$$\Sigma_{ij} = \mathrm{cov}[D_i, D_j], \quad i, j \in \{1, \ldots, J\}.$$

In this context, a portfolio takes the form $(\theta_0, \theta')'$, *where* $\theta \in \mathbb{R}^J$ *is a portfolio in the* J *risky assets and* $\theta_0 \in \mathbb{R}$ *is the position in the unit discount bond. Given any* $x \in X$, *the unique portfolio* $(\theta_0, \theta')'$ *such that* $x(1) = \theta_0 \mathbf{1} + \theta' D$ *solves*

$$\hat{x}(1) = \theta' \hat{D} \quad and \quad \theta_0 = \mathbb{E}x(1) - \theta' \mu. \tag{2.2}$$

31

2. MEAN-VARIANCE ANALYSIS

The first equation uniquely determines the risky-asset portfolio θ to match the deviations from the mean. Given θ, the bond position matches means. The portfolio $(\theta_0^{\mathbb{E}}, \theta^{\mathbb{E}'})'$ generating the cash flow $x^{\mathbb{E}}$ consists of one unit discount bond:

$$\theta^{\mathbb{E}} = 0 \quad and \quad \theta_0^{\mathbb{E}} = 1.$$

The portfolio $(\theta_0^{\Pi}, \theta^{\Pi'})'$ generating the cash flow x^{Π} is given by

$$\theta^{\Pi} = \Sigma^{-1}(S - \rho\mu) \quad and \quad \theta_0^{\Pi} = \rho - \theta^{\Pi'}\mu.$$

To see why, we note that $\hat{x}^{\Pi}(1)$ is the Riesz representation in $\hat{X}(1)$ of the linear function that maps $\hat{x}(1)$ to its present value. The rows of $\hat{D}$ form a basis for $\hat{X}(1)$ with corresponding Gram matrix Σ. The expression for θ^{Π} then follows from Proposition A.8. The expression for θ_0^{Π} follows from (2.2), with $x = x^{\Pi}$, and the fact that $\mathbb{E}x^{\Pi}(1) = \rho$. Finally, we note that, by Proposition A.7,

$$\mathrm{var}[x^{\Pi}(1)] = \theta^{\Pi'}\Sigma\theta^{\Pi} = (S - \rho\mu)'\Sigma^{-1}(S - \rho\mu).$$

2.2 MINIMUM-VARIANCE CASH FLOWS

The first minimum-variance problem we analyze is that of finding a trade that converts a given initial wealth to a time-one payoff of least variance.

Definition 2.4. *A cash flow x^* is a **globally minimum variance (g.m.v.) cash flow** if $x^* \in X$ and*

$$\mathrm{var}[x^*(1)] = \min\{\mathrm{var}[x(1)] : x(0) = x^*(0), \ x \in X\}.$$

Proposition 2.5. *If $1 \in X(1)$, the cash flow x^* is g.m.v. if and only if $x^* = \alpha(-\rho, 1)$ for some scalar α. If $1 \notin X(1)$, the cash flow x^* is g.m.v. if and only if $x^* = ax^{\Pi}$ for some scalar a.*

> *Proof.* The first claim is immediate from the definitions. Suppose $1 \notin X(1)$. Given any $x^* \in X$, we project $x^*(1)$ onto the linear span of $x^{\Pi}(1)$ to write $x^*(1) = ax^{\Pi}(1) + \varepsilon$, for some scalar a and a random variable $\varepsilon \in X(1)$ orthogonal to $x^{\Pi}(1)$. By the Pythagorean identity, $\mathrm{var}[x^*(1)] = \mathrm{var}[ax^{\Pi}(1)] + \mathrm{var}[\varepsilon]$. Since ε has zero present value, x^* is g.m.v. if and only if $\mathrm{var}[\varepsilon] = 0$. Since we assume $1 \notin X(1)$, $\mathrm{var}[\varepsilon] = 0$ if and only if $\varepsilon = 0$. ∎

Assuming $1 \notin X(1)$, the definition of the g.m.v. property of a traded cash flow x^* can be restated in geometric terms as the property that $x^*(1)$ is the projection of zero onto the linear manifold

$$M = \{x(1) \in X(1) : (x^{\Pi}(1) \mid x(1)) = -x^*(0), \ x \in X\}.$$

Let $M^{\perp} = \{x(1) \in X(1) : (x(1) \mid m) = 0 \text{ for all } m \in M\}$ denote the orthogonal-to-M linear subspace of $X(1)$. By Proposition A.23, $M^{\perp} = \text{span}(x^{\Pi}(1))$. Proposition 2.5 follows once again by noting that $x^*(1)$ is the projection of zero on M if and only if $x^*(1) \in M^{\perp}$.

A g.m.v. trade may have least payoff variance, but may also provide an unsatisfactory expected payoff. A natural next step is therefore to minimize variance given a value for the expected payoff as well as present value.

Definition 2.6. *A cash flow x^* is a **frontier cash flow** if $x^* \in X$ and*

$$\text{var}[x^*(1)] = \min\{\text{var}[x(1)] : x(0) = x^*(0), \ \mathbb{E}x(1) = \mathbb{E}x^*(1), \ x \in X\}.$$

We characterize frontier cash flows using the same argument whether a discount bond is traded or not.

Proposition 2.7. *A cash flow x^* is a frontier cash flow if and only if $x^* = ax^{\Pi} + bx^{\mathbb{E}}$ for some scalars a and b.*

Proof. Given any $x^* \in X$, we project $x^*(1)$ onto the linear span of $x^{\Pi}(1)$ and $x^{\mathbb{E}}(1)$ to write $x^*(1) = ax^{\Pi}(1) + bx^{\mathbb{E}}(1) + \varepsilon$, for some scalars a, b and a random variable $\varepsilon \in X(1)$ orthogonal to $x^{\Pi}(1)$ and $x^{\mathbb{E}}(1)$. By the Pythagorean identity, $\text{var}[x^*(1)] = \text{var}[ax^{\Pi}(1) + bx^{\mathbb{E}}(1)] + \text{var}[\varepsilon]$. Since ε has zero present value and zero expectation, x^* is a frontier cash flow if and only if $\text{var}[\varepsilon] = \mathbb{E}\varepsilon^2 = 0$, a condition that is equivalent to $\varepsilon = 0$. ∎

Alternatively, $x^* \in X$ is a frontier cash flow if and only if $x^*(1)$ is the projection of zero onto the linear manifold

$$M = \{x(1) : (x^{\Pi}(1) \mid x(1)) = -x^*(0), \ (x^{\mathbb{E}}(1) \mid x(1)) = \mathbb{E}x^*(1), \ x \in X\},$$

a property that is equivalent to $x^*(1) \in M^{\perp} = \text{span}(x^{\Pi}(1), x^{\mathbb{E}}(1))$, resulting in another derivation of Proposition 2.7.

Corollary 2.8. *Suppose x^1, x^2 are linearly independent frontier cash flows. Then the set of frontier cash flows is $\{\theta_1 x^1 + \theta_2 x^2 : \theta \in \mathbb{R}^2\}$.*

The corollary is an example of a "two-fund separation theorem." To interpret this term, suppose that a share in a traded fund $i \in \{1, 2\}$ is represented by the asset $D_i \in \mathbb{R}^K$ with spot price S_i and that $x_i = (-S_i, D_i)$ is a frontier cash flow. Suppose also that D_1 and D_2 are linearly independent, which (by Proposition 1.19) is equivalent to the linear independence of x_1 and x_2. Then any two investors who want a frontier cash flow relative to the common probability P can be served by the same two funds, even though the two investors may have entirely different attitudes toward risk.

While frontier cash flows arise naturally in portfolio-selection theory, they are also closely related to the pricing of traded payoffs, in the following sense.

Definition 2.9. *A cash flow x^* is a **pricing cash flow** if $x^* \in X$ and there exist constants ρ and q such that $q \neq 0$ and*

$$x(0) + \rho \mathbb{E}[x(1)] + q \operatorname{cov}[x^*(1), x(1)] = 0 \quad \text{for all } x \in X. \qquad (2.3)$$

If a discount bond is traded, then ρ also represents the risk-free discount factor. The two uses of ρ are consistent, as can be seen by setting $x = (-\rho, 1)$ in (2.3).

Proposition 2.10. *A cash flow x^* is a pricing cash flow if and only if $x^* = ax^{\Pi} + bx^{\mathbb{E}}$ for some $a, b \in \mathbb{R}$, where $a \neq 0$.*

Proof. The traded cash flow x^* is a pricing cash flow if and only if there exist constants p and $q \neq 0$ such that the random variable

$$\delta = -x^{\Pi}(1) + px^{\mathbb{E}}(1) + qx^*(1)$$

is orthogonal to the set $X(1)$ of traded payoffs, relative to the inner product $(\cdot \mid \cdot)$. This claim can be confirmed by rewriting (2.3) in inner-product notation, separately for the cases with and without a traded unit discount bond. Since $\delta \in X(1)$, orthogonality of δ to $X(1)$ is equivalent to $\delta = 0$, which is in turn equivalent to $x^* = ax^{\Pi} + bx^{\mathbb{E}}$, where $a = 1/q$ and $b = -p/q$. ∎

Corollary 2.11. *If x^Π and $x^{\mathbb{E}}$ are linearly independent, then $x \in X$ is a pricing cash flow if and only if it is a frontier cash flow that is not colinear with $x^{\mathbb{E}}$.*

2.3 MINIMUM-VARIANCE RETURNS

Last section's analysis is often applied in terms of returns, in which case one must exercise some caution in ensuring returns are well-defined. With that in mind, we define the market X to be **purely forward** if $x(0) = 0$ for all $x \in X$ or, equivalently, if the set of traded returns $\mathcal{R}$ is empty.

Lemma 2.12. *The market X is purely forward if and only if $x^\Pi(0) = 0$.*

Proof. By the definition of x^Π, the market X is purely forward if and only if $x^\Pi(1) = 0$. Since $(x^\Pi(1) \mid x^\Pi(1)) = -x^\Pi(0)$, $x^\Pi(1) = 0$ if and only if $x^\Pi(0) = 0$. ∎

In the remainder of this section, we assume that the market is not purely forward and therefore x^Π has a well-defined return, denoted

$$R^\Pi = -\frac{x^\Pi(1)}{x^\Pi(0)}.$$

Definition 2.13. *(a) R^* is a **globally minimum variance (g.m.v.) return** if $R^* \in \mathcal{R}$ and*

$$\text{var}[R^*] = \min\{\text{var}[R] : R \in \mathcal{R}\}.$$

*(b) R^* is a **frontier return** if $R^* \in \mathcal{R}$ and*

$$\text{var}[R^*] = \min\{\text{var}[R] : \mathbb{E}R = \mathbb{E}R^*, R \in \mathcal{R}\}.$$

Clearly, a g.m.v. return is the return of a g.m.v. cash flow, and a frontier return is the return of a frontier cash flow. It is possible, however, that a frontier cash flow does not have a well-defined return. A traded return $R \in \mathcal{R}$ can be written as $R = x(1)$ for some $x \in X$ such that $x(0) = -1$. The g.m.v. and frontier returns can therefore be visualized in terms of the projection of zero on a suitable linear manifold as explained in the last section (with $x^*(0) = -1$).

If $\mathbf{1} \in X(1)$, then the unique g.m.v. return is the return of $(-\rho, \mathbf{1}) \in X$. If $\mathbf{1} \notin X(1)$, then the unique g.m.v. return is the projection of zero onto

35

$\mathcal{R}$ and necessarily equal to R^Π (since $(-1, R^\Pi)$ is a g.m.v. cash flow). Applying the orthogonal projection theorem, we obtain the following characterization.

Proposition 2.14. *Suppose* $1 \notin X(1)$ *and the market is not purely forward.*

(a) R^Π *is the unique globally minimum variance return.*

(b) R^Π *is uniquely characterized by the condition:* $R^\Pi \in \mathcal{R}$ *and* R^Π *is orthogonal to the linear manifold* $\mathcal{R}$. *The latter orthogonality condition can be stated as*

$$\text{cov}[R^\Pi, R] = \text{Var}[R^\Pi], \quad R \in \mathcal{R} \qquad (1 \notin X(1)). \qquad (2.4)$$

Example 2.15. *In the setting of Example 2.2, suppose* $1 \notin X(1)$ *and therefore* $(D \mid D') = \Sigma$, *the variance-covariance matrix of* D. *The minimum variance of a traded return can be computed using the expression for* $\text{var}[x^\Pi(1)] = -x^\Pi(0)$ *derived in Example 2.2 as*

$$\text{var}[R^\Pi] = \frac{1}{S'\Sigma^{-1}S} \qquad (1 \notin X(1)).$$

Having understood g.m.v. returns, we turn our attention to frontier returns, starting with a two-fund separation result.

Proposition 2.16. *Suppose* $R^1, R^2 \in \mathcal{R}$ *are distinct frontier returns. Then a return* $R^* \in \mathcal{R}$ *is a frontier return if and only if* $R^* = R^1 + \alpha(R^2 - R^1)$ *for some scalar* α.

Proof. By Proposition 2.7, $R \in \mathcal{R}$ is a frontier return if and only if there exist scalars a and b such that

$$R = ax^\Pi(1) + bx^\mathbb{E}(1) \quad \text{and} \quad ax^\Pi(0) + bx^\mathbb{E}(0) = -1. \qquad (2.5)$$

Since the market is not purely forward, Lemma 2.12 implies that $x^\Pi(0) \neq 0$. Eliminating a in the above representation shows that the set ℓ of frontier returns is either a point or a line (one-dimensional manifold). Since ℓ contains the distinct returns R_1 and R_2, it follows that $\ell = \{R^1 + \alpha(R^2 - R^1) : \alpha \in \mathbb{R}\}$. ∎

Our next task is to determine exactly when two distinct frontier returns exist. For this purpose, we define the non-purely-forward market X to be **degenerate** if $\mathbb{E}R^1 = \mathbb{E}R^2$ for all $R^1, R^2 \in \mathcal{R}$. Clearly, in a degenerate market a return is a frontier return if and only if it is the g.m.v. return.

Proposition 2.17. *Suppose the market X is not purely forward. Then the following conditions are equivalent:*

1. *X is degenerate.*
2. *The set of frontier returns is a singleton.*
3. *$x^{\mathbb{E}} \in \text{span}(x^{\Pi})$.*

Proof. (1 $\implies$ 2)   Immediate.

(2 $\implies$ 3)   Suppose $x^{\mathbb{E}} \notin \text{span}(x^{\Pi})$. By Proposition 2.7, $R \in \mathcal{R}$ is a frontier return if and only if (2.5) holds for some scalars a and b. Since X is not purely forward, $x^{\Pi}(0) \neq 0$. If $x^{\mathbb{E}}(0) = 0$, then $x^{\mathbb{E}}(1) \neq 0$ (since $0 \in \text{span}(x^{\Pi})$) and therefore there are two values of b delivering two distinct frontier returns. If $x^{\mathbb{E}}(0) \neq 0$, there are two distinct values of (a, b) defining distinct frontier returns through equations (2.5).

(3 $\implies$ 1)   Suppose $x^{\mathbb{E}} = \mu x^{\Pi}$ for some $\mu \in \mathbb{R}$. If R is the return of the traded cash flow x, then

$$\mathbb{E}R = \frac{(x^{\mathbb{E}}(1) \mid x(1))}{(x^{\Pi}(1) \mid x(1))} = \mu.$$

Therefore, all traded returns have the same expectation. $\blacksquare$

Summarizing, in a non-purely-forward nondegenerate market, the set of frontier returns is a line containing R^{Π}. Equations (2.5) can be used to construct two distinct frontier returns that define the entire line of frontier returns. If $(-\rho, 1) \in X$, the line of frontier returns passes through the distinct points R^{Π} and $\rho^{-1}\mathbf{1}$. If $\mathbf{1} \notin X(1)$, then the g.m.v. return R^{Π} is orthogonal to $\mathcal{R}$ and therefore also to the line of frontier returns.

2.4 BETA PRICING

Just as frontier cash flows are closely related to pricing cash flows, frontier returns are closely related to beta-pricing returns. The beta-pricing equation below is a return version of the covariance pricing equation (2.3).

Definition 2.18. R^* *is a **beta-pricing return** if* $R^* \in \mathcal{R}$ *and there exists some* $R^0 \in \mathcal{R}$ *such that* $\mathbb{E}R^0 \neq 0$ *and*

$$\mathbb{E}[R - R^0] = \frac{\text{cov}[R^*, R]}{\text{var}[R^*]}\mathbb{E}[R^* - R^0] \quad \text{for all } R \in \mathcal{R}. \tag{2.6}$$

Remark 2.19. *If* $\mathbb{E}R^0 = 0$, *the denominator of* $R = -x(1)/x(0)$ *cancels out in equation* (2.6), *resulting in a statement about expected payoffs, not present values. In a nondegenerate market, equation* (2.6) *holds with* $\mathbb{E}R^0 = 0$ *if and only if* $\mathbf{1} \notin X(1)$ *and* $R^* \in \text{span}(x^{\mathbb{E}}(1))$.

The quantity $\text{cov}[R^*, R]/\text{var}[R^*]$ is known as the **beta** of R with respect to R^*, a terminology derived from conventional notation in linear regression theory. In this section we give a theoretical characterization of beta-pricing returns, followed by a brief discussion of a potential pitfall in its application. To avoid trivialities, we assume throughout the section that the market is neither purely forward nor degenerate. Equivalently, we assume that there exist $R^1, R^2 \in \mathcal{R}$ such that $\mathbb{E}R^1 \neq \mathbb{E}R^2$.

Suppose that R^* is a beta-pricing return and let R^0 be any traded return so that the beta-pricing equation (2.6) holds. Market nondegeneracy implies that $\mathbb{E}R^* \neq \mathbb{E}R^0$ and therefore R^0 and R^* are necessarily uncorrelated. Moreover, equation (2.6) implies that all traded returns that are uncorrelated with R^* have the same expected value. So if R^* is a beta-pricing return, any traded return R^0 that is uncorrelated with R^* can be used in equation (2.6). If $(-\rho, 1) \in X$, then $\mathbb{E}R^0 = 1/\rho$.

Before we characterize all beta-pricing returns, we argue that the g.m.v. return is *not* a beta-pricing return. If $\mathbf{1} \in X(1)$, the g.m.v. return $\rho^{-1}\mathbf{1}$ has zero variance and corresponding betas are not defined. If $\mathbf{1} \notin X(1)$, any $x \in X$ such that $x(1)$ is uncorrelated with the g.m.v. return R^{Π} satisfies $x(0) = -\text{cov}[x^{\Pi}(1), x(1)] = 0$ and therefore does not have a well-defined return. Alternatively, the orthogonality condition (2.4) implies that R^{Π} cannot be uncorrelated with a traded return. In either case, we rule out the g.m.v. return as a beta-pricing candidate.

Every traded return other than the g.m.v. return does have an uncorrelated traded return. This is obvious if the market allows riskless lending and is confirmed in the following result otherwise.

Lemma 2.20. *Suppose* $\mathbf{1} \notin X(1)$ *and the market is not purely forward. Given any return* $R^* \in \mathcal{R}$ *that does not equal the g.m.v. return* R^{Π}, *there exists a*

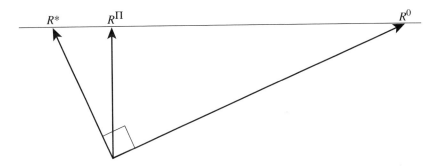

Figure 2.1 Uncorrelated traded returns on the same line.

unique scalar α such that the return $R^0 = R^\Pi + \alpha(R^* - R^\Pi) \in \mathcal{R}$ is uncorrelated with R^*. If R^* is a frontier return, then the uncorrelated return R^0 constructed this way is also a frontier return.

Proof. Since R^Π is orthogonal to $\mathcal{R}$, R^Π is also orthogonal to the line

$$\{R^\Pi + \alpha(R^* - R^\Pi) : \alpha \in \mathbb{R}\}.$$

Consulting Figure 2.1, we note that the return R^0 is the unique vector on this line that is orthogonal to R^*. If the line is that of frontier returns (see Proposition 2.16), then R^0 is also a frontier return. An algebraic version of this argument is left as an exercise. ∎

The construction of Figure 2.1 gives another view of why R^Π cannot be a beta return: as R^* approaches R^Π, the uncorrelated return R^0 goes to infinity.

We are now in a position to relate beta-pricing returns to pricing cash flows.

Proposition 2.21. *Suppose $R^* \in \mathcal{R}$ is not the g.m.v. return and the market X is not degenerate. Then R^* is a beta-pricing return if and only if it is the return of a pricing cash flow.*

Proof. Suppose $x^* \in X$ has a well-defined return R^* that is not g.m.v. If $(-\rho, \mathbf{1}) \in X$, define $R^0 = \rho^{-1}\mathbf{1}$. If $\mathbf{1} \notin X(1)$, select, using Lemma 2.20, some $R^0 \in \mathcal{R}$ that is uncorrelated with R^* and define $x^0 = (-1, R^0) \in X$.

2. MEAN-VARIANCE ANALYSIS

"if" Suppose x^* is a pricing cash flow. Equation (2.3) with $x = x^0$ implies that $\mathbb{E}R^0 \neq 0$ and $\rho = 1/\mathbb{E}R^0$. Therefore, for some constant $a \neq 0$, $\mathbb{E}[R - R^0] = a \operatorname{cov}[R^*, R]$ for all $R \in \mathcal{R}$. Dividing this equation with its special case obtained by letting $R = R^*$ results in the beta-pricing equation (2.6).

"only if" Suppose R^* is a beta-pricing return. Given any $x \in X$, choose a scalar α so that $x^\alpha = x + \alpha x^0$ has a well-defined return, denoted R^α. Applying equation (2.6) with $R = R^\alpha$, we find $-x^\alpha(0)$ $\mathbb{E}[R^\alpha - R^0] = a \operatorname{cov}[x(1), x^*(1)]$, where a is a nonzero constant that does not depend on the choice of x or α. Simplifying, we obtain the covariance pricing equation (2.3) with $\rho = 1/\mathbb{E}R^0$ and $q = -a/\mathbb{E}R^0$. ∎

The last two results together with Proposition 2.10 deliver the following characterization of beta-pricing returns.

Theorem 2.22. *Suppose $R^* \in \mathcal{R}$ and the market X is not degenerate. Then R^* is a beta-pricing return if and only if it is a frontier return that is not equal to the g.m.v. return and is not the return of $x^{\mathbb{E}}$. Moreover, if R^* is a beta-pricing return, the uncorrelated return $R^0 \in \mathcal{R}$ of the beta-pricing equation can be uniquely selected to be a frontier return.*

In practice, because of measurement error, we are never able to identify a return R^* that is exactly a frontier return. Instead, beta pricing is applied using, in place of R^*, some proxy $R^p = R^* + \varepsilon$, where the error ε is judged to be small. An arbitrarily small value of $\mathbb{E}\varepsilon^2$ is, however, consistent with the existence of a traded return whose beta with respect to R^p is arbitrarily different from its beta with respect to R^*. This pitfall is avoided if expected excess returns are normalized by standard deviations, as explained in the following section.

2.5 SHARPE RATIOS

Fixing a reference traded return R^0, the **Sharpe ratio** of a risky traded return R (relative to R^0) is defined by

$$S[R] = \frac{\mathbb{E}[R - R^0]}{\operatorname{stdev}[R]}. \tag{2.7}$$

40

The beta-pricing equation (2.6) can be formulated in terms of Sharpe ratios as

$$S[R] = \text{corr}[R^*, R]S[R^*] \quad \text{for all } R \in \mathcal{R} \text{ such that var}[R] > 0. \quad (2.8)$$

Condition (2.8) is robust to replacing R^* with a highly correlated proxy R^p, in the following sense.

Proposition 2.23. *Suppose the traded returns R^* and R^p have positive variance, R^* satisfies (2.8), and*

$$\text{corr}[R^*, R^p] = 1 - \delta, \quad \text{where } \delta \in [0, 1].$$

Then for any traded return R of positive variance,

$$\left| S[R] - \text{corr}[R^p, R]S[R^p] \right| \leq \left| S[R^*] \right| \sqrt{2\delta - \delta^2}.$$

Proof. Given any positive-variance random variable z, we use the notation

$$\tilde{z} = \frac{z - \mathbb{E}z}{\text{stdev}[z]} \in \hat{L}$$

and note the identities

$$(\tilde{z} \mid \tilde{z}) = 1 \quad \text{and} \quad (\tilde{z}_1 \mid \tilde{z}_2) = \text{corr}[z_1, z_2].$$

Condition (2.8) implies that

$$S[R] = (\tilde{R}^* \mid \tilde{R})S[R^*] \quad \text{and} \quad S[R^p] = (1 - \delta)S[R^*].$$

Therefore,

$$\left| S[R] - \text{corr}[R^p, R]S[R^p] \right| = \left| S[R^*] \right| \left| (\tilde{R}^* - (1-\delta)\tilde{R}^p \mid \tilde{R}) \right|.$$

The claimed bound follows by applying the Cauchy-Schwarz inequality:

$$\left| (\tilde{R}^* - (1-\delta)\tilde{R}^p \mid \tilde{R}) \right| \leq \sqrt{(\tilde{R}^* - (1-\delta)\tilde{R}^p \mid \tilde{R}^* - (1-\delta)\tilde{R}^p)},$$

and multiplying through the last term to find that it equals $\sqrt{2\delta - \delta^2}$. ∎

Summarizing and extending some of our earlier results, we characterize frontier returns in terms of Sharpe ratios.

Theorem 2.24. *Suppose $R^*, R^0 \in \mathcal{R}$ are uncorrelated returns, $\mathrm{var}[R^*] > 0$, and the market X is not degenerate. Then the following conditions are equivalent:*

1. *R^* is a frontier return.*
2. *Condition (2.8) holds.*
3. *$|\mathcal{S}[R^*]| = \max\{|\mathcal{S}[R]| : \mathrm{var}[R] > 0, \ R \in \mathcal{R}\}$.*

Proof. $(1 \Longrightarrow 2)$ The assumptions on R^* and R^0 imply that R^* is not g.m.v. (why?), while condition (2.8) is merely a rearrangement of the beta-pricing equation (2.6). The claim, therefore, follows from Theorem 2.22 and Remark 2.19.

$(2 \Longrightarrow 3)$ By the Cauchy-Schwarz inequality, $|\mathrm{corr}[R^*, R]| \le 1$.

$(3 \Longrightarrow 1)$ Suppose that for some $R \in \mathcal{R}$, $\mathbb{E}R = \mathbb{E}R^*$ but $\mathrm{var}[R] < \mathrm{var}[R^*]$. By replacing R with the average of R and R^* if necessary, we can conclude that $\mathrm{var}[R] > 0$ and $|\mathcal{S}[R]| > |\mathcal{S}[R^*]|$. ∎

In the remainder of this section, we assume that $(-\rho, 1) \in X$ and Sharpe ratios are defined relative to the return of the default-free bond:

$$\mathcal{S}[R] = \frac{\mathbb{E}[R] - \rho^{-1}}{\mathrm{stdev}[R]}. \tag{2.9}$$

We compute the maximum absolute Sharpe ratio in the market, based on the observation that default-free borrowing or lending does not modify the absolute Sharpe ratio of a portfolio. We state this observation as a lemma, with the proof left as an exercise.

Lemma 2.25. *For any $R \in \mathcal{R}$ of positive variance and any scalar α,*

$$\left|\mathcal{S}[(1 - \alpha)\rho^{-1}\mathbf{1} + \alpha R]\right| = \left|\mathcal{S}[R]\right|.$$

Proposition 2.26. *Suppose $(-\rho, 1) \in X$, R^* is any frontier return of positive variance, and Sharpe ratios are computed as in (2.9). Then*

$$\left|\mathcal{S}[R^*]\right| = \left|\mathcal{S}[R^\Pi]\right| \quad and \quad \mathcal{S}[R^\Pi] = -\frac{1}{\rho}\,\mathrm{stdev}[x^\Pi(1)].$$

Proof. The first equality follows from the last lemma and the fact that $R^* = (1 - \alpha)\rho^{-1}\mathbf{1} + \alpha R^\Pi$, for some $\alpha \in \mathbb{R}$. The definition of x^Π implies

$$\mathbb{E}x^{\Pi}(1) = \rho \quad \text{and} \quad -x^{\Pi}(0) = \mathbb{E}[x^{\Pi}(1)^2] = \text{var}[x^{\Pi}(1)] + \rho^2.$$

Substituting these expressions in the definition of $\mathcal{S}[R^{\Pi}]$ and simplifying gives the second equality. ∎

Example 2.27. *In the context of Example 2.3, let* $F = (F_1, \ldots, F_J)'$ *be the column vector of the risky-asset forward prices:* $F_j = S_j/\rho$. *Theorem 2.24 and the last proposition with the calculation of Example 2.3 imply that for any frontier return* R^* *of positive variance,*

$$\max\{\mathcal{S}[R]^2 : \text{var}[R] > 0, \ R \in \mathcal{R}\} = \mathcal{S}[R^*]^2 = (F - \mu)'\Sigma^{-1}(F - \mu).$$

The last expression is known as the **Hansen-Jagannathan bound***. By Proposition 1.23, it is a lower bound to the variance of any EMM density.*

2.6 MEAN-VARIANCE EFFICIENCY

A frontier return has minimum variance given its expected value, but it may or may not have maximum expected value given its variance. This concern leads to the definition of mean-variance efficiency.

Definition 2.28. *The return* R^* *is* **mean-variance efficient** *if it is a frontier return and* $\mathbb{E}R^* = \max\{\mathbb{E}R : \text{var}[R] = \text{var}[R^*], \ R \in \mathcal{R}\}$.

An instructive way of picturing mean-variance efficient returns is through a plot on the plane of the **minimum-variance frontier**, defined as the set

$$\mathcal{E} = \{(\text{stdev}[R], \mathbb{E}R) \ : \ R \text{ is a frontier return}\}.$$

In the remainder of this section, we assume that the market is neither purely forward nor degenerate. We consider the cases with and without default-free lending separately.

THE CASE WITH A TRADED DEFAULT-FREE BOND

Suppose that $(-\rho, 1) \in X$ and that Sharpe ratios are computed relative to ρ^{-1}, as in equation (2.9). On the plane, the Sharpe ratio $\mathcal{S}[R]$ is the slope of the line connecting the points $(0, \rho^{-1})$ and $(\text{stdev}[R], \mathbb{E}R)$.

Let R^* be any traded return of positive variance. Combining R^* with default-free lending or borrowing results in returns of the form

$$R^\alpha = (1 - \alpha)\rho^{-1}\mathbf{1} + \alpha R^*, \quad \alpha \in \mathbb{R}. \tag{2.10}$$

By Lemma 2.25, each R^α of positive variance has the same absolute Sharpe ratio as R^*. The set $\{(\text{stdev}[R^\alpha], \mathbb{E}R^\alpha) : \alpha \in \mathbb{R}\}$ on the plane consists of two half-lines emanating from $(0, \rho^{-1})$ with slopes $\pm S[R^*]$.

If R^* is a frontier return, then these two half-lines define the minimum variance frontier

$$\mathcal{E} = \{(0, \rho^{-1})\} \cup \left\{(\sigma, \mu) : \frac{|\mu - \rho^{-1}|}{\sigma} = |S[R^*]| = |S[R^\Pi]|, \ \sigma > 0\right\}, \tag{2.11}$$

which is plotted in Figure 2.2. The value $S[R^\Pi]$ was computed in Proposition 2.26 and is a negative number. The upper open half-line of $\mathcal{E}$ is traced by all traded returns with Sharpe ratio $-S[R^\Pi]$, which is the maximum Sharpe ratio in the market. The lower open half-line of $\mathcal{E}$ is traced by all traded returns with Sharpe ratio $S[R^\Pi]$, which is the minimum Sharpe ratio in the market.

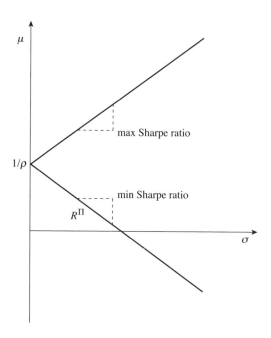

Figure 2.2 The minimum-variance frontier with a traded default-free bond.

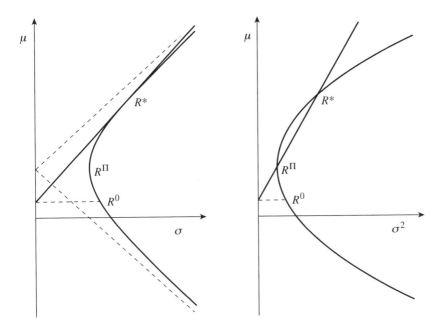

Figure 2.3 The minimum-variance frontier without a traded default-free bond.

The mean-variance efficient returns are the frontier returns that correspond to the upper closed half-line of $\mathcal{E}$. The return R^{Π} is a frontier return but is not mean-variance efficient. If R^* is any positive-variance mean-variance efficient return, the set of all mean-variance efficient returns is $\{R^{\alpha} : \alpha \geq 0\}$, where R^{α} is defined in (2.10).

THE CASE WITHOUT A TRADED DEFAULT-FREE BOND

Suppose that $\mathbf{1} \notin X(1)$, let R^* be any frontier return other than the g.m.v. return R^{Π} and define $\Delta = R^* - R^{\Pi}$. Any frontier return takes the form $R = R^{\Pi} + \alpha\Delta$ for some $\alpha \in \mathbb{R}$, determined by $\mathbb{E}R = \mathbb{E}R^{\Pi} + \alpha\mathbb{E}\Delta$. By the orthogonality equation (2.4), $\mathrm{var}[R] = \mathrm{var}[R^{\Pi}] + \alpha^2\mathrm{var}[\Delta]$. The last two equalities give the minimum-variance frontier as

$$\mathcal{E} = \left\{ (\sigma, \mu) : \frac{\sigma^2}{\mathrm{var}[\Delta]} - \frac{(\mu - \mathbb{E}R^{\Pi})^2}{(\mathbb{E}\Delta)^2} = \frac{\mathrm{var}[R^{\Pi}]}{\mathrm{var}[\Delta]}, \ \sigma > 0 \right\}. \qquad (2.12)$$

$\mathcal{E}$ is the right branch of a sideways hyperbola, plotted in the first diagram of Figure 2.3. The upper half of the frontier corresponds to the mean-variance efficient returns.

45

Suppose that the traded return R^0 is uncorrelated with R^*. As indicated on the first diagram of Figure 2.3, the line connecting $(0, \mathbb{E}R^0)$ to $(\text{stdev}[R^*], \mathbb{E}R^*)$ is tangent to $\mathcal{E}$. The reason is that for any traded return R of positive variance, the slope of the line connecting $(0, \mathbb{E}R^0)$ and $(\text{stdev}[R], \mathbb{E}R)$ is the Sharpe ratio $\mathcal{S}[R]$ relative to R^0. By Theorem 2.24, $|\mathcal{S}[R]|$ is maximized for $R = R^*$ and therefore the corresponding line cannot include an interior point of the convex hull of $\mathcal{E}$.

The second diagram of Figure 2.3 provides another graphical representation of $\mathbb{E}R^0$ on a plot of all points of the form $(\text{var}[R], \mathbb{E}R)$ as R traces the frontier returns. The resulting shape is a parabola, and $\mathbb{E}R^0$ is the vertical-axis intercept of the line that passes through $(\text{var}[R^*], \mathbb{E}R^*)$ and the globally minimum variance point $(\text{var}[R^{\Pi}], \mathbb{E}R^{\Pi})$. Equivalently, the following slope condition holds:

$$\frac{\mathbb{E}R^* - \mathbb{E}R^0}{\text{var}[R^*]} = \frac{\mathbb{E}R^{\Pi} - \mathbb{E}R^0}{\text{var}[R^{\Pi}]}.$$

This equation follows from the beta-pricing condition (2.6) and the orthogonality equation (2.4).

Finally, it is worth noting through either diagram of Figure 2.3 that as R^* approaches R^{Π}, the corresponding uncorrelated return R^0 recedes to infinity, just as we observed in Figure 2.1. This is yet another representation of the fact that R^{Π} is not a beta-pricing return.

2.7 FACTOR PRICING

While in theory frontier cash flows can be used as pricing cash flows, in practice the reliable estimation of the minimum variance frontier becomes difficult or impossible as the number of independent traded assets increases. A popular approach around this difficulty is to impose further structure on the model through the use of postulated factors, whose number is much smaller than the number of independent assets. In this section we characterize the validity of factor pricing, given an exogenously specified set of factors.

We recall the definition of $\hat{L}$ as the space of zero-mean random variables with the covariance inner product, as well as the notation $\hat{z} = z - \mathbb{E}z$ and $\hat{X}(1) = \{\hat{x}(1) : x \in X\}$, a subspace of $\hat{L}$.

Given are d linearly independent elements in $\hat{L}$, called **factors**, forming the rows of the matrix

$$B = \begin{pmatrix} B_1 \\ \vdots \\ B_d \end{pmatrix}.$$

The **factor space** is the linear subspace of $\hat{L}$ having B as its basis. The corresponding Gram matrix $(B \mid B')$ is the variance-covariance matrix of B:

$$(B \mid B')_{ij} = \text{cov}[B_i, B_j] = \mathbb{E}[B_i B_j], \quad i, j = 1, \ldots, d.$$

We do *not* require that the factors lie in $X(1)$.

For any $x \in X$, $\hat{x}(1)$ can be projected onto the factor space to obtain the orthogonal decomposition

$$x(1) = \mathbb{E}x(1) + \sigma^x B + \varepsilon^x, \tag{2.13}$$

for a unique row vector $\sigma^x \in \mathbb{R}^d$, whose elements are the **factor loadings** of x, and a zero-mean random variable ε^x that is uncorrelated with all the factors. By Proposition A.23, the factor loadings of x can be computed as

$$\sigma^x = (\text{cov}[x(1), B_1], \ldots, \text{cov}[x(1), B_d])(B \mid B')^{-1}. \tag{2.14}$$

Definition 2.29. *A column vector $\lambda \in \mathbb{R}^d$ is a **factor-pricing vector** (relative to B) if there exists a scalar ρ such that*

$$x(0) + \rho \mathbb{E}x(1) + \sigma^x \lambda = 0 \quad \text{for all } x \in X. \tag{2.15}$$

If R^0 is a traded return that is uncorrelated with every factor (for example, the return of a default-free discount bond), the factor-pricing equation (2.15) implies that $\rho = 1/\mathbb{E}R^0$.

Factor pricing is characterized in terms of pricing cash flows as follows.

Proposition 2.30. *A factor-pricing vector exists if and only if there exists some pricing cash flow x^* such that*

$$x^*(1) = \mathbb{E}x^*(1) + \sigma^* B + \varepsilon^*,$$

for some row vector $\sigma^* \in \mathbb{R}^d$ and a (necessarily zero-mean) random variable ε^* that is orthogonal to $\hat{X}(1)$ (that is, uncorrelated with every traded payoff).

Proof. Given $\rho, q \in \mathbb{R}$ and column vector $b \in \mathbb{R}^d$, consider the equation

$$x(0) + \rho \mathbb{E}x(1) + q \operatorname{cov}[x(1), b'B] = 0, \quad \text{for all } x \in X. \quad (2.16)$$

"only if" Suppose λ is a factor-pricing vector and define $b = (B \mid B')^{-1}\lambda$. By equation (2.14), the factor-pricing equation (2.15) is equivalent to equation (2.16) with $q = 1$. Projecting $b'B$ on $\hat{X}(1)$, we can write $b'B = \hat{x}^*(1) - \varepsilon^*$, for some $x^* \in X$ and some $\varepsilon^* \in \hat{L}$ that is orthogonal to $\hat{X}(1)$. It follows that x^* is a pricing cash flow.

"if" Suppose x^* is a pricing cash flow and $\hat{x}^*(1) = b'B + \varepsilon^*$, where $\varepsilon^* \in \hat{L}$ is orthogonal to $\hat{X}(1)$. Then there exist constants ρ and $q \neq 0$ such that equation (2.16) holds. It follows that $\lambda = q(B \mid B')b$ is a factor-pricing vector. ∎

Corollary 2.31. *If a factor-pricing vector with respect to the factors B exists, then there also exists a factor-pricing vector with respect to the projection of these factors onto $\hat{X}(1)$. If the factors are in $\hat{X}(1)$, then a factor-pricing vector exists if and only if there exists a pricing cash flow x^* such that $\hat{x}^*(1)$ is in the linear span of the factors.*

The preceding characterization shows that factor pricing imposes a nontrivial restriction on the way assets are priced. On the other hand, once the assumption of the possibility of factor pricing relative to some given factors has been imposed, there is no further loss in generality in assuming that these factors are demeaned versions of traded payoffs.

Factor pricing can also be expressed in terms of expected excess returns, provided these are well-defined. Given any traded return R, we define the corresponding factor loadings as $\sigma^R = \sigma^x$, where $x = (-1, R) \in X$.

Proposition 2.32. *Suppose $R^0 \in \mathcal{R}$ is uncorrelated with all the factors, and the market is not degenerate. Then λ is a factor-pricing vector if and only if the vector $\eta = -\lambda \mathbb{E}R^0$ satisfies*

$$\mathbb{E}[R - R^0] = \sigma^R \eta \quad \text{for all } R \in \mathcal{R}. \quad (2.17)$$

Proof. "only if" Given any $R \in \mathcal{R}$, applying the factor-pricing equation (2.15) with $x = (-1, R)$ gives $\rho \mathbb{E}R + \sigma^R \lambda = 1$. Letting $R = R^0$, we obtain $\rho \mathbb{E} R^0 = 1$, which when used back into $\rho \mathbb{E} R + \sigma^R \lambda = 1$ results in (2.17).

"if" Consider any $x \in X$. By Lemma 2.12, there exists a scalar α such that $x^\alpha = x + \alpha x^\Pi$ has a well-defined return R^α. Noting that

$$-x^\alpha(0)\sigma^{R^\alpha} = \sigma^x + \alpha \sigma^{x^\Pi},$$

equation (2.17) applied with $R = R^\alpha$ can be rearranged to

$$\mathbb{E}x(1) + \mathbb{E}R^0(x(0) + \sigma^x \lambda) + \alpha(\mathbb{E}x^\Pi(1) + \mathbb{E}R^0(x^\Pi(0) + \sigma^{x^\Pi}\lambda)) = 0.$$

The same calculation applied with $\alpha = 0$ and $x = x^\Pi$ shows that the coefficient of α above vanishes. Therefore, $\mathbb{E}x(1) + \mathbb{E}R^0(x(0) + \sigma^x \lambda) = 0$ for all $x \in X$. The latter condition with $\mathbb{E}R^0 = 0$ would imply a degenerate market. Therefore, $\mathbb{E}R^0 \neq 0$ and the factor-pricing equation (2.15) holds with $\rho = 1/\mathbb{E}R^0$. ∎

2.8 EXERCISES

1. Show through a convincing example that an investor who is concerned with maintaining a subsistence level can be better off choosing a portfolio that does not minimize variance given an initial investment and expected return.

2. Suppose the market is implemented by spot trading in the linearly independent assets $D_1, \ldots, D_J$ with respective spot prices $S_1, \ldots, S_J$. Compute the covariance of the payoffs of any two frontier portfolios (distinct or not) in terms of the S_j and D_j. Repeat the calculation in terms of portfolio weights and asset returns alone (assuming these are well-defined), using the results and notation of Exercise 4.

3. In the context of Example 2.3, let G be the Gram matrix corresponding to the basis $1, D_1, \ldots, D_J$, and show that

$$G = \begin{bmatrix} 1 & \mu' \\ \mu & \Sigma + \mu\mu' \end{bmatrix} \quad \text{and} \quad G^{-1} = \begin{bmatrix} 1 + \mu'\Sigma^{-1}\mu & -\mu'\Sigma^{-1} \\ -\Sigma^{-1}\mu & \Sigma^{-1} \end{bmatrix}.$$

Use these expressions and the results of Example 2.2 to derive the formulas of Example 2.3.

4. Assume the context of Example 1.21 and define

$$\mu^R = (\mathbb{E}R_1, \dots, \mathbb{E}R_J)' \quad \text{and} \quad \iota = (1, \dots, 1)' \in \mathbb{R}^J.$$

(a) Show that

$$x^\Pi = \iota'(R \mid R')^{-1}(-\iota, R) \quad \text{and} \quad x^{\mathbb{E}} = \mu^{R'}(R \mid R')^{-1}(-\iota, R),$$

and that the portfolio weights ψ^Π and $\psi^{\mathbb{E}}$ such that $R^\Pi = \psi^{\Pi'} R$ and $R^{\mathbb{E}} = \psi^{\mathbb{E}'} R$ are given by

$$\psi^\Pi = \frac{(R \mid R')^{-1}\iota}{\iota'(R \mid R')^{-1}\iota} \quad \text{and} \quad \psi^{\mathbb{E}} = \frac{(R \mid R')^{-1}\mu^R}{\iota'(R \mid R')^{-1}\mu^R}.$$

(b) Simplify the calculations of part (a), assuming a unit discount bond is traded.

(c) Suppose $1 \notin X(1)$ and R^Π solves the problem of minimizing $\text{var}(\psi'R) = \psi'(R \mid R')\psi$ subject to the constraint $\psi'\iota = 1$. Use a projection argument to compute ψ^Π and to prove that for all $\psi \in \mathbb{R}^J$ such that $\psi'\iota = 1$,

$$\text{var}[R^\Pi] = \text{cov}[R^\Pi, \psi'R] = \frac{1}{\iota'(R \mid R')^{-1}\iota}.$$

5. On the set $L = \mathbb{R}^K$ of all random variables, define the inner product $(x \mid y)_L = \mathbb{E}[xy]$. In this exercise, we endow $X(1)$ with the inner product $(\cdot \mid \cdot)_L$ inherited from L, which differs from the inner product $(\cdot \mid \cdot)$ if $1 \notin X(1)$. A default-free bond may or may not be traded. Let π be any state-price density that is normalized so that $\pi(0) = 1$. The random variable $m \in X(1)$ is the Riesz representation of the present-value functional on $X(1)$, and $n \in X(1)$ is the Riesz representation of the expectation functional on $X(1)$.

(a) Show that m is the projection of $\pi(1)$ on $X(1)$, and n is the projection of 1 on $X(1)$.

(b) Characterize $\min\{\mathbb{E}R^2 : \mathbb{E}[\pi(1)R] = 1, R \in L\}$.

(c) Show that if $(-\rho, 1) \in X$, then $\rho = \mathbb{E}m$.

(d) Show that if $1 \notin X(1)$ and $\mathbb{E}m \neq 0$, then the market spanned by X and $(-\mathbb{E}m, 1)$ satisfies the law of one price, meaning that it does not contain the cash flow 1^0.

(e) Construct examples that show that the pricing kernel m need not be strictly positive, and the enlarged market span$\{X, (-\mathbb{E}m, 1)\}$ may not be arbitrage-free.

(f) Let x^Π and $x^\mathbb{E}$ be given as in Definition 2.1, relative to the inner product $(\cdot \mid \cdot)$, not $(\cdot \mid \cdot)_L$. Show that if $1 \notin X(1)$, then $\mathbb{E}n < 1$ and

$$x^\Pi(1) = m + (\mathbb{E}m)x^\mathbb{E}(1) \quad \text{and} \quad x^\mathbb{E}(1) = n/(1 - \mathbb{E}n) \quad (1 \notin X(1)).$$

Finally, express the entire cash flows x^Π and $x^\mathbb{E}$ in terms of m and n (both for $1 \notin X(1)$ and $1 \in X(1)$).

(g) Suppose the market is implemented by spot trading in the linearly independent assets $D_1, \ldots, D_J$, with corresponding spot prices $S_1, \ldots, S_J$. Compute m and n in terms of the S_j and D_j.

6. Suppose the arbitrage-free market X is implemented by forward trading in the linearly independent assets $D_1, \ldots, D_J$. You wish to hedge a time-one risk exposure z, a random variable that is not necessarily in $X(1)$. Construct a portfolio (hedge) in the J forward contracts that minimizes the variance of the overall time-one cash flow.

7. Characterize the set of markets in which $x^\mathbb{E}$, and therefore any nonzero element of span$(x^\mathbb{E})$, is a pricing cash flow. Explain why your answer is consistent with Proposition 2.10.

8. Suppose that $1 \notin X(1)$ and let R^1 and R^2 be any distinct frontier returns. Use a projection argument to show that

$$R^\Pi = R^1 - \frac{\text{cov}[R^1, R^2 - R^1]}{\text{var}[R^2 - R^1]}(R^2 - R^1).$$

9. Prove Remark 2.19.

10. Suppose $1 \notin X(1)$. Given any traded return $R \neq R^\Pi$, determine a value of the scalar α such that $R^\Pi + \alpha(R - R^\Pi)$ is uncorrelated with R, and show that this value is unique, hence proving Lemma 2.20.

11. Prove the claim of the second-last sentence of Section 2.4.

12. Assume that $g : \mathbb{R} \to \mathbb{R}$ has a continuous derivative $g' : \mathbb{R} \to \mathbb{R}$.

(a) Stein's lemma states that if x is a normally distributed random variable, then $\text{cov}[g(x), x] = \mathbb{E}[g'(x)]\text{var}[x]$. Prove this claim, by first reducing it to its special case in which $\mathbb{E}X = 0$ and $\text{var}[X] = 1$.

51

(b) Use Stein's lemma and an orthogonal decomposition argument to show that if the random variables x and y are jointly normally distributed, then $\operatorname{cov}[g(x), y] = \mathbb{E}[g'(x)]\operatorname{cov}[x, y]$.

(c) Consider a version of this chapter's model in which the time-one states are the real line, and all time-one traded payoffs have finite variance. Suppose that R^* is a beta-pricing return with uncorrelated traded return R^0. Show that if R is a traded return such that (R, R^*) is normally distributed, then

$$\mathbb{E}[g(R) - R^0] = \mathbb{E}[g'(R)]\mathbb{E}[R - R^0].$$

13. Suppose that $(-\rho, 1) \in X$ and R is a traded return. Confirm, using this chapter's results, that $|\mathcal{S}[R]| \leq \rho^{-1}\operatorname{stdev}[x^\Pi(1)]$. Suppose further that π is a state-price density. Using a projection argument, show that

$$\operatorname{stdev}[x^\Pi(1)] \leq \operatorname{stdev}\left[\frac{\pi(1)}{\pi(0)}\right],$$

hence providing another proof of the absolute Sharpe ratio bound of Proposition 1.23.

14. Plot the set of all pairs $(\operatorname{stdev}[R], \mathbb{E}R)$ as R ranges over all returns of portfolios in a given default-free bond and a given risky asset. Confirm both geometrically and algebraically that all of these returns have the same absolute Sharpe ratio, hence proving Lemma 2.25.

15. (a) Define an orthogonal matrix that transforms the set $\{(x, y) : xy = 1\}$ to the set $\{(v, w) : v^2 - w^2 = 1\}$. Explain in words what the transformation does and illustrate with diagrams.

(b) Use part (a) and whatever other linear transformations are needed to transform a plot of $\{(x, y) : xy = 1\}$ to the minimum variance frontier for the case in which $1 \notin X(1)$. Make a rough plot of each stage, but be sure to label the slope and intercept of any asymptotes, as well as the coordinates of the globally minimum-variance traded return.

16. Suppose $1 \notin X(1)$, and R^* and R^0 are uncorrelated frontier returns. Consider the enlarged set of returns

$$\mathcal{R}^0 = \{\mathbb{E}R^0 + \alpha(R - \mathbb{E}R^0) : \alpha \in \mathbb{R}, \ R \in \mathcal{R}\}.$$

Show that if R^* is a frontier return relative to $\mathcal{R}$, then it is also a frontier return relative to $\mathcal{R}^0$, meaning that there exists no $R \in \mathcal{R}^0$

such that $\mathbb{E}R = \mathbb{E}R^*$ but $\mathrm{var}[R] < \mathrm{var}[R^*]$. Provide a geometric interpretation of this observation.

17. Prove Corollary 2.31. In the context of Example 2.3 compute the projection of the factors B onto $\hat{X}(1)$. Relate factor loadings and prices relative to B to the respective quantities relative to the projection of B on $\hat{X}(1)$.

18. (Approximate Factor Pricing) This exercise outlines an argument that is sometimes used to justify factor pricing as an approximate pricing technique. In the context of Section 2.7, further assume that $(-\rho, 1) \in X$ for a risk-free discount factor $\rho > 0$. The maximum absolute Sharpe ratio of all traded returns is denoted

$$s = \frac{1}{\rho}\,\mathrm{stdev}[x^{\Pi}(1)].$$

The notation for the factor loadings and residual of x^{Π} in its factor decomposition (2.13) is simplified to σ^{Π} and ε^{Π}, respectively. Factor prices, in an approximate sense to be explained shortly, are assumed to be given by

$$\lambda_i = \mathrm{cov}[x^{\Pi}(1), B_i], \quad i = 1, \dots, d.$$

(a) Show that for all $x \in X$,

$$|x(0) + \rho\mathbb{E}x(1) + \sigma^x\lambda| = |\mathrm{cov}[\varepsilon^{\Pi}, \varepsilon^x]| \le s\rho\,\mathrm{stdev}[\varepsilon^x].$$

(b) Assume that the market X is implemented by default-free lending and spot trading in the assets $D_1, \dots, D_J$, with corresponding spot prices $S_1, \dots, S_J$ (as in Example 2.3). Writing σ_j for the factor loadings of asset j, we have

$$D_j = \mathbb{E}D_j + \sigma_j B + \varepsilon_j, \quad j = 1, \dots, J,$$

where ε_j is zero-mean and uncorrelated with the factors. Suppose further that the terms ε_j are uncorrelated with each other, and define

$$\sigma = \max_j\,\mathrm{stdev}[\varepsilon_j].$$

The **factor pricing error** of contract j is defined as

$$e_j = |S_j - \rho\mathbb{E}D_j - \sigma_j\lambda|.$$

Given any $\delta > 0$, show that the number of assets with factor pricing error greater than δ is less than $(\sigma s\rho/\delta)^2$.

Hints: First show that $\varepsilon^\Pi \in \mathrm{span}(\varepsilon_1, \ldots, \varepsilon_J)$. Using the Pythagorean identity, argue that

$$\sigma^2(\varepsilon^\Pi \mid \varepsilon^\Pi) \geq \sum_j (\varepsilon^\Pi \mid \varepsilon_j)^2.$$

Using part (a) to compute e_j, show that

$$\sum_j e_j^2 \leq (\sigma s \rho)^2.$$

2.9 NOTES

The mean-variance theory of portfolio choice is due to Markowitz (1952, 1959) and Tobin (1958) (see also Merton (1972)). The connection to beta pricing is pointed out by Ross (1976b) and utilized by Roll (1977, 1978), who emphasized the problem with beta pricing relative to a proxy that is not on the frontier. The bound of Example 2.27 is due to Hansen and Jagannathan (1991). Proposition 2.23 is, to my knowledge, new.

A single-factor model, with the market acting as the single factor, was studied by Sharpe (1963). (This is the same Sharpe after whom Sharpe ratios are named.) An equilibrium giving rise to such a market-factor pricing model is known as the Capital Asset Pricing Model (CAPM) and is discussed in the following chapter. Factor pricing theory more generally (including approximate factor pricing as in Exercise 18) was introduced by Ross (1976a) under the name Arbitrage Pricing Theory (APT). Some of the early contributions to this literature include Chamberlain (1983b), Chamberlain and Rothschild (1983), Dybvig (1983), Grinblatt and Titman (1983) and Huberman (1983). Equilibrium models of factor pricing include Connor (1984), Milne (1988), Connor and Korajczyk (1989), Werner (1997) and Kim (1998).

The chapter's main results apply essentially unchanged in a setting with infinitely many states, provided the market is implemented by a finite number of contracts and all random variables are restricted to have finite variance. A suitable formal setting for such an extension is a Hilbert space, as in Chamberlain and Rothschild (1983) (but also see Reisman (1988)).

CHAPTER THREE

Optimality and Equilibrium

STRENGTHENING THE ASSUMPTION of an arbitrage-free market, in this chapter we relate state prices to preferences and endowments of agents in a competitive equilibrium, and we refine the concept of market completeness with that of effective market completeness. Equilibrium pricing is illustrated with the CAPM and representative-agent pricing, which are models that have played important roles in the development of asset pricing theory. The associated optimality theory sets the foundations for understanding optimal portfolio theory beyond last chapter's mean-variance analysis. The chapter's mathematical background is contained in Appendix A. Familiarity with Chapter 2 is assumed only in the CAPM example of Section 3.2.

3.1 PREFERENCES, OPTIMALITY AND STATE PRICES

The underlying uncertainty model is the same as in previous chapters: there are $1 + K$ spots, with spot zero representing time zero and the other K spots representing time-one states. Unless otherwise indicated, we make no use of an underlying probability. We recall the formal definition of a market X as a linear subspace of the set $\mathbb{R}^{1+K}$ of all cash flows, reflecting our informal assumption of a perfectly competitive financial market that can be incomplete but is otherwise unconstrained and free of transaction costs.

We consider an agent who may want to use a market to trade into a preferred consumption plan. For our purposes, a **consumption plan** is any cash flow, that is, any vector $c \in \mathbb{R}^{1+K}$, with c_k representing an amount consumed at spot k. Of course, in reality consumption consists of bundles of multiple goods. By assuming that consumption is one-dimensional at every spot, we are implicitly taking relative spot prices of goods as given and we measure consumption in some unit of account. The agent has preferences over consumption plans within a **consumption set** C, defined as any subset of $\mathbb{R}^{1+K}$. In a typical application we assume either that $C = \mathbb{R}^{1+K}$ or that C is the set of every consumption plan c satisfying a subsistence condition, $c_k > \ell$ for a given scalar ℓ.

The agent's preferences are modeled by a **binary relation** on C, that is, a subset $\succ$ of $C \times C$. The condition $(a, b) \in \succ$, denoted $a \succ b$, should be interpreted as the agent's willingness to switch from plan b to plan a if presented with the opportunity to do so at a sufficiently low but positive cost. Note that the statement $a \succ b$ implies $a, b \in C$. At this stage, we do not require that any two consumption plans be comparable. For example, not $a \succ b$ could mean that the agent finds a too complex to compare to b.

The preference properties of monotonicity and continuity are imposed throughout the text and are therefore made part of the definition of a preference below. Additional properties, like convexity, are imposed as needed. In defining continuity, we use the ball notation:

$$B(c; \varepsilon) = \{x \in \mathbb{R}^{1+K} : \|x - c\| \le \varepsilon\}, \quad c \in \mathbb{R}^{1+K}, \quad \varepsilon \in (0, \infty),$$

where $\| \cdot \|$ denotes the Euclidean norm (although, as explained in Section A.5, the definition of continuity would remain the same if one were to use any other norm on $\mathbb{R}^{1+K}$).

Definition 3.1. *A preference is a binary relation $\succ$ on some consumption set C that satisfies:*

1. *(irreflexivity) There is no c such that $c \succ c$.*

2. *(monotonicity) For every arbitrage cash flow h,*

$$(c \in C \implies c + h \succ c) \quad and \quad (b \succ c \implies b + h \succ c).$$

3. *(continuity) If $a \succ b$, then there exists a sufficiently small scalar $\varepsilon > 0$ such that $x \succ y$ for every $x \in B(a; \varepsilon)$ and $y \in B(b; \varepsilon)$.*

*A preference $\succ$ is **convex** if the set $\{c : c \succ b\}$ is convex for every $b \in C$.*

Remark 3.2. *Since a preference $\succ$ on C is a subset of $C \times C$, the above restrictions on $\succ$ imply that C is open and monotone in the sense that $c \in C$ and $h \in \mathbb{R}_+^{1+K}$ implies $c + h \in C$.*

For the remainder of this section, we fix a consumption set C, a preference $\succ$ on C, a reference consumption plan c in C, and a market X.

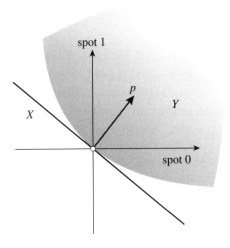

Figure 3.1 Optimality and state-price vector.

Definition 3.3. *The consumption plan c is **optimal** if $c + y \succ c$ implies $y \notin X$. Given any vector p in $\mathbb{R}^{1+K}$, the consumption plan c is p-**optimal** if $c + y \succ c$ implies $p \cdot y > 0$.*

Remark 3.4. *By the monotonicity of $\succ$, if c is optimal, then X is necessarily arbitrage-free. Similarly, if c is p-optimal, then p is strictly positive.*

Optimality and p-optimality are related as follows.

Proposition 3.5. *(a) If c is p-optimal for some state-price vector p, then c is optimal.*

(b) Suppose $\succ$ is convex. If c is optimal, then c is p-optimal for some state-price vector p.

(c) Suppose the market X is complete with state-price vector p. Then c is optimal if and only if c is p-optimal.

Proof. We first note that c is optimal if and only if $X \cap Y = \emptyset$, where

$$Y = \{y \in \mathbb{R}^{1+K} : c + y \succ c\}.$$

(a) If p is a state-price vector and c is p-optimal, then

$$(x \in X \implies p \cdot x \le 0) \quad \text{and} \quad (y \in Y \implies p \cdot y > 0). \qquad (3.1)$$

Therefore, $X \cap Y = \emptyset$.

(b) Suppose c is optimal and therefore $X \cap Y = \emptyset$. Since $\succ$ is assumed convex, Y is convex. The separating hyperplane theorem (Corollary A.30) implies that there exists a nonzero vector $p \in \mathbb{R}^{1+K}$ such that $p \cdot x \leq 0$ for all $x \in X$ and $p \cdot y \geq 0$ for all $y \in Y$. Since $\succ$ is continuous, Y is open and therefore (3.1) must hold. (To see why, suppose $p \cdot y = 0$ for some $y \in Y$ and let $\varepsilon > 0$ be small enough so that $y - \varepsilon p \in Y$. We then have the contradiction $0 \leq p \cdot (y - \varepsilon p) < 0$.) The second part of (3.1) implies that c is p-optimal and p is strictly positive. Finally, the first part of (3.1) implies that p is a state-price vector.

(c) Suppose c is optimal. The assumptions on X and p imply that

$$X = \{x \in \mathbb{R}^{1+K} : p \cdot x = 0\}.$$

By preference monotonicity, if there exists some x such that $c + x \succ c$ and $p \cdot x \leq 0$, then there exists some x such that $c + x \succ c$ and $p \cdot x = 0$, in contradiction to the optimality of c. Therefore c is p-optimal. The converse follows from part (a). ∎

The geometry of the foregoing proof should be compared to that of the first fundamental theorem of asset pricing. In the latter, a state-price vector p strictly separates X from the set of arbitrage cash flows. The dual optimality condition (3.1) on the other hand requires the strict separation of X from the set Y, which is generally a strict superset of the set of arbitrage cash flows.

3.2 EQUILIBRIUM

We introduce a simple version of competitive equilibrium, in which agents use a market to trade into optimal consumption plans and their trades clear the market. We have already defined an agent's consumption set and preference. The formal definition of an agent is completed by introducing endowments.

Definition 3.6. An **agent** is a triple $(C, \succ, e)$, where C is a consumption set, $\succ$ is a preference on C, and e is a consumption plan, called the agent's **endowment**. The cash flow x is an **optimal trade** for agent $(C, \succ, e)$ given a market X if $e + x \in C$, $x \in X$ and there exists no $y \in X$ such that $e + x + y \succ e + x$.

Remark 3.7. *For any $x \in X$, $e + x$ is an optimal consumption plan in C relative to the preference $\succ$ and market X (Definition 3.3) if and only if x is an optimal trade for agent $(C, \succ, e)$ given X.*

We define equilibrium in terms of the agents

$$(C^i, \succ^i, e^i), \quad i = 1, \ldots, I, \tag{3.2}$$

who are fixed throughout, with corresponding **aggregate endowment**

$$e = \sum_{i=1}^{I} e^i.$$

An **allocation** is any vector of consumption plans of the form

$$\mathbf{c} = (c^1, \ldots, c^I) \in C^1 \times \cdots \times C^I.$$

In an equilibrium all agents must find their individual consumption optimal given the market X, and the aggregate consumption must equal the aggregate endowment.

Definition 3.8. *An **equilibrium** is a pair $(\mathbf{c}, X)$ of an allocation $\mathbf{c}$ and a market X such that the following conditions hold:*

1. *(individual optimality) For every agent i, $c^i - e^i$ is an optimal trade for agent i given X.*
2. *(market clearing) The agents' trades $c^i - e^i$ sum up to zero. Equivalently, aggregate consumption matches the aggregate endowment:*

$$\sum_{i=1}^{I} c^i = e.$$

Example 3.9 (Spot-Market Equilibrium). *We take as given J assets whose payoffs form the rows of the $J \times K$ matrix D. A **spot-price vector** is any column vector $S \in \mathbb{R}^J$. A portfolio $\theta^i \in \mathbb{R}^J$ is **optimal** for agent i given the prices S if the corresponding consumption plan $c^i = e^i + \theta^{i\prime}(-S, D)$ is in C^i and there exists no portfolio $\alpha \in \mathbb{R}^J$ such that $e^i + \alpha'(-S, D) \succ^i c^i$. A **portfolio profile** is a $J \times I$ matrix $\theta = (\theta^1, \ldots, \theta^I)$, with θ^i interpreted as a portfolio of agent i. A **spot-market equilibrium** is a pair (θ, S) of a portfolio profile and a spot-price vector such that*

1. *θ^i is optimal for agent i given S, for every agent i.*
2. *θ **clears the market**, meaning that $\sum_i \theta^i = 0$.*

59

To relate a spot-market equilibrium to Definition 3.8, we define the implemented market corresponding to a spot-price vector S as

$$X_S = \{\alpha'(-S, D) : \alpha \in \mathbb{R}^J\}.$$

The portfolio θ^i finances the consumption plan $c^i = e^i + \theta^{i\prime}(-S, D)$. The portfolio profile $\boldsymbol{\theta}$ finances the allocation $\mathbf{c}$ if θ^i finances c^i for every agent i. Suppose $(\boldsymbol{\theta}, S)$ is a spot-market equilibrium and let $\mathbf{c}$ be the corresponding financed allocation. Then $(\mathbf{c}, X_S)$ is an equilibrium. Conversely, suppose $(\mathbf{c}, X_S)$ is an equilibrium for some spot-price vector S. Then there exists a portfolio profile $\boldsymbol{\theta}$ that finances $\mathbf{c}$ and $(\boldsymbol{\theta}, S)$ is a spot-market equilibrium. Such a portfolio profile can be constructed by selecting the portfolio θ^i to finance c^i for every agent $i \geq 2$ and defining $\theta^1 = -\sum_{i=2}^I \theta^i$. By market clearing of $\mathbf{c}$ and the linearity of the financing condition, θ^1 finances c^1.

A simple equilibrium pricing argument that has played a prominent role in the early development of asset pricing theory is the Capital Asset Pricing Model, or CAPM for short. We outline a version of the CAPM based on the results of Chapter 2. (Variants are given in Exercise 2 of this chapter and Exercise 12 of the following chapter.)

Example 3.10 (CAPM). *We fix an underlying strictly positive probability P and we consider an arbitrage-free market X with the special cash flows x^Π and $x^\mathbb{E}$ of Definition 2.1. A default-free discount bond may or may not be traded. We derive the CAPM under the following assumptions:*

- *(equilibrium) $(\mathbf{c}, X)$ is an equilibrium relative to the agents*

$$(\mathbb{R}^{1+K}, \succ^i, e^i), \quad i = 1, \ldots, I.$$

- *(marketed endowments) For every agent i, e^i is marketed.*

- *(variance-averse preferences) For any agent i, if a and b are marketed cash flows such that $a(0) = b(0)$ and $\mathbb{E}a(1) = \mathbb{E}b(1)$, then*

$$\text{var}[a(1)] < \text{var}[b(1)] \quad \text{implies} \quad a \succ^i b.$$

- *(regularity) $e(1)$ is not colinear with $x^\mathbb{E}(1)$.*

By the marketed-endowment assumption, the equilibrium consumption plan of agent i can be written as

$$c^i = w^i \mathbf{1}^0 + x^i, \quad \text{for some } w^i \in \mathbb{R} \text{ and } x^i \in X.$$

By the optimality of c^i and variance aversion, x^i is necessarily a frontier cash flow and therefore

$$x^i = a^i x^{\Pi} + b^i x^{\mathbb{E}}, \quad \text{for some } a^i, \ b^i \in \mathbb{R}.$$

Let us define the scalars $w = \sum_i w^i$, $a = \sum_i a^i$ and $b = \sum_i b^i$. Adding up over all agents, and using market clearing and the regularity assumption, we conclude that

$$e = w\mathbf{1}^0 + x, \quad \text{where } x = ax^{\Pi} + bx^{\mathbb{E}} \text{ and } a \neq 0. \tag{3.3}$$

*By Proposition 2.10, the trade x is a pricing cash flow. This is the essential CAPM conclusion, although the CAPM is usually stated in terms of beta pricing. Assuming that $x(0) \neq 0$, we define the **market return** as*

$$M = -\frac{x(1)}{x(0)} = \frac{e(1)}{\text{present value of } e(1)} = \frac{e(1)}{w - e(0)}.$$

Assuming further that M is not the g.m.v. return, Theorem 2.22 implies that M is a beta-pricing return, which is the usual CAPM conclusion. (Note that X is not degenerate by equation (3.3), the regularity assumption and Proposition 2.17.) A concrete construction of a CAPM equilibrium is part of Exercise 8.

Equilibrium as just defined is related to the following version of the standard competitive equilibrium notion for exchange economies, where Arrow cash flows play the traditional role of commodities, and state prices play the role of commodity prices.

Definition 3.11. *An **Arrow-Debreu equilibrium** is a pair $(\mathbf{c}, p)$ of an allocation $\mathbf{c}$ and a vector $p \in \mathbb{R}^{1+K}$ such that the following conditions hold:*

1. *(individual optimality) For every agent i,*

$$(p \cdot c^i \leq p \cdot e^i) \quad \text{and} \quad (c \succ c^i \implies p \cdot c > p \cdot e^i).$$

2. *(market clearing) $\sum_{i=1}^{I} c^i = e$.*

Remark 3.12. *By preference monotonicity, the individual optimality condition is equivalent to*

$$(p \cdot c^i = p \cdot e^i) \quad \text{and} \quad (c^i + y \succ^i c^i \implies p \cdot y > 0).$$

The second part of this condition is p-optimality of c^i relative to $\succ^i$.

Proposition 3.13. *Suppose p is a state-price vector relative to the market X, and* **c** *is an allocation such that* $c^i - e^i \in X$ *for every i. If* $(\mathbf{c}, p)$ *is an Arrow-Debreu equilibrium, then* $(\mathbf{c}, X)$ *is an equilibrium. Conversely, if* $(\mathbf{c}, X)$ *is an equilibrium and X is complete, then* $(\mathbf{c}, p)$ *is an Arrow-Debreu equilibrium.*

Proof. Suppose $(\mathbf{c}, p)$ is an Arrow-Debreu equilibrium and $c^i - e^i \in X$. Remarks 3.7 and 3.12 and Proposition 3.5(a) imply that $c^i - e^i$ is an optimal trade for agent i and therefore $(\mathbf{c}, X)$ is an equilibrium. Conversely, suppose $(\mathbf{c}, X)$ is an equilibrium and X is complete. Since $c^i - e^i \in X$ and p is a state-price vector, $p \cdot c^i = p \cdot e^i$. By Proposition 3.5(c), c^i is p-optimal relative to $\succ^i$ and therefore $(\mathbf{c}, p)$ is an Arrow-Debreu equilibrium. ∎

Proposition 3.13 leaves open the question of whether an incomplete-market equilibrium allocation is necessarily an allocation of some Arrow-Debreu equilibrium. Proposition 3.5(b) shows that, given preference convexity, optimality for agent i implies p^i-optimality for some state-price vector p^i. Since there are many linearly independent state-price vectors relative to an incomplete market, it is not clear that we can select the p^i to be common among agents. In fact, we argue in the following section that this is the case if and only if the market is effectively complete.

3.3 EFFECTIVE MARKET COMPLETENESS

We continue in last section's setting, where allocations and equilibrium are defined relative to the given agents (3.2). Individual-agent optimality requires that an agent has no incentive to trade away from the optimal plan. Even when faced with individually optimal plans, however, agents may still have an incentive to trade as a group and break up the traded cash flow among them. This motivates the following definition of allocational optimality given a market.

Definition 3.14. *The allocation* **c** *is* **optimal given the market** *X if*

$$c^i + y^i \succ^i c^i \text{ for every agent } i \quad \text{implies} \quad \sum_{i=1}^{I} y^i \notin X.$$

Allocational optimality is equivalent to the apparently stronger requirement of allocational optimality relative to every subset of agents.

Proposition 3.15. *The allocation* **c** *is optimal given the market* X *if and only if for any set* $L \subseteq \{1, \ldots, I\}$ *of agents,*

$$c^i + y^i \succ^i c^i \text{ for all } i \in L \quad \text{implies} \quad \sum_{i \in L} y^i \notin X.$$

Proof. Given any $L \subseteq \{1, \ldots, I\}$, suppose $c^i + x^i \succ c^i$ for all $i \in L$, where $\sum_{i \in L} x^i = x \in X$. Let $x^i = 0$ for $i \notin L$, and fix any agent $l \in L$. By preference continuity, there exists some $\varepsilon > 0$ such that $c^l + x^l - \varepsilon \mathbf{1} \succ c^l$. Let $y^l = x^l - \varepsilon \mathbf{1}$ and $y^i = x^i + \varepsilon \mathbf{1}/(I-1)$ for $i \neq l$. Then $\sum_{i=1}^{I} y^i = x \in X$ and $c^i + y^i \succ^i c^i$ for every agent i. Therefore, **c** is not optimal given X. The converse is immediate. ∎

Corollary 3.16. *If an allocation* **c** *is optimal given the market* X, *then each* c^i *is individually optimal:* $c^i + y \succ^i c^i \implies y \notin X$.

Suppose an allocation is not optimal given the market X. Then a market maker can step in and offer strictly desirable trades for a positive fee, while perfectly hedging the aggregate position in the market X. An effectively complete market, formally defined below, is one that presents no market-making opportunities of this type. In reality, fundamental economic forces, such as moral-hazard or liquidity concerns, can prevent the market maker from fully exploiting a missing market, leading to equilibria in which markets are not effectively complete.

Definition 3.17. *An **effectively complete market equilibrium** is an equilibrium* $(\mathbf{c}, X)$ *such that the allocation* **c** *is optimal given the market* X.

In the remainder of this section, we characterize allocational optimality given a market and we show that, at least for convex preferences, the set of effectively complete market equilibrium allocations is the same as the set of Arrow-Debreu equilibrium allocations.

We begin by extending the definition of p-optimality to allocations.

Definition 3.18. *Given any* $p \in \mathbb{R}^{1+K}$, *the allocation* **c** *is p-**optimal** if*

$$c^i + y^i \succ^i c^i \text{ for every agent } i \quad \text{implies} \quad p \cdot \sum_{i=1}^{I} y^i > 0.$$

The following result generalizes Proposition 3.5 (which corresponds to the single-agent case, $I = 1$).

Proposition 3.19. *The following are true for any allocation* **c** *and market* X.

(a) *Suppose* p *is a state-price vector relative to* X. *If* **c** *is* p-*optimal, then* **c** *is optimal given* X.

(b) *If each* $\succ^i$ *is convex and* **c** *is an optimal allocation given the market* X, *then there exists some state-price vector* p *(relative to* X *) such that* **c** *is* p-*optimal.*

(c) *Suppose the market* X *is complete and* p *is a corresponding state-price vector. Then the allocation* **c** *is optimal given* X *if and only if it is* p-*optimal.*

Proof. Note that **c** is optimal given X if and only if $X \cap Y = \emptyset$, where

$$Y = \left\{ y \in \mathbb{R}^{1+K} : y = \sum_{i=1}^{I} y^i, \ c^i + y^i \succ^i c^i \right\}.$$

Given this new definition of Y, the proof of parts (a) and (b) is the same as that of the respective parts of Proposition 3.5, with **c** in place of c. For part (c), the argument is analogous to the proof of Proposition 3.5(c): Suppose **c** is optimal given the complete market $X = \{x \in \mathbb{R}^{1+K} : p \cdot x = 0\}$. By preference monotonicity, if there exist agent trades x^i such that $c^i + x^i \succ^i c^i$ and $p \cdot x \leq 0$ for $x = \sum_i x^i$, then there exist trades x^i satisfying the same condition but with $p \cdot x = 0$. Therefore, **c** is p-optimal. The converse follows from part (a). ■

The argument of Proposition 3.13 on the relationship between equilibria and Arrow-Debreu equilibria can now be extended as follows.

Proposition 3.20. (a) *Suppose* p *is a state-price vector relative to the market* X *and* **c** *is an allocation such that* $c^i - e^i \in X$ *for every* i. *If* $(\mathbf{c}, p)$ *is an Arrow-Debreu equilibrium, then* $(\mathbf{c}, X)$ *is an effectively complete market equilibrium.*

(b) *If each* $\succ^i$ *is convex and* $(\mathbf{c}, X)$ *is an effectively complete market equilibrium, then there exists a state-price vector* p *relative to* X *such that* $(\mathbf{c}, p)$ *is an Arrow-Debreu equilibrium.*

Proof. (a) Suppose that $(\mathbf{c}, p)$ is an Arrow-Debreu equilibrium and $c^i + y^i \succ c^i$ for every agent i. Since c^i is p-optimal, $p \cdot y^i > 0$ for every i and therefore $p \cdot \sum_i y^i > 0$. If p is a state-price vector, then $\sum_i y^i \notin X$, proving that **c** is optimal given X. The allocation **c** clears the market since $(\mathbf{c}, p)$ is an Arrow-Debreu equilibrium. Given the assumption $c^i - e^i \in X$ and Corollary 3.16, it follows that $(\mathbf{c}, X)$ is an effectively complete market equilibrium.

(b) Given the assumptions of part (b), Proposition 3.19(b) implies that there exists some state-price vector p (relative to X) such that **c** is p-optimal, and therefore **c** is optimal given the complete market $X_p = \{x \in \mathbb{R}^{1+K} : p \cdot x = 0\}$. By Corollary 3.16, for every agent i, c^i is optimal given X_p and therefore p-optimal. Therefore, $(\mathbf{c}, p)$ is an Arrow-Debreu equilibrium. ∎

Finally, we consider another interpretation of effective market completeness, based on the idea that in an equilibrium $(\mathbf{c}, X)$ agents may be optimizing relative to an implicit complete market X_p that includes X. In such an equilibrium, the possible incompleteness of X is nonbinding.

Proposition 3.21. *Given any equilibrium* $(\mathbf{c}, X)$, *consider the following conditions:*

1. *There exists a complete market X_p such that $X \subseteq X_p$ and $(\mathbf{c}, X_p)$ is an equilibrium.*

2. $(\mathbf{c}, X)$ *is an effectively complete market equilibrium.*

Condition 1 implies condition 2. Conversely, if each $\succ^i$ is convex, condition 2 implies condition 1.

Proof. Defining $X_p = \{x \in \mathbb{R}^{1+K} : p \cdot x = 0\}$, Proposition 3.13 implies that $(\mathbf{c}, p)$ is an Arrow-Debreu equilibrium if and only if $(\mathbf{c}, X_p)$ is an equilibrium. Also p is a state-price vector relative to X if and only if $X \subseteq X_p$. Given these observations, the result follows from Proposition 3.20. ∎

3.4 REPRESENTATIVE-AGENT PRICING

Representative-agent pricing refers to equilibrium pricing models in which market prices are characterized as being in equilibrium relative to a single agent, the representative agent, whose endowment is the aggregate endowment in the economy, and whose preferences are defined independently of how the aggregate endowment is initially allocated. Such models produce specific predictions on the relationship between aggregate consumption and asset prices.

This section provides sufficient conditions on the structure of preferences and endowments for representative-agent pricing to be possible. As we will see in the following section, if preferences are also assumed to have an additive utility representation, this section's restrictions imply specific parameterizations (namely, power, logarithmic or exponential utilities). The arguments presented here apply in more general settings, however, including the recursive utility framework of Chapter 6. The scale/translation invariance restrictions on preferences introduced in this section also play an important role in the dynamic theory of optimal consumption/ portfolio choice of Chapter 6.

A reference market X is given throughout and is characterized as part of an equilibrium under special assumptions on the agents.

3.4.1 Aggregation Based on Scale Invariance

We first consider an argument based on a scale-invariance[1] restriction on preferences, which is related to a notion of constant relative risk aversion in the following chapter. Although the assumptions are stated in terms of preferences, the monotonicity and continuity restrictions on preferences play no role in what follows. A variant of the argument that includes CAPM equilibria is given in Exercise 8.

Definition 3.22. *A preference $\succ^*$ is* **scale invariant** *(SI) if*

$$\tilde{c} \succ^* c \quad \text{implies} \quad s\tilde{c} \succ^* sc \text{ for all } s \in (0, \infty).$$

For the remainder of this subsection, we fix a reference agent

$$(\mathbb{R}_{++}^{1+K}, \succ^*, e^*), \quad \text{where } \succ^* \text{ is scale invariant.} \tag{3.4}$$

For the purposes of this discussion, we define an agent $(C, \succ, e)$ to be an **SI agent with characteristics** (b, w, y) if b is a cash flow, w is a positive scalar, y is a trade in X, and the agent is specified in terms of the reference

---

[1] The term "homothetic" is often used instead of "scale-invariant" in the literature.

agent (3.4) by

$$C = \{c : c - b \in \mathbb{R}_{++}^{1+K}\}, \quad \tilde{c} \succ c \iff \tilde{c} - b \succ^* c - b,$$
$$e = b + we^* + y. \tag{3.5}$$

We interpret b as the agent's subsistence plan, w as the agent's wealth above subsistence measured in multiples of the reference plan e^*, and y as an endowed trade (whose present value is zero). For example, if $e^* = \mathbf{1}^0$, then the present value of the endowment in excess of subsistence, $e - b$, is equal to w. We do not assume, however, that e^* is marketed.

Our first key observation is the following lemma, which shows that given the existence of an optimum, every SI agent finds it optimal to consume in excess of subsistence the same plan scaled by the specific agent's wealth above subsistence.

Lemma 3.23. *Suppose $(C, \succ, e)$ is an SI agent with characteristics (b, w, y) and the cash flows x and x^* are related by $x + y = wx^*$. Then x is an optimal trade for agent $(C, \succ, e)$ if and only if x^* is an optimal trade for the reference agent (3.4). The corresponding optimal consumption plans $c = e + x$ and $c^* = e^* + x^*$ are related by*

$$c - b = wc^*. \tag{3.6}$$

Proof. Suppose $x + y = wx^*$ and therefore $x \in X \iff x^* \in X$. By the definition of the endowment e, the consumption plans $c = e + x$ and $c^* = e^* + x^*$ are related by (3.6). Suppose $\tilde{x}$ and $\tilde{x}^*$ are also related by $\tilde{x} + y = w\tilde{x}^*$, and let $\tilde{c} = e + \tilde{x}$ and $\tilde{c}^* = e^* + \tilde{x}^*$ and therefore $\tilde{c} - b = w\tilde{c}^*$. The claim follows from the equivalences

$$\tilde{c} \succ c \iff \tilde{c} - b \succ^* c - b \iff w\tilde{c}^* \succ^* wc^* \iff \tilde{c}^* \succ^* c^*. \quad \blacksquare$$

We now consider an economy of SI agents, with the characteristics of agent i denoted (b^i, w^i, y^i). We define the **representative agent** as the SI agent with characteristics (b, w, y), where

$$b = \sum_i b^i, \quad w = \sum_i w^i, \quad y = \sum_i y^i. \tag{3.7}$$

It follows that the endowment of the representative agent is the aggregate endowment $e = \sum_i e^i$. Using Lemma 3.23, we construct an equilibrium in which all agents consume in excess of subsistence the same amount scaled by their individual wealth above subsistence. Given market clearing, we can think of the resulting allocation as being the result of first allocating to all agents their subsistence plans and then allocating the remaining aggregate endowment $e - b$ in proportion to each agent's wealth above subsistence. As a result, agent i consumes

$$c^i = b^i + \frac{w^i}{w}(e - b). \tag{3.8}$$

We argue that such an equilibrium is equivalent to the optimality of the aggregate endowment for the representative agent. Finally, given convex preferences, in this equilibrium the market is effectively complete.

Proposition 3.24. *Suppose that for every $i \in \{1, \ldots, I\}$, $(C^i, \succ^i, e^i)$ is an SI agent with characteristics (b^i, w^i, y^i). The **representative agent** $(C, \succ, e)$ is defined as the SI agent with characteristics (b, w, y) given in equations* (3.7). *The allocation $\mathbf{c} = (c^1, \ldots, c^I)$ is defined in* (3.8). *Then $(\mathbf{c}, X)$ is an equilibrium if and only if e is an optimal consumption plan for the representative agent given the market X. Finally, if $\succ^*$ is convex and $(\mathbf{c}, X)$ is an equilibrium, then $(\mathbf{c}, X)$ is an effectively complete market equilibrium.*

Proof. Defining $c^* = (1/w)(e - b)$, note that

$$c^i = b^i + w^i c^*, \quad i = 1, \ldots, I.$$

It follows that $\sum_i c^i = b + wc^* = e$ and therefore the allocation $\mathbf{c}$ clears the market. Let $x^i = c^i - e^i$ and $x^* = c^* - e^*$. The definition of c^i and e^i implies that $x^i + y^i = w^i x^*$. Adding up over i, we also have $0 + y = wx^*$. By Lemma 3.23, x^i is an optimal trade for trader i if and only if x^* is an optimal trade for agent $(\mathbb{R}^{1+K}_{++}, \succ^*, e^*)$, if and only if zero is an optimal trade for the representative agent. Therefore, $(\mathbf{c}, X)$ is an equilibrium if and only if e is optimal for the representative agent.

Finally, suppose $\succ^*$ is convex and $(\mathbf{c}, X)$ is an equilibrium. We argue that the allocation $\mathbf{c}$ is optimal given X. Suppose that $c^i + \tilde{x}^i \succ^i c^i$ for all i and $\tilde{x} = \sum_i \tilde{x}_i$. By the definition of $\succ^i$, c^i and c^*,

$$\frac{w^i}{w}(e - b) + \tilde{x}^i \succ^* \frac{w^i}{w}(e - b).$$

By scale invariance,

$$e - b + \frac{w}{w^i}\tilde{x}^i \succ^* e - b.$$

Since $\tilde{x}$ is a convex combination of the $(w/w^i)\tilde{x}^i$, convexity of $\succ^*$ implies $e - b + \tilde{x} \succ^* e - b$, which is the same as $e + \tilde{x} \succ e$. Since e is an optimal consumption plan for the representative agent, it follows that $\tilde{x} \notin X$. ∎

3.4.2 Aggregation Based on Translation Invariance

Another version of the aggregation argument is based on a translation-invariance assumption on preferences, which is related to a notion of constant absolute risk aversion in the following chapter. As in the last subsection, the monotonicity and continuity assumptions on preferences play no role. For our purposes, translation invariance means translation invariance in the direction of the unit cash flow $\mathbf{1} = (1, \dots, 1)$ (although the arguments that follow remain valid if the symbol $\mathbf{1}$ is assumed to represent any other fixed reference cash flow).

Definition 3.25. *A preference $\succ^*$ is* **translation invariant (TI)** *if*

$$\tilde{c} \succ^* c \quad \text{implies} \quad \tilde{c} + \theta\mathbf{1} \succ^* c + \theta\mathbf{1} \text{ for all } \theta \in \mathbb{R}.$$

For the remainder of this subsection, we fix a reference agent

$$(\mathbb{R}^{1+K}, \succ^*, e^*), \quad \text{where } \succ^* \text{ is translation-invariant.} \tag{3.9}$$

We define an agent $(C, \succ, e)$ to be a **TI agent with characteristics** (α, θ, y) if α is a positive scalar, θ is a scalar, y is a trade in X, and

$$C = \mathbb{R}^{1+K}, \quad \tilde{c} \succ c \iff \frac{1}{\alpha}\tilde{c} \succ^* \frac{1}{\alpha}c, \quad e = \alpha e^* + \theta\mathbf{1} + y. \tag{3.10}$$

In the following chapter we show that if the agent consumes only at time one and $\succ^*$ is risk averse, then α represents an ordinal measure of risk tolerance: the lower its value, the more risk averse the agent. More generally, however, α also relates to the agent's time preferences.

The translation-invariant analog to Lemma 3.23 follows.

Lemma 3.26. *Suppose $(C, \succ, e)$ is an TI agent with characteristics (α, θ, y), and the cash flows x and x^* are related by $x + y = \alpha x^*$. Then x is an optimal trade for agent $(C, \succ, e)$ if and only if x^* is an optimal trade for the reference* *agent* (3.9). *The corresponding optimal consumption plans* $c = e + x$ *and* $c^* = e^* + x^*$ *are related by*

$$c = \alpha c^* + \theta 1. \tag{3.11}$$

Proof. Suppose $x + y = \alpha x^*$ and therefore $x \in X \iff x^* \in X$. By the definition of the endowment e, the consumption plans $c = e + x$ and $c^* = e^* + x^*$ are related by (3.11). Suppose $\tilde{x}$ and $\tilde{x}^*$ are also related by $\tilde{x} + y = \alpha \tilde{x}^*$ and let $\tilde{c} = e + \tilde{x}$ and $\tilde{c}^* = e + \tilde{x}^*$ and therefore $\tilde{c} = \alpha \tilde{c}^* + \theta 1$. The claim follows from the equivalences

$$\tilde{c} \succ c \iff \frac{1}{\alpha}\tilde{c} \succ^* \frac{1}{\alpha}c \iff \tilde{c}^* + \frac{\theta}{\alpha}1 \succ^* c^* + \frac{\theta}{\alpha}1 \iff \tilde{c}^* \succ^* c^*. \qquad \blacksquare$$

We now consider an economy of TI agents, with the characteristics of agent i denoted $(\alpha^i, \theta^i, y^i)$. We define the **representative agent** as the TI agent with characteristics (α, θ, y), where

$$\alpha = \sum_i \alpha^i, \quad \theta = \sum_i \theta^i, \quad y = \sum_i y^i. \tag{3.12}$$

Therefore, the representative agent's endowment is the aggregate endowment $e = \sum_i e^i$. Using Lemma 3.26, we construct below an equilibrium in which all agents consume their endowed annuities $\theta^i 1$ and they are allocated the remaining aggregate endowment $e - \theta 1$ in proportion to each agent's coefficient α^i. As a result agent i consumes

$$c^i = \theta^i 1 + \frac{\alpha^i}{\alpha}(e - \theta 1). \tag{3.13}$$

As in the scale-invariant formulation, such an equilibrium is equivalent to the optimality of the aggregate endowment for the representative agent, and given convex preferences, the equilibrium implies an effectively complete market.

Proposition 3.27. *Suppose that for every $i \subset \{1, \ldots, I\}$, $(C^i, \succ^i, e^i)$ is a TI agent with characteristics $(\alpha^i, \theta^i, y^i)$. The **representative agent** $(C, \succ, e)$ is defined as the TI agent with characteristics (α, θ, y) given in equations (3.12). The allocation $\mathbf{c} = (c^1, \ldots, c^I)$ is defined by (3.13). Then $(\mathbf{c}, X)$ is an equilibrium if and only if e is an optimal consumption plan for the representative agent given the market X. Finally, if $\succ^*$ is convex and $(\mathbf{c}, X)$ is an equilibrium, then $(\mathbf{c}, X)$ is an effectively complete market equilibrium.*

Proof. Letting $c^* = (1/\alpha)(e - \theta\mathbf{1})$, we have

$$c^i = \theta^i\mathbf{1} + \alpha^i c^*, \quad i = 1, \ldots, I,$$

and therefore $\sum_i c^i = \theta\mathbf{1} + \alpha c^* = e$, which confirms market clearing. Let $x^i = c^i - e^i$ and $x^* = c^* - e^*$. The definition of c^i and e^i implies that $x^i + y^i = \alpha^i x^*$. Adding up over i, we also have $0 + y = \alpha x^*$. By Lemma 3.26, x^i is an optimal trade for trader i if and only if x^* is an optimal trade for agent $(\mathbb{R}^{1+K}, \succ^*, e^*)$, if and only if zero is an optimal trade for the representative agent. Therefore, $(\mathbf{c}, X)$ is an equilibrium if and only if e is optimal for the representative agent.

Finally, suppose $\succ^*$ is convex and $(\mathbf{c}, X)$ is an equilibrium. We argue that the allocation $\mathbf{c}$ is optimal given X. Suppose that $c^i + \tilde{x}^i \succ^i c^i$ for all i and $\tilde{x} = \sum_i \tilde{x}^i$. Substituting the definitions of $\succ^i$, c^i and c^* in the condition $c^i + \tilde{x}^i \succ^i c^i$, and using the translation invariance of $\succ^*$ to cancel out multiples of $\mathbf{1}$ on both sides, we conclude that

$$\frac{1}{\alpha}e + \frac{1}{\alpha^i}\tilde{x}^i \succ^* \frac{1}{\alpha}e.$$

Since $\tilde{x}/\alpha$ is a convex combination of the $\tilde{x}^i/\alpha^i$, the convexity of $\succ^*$ implies

$$\frac{1}{\alpha}(e + \tilde{x}) \succ^* \frac{1}{\alpha}e,$$

which is the same as $e + \tilde{x} \succ e$. Since e is an optimal consumption plan for the representative agent, it follows that $\tilde{x} \notin X$. $\blacksquare$

3.5 UTILITY

Utility functions provide a useful way of quantifying preferences that will play an important role in the remainder of this text. The first subsection below characterizes preferences admitting a utility representation and relates last section's scale- or translation-invariance preference properties to restrictions on the functional form of utilities. The second subsection characterizes preferences with an additive utility representation and shows that the combination of additivity with scale or translation invariance results in specific parametric utility forms.

3.5.1 Compensation Function Construction of Utilities

For simplicity, from now on we assume that a consumption set takes the form

$$C = (\ell, \infty)^{1+K} \text{ for some } \ell \in [-\infty, 1). \tag{3.14}$$

It is convenient for our purposes to define utility functions to be monotone and continuous, although these restrictions are not standard in the literature. A function $U : C \to \mathbb{R}$ is **increasing** if $U(c + h) > U(c)$ for any arbitrage cash flow h and any $c \in C$.

Definition 3.28. *A **utility** (function) is any continuous and increasing real-valued function on some consumption set of the form* (3.14). *The utility U **represents** the preference $\succ$ on C if it has C as its domain and*

$$a \succ b \iff U(a) > U(b).$$

*Two utilities are **ordinally equivalent** if they represent the same preference.*

Proposition 3.29. *Suppose U and $\tilde{U}$ are utilities on the common consumption set* (3.14). *Then the sets $S = \{U(c) : c \in C\}$ and $\tilde{S} = \{\tilde{U}(c) : c \in C\}$ are open (connected) intervals. Finally, the utilities U and $\tilde{U}$ are ordinally equivalent if and only if there exists a unique increasing continuous function of the form $f : S \to \tilde{S}$ such that $\tilde{U} = f \circ U$.*

Proof. The consumption set restriction (3.14) implies that

$$\text{for any } c \in C, \text{ there exist } \alpha, \beta \in (\ell, \infty)$$
$$\text{such that } \alpha\mathbf{1} < c < \beta\mathbf{1}. \tag{3.15}$$

It follows that $S = \{U(s\mathbf{1}) : s \in (\ell, \infty)\}$ and $\tilde{S} = \{\tilde{U}(s\mathbf{1}) : s \in (\ell, \infty)\}$, which are connected sets since utilities are continuous. Consider the function $g : S \to (\ell, \infty)$ defined by $g(U(s\mathbf{1})) = s$. Since U is increasing, g is well-defined, increasing and onto, and consequently continuous. Therefore, $S = g^{-1}(\ell, \infty)$ is an open set. This proves that S and $\tilde{S}$ are open connected sets. Finally, suppose U and $\tilde{U}$ are ordinally equivalent and let the function $f : S \to \tilde{S}$ be defined by $f(U(s\mathbf{1})) = \tilde{U}(s\mathbf{1}), s \in (\ell, \infty)$. Clearly, f is increasing and onto, and therefore continuous. The uniqueness of f and the converse are immediate. ∎

Consider any given preference $\succ$ on a consumption set C of the form (3.14). A natural candidate for a utility representation of $\succ$ is its **compensation function** $U : C \to \mathbb{R}$, which we define by

$$U(c) = \inf\{\theta \in \mathbb{R} : \theta\mathbf{1} \succ c\}, \quad c \in C. \tag{3.16}$$

Condition (3.15) of the preceding proof and the monotonicity of $\succ$ ensure that U is well-defined. If $\succ$ has a utility representation $\tilde{U}$, then the compensation function of $\succ$ is the ordinally equivalent utility

$$U = f^{-1} \circ \tilde{U}, \quad \text{where} \quad f(\theta) = \tilde{U}(\theta\mathbf{1}), \quad \theta \in (\ell, \infty).$$

The compensation function of $\succ$ is, however, well-defined even if $\succ$ admits no utility representation. The existence of a utility representation can be characterized in terms of the **weak preference** $\succeq$ corresponding to $\succ$, which we define as the relation

$$a \succeq b \iff \text{not } b \succ a, \quad a, b \in C.$$

The weak preference $\succeq$ is

- **complete** if for all $a, b \in C$, either $a \succeq b$ or $b \succeq a$ or both;
- **transitive** if $a \succeq b$ and $b \succeq c$ implies $a \succeq c$.

Proposition 3.30. *A preference on a consumption set of the form* (3.14) *admits a utility representation if and only if the corresponding weak preference is complete and transitive.*

Proof. The "only if" part is immediate. For the converse, one can use completeness and transitivity of $\succeq$ to verify that the compensation function of $\succ$ is a utility representation of $\succ$. The details are left as an exercise. ∎

To relate last section's scale/translation invariance properties to utilities, we define a function $U : C \to \mathbb{R}$ to be

- **homogeneous of degree one** if $C = \mathbb{R}_{++}^{1+K}$ and

$$U(sc) = sU(c) \quad \text{for all } s \in (0, \infty) \text{ and } c \in C;$$

- **quasilinear with respect to 1** if $C = \mathbb{R}^{1+K}$ and

$$U(c + \theta\mathbf{1}) = U(c) + \theta \quad \text{for all } \theta \in \mathbb{R} \text{ and } c \in C.$$

73

Suppose U is the compensation function of the preference $\succ$. If $\succ$ is scale invariant, then U is homogeneous of degree one. Similarly, if $\succ$ is translation invariant, then U is quasilinear with respect to $\mathbf{1}$. Given these observations, the following result is immediate.

Proposition 3.31. *(a) Suppose $\succ$ is a preference on $\mathbb{R}^{1+K}_{++}$ that admits some utility representation. Then $\succ$ is scale invariant if and only if it can be represented by a utility that is homogeneous of degree one.*

(b) Suppose $\succ$ is a preference on $\mathbb{R}^{1+K}$ that admits some utility representation. Then $\succ$ is translation invariant if and only if it can be represented by a utility that is quasilinear with respect to $\mathbf{1}$.

Finally, we show the useful fact that convexity of a scale- or translation-invariant preference is equivalent to the concavity of the corresponding compensation function, assuming the latter is also a utility representation.

Lemma 3.32. *Suppose that the utility function $U : \mathbb{R}^{1+K}_{++} \to \mathbb{R}$ is homogeneous of degree one. Then the following conditions are equivalent:*

1. For every $x, y \in \mathbb{R}^{1+K}_{++}$ and $p \in (0,1)$,

$$U(x) = U(y) \implies U(px + (1-p)y) \geq U(x). \tag{3.17}$$

2. For every $x, y \in \mathbb{R}^{1+K}_{++}$, $U(x+y) \geq U(x) + U(y)$.

3. U is concave.

Proof. $(1 \implies 2)$ Given any $x, y \in \mathbb{R}^{1+K}_{++}$, the continuity and strict monotonicity of U implies that the constants $\alpha, \beta \in \mathbb{R}_{++}$ are well-defined by

$$U(x+y) = U(\alpha x) = U(\beta y).$$

By the homogeneity of U and condition 1, we have

$$\frac{\alpha\beta}{\alpha+\beta} U(x+y) = U\left(\frac{\beta}{\alpha+\beta}(\alpha x) + \frac{\alpha}{\alpha+\beta}(\beta y)\right) \geq U(x+y).$$

Since U is increasing, it follows that $\alpha\beta/(\alpha+\beta) \geq 1$, which is equivalent to $1 \geq \alpha^{-1} + \beta^{-1}$. Therefore,

$$U(x+y) \geq \frac{U(\alpha x)}{\alpha} + \frac{U(\beta y)}{\beta} = U(x) + U(y).$$

$(2 \Longrightarrow 3)$ For any $x, y \in \mathbb{R}_{++}^{1+K}$ and $p \in (0,1)$,

$$U(px + (1-p)y) \geq U(px) + U((1-p)y) = pU(x) + (1-p)U(y).$$

$(3 \Longrightarrow 1)$ Immediate. ∎

Proposition 3.33. *Suppose the utility function U represents the preference $\succ$ on $\mathbb{R}_{++}^{1+K}$ (respectively, $\mathbb{R}^{1+K}$), and U is homogeneous of degree one (respectively, quasilinear with respect to $\mathbf{1}$). Then $\succ$ is convex if and only if U is concave.*

Proof. The "if" statements are immediate. We show the "only if" claims.

Scale-invariant case. Suppose that the convex preference $\succ$ on $\mathbb{R}_{++}^{1+K}$ is represented by the homogeneous-of-degree-one utility function U. By the last lemma, it suffices to verify condition (3.17), given any $x, y \in \mathbb{R}_{++}^{1+K}$ and $p \in (0,1)$. Assuming $U(x) = U(y)$, we have, for any positive integer n,

$$x + \frac{1}{n}\mathbf{1} \succ x \quad \text{and} \quad y + \frac{1}{n}\mathbf{1} \succ x.$$

By the convexity of $\succ$, it follows that

$$U\left(px + (1-p)y + \frac{1}{n}\mathbf{1}\right) > U(x).$$

Letting n go to infinity and using the continuity of U, condition (3.17) is confirmed.

Translation-invariant case. Suppose that the convex preference $\succ$ on $\mathbb{R}^{1+K}$ is represented by the quasilinear-with-respect-to-$\mathbf{1}$ utility function U. Given any $x, y \in \mathbb{R}^{1+K}$ and $p \in (0,1)$, we are to show that

$$U(px + (1-p)y) \geq pU(x) + (1-p)U(y).$$

We choose $\theta \in \mathbb{R}$ so that $U(x) = U(y + \theta \mathbf{1})$. By the quasilinearity of U, the above inequality is equivalent to its version obtained by replacing y with $y + \theta \mathbf{1}$. Therefore, concavity follows again from the apparently weaker condition (3.17), which follows from the convexity of $\succ$ exactly as in the scale-invariant case. ∎

3.5.2 Additive Utilities

Utility functions are often assumed in the literature to take an additive form. Utility additivity is characterized in this section and is shown to result in expected discounted power, logarithmic or exponential utility when combined with scale- or translation-invariance assumptions. A main theme of the dynamic theory of Chapter 6 is that utility additivity across both time and states imposes a strong ad hoc restriction on the relationship between an agent's time preferences and risk aversion. On the other hand, this section's theory is reinterpreted in the following chapter to apply to atemporal preferences, forming the basis for a theory of risk aversion that plays a key role in the recursive formulation of Chapter 6.

Definition 3.34. *A utility* $U : (\ell, \infty)^{1+K} \to \mathbb{R}$ *is* **additive** *if there exist functions* $U_k : (\ell, \infty) \to \mathbb{R}$ *such that*

$$U(x) = \sum_{k=0}^{K} U_k(x_k), \quad x \in (\ell, \infty)^{1+K}. \tag{3.18}$$

Given any cash flows x, y and set of spots $A \subseteq \{0, 1, \dots, K\}$, we define the cash flow $x_A y_{-A}$ by

$$(x_A y_{-A})_k = \begin{cases} x_k, & \text{if } k \in A; \\ y_k, & \text{if } k \notin A. \end{cases}$$

The key properties characterizing additive utilities are as follows.

Definition 3.35. *(a) A preference* $\succ$ *is* **separable** *if*

$$x_A z_{-A} \succ y_A z_{-A} \quad \Longleftrightarrow \quad x_A \tilde{z}_{-A} \succ y_A \tilde{z}_{-A}, \tag{3.19}$$

for any $x, y, z, \tilde{z} \in (\ell, \infty)^{1+K}$ *and* $A \subseteq \{0, 1, \dots, K\}$.

(b) Two additive utilities U *and* $\tilde{U}$ *on* $(\ell, \infty)^{1+K}$ *are* **related by a positive affine transformation** *if there exist some* $a \in \mathbb{R}_{++}$ *and* $b \in \mathbb{R}^{1+K}$ *such that*

$$\tilde{U}_k = a U_k + b_k, \quad \text{for all } k \in \{0, 1, \dots, K\}.$$

It is immediate that a preference that admits an additive utility representation is separable, and that two additive utilities that are related by a positive affine transformation are ordinally equivalent. The following result includes converse statements, which are part of a broader additive representation theory cited in the notes.

Theorem 3.36. *(a) (Existence) Suppose $K > 1$ and $\succ$ is a preference on $(\ell, \infty)^{1+K}$ that admits some utility representation. Then $\succ$ admits an additive utility representation if and only if it is separable.*

(b) (Uniqueness) Two additive utilities on $(\ell, \infty)^{1+K}$ are ordinally equivalent if and only if they are related by a positive affine transformation.

Part (a) is not valid for $K = 1$, in which case an ordinal condition more elaborate than (3.19) is required. In applications the assumption $K > 1$ is without loss in generality, since one can always expand the state space by introducing a coin toss.

Of special interest are additive utilities that represent scale- or translation-invariant preferences, as in the representative-agent pricing theory of Section 3.4. This class of utilities is fully characterized below, under only a minor regularity assumption (which can weakened, based on results cited in the notes).

Theorem 3.37. *Suppose that the preference $\succ$ on $(\ell, \infty)^{1+K}$ admits an additive utility representation (3.18), where each U_k is continuously differentiable on some (arbitrarily small) interval.*

(a) Suppose $\ell = 0$. The preference $\succ$ is scale invariant if and only if there exists a strictly positive probability P and a positive scalar β such that $\succ$ admits an additive utility representation of the form

$$U(c) = u(c_0) + \beta \sum_k u(c_k)P_k = u(c(0)) + \beta \mathbb{E}[u(c(1))], \qquad (3.20)$$

where the function $u : (0, \infty) \to \mathbb{R}$ is given in terms of a parameter $\gamma \in \mathbb{R}$ by

$$u(x) = \frac{x^{1-\gamma} - 1}{1 - \gamma} \qquad (= \log(x) \quad \text{if } \gamma = 1). \qquad (3.21)$$

(b) Suppose $\ell = -\infty$. The preference $\succ$ is translation invariant if and only if there exists a strictly positive probability P and a positive scalar β such that $\succ$ admits an additive utility representation of the form (3.20), where the function $u : \mathbb{R} \to \mathbb{R}$ is given in terms of a parameter $\gamma \in \mathbb{R}$ by

$$u(x) = \frac{1 - \exp(-\gamma x)}{\gamma} \qquad (= x \quad \text{if } \gamma = 0). \qquad (3.22)$$

77

Proof. Suppose the preference $\succ^{\log}$ on $\mathbb{R}^{1+K}_{++}$ and the preference $\succ$ on $\mathbb{R}^{1+K}$ are related by

$$x \succ^{\log} y \quad \Longleftrightarrow \quad \log x \succ \log y.$$

Then $\succ^{\log}$ is scale invariant if and only if $\succ$ is translation invariant. We can therefore prove either part and the other follows by a change of variables. We show part (b).

Let U be any additive utility representation of the translation-invariant preference $\succ$ on $\mathbb{R}^{1+K}$. Given any scalar y, $U(x+y\mathbf{1})$ as a function of $x \in \mathbb{R}^{1+K}$ defines another additive utility that is ordinally equivalent to U. Since additive representations are unique up to positive affine transformations, there exist $a(y) \in \mathbb{R}_{++}$ and $b(y) \in \mathbb{R}^{1+K}$ such that

$$U_k(x+y) = a(y)U_k(x) + b_k(y), \quad x \in \mathbb{R}. \tag{3.23}$$

Applying this condition twice, once with $x = 0$ and once with any other $x \neq 0$, shows that

$$\frac{U_k(x+y) - U_k(y)}{x} = a(y)\frac{U_k(x) - U_k(0)}{x}, \quad x \in \mathbb{R}\setminus\{0\}.$$

Consider what happens as x approaches zero. By the regularity assumption, there exists some $y \in (\ell, \infty)$ such that the left-hand side converges to $U'_k(y)$. The right-hand side must also converge. But then the left-hand side must converge for any choice of $y \in (\ell, \infty)$, with $a(y) = U'_k(y)/U'_k(0)$. Differentiating (3.23) with respect to x gives $U'_k(x+y) = a(y)U'_k(x)$. The last two equations imply that the function $f(x) = \log(U'_k(x)/U'_k(0))$ satisfies

$$f(x+y) = f(x) + f(y), \quad x, y \in \mathbb{R}. \tag{3.24}$$

An exercise shows that if f is continuous at some point, then it is continuous everywhere. Therefore, $f(x) = -\gamma x$ for some scalar γ. Letting $P_k = U'_k(0)/\sum_k U'_k(0)$ and solving for U_k concludes the proof. ∎

A consumption plan is **deterministic** if it takes the form $(x_0, x_1\mathbf{1})$ for scalar x_0, x_1. In the preceding representations, the coefficients β and γ are determined by preferences over deterministic consumption plans, that is, by the preference $\succ^d$ on $(\ell, \infty)^2$ defined by $x \succ^d y \iff (x_0, x_1\mathbf{1}) \succ (y_0, y_1\mathbf{1})$.

A utility representation of $\succ^d$ is obtained by restricting the utility U of equation (3.20) to the set of deterministic plans:

$$x \succ^d y \iff u(x_0) + \beta u(x_1) > u(y_0) + \beta u(y_1), \quad x, y \in (\ell, \infty)^2.$$

By Theorem 3.36(b), any other additive utility representation of $\succ^d$ must be of the form $(au(x_0) + b_0) + (a\beta u(x_1) + b_1)$, for some $a \in \mathbb{R}_{++}$ and $b \in \mathbb{R}^2$. Any such utility representation uniquely determines the ratios

$$\frac{\beta u'(x_1)}{u'(x_0)} \quad \text{and} \quad -\frac{u''(x_1)}{u'(x_1)}$$

and therefore the values of β and γ. On the other hand, the coefficient γ is also determined by preferences over time-one payoffs given, say, unit time-zero consumption, that is, by comparisons of the form $(1, x) \succ (1, y)$, $x, y \in \mathbb{R}^K$. This claim can again be shown by the uniqueness property of additive representations, which implies that the ratio $-u''/u'$ is determined. In the following chapter we show that for fixed time-zero consumption, the parameter γ is a coefficient of absolute risk aversion in the translation-invariant representation (3.22) and a coefficient of relative risk aversion in the scale-invariant representation (3.21). The fact that γ is a coefficient of risk aversion that is determined by the agent's preferences over deterministic plans reflects a strong relationship between time preferences and risk aversion implied by additivity across all spots. We return to this issue in Chapter 6.

3.6 UTILITY AND INDIVIDUAL OPTIMALITY

This section provides optimality characterizations for an agent $(C, \succ, e)$, where $C = (\ell, \infty)^{1+K}$ and $\succ$ has a utility representation $U : C \to \mathbb{R}$. In this case we refer directly to the agent (C, U, e). Optimality is defined relative to a given market X, which is fixed throughout. Besides continuity and monotonicity of U, which are part of the utility definition, differentiability or concavity assumptions are imposed as needed.

We begin with an existence result.

Proposition 3.38. *Suppose that the set $\{c \in C : U(c) \geq U(e)\}$ is closed and bounded below. If the market is arbitrage-free, then an optimal trade for the agent (C, U, e) exists.*

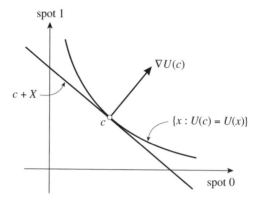

Figure 3.2 Optimality in terms of the utility gradient.

Proof. Since the market is arbitrage-free, there exists a state-price vector p. The set

$$S = \{c \in C : U(c) \geq U(e)\} \cap \{e + x : x \in X, p \cdot x \leq 0\}$$

is nonempty, closed and bounded, and therefore compact. Since U is continuous, it is maximized over S by some $c = e + x \in S$. By the definition of the set S, it follows that c is p-optimal. By Proposition 3.5, c is optimal and therefore x is an optimal trade. ∎

Next we formulate a simple characterization of the optimality of a consumption plan c in terms of the gradient vector $\nabla U(c)$. Provided the latter exists, it is specified by

$$\nabla U(c) \cdot x = \lim_{\alpha \downarrow 0} \frac{U(c + \alpha x) - U(c)}{\alpha}, \quad x \in \mathbb{R}^{1+K}.$$

The optimality condition is illustrated in Figure 3.2.

Proposition 3.39. *Given any $c \in C$, suppose the gradient vector $\nabla U(c)$ exists and is strictly positive. If c is optimal, then $\nabla U(c)$ is a state-price vector. Conversely, if U is concave and $\nabla U(c)$ is a state-price vector, then c is optimal.*

Proof. Suppose c is optimal. Using the fact that C is open, given any $x \in X$, we select $\varepsilon > 0$ small enough so that $c + \alpha x \in C$ for all

$\alpha \in [0, \varepsilon]$. The function $f(\alpha) = U(c + \alpha x)$, $\alpha \in [0, \varepsilon]$, is maximized at zero and therefore has a nonpositive right derivative at zero: $f'_+(0) = \nabla U(c) \cdot x \leq 0$. This proves that $\nabla U(c)$ is a state-price vector.

Conversely, suppose that U is concave and $p = \nabla U(c)$ is a state-price vector. For any $x \in X$ such that $c + x \in C$, the gradient inequality and the fact that $p \cdot x \leq 0$ imply that $U(c + x) \leq U(c) + p \cdot x \leq U(c)$, which proves the optimality of c. ∎

Example 3.40. *Suppose that* $C = \mathbb{R}_{++}^{1+K}$ *and the utility* $U : C \to \mathbb{R}$ *is given by*

$$U(x) = u(x_0) + \beta \sum\nolimits_{k=1}^{K} u(x_k) P_k,$$

where $u : (0, \infty) \to \mathbb{R}$ *is a concave differentiable function,* $\beta \in (0, \infty)$ *and* P *is a strictly positive probability. If* $\nabla U(c)$ *is a state-price vector, a corresponding state-price density* π *satisfies*

$$\frac{\pi_k}{\pi_0} = \beta \frac{u'(c_k)}{u'(c_0)}, \quad k = 1, \ldots, K.$$

Assuming the utility U is concave, optimality at $c \in C$ can be characterized in terms of the superdifferential

$$\partial U(c) = \{d \in \mathbb{R}^{1+K} : U(\tilde{c}) \leq U(c) + d \cdot (\tilde{c} - c) \text{ for all } \tilde{c} \in C\},$$

without assuming the existence of a utility gradient. As shown in Section A.7, if U is concave, then $\partial U(c)$ is nonempty. As shown in Section A.9, if $\partial U(c)$ is nonempty and the gradient $\nabla U(c)$ exists, then $\partial U(c) = \{\nabla U(c)\}$. We first apply the optimality conditions of Section A.8 to p-optimality (Definition 3.3).

Proposition 3.41. *Suppose* $p \in \mathbb{R}_{++}^{1+K}$ *and* $J : \mathbb{R} \to \mathbb{R} \cup \{\pm\infty\}$ *is defined by*

$$J(\delta) = \sup\{U(e + x) : p \cdot x \leq \delta, \ e + x \in C\} \quad (\inf \emptyset = -\infty). \quad (3.25)$$

Then the following are true for any c *in* C *such that* $p \cdot c = p \cdot e$.

(a) If $\lambda p \in \partial U(c)$ *for some* $\lambda \in (0, \infty)$, *then* c *is* p-*optimal and* $\lambda \in \partial J(0)$.

(b) Suppose U *is concave and* c *is* p-*optimal. Then* $\partial J(0)$ *is nonempty and* $\lambda p \in \partial U(c)$ *for every* $\lambda \in \partial J(0)$. *Assuming further that* $\nabla U(c)$

81

exists, then J is differentiable at zero and

$$\lambda = J'(0) = \nabla U(c) \cdot h \quad \text{for all } h \in \mathbb{R}^{1+K} \text{ such that } p \cdot h = 1. \quad (3.26)$$

Proof. The result follows from Theorem A.33 and Proposition A.35, noting that condition (b) of Theorem A.33 in this context can be written as $\lambda p \in \partial U(c)$ for some $\lambda \in (0, \infty)$. (The positivity of λ follows from the monotonicity of U.) To confirm condition (3.26), we note that if U is concave and $\nabla U(c)$ exists for a p-optimal c, then $\partial U(c) = \{\nabla U(c)\}$ and therefore $\lambda \in \partial J(0)$ implies $\nabla U(c) = \lambda p$. This proves that $\partial J(0)$ is a singleton and therefore $\lambda = J'(0)$. Finally, if $p \cdot h = 1$, then $\nabla U(c) \cdot h = \lambda p \cdot h = \lambda$. ∎

Condition (3.26) implies that if the agent's initial wealth $p \cdot e$ were changed by a small amount δ, the resulting optimal utility $J(\delta)$ would be approximately equal to $U(c + \delta h)$, where c is p-optimal and costs $p \cdot c = p \cdot e$ and h is any cash flow such that $p \cdot h = 1$. (This is an instance of a more general class of so-called envelope theorems.)

Example 3.42 (Scale/Translation Invariance). *Let $w = p \cdot e$ be the agent's initial wealth. If $C = \mathbb{R}^{1+K}_{++}$, $w > 0$ and U is homogeneous of degree one, then there exists a $\lambda \in (0, \infty)$ such that*

$$J(\delta) = \lambda(w + \delta) \quad \text{for all } \delta \in (-w, \infty).$$

Analogously, if $C = \mathbb{R}^{1+K}$ and U is quasilinear with respect to $\mathbf{1}$, then there exists a scalar y such that

$$J(\delta) = \frac{1}{p \cdot \mathbf{1}}(y + \delta) \quad \text{for all } \delta \in \mathbb{R}.$$

In both cases, the shadow price of wealth $\lambda = J'(0)$ is independent of the wealth level w.

Finally, we characterize an agent's optimal trade (Definition 3.6) in terms of the utility superdifferential.

Proposition 3.43. *Suppose $x \in X$. If there exists a state-price vector $p \in \partial U(e + x)$, then x is an optimal trade for agent (C, U, e). Conversely, if x is an optimal trade for agent (C, U, e) and U is concave, then there exists a state-price vector $p \in \partial U(e + x)$.*

Proof. This is a corollary of Propositions 3.5 and 3.41. It is worth noting, however, that the simple verification argument used in Proposition 3.39 also applies here: If $p \in \partial U(e+x)$ is a state-price vector, then

$$U(e+x+y) \leq U(e+x) + p \cdot y \leq U(e+x) \quad \text{for all } y \in X.$$

and therefore x is an optimal trade. ∎

3.7 UTILITY AND ALLOCATIONAL OPTIMALITY

We have seen that, under some regularity, individual optimality is characterized by the existence of a state-price vector that belongs to the utility superdifferential at the optimum or is colinear with the utility gradient at the optimum if such a gradient exists. Specializing an idea introduced in Proposition 3.19, in this section we show that allocational optimality corresponds to the existence of a common state-price vector that satisfies the individual optimality conditions for all agents at once. This fact leads to a characterization of an effectively complete market equilibrium in terms of the optimality of the aggregate endowment for a suitably constructed single agent. As a consequence, given special additive-utility structure, a state-price density in an effectively complete market equilibrium can be expressed, spot by spot, as a deterministic function of aggregate consumption.

Allocations and equilibria are defined relative to the agents

$$(C^i, U^i, e^i), \quad i = 1, \ldots, I,$$

where each $U^i : C^i \to \mathbb{R}$ is a utility and

$$C^i = (\ell^i, \infty)^{1+K} \text{ for some } \ell^i \in [-\infty, 1).$$

We recall that an allocation $\mathbf{c}$ is optimal given the market X if and only if for any other allocation $\tilde{\mathbf{c}}$,

$$U^i(\tilde{c}^i) > U^i(c^i) \text{ for all } i \implies \sum_i (\tilde{c}^i - c^i) \notin X.$$

Given our standing assumption of preference monotonicity and continuity, we show that the allocational optimality condition is equivalent to an apparently stronger version of the condition.

Proposition 3.44. *The allocation* **c** *is optimal given a market* X *if and only if for any other allocation* $\tilde{\mathbf{c}}$,

$$U^i(\tilde{c}^i) \geq U^i(c^i) \text{ for all } i, \text{ and } U^i(\tilde{c}^i) > U^i(c^i) \text{ for some } i$$
$$\implies \sum_i (\tilde{c}^i - c^i) \notin X.$$

Proof. If $U^i(\tilde{c}^i) \geq U^i(c^i)$ for all i and $U^j(\tilde{c}^j) > U^j(c^j)$ for some agent j, we can reduce $\tilde{c}^j$ by a small positive amount, which can then be equally divided among the remaining agents, making them strictly better off. More formally, the result is a corollary of Proposition 3.15. ∎

Remark 3.45. *An allocation* **c** *that clears the market and is optimal given the trivial market* $\{0\}$ *is known as a **Pareto optimal** allocation. Clearly, allocations arising in effectively complete market equilibria are Pareto optimal. Pareto optimality is further explored in Exercise 18.*

Proposition 3.39 characterized individual optimality in terms of the state-price property of the utility gradient. The result is extended below to allocational optimality.

Proposition 3.46. *Given the allocation* **c**, *suppose that for every agent* i, *the gradient* $\nabla U^i(c^i)$ *exists and is strictly positive.*

(a) *Suppose* **c** *is optimal given the market* X. *Then there exists a state-price vector* p *and a vector* $\mu \in \mathbb{R}^I_{++}$ *such that*

$$p = \mu_i \nabla U^i(c^i), \quad i = 1, \ldots, I. \tag{3.27}$$

(b) *If each* U^i *is concave and* p *is a state-price vector such that* (3.27) *holds for some* $\mu \in \mathbb{R}^I_{++}$, *then* **c** *is optimal given* X.

Proof. (a) Suppose **c** is optimal given X. For any two agents i and j, let F_{ij} be the set of all $x \in \mathbb{R}^{1+K}$ such that $c^i + x \in C^i$ and $c^j - x \in C^j$. Since C^i and C^j are open sets, F_{ij} contains an open ball centered at zero. Since $0 \in X$, optimality of **c** given X implies that $x = 0$ maximizes $U^i(c^i + x)$ subject to the constraint $U^j(c^j - x) \geq U^j(c^j), x \in F_{ij}$. Applying Theorem A.39 to this optimization problem shows the gradient colinearity restriction (3.27) for some $\mu \in \mathbb{R}^I_{++}$ and $p \in \mathbb{R}^K$. Since optimality of $\mathbf{c}$ given X implies optimality of c^i for agent i, Proposition 3.39 implies that p is a state-price vector.

(b) Suppose the cash flows $x^1, \ldots, x^I$ add up to $x \in X$ and $c^i + x^i \in C^i$ for all i. Multiplying the gradient inequality $U(c^i + x^i) \le U(c^i) + \nabla U(c^i) \cdot x^i$ by μ_i, adding up over i, and using (3.27) and the fact that $p \cdot x = 0$, we find that

$$\sum_i \mu_i U^i(c^i + x^i) \le \sum_i \mu_i U^i(c^i).$$

Since $\mu \in \mathbb{R}^I_{++}$, it is not the case that $U^i(c^i + x^i) > U^i(c^i)$ for all i. ∎

Corollary 3.47. *Suppose $(\mathbf{c}, X)$ is an equilibrium and for every agent i, U^i is concave and $\nabla U^i(c^i)$ exists. Then $(\mathbf{c}, X)$ is an effectively complete market equilibrium if and only if every $\nabla U^i(c^i)$ is a state-price vector that defines the same present-value function.*

To further discuss allocational optimality, we introduce the consumption set

$$C = (\ell, \infty)^{1+K}, \quad \text{where} \quad \ell = \sum_{i=1}^I \ell^i,$$

and for every $\mu \in \mathbb{R}^I_{++}$, the utility $U^\mu : C \to \mathbb{R}$ defined by

$$U^\mu(c) = \sup\left\{\sum_{i=1}^I \mu_i U^i(c^i) : \sum_{i=1}^I c^i \le c, \ c^i \in C^i\right\}. \tag{3.28}$$

Throughout the remainder of this section, we assume that

$$e \in C \quad \text{and} \quad U^\mu(e) < \infty.$$

Note that if each U^i is concave, then U^μ is also concave and $\partial U^\mu(e) \ne \emptyset$ (since C is open). For any scalar μ_i, we define

$$\mu_i \partial U^i(c^i) = \{\mu_i d : d \in \partial U^i(c^i)\}.$$

Lemma 3.48. *For any allocation $\mathbf{c}$ such that $\sum_i c^i = e$ and any $\mu \in \mathbb{R}^I_{++}$, the following two conditions are equivalent:*

1. $U^\mu(e) = \sum_{i=1}^I \mu_i U^i(c^i)$ *and* $p \in \partial U^\mu(e)$.
2. $p \in \bigcap_{i=1}^I \mu_i \partial U^i(c^i)$.

Proof. We apply Theorem A.33 to the problem (3.28) defining $U^\mu(e)$, with $J(\delta) = U^\mu(e + \delta)$ and $\lambda = p$. Condition 2 of Theorem A.33 in this context is equivalent to

$$U^\mu(e) = \sum\nolimits_{i=1}^{I} \max\{\mu_i U^i(x^i) - p \cdot (x^i - e^i) : x^i \in C^i\}, \quad p \in \mathbb{R}_{++}^{1+K},$$

where strict positivity of p follows from the (strict) monotonicity of the utilities. The result follows by noting that $p \in \mu_i \partial U^i(c^i)$ if and only if c^i maximizes the ith term of the above sum. ∎

The section's main result on effectively complete market equilibria follows.

Proposition 3.49. *Suppose each utility U^i is concave and the allocation **c** and market X satisfy $c^i - e^i \in X$ for every agent i. Then the following two conditions are equivalent:*

1. $(\mathbf{c}, X)$ is an effectively complete market equilibrium.

*2. There exists some $\mu \in \mathbb{R}_{++}^{I}$ such that zero trade is optimal for the agent (C, U^μ, e) given the market X and the allocation **c** solves the maximization problem defining $U^\mu(e)$, that is, $U^\mu(e) = \sum_i \mu_i U^i(c^i)$ and $\sum_i c^i \leq e$.*

Suppose these conditions are satisfied. Then there exists a state-price vector p (relative to X) such that

$$p \in \partial U^\mu(e) = \bigcap\nolimits_{i=1}^{I} \mu_i \partial U^i(c^i).$$

If the gradient vectors $\nabla U^i(c^i)$ exist, then $\nabla U^\mu(e)$ also exists and

$$p = \nabla U^\mu(e) = \mu_i \nabla U^i(c^i), \quad i = 1, \dots, I.$$

Proof. Suppose $(\mathbf{c}, X)$ is an effectively complete market equilibrium. By Proposition 3.20, $(\mathbf{c}, p)$ is an Arrow-Debreu equilibrium for some state-price vector p. Individual optimality for agent i implies that $\lambda_i p \in \partial U^i(c^i)$ and $\lambda_i > 0$. Let $\mu_i = 1/\lambda_i$. Lemma 3.48 shows that $U^\mu(e) = \sum_i \mu_i U^i(c^i)$ and $p \in \partial U^\mu(e)$. By applying Proposition 3.43, it follows that the zero trade is optimal for (C, U^μ, e). The converse is proved by reversing the above steps. The remaining claims are immediate from Lemma 3.48. ∎

The vector μ of the foregoing construction is generally a function of the entire endowed allocation $(e^1, \ldots, e^I)$ and not just the aggregate endowment e. In the representative-agent pricing contexts of Propositions 3.24 and 3.27, assuming $\succ^*$ has a concave utility representation, one can apply Proposition 3.49 with a vector μ that does not depend on the initial allocation of the aggregate endowment, using the argument of Example 3.42.

The following example gives an application of Proposition 3.49 in which the vector μ generally depends on the endowment allocation, but special additive preference structure allows one to write a state-price density as a deterministic function of the aggregate endowment. As discussed in Section 3.5.2 and further in Chapter 6, utility additivity in a dynamic setting implies strong restrictions on risk aversion.

Example 3.50 (Additive Aggregation). *Given the strictly positive probability P, suppose that*

$$U^i(c) = u^i(c_0) + \beta \sum_{k=1}^{K} u^i(c_k) P_k, \quad c \in C^i,$$

where $u^i : (\ell^i, \infty) \to \mathbb{R}$ is a concave differentiable function and $\beta \in (0, \infty)$ is common among agents. For any vector of agent weights $\mu \in \mathbb{R}_{++}^I$, the utility U^μ defined in (3.28) also has the above representation, with $i = \mu$, where

$$u^\mu(x) = \sup \left\{ \sum_{i=1}^{I} \mu_i u^i(x_i) : \sum_{i=1}^{I} x_i \leq x, \ x_i \in (\ell^i, \infty) \right\}.$$

If $(\mathbf{c}, X)$ is an effectively complete market equilibrium, then there exists $\mu \in \mathbb{R}_{++}^I$ such that $\nabla U^\mu(e)$ is a state-price vector. Therefore, for every spot k, the corresponding normalized state-price density

$$\frac{\pi_k}{\pi_0} = \beta \frac{u^{\mu\prime}(e_k)}{u^{\mu\prime}(e_0)}$$

is a deterministic function of the spot-k aggregate endowment e_k.

3.8 EXERCISES

1. (a) Construct an example of an agent and an arbitrage-free market such that an optimal consumption plan does not exist, based on the existence of cycles: $c^1 \succ c^2 \succ \cdots \succ c^1$.

(b) Given the agent $(C, \succ, e)$, suppose that $\succ$ is convex and there exists a bounded-below and closed set $B \subseteq C$ such that $c \in C$ and $b \notin B$ implies not $b \succ c$. If the market is arbitrage-free, then an optimal consumption plan exists. Show that this claim follows from the following fact (which is proved, for example, in Aliprantis and Border (1999)): *Suppose the preference $\succ$ is convex and K is a compact subset of C. Then there exists $\hat{c} \in K$ such that $c \succ \hat{c}$ implies $c \notin K$.* (Note: This fact is valid without the monotonicity assumption on $\succ$, and so is the existence claim that follows from it.)

2. In the context of Example 3.10, modify the assumption of mean-variance preferences to the following: For all marketed cash flows a and b such that $a(0) = b(0)$ and $\mathrm{var}(a(1)) = \mathrm{var}(b(1))$,

$$\mathbb{E}a(1) > \mathbb{E}b(1) \implies a \succ^i b.$$

Suppose also that the cash flows x^Π and $x^\mathbb{E}$ are not colinear.

(a) Show that there exists $x^* \in X$ such that $x^*(0) = 0$ and $\mathbb{E}x^*(1) > 0$.

(b) Suppose $\bar{x}(0) = x(0)$, $\mathbb{E}\bar{x}(1) = \mathbb{E}x(1)$ and $\mathrm{var}[\bar{x}(1)] < \mathrm{var}[x(1)]$. Given the x^* of part (a), compute a value $\alpha > 0$ such that $x^\alpha = \bar{x} + \alpha x^*$ satisfies $x^\alpha(0) = x(0)$, $\mathbb{E}x^\alpha(1) > \mathbb{E}x(1)$ and $\mathrm{var}[x^\alpha(1)] = \mathrm{var}[x(1)]$.

(c) Derive the CAPM under the modified assumptions.

3. Suppose X is an arbitrage-free and nondegenerate market, $(-\rho, 1) \in X$ and x^Π is specified by Definition 2.1.

(a) Show that there exists an arbitrage-free complete market X_c such that $X \subseteq X_c$. Given such a market X_c, let $x_c^\Pi \in X_c$ be defined in X_c the way x^Π is defined in X. How do the cash flows x^Π and x_c^Π relate to each other?

(b) Consider the CAPM of Example 3.10 in this context, with the added assumption that each $\succ^i$ is variance averse on the entire consumption set $\mathbb{R}^{1+K}$ (and not just for marketed cash flows). Show that $(\mathbf{c}, X)$ is an effectively complete market equilibrium.

4. In the context of Example 3.9, assume that the market is incomplete and let $M = \mathrm{span}(1^0, X_S)$ be the corresponding marketed subspace. Show that M does not depend on S, formulate an M-constrained notion of Arrow-Debreu equilibrium, and show its equivalence to a spot-market equilibrium. Also define an M-constrained notion of

allocational optimality, and prove that if (θ, p) is a spot-market equilibrium, then θ implements an M-constrained optimal allocation. (Unfortunately, these arguments are limited to the special single-period model of Example 3.9. In a dynamic extension of the model, the marketed subspace would typically depend on the equilibrium spot prices.)

5. Formulate a competitive equilibrium notion for a forward market in J given assets, and relate it to the main market equilibrium notion of this chapter, as well as to Arrow-Debreu equilibrium.

6. Define and characterize frontier cash flows for a purely forward market. Based on this characterization, formulate the CAPM for a purely forward market. *Hint:* A forward-value functional should play the role of the present-value functional.

7. Provide an alternative dual approach to the last step of the proof of Propositions 3.24 and 3.27, proving effective market completeness by using the optimality of the aggregate endowment for the representative agent to show the existence of a suitable market completion as defined in Proposition 3.21.

8. Remove the assumption of monotonicity in the definition of a preference and show the following version of Proposition 3.24. Suppose the agents $(C^i, \succ^i, e^i)$, $i = 1, \ldots, I$, are specified in terms of a scale-invariant preference $\succ^*$ on $\mathbb{R}^{1+K}_{++}$ and the parameters $b^1, \ldots, b^I \in \mathbb{R}^{1+K}$ by

$$C^i = \{c \in \mathbb{R}^{1+K} : b^i - c \in \mathbb{R}^{1+K}_{++}\} \text{ and } \tilde{c} \succ^i c \iff b^i - \tilde{c} \succ^* b^i - c.$$

Suppose further that for each agent i, there exist $v^i, w^i \in \mathbb{R}$ such that

$$e^i - w^i \mathbf{1}^0 \in X, \quad b^i - v^i \mathbf{1}^0 \in X \quad \text{and} \quad w^i < v^i,$$

and define $b = \sum_i b^i$, $e = \sum_i e^i$, $v = \sum_i v^i$, $w = \sum_i w^i$. The allocation $\mathbf{c}$ is defined by

$$c^i = b^i - \frac{v^i - w^i}{v - w}(b - e), \quad i = 1, \ldots, I.$$

Then $(\mathbf{c}, X)$ is an equilibrium if and only if e is the optimal consumption plan for the agent $(C, \succ, e)$, where

$$C = \{c \in \mathbb{R}^{1+K} : b - c \in \mathbb{R}^{1+K}_{++}\} \quad \text{and} \quad \tilde{c} \succ c \iff b - \tilde{c} \succ^* b - c.$$

If $(\mathbf{c}, X)$ is an equilibrium and $\succ^*$ is convex, then $(\mathbf{c}, X)$ is an effectively complete market equilibrium. Give an example of a CAPM equilibrium in this setting in which the preference $\succ^*$ has an additive utility representation of the form used in Example 3.40.

9. Suppose that the representative-agent equilibria of Propositions 3.24 and 3.27 are implemented by spot-market equilibria, as in Example 3.9. What are the equilibrium trades for the scale-invariant case and for the translation-invariant case? To what extent can you generalize the equilibria of these two propositions to include trading constraints as in Section 1.7?

10. (a) Suppose that $\succ$ is a preference, and $a \succeq b \iff$ not $b \succ a$. Show that $\succeq$ is complete if and only if $a \succ b$ implies $a \succeq b$.

(b) Show that if $\succeq$ is a complete and transitive binary relation on a finite set S, then there exists some $\hat{s} \in S$ such that $\hat{s} \succeq s$ for all $s \in S$. Is the conclusion true if completeness or transitivity is relaxed? Provide proofs or counterexamples.

11. Let $C = \mathbb{R} \times \{0, 1\}$ and define the binary relation $\succ$ on C by

$$(x_1, x_2) \succ (y_1, y_2) \iff (x_1 > y_1) \text{ or } (x_1 = y_1 \text{ and } x_2 > y_2).$$

Show that the relation $\succeq$ defined by $a \succeq b \iff$ not $b \succ a$ is complete and transitive, but there exists no function $U : C \to \mathbb{R}$ such that $a \succ b \iff U(a) > U(b)$. Explain why this is not a counterexample to Proposition 3.30.

12. Complete the proof of Proposition 3.30.

13. (a) Give an example of a differentiable utility that is strictly increasing but whose gradient is not strictly positive.

(b) Suppose C is an open set of consumption plans, and $U : C \to \mathbb{R}$ is concave and satisfies $U(c + x) > U(c)$ if x is an arbitrage and $c, c + x \in C$. Show that every element of $\partial U(c)$ is strictly positive.

14. In the context of Section 3.4, suppose that the preference $\succ^*$ has a concave utility representation. Are the equilibria described in Section 3.4 unique in this case? Provide a proof or give a counterexample together with sufficient conditions for uniqueness.

15. Prove the assertions of Example 3.42.

16. Consider the context of Proposition 3.46, with every U^i concave and differentiable.

(a) Suppose that $(\mathbf{c}, X)$ is an effectively complete market equilibrium and let $(\mathbf{c}, p)$ be a corresponding Arrow-Debreu equilibrium, constructed as in Proposition 3.20. Assume the state-price vector p is normalized so that $p_0 = 1$, and let J^i be defined in terms of U^i just as J was defined in terms of U in (3.25). Express the vector μ of condition (3.27) in terms of J^i.

(b) Specialize part (a) to the context of Example 3.42.

17. Show that the supremum in (3.28) is achieved if $\ell^i > -\infty$ for every i, and provide an alternative sufficient condition for the supremum to be a maximum if $\ell^i = -\infty$ for some i.

18. (Pareto Optimality) In the context of Section 3.7, let $\mathbf{c}$ be an allocation that clears the market: $\sum_i c^i = \sum_i e^i = e$. The allocation $\mathbf{c}$ is **Pareto optimal** if there exists no allocation $\tilde{\mathbf{c}}$ such that $\sum_i \tilde{c}^i = e$, $U^i(\tilde{c}^i) \geq U^i(c^i)$ for every agent i and $U^i(\tilde{c}^i) > U^i(c^i)$ for some agent i.

(a) Show that if $\mathbf{c}$ is a Pareto optimal allocation and the gradient vector $\nabla U^i(c^i)$ exists for each agent i, then there exists a vector $\mu \in \mathbb{R}^I_+$ such that

$$\mu_i \nabla U^i(c^i) = \mu_j \nabla U^j(c^j) \quad \text{for all } i, j \in \{1, \dots, I\}.$$

(b) If $U^\mu(e) = \sum_i \mu_i U^i(c^i)$ for some $\mu \in \mathbb{R}^I_{++}$, then $\mathbf{c}$ is Pareto optimal. Conversely, if each U^i is concave and $\mathbf{c}$ is Pareto optimal, then $U^\mu(e) = \sum_i \mu_i U^i(c^i)$ for some $\mu \in \mathbb{R}^I_{++}$. Prove this claim from first principles using the separating hyperplane theorem in $\mathbb{R}^I_{++}$.

(c) Show that if $p \in \bigcap_{i=1}^I \mu_i \partial U^i(c^i)$ for some $\mu \in \mathbb{R}^I_{++}$, then $\mathbf{c}$ is Pareto optimal and $p \in \partial U^\mu(e)$.

(d) Suppose that each U^i is concave and $\mathbf{c}$ is Pareto optimal. Then there exists $\mu \in \mathbb{R}^I_{++}$ such that

$$\partial U^\mu(e) = \bigcap_{i=1}^I \mu_i \partial U^i(c^i) \neq \emptyset.$$

If the gradient vectors $\nabla U^i(c^i)$ exist, then

$$\nabla U^\mu(e) = \mu_i \nabla U^i(c^i), \quad i = 1, \dots, I.$$

3.9 NOTES

While the notion of competitive equilibrium dates back to Walras (1874), this chapter's formalism is based on the theory developed in the 1950s by Arrow (1951, 1953), Arrow and Debreu (1954), Debreu (1952, 1959) and McKenzie (1954, 1955, 1959). The term "Arrow-Debreu equilibrium" reflects the contributions of Arrow (1953) and Debreu (1959) in reinterpreting classical commodities as contingent claims, also known as "Arrow-Debreu commodities." The theory was extended to allow for preferences that are not complete or transitive by Sonnenschein (1971), Mas-Colell (1974b), Shafer (1974), Gale and Mas-Colell (1975) and Shafer and Sonnenschein (1975). Textbook accounts of competitive equilibrium analysis include Ellickson (1993), Hildenbrand and Kirman (1988), Mas-Colell, Whinston, and Green (1995) and Vohra (2005). Mas-Colell (1985) and Balasko (1988) present a differentiable approach. These texts discuss economies with multiple commodities and no uncertainty, but they can be reinterpreted as applying to complete markets Arrow-Debreu economies. Incomplete markets with an exogenous asset structure first appeared in Diamond (1967). The challenges presented by the examples of Hart (1974, 1975) stimulated a large literature on the existence and (sub)optimality of incomplete-markets equilibria that is surveyed by Magill and Shafer (1991). A textbook introduction to the incomplete-markets theory is given by Magill and Quinzii (1996).

While general equilibrium theory has focused on theoretical issues of existence and allocational optimality, asset pricing theory developed in the direction of more specific models with the aim of deriving testable implications, with a primary concern being the explanation of how the market prices risk. The CAPM was developed in that spirit by Treynor (1962), Sharpe (1964), Lintner (1965) and Mossin (1966). The CAPM without a risk-free asset first appears in Lintner (1969) and Black (1972). The derivation of Example 3.10 is closest to the account of Duffie (1991). The assumption of mean-variance preferences in the sense of Example 3.10 and Exercise 2 can be justified by assuming expected utility (defined in the following chapter) and special distributional restrictions on the asset returns. Tobin (1958) first showed that normally distributed returns suffice (see Exercise 12 of Chapter 4). Agnew (1971) showed that the normal distribution is only a special instance of the class of distributions implying mean-variance preferences. The latter was then fully characterized by Chamberlain (1983a). Equilibrium asset pricing models evolved from the CAPM to consumption-based dynamic models that are discussed in Chapter 6, as well as the multifactor extensions discussed in the notes of the last chapter.

The aggregation notion of Section 3.4 dates back, at least, to Gorman (1953) (see also Chipman (1974)). The role of additive exponential, logarithmic and exponential utility forms in the aggregation argument already appears in the work of Wilson (1968) and Pollak (1971) (see also Milne (1979)), although it received more attention in finance through the work of Rubinstein (1974) and Brennan and Kraus (1978). The notion of Gorman aggregation was extended to economies with asymmetrically informed agents and possibly partially informative prices by DeMarzo and Skiadas (1998, 1999). The characterization of scale- or translation-invariant additive representations given in Theorem 3.37 is based on the solution of the so-called Cauchy equation (3.24), a detailed analysis of which can be found in Aczél and Dhombres (1989) (and can be used to weaken the regularity assumption of Theorem 3.37). Lemmas 3.23 and 3.26, as well as the form of the CAPM optimal trades in Example 3.10, are instances of two-fund separation results, originating in Tobin (1958). A more general fund-separation theory includes the contributions of Cass and Stiglitz (1970) and Ross (1978a) and is discussed in textbook form by Ingersoll (1987). The relationship of the preference restrictions allowing aggregation to recursive utility is discussed in Chapter 6. Some authors (for example, Duffie (2001)) use the term representative-agent pricing to refer to the type of argument used in Proposition 3.49 and Example 3.50 (where the agent weights depend on the agent initial endowments). The basic argument behind this approach dates back to Negishi (1960).

Chapter 6 of Debreu (1983), which is based on a 1952 working paper, shows the existence of a continuous utility representation of a continuous, complete and transitive binary relation, without monotonicity. In Chapter 9 of the same monograph, Debreu characterized continuous additive utility representations in a way that includes Theorem 3.36. Debreu's theorems are part of a broader theory of measurement, which is reviewed in the monographs of Krantz, Luce, Suppes and Tversky (1971) and Narens (1985). These authors present an algebraic theory that generalizes Debreu's topological results (see also Wakker (1988)). The problem of the representation of a convex preference order by a concave utility function was studied by Mas-Colell (1974a) and Kannai (1974, 1977, 1981). The representation of separable preferences by concave utilities is discussed in the following chapter. Finally, Candeal and Induráin (1995) discuss the relationship between scale invariance of indifferences and scale invariance of preferences, showing that the two notions coincide given continuity.

CHAPTER FOUR

Risk Aversion

A CENTRAL CONCERN of asset pricing theory is the modeling of the premia that agents require in equilibrium as compensation for bearing risk. A formal representation of risk aversion is therefore required. Risk aversion also plays a key role in an agent's optimal portfolio decisions. We are interested in risk aversion both in an absolute sense (is an agent risk averse?) and a comparative sense (is an agent more risk averse than another?). This chapter begins with general formal definitions of absolute and comparative risk aversion. Little can be said, however, without additional special structure of preferences, including some notion of beliefs. For this reason, the chapter introduces a foundation for an expected utility representation of preferences, which is followed by an analysis of risk aversion in the context of expected utility. Although the setting is that of static choice, the chapter's material is used as a building block in the theory of recursive utility in Chapter 6. Familiarity with some of last chapter's definitions and results regarding preferences is assumed.

4.1 ABSOLUTE AND COMPARATIVE RISK AVERSION

Preferences over consumption plans relate to risk aversion as well as preferences for substitution over time. As we will see in Chapter 6, the two notions are generally intertwined. In this chapter, however, we focus on risk aversion alone by assuming consumption occurs at time one only, or consumption at time zero is fixed.[1] Preferences and utilities are therefore defined on the set $(\ell, \infty)^K$, where $\ell \in [-\infty, 1)$. To avoid trivialities, we assume that $K \geq 2$ throughout the chapter. Our earlier results all apply in this context, with time zero reinterpreted as another time-one state. This section's objective is to provide ordinal definitions of absolute and comparative risk aversion.

---

[1] If time-zero consumption is fixed at some level $h \in (\ell, \infty)$, then a preference $\succ$ on $(\ell, \infty)^{1+K}$ induces a preference $\succ_h$ on $(\ell, \infty)^K$ defined by $a \succ_h b \iff (h, a) \succ (h, b)$.

94

We define a preference to be risk averse if, relative to any deterministic payoff, an undesirable trade remains undesirable if scaled up. A more formal statement follows, using the preference notion of Definition 3.1.

Definition 4.1. *The preference $\succ$ on $(\ell, \infty)^K$ is **risk averse** if for any $w \in (\ell, \infty)$, $x \in (\ell - w, \infty)^K$ and scalar s such that $w\mathbf{1} + sx \in (\ell, \infty)^K$,*

$$w\mathbf{1} \succ w\mathbf{1} + x \text{ and } s \in (1, \infty) \implies w\mathbf{1} \succ w\mathbf{1} + sx. \qquad (4.1)$$

Remark 4.2. *Let the relation $\succeq$ be the weak preference corresponding to $\succ$ (defined by $a \succeq b \iff$ not $b \succ a$) and consider the condition: for any $w \in (\ell, \infty)$,*

$$a \succeq w\mathbf{1} \text{ and } b \succeq w\mathbf{1} \implies \phi a + (1 - \phi)b \succeq w\mathbf{1} \text{ for all } \phi \in (0, 1). \qquad (4.2)$$

This condition expresses a notion of preference for diversification and can therefore also be interpreted as risk aversion. Condition (4.1)) is weaker, since it is implied from (4.2) by letting $a = w\mathbf{1}, b = w\mathbf{1} + sx$ and $\phi = 1 - s^{-1}$. We will see in Section 4.3 that the two conditions are equivalent if $\succ$ admits an expected utility representation.

In the following definition, a preference is said to be more risk averse than another if a trade that is rejected relative to a deterministic payoff by the second preference is also rejected relative to the same payoff by the first. We use the term "more risk averse" here to really mean "at least as risk averse." This inconsistency of terminology is common in the literature and we follow it for simplicity.

Definition 4.3. *A preference $\succ^1$ on $(\ell, \infty)^K$ is **more risk averse** than a preference $\succ^2$ on $(\ell, \infty)^K$ if for any scalar $w \in (\ell, \infty)$ and payoff $c \in (\ell, \infty)^K$,*

$$w\mathbf{1} \succ^2 c \implies w\mathbf{1} \succ^1 c. \qquad (4.3)$$

*Two preferences are **equally risk averse** if each is more risk averse than the other.*

As in Section 3.5.1, we define the **compensation function** $\upsilon : (\ell, \infty)^K \to (\ell, \infty)$ of a preference $\succ$ on $(\ell, \infty)^K$ by

$$\upsilon(c) = \inf\{w \in (\ell, \infty) : w\mathbf{1} \succ c\}.$$

95

In this context, a compensation function that is also a utility representation is known as a **certainty equivalent**. The following characterization of comparative risk aversion is an immediate consequence of the definitions; it is valid with or without the existence of a utility representation.

Proposition 4.4. *For each $i \in \{1, 2\}$, suppose $\succ^i$ is a preference on $(\ell, \infty)^K$ with compensation function v^i. Then $\succ^1$ is more risk averse than $\succ^2$ if and only if $v^1(c) \leq v^2(c)$ for all $c \in (\ell, \infty)^K$.*

Comparative risk aversion can be usefully applied to a single preference at different scales or relative to different additive deterministic wealth levels. We illustrate with a discussion that will help us understand the preference restrictions of the representative-agent pricing theory of Section 3.4, starting with the relationship between scale invariance and risk aversion. Given a preference $\succ$ on $(0, \infty)^K$, we define, for every $s \in (0, \infty)$, a new preference $\succ_s^R$ on $(0, \infty)^K$ by

$$x \succ_s^R y \iff sx \succ sy. \tag{4.4}$$

The preference $\succ$ exhibits **constant relative risk aversion**, or is **CRRA** for short, if the preferences $\succ_s^R$ are equally risk averse for all values of $s \in (0, \infty)$. More directly, $\succ$ is CRRA if and only if

$$w \in (0, \infty) \text{ and } w\mathbf{1} \succ c \quad \text{implies} \quad sw\mathbf{1} \succ sc \text{ for all } s \in (0, \infty). \tag{4.5}$$

We interpret the CRRA condition to mean that risk aversion does not change with scale.

Proposition 4.5. *Suppose $\succ$ is a preference on $(0, \infty)^K$ with compensation function v.*

(a) If $\succ$ is scale invariant, then $\succ$ is CRRA.

(b) $\succ$ is CRRA if and only if v is homogeneous of degree one.

(c) Suppose further that $\succ$ admits a utility representation. Then $\succ$ is scale invariant if and only if it is CRRA.

Proof. Condition (4.5) proves part (a) and justifies the following calculation of the compensation function of $\succ_s^R$:

$$v_s^R(c) = \inf\{w : w\mathbf{1} \succ_s^R c\} = \frac{1}{s}\inf\{sw : sw\mathbf{1} \succ sc\} = \frac{1}{s}v(sc).$$

By Proposition 4.4, it follows that $\succ$ is CRRA if and only if $s^{-1}v(sc)$ is constant in $s > 0$, which proves part (b). Finally, if v is a utility representation of $\succ$ that is homogeneous of degree one, then $\succ$ is scale invariant and therefore CRRA. This shows part (c). ∎

Consider the class of preferences appearing in the aggregation argument of Section 3.4 based on translation invariance. In particular, we are interested in the interpretation of the parameter α in the TI agent specification (3.10) as a coefficient of risk tolerance. Given any preference $\succ$ on $\mathbb{R}^K$, we define the preference $\succ_s^R$ on $\mathbb{R}^K$ by (4.4), and we say that $\succ$ exhibits **increasing relative risk aversion**, or **is IRRA** for short, if $s_1 \geq s_2 > 0$ implies that $\succ_{s_1}^R$ is more risk averse than $\succ_{s_2}^R$. More directly, $\succ$ is IRRA if and only if

$$w \in \mathbb{R} \text{ and } w\mathbf{1} \succ c \quad \text{implies} \quad sw\mathbf{1} \succ sc \text{ for all } s \in (1,\infty). \qquad (4.6)$$

In other words, IRRA means that risk aversion does not decrease with increasing scale. In Proposition 3.27, with all spots reinterpreted as time-one states, the preference $\succ^i$ on $\mathbb{R}^K$ is defined in terms of the positive scalar α^i by $\tilde{c} \succ^i c \iff (1/\alpha^i)\tilde{c} \succ^* (1/\alpha^i)c$. It follows from the definitions that if $\succ^*$ is IRRA, then $\alpha^i \geq \alpha^j > 0$ implies that $\succ^j$ is more risk averse than $\succ^i$. The following characterization of the IRRA property can be proved analogously to Proposition 4.5.

Proposition 4.6. *Suppose $\succ$ is a preference on $\mathbb{R}^K$ with compensation function v. If $\succ$ is IRRA, then $v(sc) \leq sv(c)$ for all $s \in (1,\infty)$. The converse is also true if $\succ$ admits a utility representation.*

Let us now consider the risk-aversion interpretation of translation invariance. As the proof of Proposition 4.7 below shows, the analysis is mathematically isomorphic to the above discussion of scale invariance, although the economic interpretation is distinctly different. Given the preference $\succ$ on $\mathbb{R}^K$, we define, for any $\theta \in \mathbb{R}$, the preference $\succ_\theta^A$ on $\mathbb{R}^K$ by

$$x \succ_\theta^A y \iff \theta\mathbf{1} + x \succ \theta\mathbf{1} + y.$$

The preference $\succ$ exhibits **constant absolute risk aversion**, or **is CARA** for short, if $\succ_\theta^A$ is equally risk averse for all values of θ. More directly, $\succ$ is

97

CARA if and only if

$$\theta \in \mathbb{R} \text{ and } \theta 1 \succ c \quad \text{implies} \quad \theta 1 + w 1 \succ c + w 1 \text{ for all } w \in \mathbb{R}. \quad (4.7)$$

Proposition 4.7. *Suppose* $\succ$ *is a preference on* $\mathbb{R}^K$ *with compensation function* v.

(a) If $\succ$ *is translation invariant, then* $\succ$ *is CARA.*

(b) $\succ$ *is CARA if and only if* v *is quasilinear with respect to* **1**.

(c) Suppose further that $\succ$ *admits a utility representation. Then* $\succ$ *is translation invariant if and only if it is CARA.*

Proof. Define the preference $\succ^{\log}$ on $(0, \infty)^K$ by

$$x \succ^{\log} y \iff \log(x) \succ \log(y).$$

Then $\succ$ is translation invariant (CARA) if and only if $\succ^{\log}$ is scale invariant (CRRA). The compensation function of $\succ^{\log}$ can be computed as

$$v^{\log}(c) = \inf\{w : \log w 1 \succ \log c\}$$
$$= \exp \inf\{w : w 1 \succ \log c\} = \exp v(\log c).$$

Therefore, v is quasilinear with respect to **1** if and only if $v^{\log}$ is homogeneous of degree one. Through these transformations, the claimed result is isomorphic to Proposition 4.5. ■

Finally, we characterize CARA preferences that are IRRA in the following proposition, which further clarifies the extent to which the coefficients α^i in Proposition 3.27 are measures of risk tolerance.

Proposition 4.8. *Suppose* $\succ$ *is a CARA preference on* $\mathbb{R}^K$. *Then* $\succ$ *is IRRA if and only if it is risk averse.*

Proof. Suppose $\succ$ is CARA. For any $\theta \in \mathbb{R}$ and $s \in (1, \infty)$, we have

$$\theta 1 \succ c \iff 0 \succ c - \theta 1 \quad \text{and} \quad s\theta 1 \succ sc \iff 0 \succ s(c - \theta 1).$$

The result follows from the definition of risk aversion (with $x = c - \theta 1$) and the definition of IRRA. ■

4.2 EXPECTED UTILITY

A particularly rich theory of risk aversion is possible in the context of expected utility theory, which is our focus in the remainder of this chapter. In this section we define expected utility representations and we characterize their existence and uniqueness. We continue to study preferences on a set of **payoffs** $(\ell, \infty)^K$, for some $\ell \in [-\infty, 1)$. We regard a payoff either as a row vector of the form $x = (x_1, \ldots, x_K)$ or as a random variable. We write $\mathbb{E}$ for the expectation operator relative to whatever probability is denoted P in the given context; that is, $\mathbb{E}x = \sum_k x_k P_k$.

Definition 4.9. *An **expected utility (EU) representation** of a preference $\succ$ on $(\ell, \infty)^K$ is a pair (P, u) of a strictly positive probability P and an increasing and continuous function $u : (\ell, \infty) \to \mathbb{R}$ such that $x \succ y$ is equivalent to $\mathbb{E}u(x) > \mathbb{E}u(y)$, for all $x, y \in (\ell, \infty)^K$. Two EU representations are **ordinally equivalent** if they represent the same preference.*

A utility of the form $U(c) = \mathbb{E}u(c)$, for some $u : (\ell, \infty) \to \mathbb{R}$, is clearly additive. By the uniqueness part of Theorem 3.36, we have the following uniqueness result for EU.

Theorem 4.10. *If (P, u) and $(\tilde{P}, \tilde{u})$ are ordinally equivalent EU representations, then $\tilde{P} = P$ and $\tilde{u} = au + b$ for some $a \in \mathbb{R}_{++}$ and $b \in \mathbb{R}$.*

Given an EU representation (P, u) of a preference $\succ$, the probability P is uniquely determined by $\succ$ and is consistent with the beliefs of an agent with preferences $\succ$, in the following sense. Relative to a plan that results in equal contingent consumption at states k and m, the agent would strictly prefer to increase consumption by a given amount at state k rather than at state m if and only if k is more likely than m. More formally, for any $x \in (\ell, \infty)^K$ and positive scalar α,

$$\text{if } x_k = x_m, \text{ then } \quad x + \alpha \mathbf{1}^k \succ x + \alpha \mathbf{1}^m \iff P_k > P_m, \qquad (4.8)$$

where

$$\mathbf{1}_i^k = \begin{cases} 1, & \text{if } i = k; \\ 0, & \text{if } i \neq k. \end{cases}$$

99

Implicit in this discussion is the assumption of an informal notion of state independence, in the sense that a unit of consumption is valued the same by the agent at state k as at state m. If U is an additive utility, then, given any strictly positive probability P, we can write

$$U(c) = \sum\nolimits_{k=1}^{K} u_k(c_k)P_k, \quad \text{where} \quad u_k = \frac{U_k}{P_k}.$$

An EU representation further requires that for some (unique) choice of P, we can set $u_1 = \cdots = u_K = u$, reflecting the state-independent valuation of outcomes. Below we formalize this notion in a way that completely characterizes the additive utilities that are also EU representations. Important special cases in which the existence of an EU representation follows (under a mild regularity assumption) from separability alone are those of CARA and CRRA preferences, which are discussed in Section 4.5.

Given a preference $\succ$ on $(\ell, \infty)^K$, where $K > 2$, let us recall some facts from Section 3.5. In this text, preferences and utilities are, by definition, continuous and monotone. The preference $\succ$ admits some utility representation if and only if the corresponding weak preference is complete and transitive. Given that $\succ$ admits a utility representation and $K > 2$, it admits an additive utility representation if and only if $\succ$ is separable. In the current context, $\succ$ is **separable** if for any event $A \subseteq \{1, \ldots, K\}$ and any payoffs $x, y, z, \tilde{z} \in (\ell, \infty)^K$,

$$x_A z_{-A} \succ y_A z_{-A} \quad \Longleftrightarrow \quad x_A \tilde{z}_{-A} \succ y_A \tilde{z}_{-A}.$$

One can think of this condition as stating that a payoff x can be assessed conditionally on the realization of an event A in a way that is independent of the values x takes in states where the event A is not realized. Separability is necessary for an EU representation but not sufficient. We now state an additional state-independence condition that is necessary and sufficient for a preference that admits an additive utility representation to admit an EU representation. We state the condition in terms of the **indifference relation** $\sim$ associated with the preference $\succ$, which is defined by

$$x \sim y \quad \Longleftrightarrow \quad (\text{not } x \succ y) \text{ and } (\text{not } y \succ x).$$

Clearly, if U is a utility representation of $\succ$, then $x \sim y \Longleftrightarrow U(x) = U(y)$. The following definition applies to any preference $\succ$ on $(\ell, \infty)^K$, where $K > 2$. Its interpretation as state independence, however, assumes that $\succ$ is separable.

Definition 4.11. *The preference $\succ$ is **state independent** if, given any $w \in$ (ℓ, ∞) and any states $m \neq 1$ and $k \notin \{1, m\}$, the following is true for all sufficiently small positive scalars x_1, x_k, y, z:*

If

$$w\mathbf{1} + x_1 \mathbf{1}^m - y\mathbf{1}^1 \sim w\mathbf{1} \quad and \quad w\mathbf{1} + x_1\mathbf{1}^m \sim w\mathbf{1} + z\mathbf{1}^1, \qquad (4.9)$$

then

$$w\mathbf{1} + x_k\mathbf{1}^m - y\mathbf{1}^k \sim w\mathbf{1} \quad implies \quad w\mathbf{1} + x_k\mathbf{1}^m \sim w\mathbf{1} + z\mathbf{1}^k. \qquad (4.10)$$

We interpret Definition 4.11 with the help of Figure 4.1. Condition (4.9) defines a sense in which the intensity by which a decrease from w to $w - y$ at state one is undesirable equals the intensity by which an increase from w to $w + z$ at the same state is desirable. State independence requires that this matching of intensities is not contradicted if state one is replaced by state k. The first (respectively, second) part of condition (4.9) corresponds to the agent's indifference between the two payoffs represented by the two solid (respectively, dotted) lines on the left half of Figure 4.1. In each comparison,

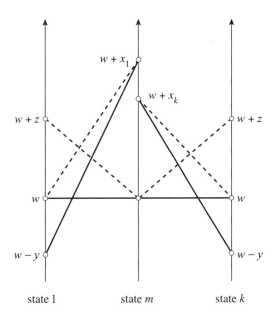

Figure 4.1 Ordinal definition of state independence for preferences admitting an additive utility representation.

a change of consumption away from w at state 1 is compensated by the same increase of x_1 at state m. The right half of Figure 4.1 is the analogous relationship with state k in place of state 1, which would be contradicted if the left-hand side of condition (4.10) were true but the right-hand side of the same condition were false. Note that the compensating amounts x_1 and x_k need not be equal, reflecting the possibly unequal likelihoods of states 1 and k. In the example of Figure 4.1, we think of state k as being less likely than state 1, since $x_k < x_1$.

Theorem 4.12. *Suppose that $K > 2$ and $\succ$ is a preference that admits a utility representation. Then $\succ$ admits an expected utility representation if and only if it is both separable and state independent.*

Proof. The "only if" part is immediate. Conversely, suppose $\succ$ is separable and state independent. Theorem 3.36 implies that $\succ$ is represented by an additive utility $U = \sum_{k=1}^{K} U_k$. For every state k, we define the open interval $I_k = \{U_k(x) : x \in (\ell, \infty)\}$ and the function $\phi_k : I_1 \mapsto I_k$ such that $U_k(x) = \phi_k(U_1(x))$ for all $x \in (\ell, \infty)$. Suppose that we can show that each ϕ_k is affine, that is, $\phi_k(U_1) = a_k U_1 + b_k$ for some $a_k \in \mathbb{R}_{++}$ and $b_k \in \mathbb{R}$. Then an EU representation (P, u) of υ results if we define $u = U_1$ and $P_k = a_k / \sum_k a_k$. There remains to show that each ϕ_k is affine. Since ϕ_k is onto and increasing, it is continuous, and therefore it suffices to confirm that given any $\alpha \in I_1$, there exists a positive ε such that

$$\phi_k(\alpha + \delta) - \phi_k(\alpha) = \phi_k(\alpha) - \phi_k(\alpha - \delta), \quad \text{for all } \delta \in (0, \varepsilon). \quad (4.11)$$

(While this claim should be intuitively clear, it can be proved formally using Lemma 4.13 of the following section, applied with $p = 1/2$.) We fix any $\alpha \in I_1$ and let $w \in (\ell, \infty)$ be defined by $U_1(w) = \alpha$. Given any states $k \neq 1$ and $m \notin \{1, k\}$, continuity implies the existence of a sufficiently small ε such that for any $\delta \in (0, \varepsilon)$ there exist positive scalars x_1, x_k, y, z that solve the equations

$$\delta = U_1(w+z) - U_1(w) = U_1(w) - U_1(w-y) = U_m(w+x_1) - U_m(w),$$
$$\text{and} \quad U_m(w+x_k) - U_m(w) = U_k(w) - U_k(w-y).$$

The first set of equalities implies that condition (4.9) is satisfied and therefore so is condition (4.10). The last equality implies the first indifference of (4.10) and therefore that $w + z\mathbf{1}^k \sim w + x_k\mathbf{1}^m$, which is in turn equivalent to $U_k(w+z) - U_k(w) = U_m(w+x_k) - U_m(w)$. This proves that $U_k(w+z) - U_k(w) = U_k(w) - U_k(w-y)$, an equality that is equivalent to that of condition (4.11). ∎

4.3 EXPECTED UTILITY AND RISK AVERSION

As noted in Remark 4.2, risk aversion of a preference $\succ$ is generally a weaker restriction than convexity of $\succ$. It is also true that an arbitrary convex preference need not admit a concave utility representation. But if $\succ$ admits an expected utility representation (P, u), then risk aversion of $\succ$ is equivalent to convexity of $\succ$, which is equivalent to concavity of u. Moreover, the more risk averse $\succ$ is, the more concave u is, and vice versa. In this section we prove these claims.

4.3.1 Comparative Risk Aversion

We begin with a preliminary lemma. The first part is Jensen's inequality, which applies in much greater generality than stated below (with essentially the same proof). The second part is a concavity criterion for continuous functions; it is a strong converse to the first part.

Lemma 4.13. *Suppose D is a real interval.*

(a) (Jensen's inequality) If the function $f : D \to \mathbb{R}$ is concave, then

$$\mathbb{E} f(x) \leq f(\mathbb{E}x), \quad \text{for every random variable } x \in D^K.$$

(b) The function $f : D \to \mathbb{R}$ is concave if there exists a fixed $p \in (0, 1)$ such that

$$pf(a) + (1-p)f(b) \leq f(pa + (1-p)b), \quad \text{for all } a, b \in D.$$

Proof. (a) Except in trivial cases, $\mathbb{E}x$ lies in the interior of D. In this case, we can select an element δ of the superdifferential of f at $\mathbb{E}x$, implying that $f(x) \leq f(\mathbb{E}x) + \delta(x - \mathbb{E}x)$. Taking expectations on both sides completes the proof.

(b) Let $J_0 = \{0, 1\}$ and $J_{n+1} = \{p\alpha + (1 - p)\beta : \alpha, \beta \in J_n\}$, $n = 1, 2, \ldots$ The set $J = \bigcup_{n=1}^{\infty} J_n$ is dense in $[0, 1]$. Fix any a and b in D and consider the closed set

$$S = \{\phi \in [0, 1] : \phi f(a) + (1 - \phi) f(b) \leq f(\phi a + (1 - \phi) b)\}.$$

An induction shows that $J \subseteq S$. Since S is closed and contains a dense subset of $[0, 1]$, it contains all of $[0, 1]$. ∎

Comparative risk aversion for expected utility is characterized in the following result.

Theorem 4.14. *For each $i \in \{1, 2\}$, suppose the preference $\succ^i$ on $(\ell, \infty)^K$ has the EU representation (P, u^i) (with common probability P). Then the following conditions are equivalent:*

1. $\succ^1$ is more risk averse than $\succ^2$.

2. $u^1 = f \circ u^2$ for a concave function $f : \{u^2(\alpha) : \alpha \in (\ell, \infty)\} \to \mathbb{R}$.

Proof. Let v^i be the compensation function (or certainty equivalent) of $\succ^i$, which is determined implicitly by

$$u^i(v^i(x)) = \mathbb{E}u^i(x), \quad x \in (\ell, \infty)^K.$$

By Proposition 4.4, $\succ^1$ is more risk averse than $\succ^2$ if and only if $v^1 \leq v^2$.

$(2 \implies 1)$ Suppose that $u^1 = f \circ u^2$ for a concave function f. Given any $x \in (\ell, \infty)^K$, let $y = u^2(x)$. By Jensen's inequality,

$$u^1(v^1(x)) = \mathbb{E}[u^1(x)] \leq f(\mathbb{E}[u^2(x)]) = f(u^2(v^2(x))) = u^1(v^2(x)).$$

Since u^1 is increasing, this shows that $v^1 \leq v^2$.

$(1 \implies 2)$ Conversely, suppose that $v^1 \leq v^2$. Since u^2 is increasing and continuous, u^2 maps (ℓ, ∞) onto an interval $D = \{u^2(\alpha) : \alpha \in (\ell, \infty)\}$. The function $f : D \to \mathbb{R}$ is therefore well-defined by

$$u^1(\alpha) = f(u^2(\alpha)), \quad \alpha \in (\ell, \infty).$$

We show that f is concave. Let $p = P_1 > 0$. Given any $a, b \in D$, we define w, α and β so that

$$u^2(w) = pa + (1 - p)b, \quad u^2(w + \alpha) = a, \quad u^2(w + \beta) = b.$$

Finally, we define $x \in \mathbb{R}^K$ by letting $x_1 = \alpha$ and $x_k = \beta$ for $k = 2, \ldots, K$. By construction, $v^2(w1 + x) = w$ and therefore $v^1(w1 + x) \leq w$. Since $u^1 = f \circ u^2$, the last inequality can be restated as $pf(a) + (1-p)f(b) \leq f(pa + (1-p)b)$. Applying Lemma 4.13(b), we conclude that f is concave. ∎

An EU representation (P, u^0) is called **risk neutral** if u^0 is affine. We say that (P, u) is **more risk averse than risk neutral** if

$$\mathbb{E}u(w1 + x) \geq u(w) \quad \text{implies} \quad \mathbb{E}x \geq 0, \qquad (4.12)$$

for any $w \in (\ell, \infty)$ and $x \in (\ell - w, \infty)^K$. To justify this terminology, consider a preference $\succ$ on $(\ell, \infty)^K$ with EU representation (P, u), and another preference $\succ^0$ on $(\ell, \infty)^K$ with the risk-neutral EU representation (P, u^0). Without loss of generality, we assume that $u^0(w) = w$. It then follows from the definitions that (P, u) is more risk averse than risk neutral if and only if $\succ$ is more risk averse than $\succ^0$. It is important to note that in making this comparison, the probability P is common in the EU representation of both preferences. Given these observations, Theorem 4.14 implies that (P, u) is more risk averse than risk neutral if and only if u is concave. An alternative graphical derivation of the "only if" part of this claim is given in Figure 4.2.

4.3.2 Absolute Risk Aversion

Suppose the preference $\succ$ on $(\ell, \infty)^K$ has the EU representation (P, u). Considering the contrapositive of the condition defining absolute risk aversion (Definition 4.1), we note that $\succ$ is risk averse if and only if

$$\mathbb{E}u(w1 + x) \geq u(w) \implies \mathbb{E}u(w1 + \phi x) \geq u(w) \text{ for all } \phi \in (0, 1), \quad (4.13)$$

for any $w \in (\ell, \infty)$ and $x \in (\ell - w, \infty)^K$. Another plausible notion of absolute risk aversion is convexity of $\succ$, which in this context is equivalent to the condition: for any $w \in (\ell, \infty)$ and $x, y \in (\ell - w, \infty)^K$,

$$\mathbb{E}u(w1 + x) \geq u(w) \text{ and } \mathbb{E}u(w1 + y) \geq u(w)$$
$$\implies \mathbb{E}u(w1 + \phi x + (1 - \phi)y) \geq u(w) \text{ for all } \phi \in (0, 1).$$

As noted in Remark 4.2, the above condition can be viewed as a diversification principle and it implies that $\succ$ is risk averse; condition (4.13) is recovered by setting $y = 0$. Therefore, if $\succ$ is convex, it is necessarily risk averse. Yet another plausible concept of absolute risk aversion is that of

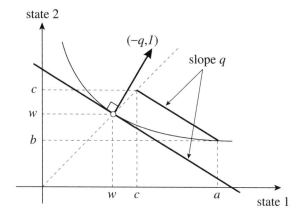

state 2

(−q,1)

slope q

c

w

b

w   c   a

state 1

Figure 4.2 Here is another proof that more risk averse than risk neutral implies concavity. Suppose (without loss in generality) that $K = 2$, and let $p = P_1$ and $q = -p/(1-p)$. Consider any payoff (a, b), and let $w = u^{-1}(pu(a) + (1-p)u(b))$. The curved line is the boundary of the set $B(w) = \{(x, y) : pu(x) + (1-p)u(y) > u(w)\}$. Suppose that $\succ$ is more risk averse than risk neutral. Condition (4.12) means that the vector $(-q, 1)$ supports the set $B(w)$ at (w, w). The orthogonal to $(-q, 1)$ line through (w, w) has slope q. Letting $c = pa + (1-p)b$, the line through (a, b) to (c, c) also has slope q and is therefore parallel to the supporting line. This shows that (c, c) lies above the point (w, w) on the diagonal, a fact that can be restated as the concavity condition $u(pa + (1-p)b) = u(c) \geq u(w) = pu(a) + (1-p)u(b)$.

being more risk averse than risk neutral, which was characterized in Section 4.3.1 (see also Exercise 4) as being equivalent to the concavity of u. If u is concave, then clearly $\succ$ is convex and therefore risk averse.

We argue that if $\succ$ is risk averse, then u is necessarily concave, thus establishing the equivalence of all of the preceding notions of absolute risk aversion when applied to expected utility. In practically all applications it is true that there exists a dense subset of (ℓ, ∞) on which u has a positive derivative.[2] In this case, the following simple argument suffices. Suppose that $\succ$ is risk averse. We will show that u is concave by verifying that (P, u) is more risk averse than risk neutral. Suppose first that $\mathbb{E}[u(w\mathbf{1} + x)] > u(w)$ for some $w \in (\ell, \infty)$ and $x \in (\ell, \infty)^K$. By perturbing w slightly if necessary, we assume that the derivative $u'(w)$ exists and is positive. Utilizing (4.13),

---

[2] An increasing function is differentiable outside a set of Lebesgue measure zero (see, for example, Chapter 5 of Royden (1988), or Theorem 7.2.7 of Dudley (2002)). It is still possible, however, that the derivative vanishes on an open interval.

it follows that

$$\mathbb{E}\left[\frac{u(w\mathbf{1}+\alpha x)-u(w)}{\alpha x}x\right] \geq 0, \quad \alpha \in (0,1). \tag{4.14}$$

Letting α go to zero, we find that $u'(w)\mathbb{E}x \geq 0$. Since $u'(w) > 0$, this proves that $\mathbb{E}x \geq 0$. If $\mathbb{E}[u(w\mathbf{1}+x)] = u(w)$, we apply the same argument with $x + \varepsilon\mathbf{1}$ in place of x, where $\varepsilon > 0$, to conclude that $\mathbb{E}x \geq -\varepsilon$. Letting $\varepsilon \downarrow 0$, we again conclude that $\mathbb{E}x \geq 0$. In either case, condition (4.12) is verified. We have therefore proved the following theorem under a mild regularity assumption. The latter is dropped in the theorem's proof for the benefit of the intellectually curious.

Theorem 4.15. *Suppose the preference $\succ$ on $(\ell,\infty)^K$ admits the EU representation (P,u). Then the following conditions are equivalent:*

1. *$\succ$ is risk averse.*
2. *$\succ$ is convex.*
3. *u is concave.*

Proof. $(3 \implies 2 \implies 1)$ See above discussion.

$(1 \implies 3)$ We assume that $K = 2$, since the general case is a corollary of the two-state case. Suppose $\succ$ is risk averse. As above, concavity of u follows if we verify the support condition (4.12). We will complete the proof by showing that the violation of (4.12) leads to a contradiction. So suppose that $\mathbb{E}u(w_0\mathbf{1}+x) \geq u(w_0)$ for some $w_0 \in (\ell,\infty)$ and $x \in (\ell,\infty)^K$ such that $\mathbb{E}x < 0$. Since u is increasing, we can slightly increase the value of x so that

$$\mathbb{E}x < 0 \quad \text{and} \quad \mathbb{E}u(w_0\mathbf{1}+x) > u(w_0), \tag{4.15}$$

which we henceforth assume. We are going to prove that

$$u \text{ is convex on } D = (w_0 - h, w_0 + h) \text{ for some } h > 0. \tag{4.16}$$

Assume this condition for now. By Lemma 4.16, which follows this proof, u must have a positive derivative at all but countably many points of D. We can therefore choose some w sufficiently close to w_0 so that $\mathbb{E}u(w\mathbf{1}+x) \geq u(w)$ and $u'(w) > 0$. By risk aversion, $\mathbb{E}u(w\mathbf{1}+\alpha x) \geq u(w)$ for all $\alpha \in (0,1)$ and therefore inequality (4.14) holds. Letting α go to zero results in $u'(w)\mathbb{E}x \geq 0$, which contradicts (4.15).

Finally, we verify the convexity condition (4.16), making use of the assumption that $K = 2$. By increasing the value of x in (4.15), we can and do assume that there exists an $x = (x_1, x_2) \in (\ell, \infty)^2$ such that

$$\mathbb{E}x = 0 \quad \text{and} \quad \mathbb{E}u(w_0 1 + x) > u(w_0).$$

Reordering the two states if necessary, we assume that $x_1 > 0 > x_2$. By continuity of u, there exists some $h \in (0, (x_1 - x_2)/2)$ such that

$$\mathbb{E}u(w1 + x) > u(w) \quad \text{for all } w \in D = (w_0 - h, w_0 + h).$$

Let $p = P_1 = 1 - P_2$. Given any $a, b \subset D$ such that $a > b$, we define

$$w = pa + (1 - p)b.$$

Combining the last equality with our assumption $px_1 + (1 - p)x_2 = 0$, we obtain

$$\frac{b - w}{a - w} = -\frac{p}{1 - p} = \frac{x_2}{x_1}.$$

This proves the existence of some $\phi > 0$ such that

$$a = w + \phi x_1 \quad \text{and} \quad b = w + \phi x_2.$$

Since $\phi(x_1 - x_2) = a - b < 2h < x_1 - x_2$, it follows that $\phi \in (0, 1)$. By risk aversion, $\mathbb{E}u(w1 + x) \geq u(w)$ implies that $\mathbb{E}u(w1 + \phi x) \geq u(w)$. The last inequality can be restated as

$$pu(a) + (1 - p)u(b) \geq u(pa + (1 - p)b).$$

Applying Lemma 4.13(b) to $-u$ completes the proof of (4.16). ∎

Lemma 4.16. Suppose the function $f : (a, b) \to \mathbb{R}$ is convex and increasing. Then f has a positive derivative at all except at most countably many elements of its domain.

Proof. Consider any point $w \in (a, b)$ and fix any point $w_1 \in (a, w)$. For $w_2 \in (w, b)$, the slope $(u(w_2) - u(w))/(w_2 - w)$ is increasing in w_2 and is bounded below by the positive slope $(u(w) - u(w_1))/(w - w_1)$.

Therefore, the right derivative $f'_+(w)$ exists and is positive. Similarly, the left derivative $f'_-(w)$ exists and $f'_-(w) \leq f'_+(w)$. Since the intervals $(f'_-(w), f'_+(w))$ are nonoverlapping as w ranges over (a, b), at most countably many of them are nonempty. This proves that for all except at most countably many values of $w \in (a, b)$, $f'(w) = f'_-(w) = f'_+(w) > 0$. ∎

4.4 RISK AVERSION AND SIMPLE PORTFOLIO CHOICE

In general, an agent's demand for a given risky asset depends not only on the agent's risk aversion, but also on other considerations, including the agent's time preferences and endowment, and the joint distribution of multiple traded risky assets. In this section we analyze a simple portfolio problem that provides a clean link between risky-asset demand and risk aversion by assuming away other considerations.

We consider an agent with deterministic time-one endowment $w\mathbf{1}$, for some $w \in (\ell, \infty)$. The agent's time-zero consumption is given at some fixed level. Given the latter, the agent's preference over the set $(\ell, \infty)^K$ of time-one payoffs has the EU representation (P, u), where $u : (\ell, \infty) \to \mathbb{R}$ is assumed to be concave, meaning that the agent is risk averse. We do *not* assume that u is everywhere differentiable. As we will see shortly, kinks of u can have interesting implications for the optimal demand of a risky asset.

The agent can trade in a forward market, while leaving time-zero consumption unchanged. (Equivalently, the agent could be assumed to trade in a spot market for D along with any borrowing or lending required to leave time-zero consumption at its fixed level.) The agent's only decision is to select a number θ of forward contracts on a single risky asset D, whose forward price is F. We define the random variables

$$Y = D - F\mathbf{1}, \quad Y^+ = \max\{0, Y\}, \quad Y^- = -\min\{0, Y\}.$$

We assume that the market is arbitrage-free and D has positive variance and therefore Y^+ and Y^- are nonzero. The time-one payoff resulting from the portfolio θ is denoted

$$x^\theta = w\mathbf{1} + \theta Y.$$

109

We also define the set of portfolios that result in admissible time-one payoffs

$$\Theta = \{\theta \in \mathbb{R} : x^\theta \in (\ell, \infty)^K\}.$$

Since Y^+ and Y^- are nonzero, Θ is a bounded open interval if $\ell > -\infty$ and $\Theta = \mathbb{R}$ if $\ell = -\infty$. The agent's problem is to maximize the concave function $U : \Theta \to \mathbb{R}$ defined by

$$U(\theta) = \mathbb{E}[u(x^\theta)], \quad \theta \in \Theta. \tag{4.17}$$

The set of maximizing values of $\theta \in \Theta$ is denoted arg max U.

If u is differentiable, then

$$\arg\max U = \{\theta \in \Theta : \mathbb{E}[u'(x^\theta)Y] = 0\}.$$

We generalize this statement by relaxing the differentiability assumption on u. Since u is assumed concave, it has well-defined right and left derivatives at any $w \in (\ell, \infty)$, denoted $u'_+(w)$ and $u'_-(w)$, respectively. We also define $\delta(w) \in \mathbb{R}_+$ by

$$u'_-(w) = u'_+(w)(1 + \delta(w)).$$

The function u is differentiable at w if and only if $\delta(w) = 0$. (Since u is concave, the intervals $(u'_+(w), u'_-(w))$ are disjoint for distinct values of w and therefore there are at most countably many $w \in (\ell, \infty)$ such that $\delta(w) > 0$.)

Proposition 4.17. *If u is concave, then $\theta \in$ arg max U if and only if*

$$\mathbb{E}[u'_+(x^\theta)Y^+] - \mathbb{E}[u'_-(x^\theta)Y^-] \le 0 \le \mathbb{E}[u'_-(x^\theta)Y^+] - \mathbb{E}[u'_+(x^\theta)Y^-].$$

Proof. Direct computation shows that the above condition is equivalent to $U'_+(\theta) \le 0 \le U'_-(\theta)$, which clearly characterizes the optimality of θ. ∎

Corollary 4.18. *Suppose u is concave and $\theta \in$ arg max U.*

(a) $[\mathbb{E}Y > 0 \implies \theta \ge 0]$ *and* $[\mathbb{E}Y < 0 \implies \theta \le 0]$.

(b) $\theta = 0$ *if and only if* $-\delta(w)\,\mathbb{E}Y^+ \le \mathbb{E}Y \le \delta(w)\,\mathbb{E}Y^-$.

(c) *If u is differentiable, then*

$$[\mathbb{E}Y > 0 \implies \theta > 0] \quad and \quad [\mathbb{E}Y < 0 \implies \theta < 0].$$

Part (a) states that it is never optimal for the agent to short the risky asset if $\mathbb{E}Y > 0$ or go long the asset if $\mathbb{E}Y < 0$, although it allows for the possibility of no trade in either case. Part (b) characterizes the cases in which no trade is optimal. It shows that if u is kinked at w, then the agent will find it optimal to not trade in D unless the expected payoff is sufficiently high and positive, or sufficiently low and negative. If u is differentiable at w, then no trade is optimal if and only if $\mathbb{E}\,Y = 0$, and therefore part (a) implies part (c).

Next we compare the risky-asset demand of two risk-averse agents that are identical to the agent studied so far, except for the function u, which is taken to be $u^i : (\ell, \infty) \to \mathbb{R}$ for agent $i \in \{1, 2\}$. Agent one is therefore more risk averse than agent two if and only if $u^1 = f \circ u^2$ for a concave function f. The functions $U^i : \Theta \to \mathbb{R}$ are defined by

$$U^i(\theta) = \mathbb{E}[u^i(x^\theta)], \quad i = 1, 2.$$

Proposition 4.19. *Suppose, for each $i \in \{1, 2\}$, that agent i is risk averse and* $\arg\max U^i = [a_i, b_i] \subseteq \mathbb{R}_+$. *If agent one is more risk averse than agent two, then $a_1 \le a_2$ and $b_1 \le b_2$.*

Proof. It suffices to confirm that for every $\theta \in \mathbb{R}_+$,

$$[U_-^{1\prime}(\theta) > 0 \implies U_-^{2\prime}(\theta) > 0] \quad \text{and}$$
$$[U_+^{2\prime}(\theta) < 0 \implies U_+^{1\prime}(\theta) < 0]. \tag{4.18}$$

To see why, consider two mountaineers who climbed a single-peaked mountain each. Let $U^i(\theta)$ be the elevation of climber i at time θ. Condition (4.18) says that when climber one was ascending so was climber two, and when climber two was descending so was climber one. Therefore, climber one summited no later than climber two ($a_1 \le a_2$), and climber two started descending no sooner than climber one ($b_1 \le b_2$). (A more formal proof is left to the interested reader.)

Suppose first that $U_-^{1\prime}(\theta) > 0$ and therefore

$$\mathbb{E}[u_-^{1\prime}(w1 + Y\theta)Y^+] > \mathbb{E}[u_+^{1\prime}(w1 + Y\theta)Y^-].$$

Let $u^1 = f \circ u^2$, where f is an increasing concave function. It follows that

$$\mathbb{E}[f_-'(u^2(w1 + Y\theta))u_-^{2\prime}(w1 + Y\theta)Y^+]$$
$$> \mathbb{E}[f_+'(u^2(w1 + Y\theta))u_+^{2\prime}(w1 + Y\theta)Y^-].$$

Since f is concave and u^2 is increasing and $\theta \ge 0$,

$$f_+'(u^2(w1)) \ge f_-'(u^2(w1 + Y\theta)) \text{ on the event } \{Y > 0\},$$

111

and

$$f'_+(u^2(w1 + Y\theta)) \geq f'_+(u^2(w1)) \text{ on the event } \{Y < 0\}.$$

Combining the last three inequalities results in

$$\mathbb{E}[f'_+(u^2(w1))u_-^{2\prime}(w1 + Y\theta)Y^+] > \mathbb{E}[f'_+(u^2(w1))u_+^{2\prime}(w1 + Y\theta)Y^-].$$

Canceling $f'_+(u^2(w1))$ on both sides results in $U_-^{2\prime}(\theta) > 0$. The second implication in (4.18) is shown similarly. ∎

4.5 Coefficients of Risk Aversion

Twice-differentiable expected utilities are parsimoniously represented by their coefficient of absolute or relative risk aversion, which are introduced in this section and are related to local notions of absolute and comparative risk aversion in the following section. The differentiability assumption is typically satisfied in applications,[3] as in the CRRA or CARA specifications arising in the context of representative-agent pricing.

We let $C^2(\ell, \infty)$ denote the set of all real-valued functions on (ℓ, ∞) with a continuous second derivative.

Definition 4.20. *Given any $u \in C^2(\ell, \infty)$, the corresponding* **coefficient of absolute risk aversion** $A^u : (\ell, \infty) \to \mathbb{R}$ *and* **coefficient of relative risk aversion** $R^u : (\ell, \infty) \to \mathbb{R}$ *are defined by*

$$A^u(w) = -\frac{u''(w)}{u'(w)} \quad and \quad R^u(w) = wA^u(w). \tag{4.19}$$

Writing equation (4.19) as $A^u(w)dw = -d \log u'(w)$, and integrating twice, we find that A^u entirely determines u up to a positive affine transformation. By combining this observation with the EU uniqueness result of Theorem 4.10, it follows that there is a one-to-one correspondence between

---

[3] From a modeling perspective, suppose that an agent does not receive a payoff x exactly, but rather receives $x + \varepsilon$, where ε is a noise term. After a suitable enlargement of the state space, suppose that ε is distributed on some bounded real interval independently of x and has a smooth density ϕ. Then the agent's expected utility can be computed as $\mathbb{E}[u(x + \varepsilon)] = \mathbb{E}[u_\varepsilon(x)]$, where $u_\varepsilon(x) = \int_\mathbb{R} u(x + \alpha)\phi(\alpha)d\alpha$. Even if u is not smooth, the reduced utility function u_ε is necessarily smooth. Here we are not modeling the noise term, but we can interpret an expected utility representation to be of the form (P, u_ε) for some implied noise term ε, in a larger probability space than the current K-state model.

preferences that admit some twice continuously differentiable EU representation and pairs of a probability and an absolute risk-aversion coefficient (see Exercise 7).

The relationship of coefficients of risk aversion to risk aversion follows from the more general discussion of Section 4.3 and is summarized below (see also Exercise 8).

Proposition 4.21. *Suppose that* $\succ, \succ^1$ *and* $\succ^2$ *are preferences with respective EU representations* $(P, u), (P, u^1)$ *and* (P, u^2), *where* $u, u^1, u^2 \in C^2(\ell, \infty)$.

(a) *The preference* $\succ$ *is risk averse if and only if* $A^u(w) \geq 0$ *for all* $w \in (\ell, \infty)$.

(b) *The preference* $\succ^1$ *is more risk averse than* $\succ^2$ *if and only if for every* $w \in (\ell, \infty)$, $A^{u^1}(w) \geq A^{u^2}(w)$.

(c) *The preference* $\succ$ *is CARA if and only if* A^u *is constant; CRRA if and only if* R^u *is constant; and IRRA if and only if* R^u *is nondecreasing.*

Proof. (a) The first claim follows from Theorem 4.15 and the fact that u is concave if and only if $A^u \geq 0$.

(b) Let the function f be defined by $u^1 = f \circ u^2$. Direct computation shows that

$$A^{u^1} = A^{u^2} + (A^f \circ u^2)u^{2\prime}. \tag{4.20}$$

Therefore f is concave ($A^f \geq 0$) if and only if $A^{u^1} \geq A^{u^2}$, and the result follows from Theorem 4.14.

(c) This is a corollary of part (b). ∎

The functional form of expected utilities with constant absolute or relative coefficient of risk aversion, which can be computed as a calculus exercise, is summarized below.

Proposition 4.22. (a) *For any* $u \in C^2(0, \infty)$ *and* $\gamma \in \mathbb{R}$, $R^u = \gamma$ *if and only if there exist* $a \in \mathbb{R}_{++}$ *and* $b \in \mathbb{R}$ *such that*

$$au(x) + b = \frac{x^{1-\gamma} - 1}{1 - \gamma} \quad (= \log(x) \ if \ \gamma = 1).$$

(b) *For any* $u \in C^2(\mathbb{R})$ *and* $\gamma \in \mathbb{R}$, $A^u = \gamma$ *if and only if there exist* $a \in \mathbb{R}_{++}$ *and* $b \in \mathbb{R}$ *such that*

$$au(x) + b = \frac{1 - \exp(-\gamma x)}{\gamma} \quad (= x \ if \ \gamma = 0).$$

113

While the last two propositions characterize CARA or CRRA smooth expected utilities, a stronger result was given in Theorem 3.37, which in the current context can be restated as follows.

Theorem 4.23. *Suppose the preference* $\succ$ *on* $(\ell, \infty)^K$ *admits an additive utility representation* U *such that each* U_k *is continuously differentiable somewhere in its domain. Then* $\succ$ *is CRRA (CARA) if and only if it has an EU representation with constant coefficient of relative (absolute) risk aversion.*

The remarkable aspect of this theorem is that only additivity is assumed; state independence, and hence the existence of an expected utility representation, is a consequence of scale or translation invariance and a minor regularity assumption.

The combination of expected utility and the preference restrictions used in the representative-agent pricing arguments of Section 3.4 naturally gives rise to the class of expected utilities with hyperbolic absolute risk aversion (HARA). The real-valued function u is **HARA with coefficients**[4] $(\alpha, \beta) \in \mathbb{R}^2$ if it belongs to $C^2(\{w : \alpha + \beta w > 0\})$ and

$$A^u(w) = \frac{1}{\alpha + \beta w}, \quad \alpha + \beta w > 0. \tag{4.21}$$

Assuming it is nonempty, the domain $\{w : \alpha + \beta w > 0\}$ is unbounded above if and only if $\beta \geq 0$. Risk-averse CRRA and CARA expected utilities that are not risk neutral are HARA utilities with coefficients $(0, 1/\gamma)$ and $(1/\gamma, 0)$, respectively, where $\gamma > 0$. A calculus exercise shows:

Proposition 4.24. *The function* $u \in C^2(\{w : \alpha + \beta w > 0\})$ *is HARA with coefficients* (α, β) *if and only if there exist scalars* a *and* b *such that*

$$au(w) + b = \begin{cases} \frac{1}{\beta-1}(\alpha + \beta w)^{(\beta-1)/\beta}, & \text{if } \beta \neq 0 \text{ and } \beta \neq 1; \\ \log(\alpha + w), & \text{if } \beta = 1; \\ -\alpha \exp(-w/\alpha), & \text{if } \beta = 0 \text{ and } \alpha > 0. \end{cases} \tag{4.22}$$

The representative-agent equilibria of Propositions 3.24 and 3.27, under the additional assumption that $\succ^*$ has an EU representation (P, u^*), result

---

[4] The coefficient of absolute risk tolerance is defined as $1/A^u$. For this reason, some authors use the term linear risk tolerance (LRT) in place of HARA (although affine risk tolerance would have been more accurate). The coefficient β is sometimes referred to as a coefficient of cautiousness.

in a formulation in which agent i has preferences with an EU representation (P, u^i) that is HARA with coefficients (α^i, β). As the notation suggests, the parameters P and β must be common among agents for the aggregation argument to apply. The scale-invariance and translation-invariance arguments of aggregation are combined in the following example of equilibrium forward pricing. While our preference monotonicity assumption requires that $\beta \geq 0$, the stated equilibrium is valid for any value of β, including the quadratic utility case ($\beta = -1$), which results in a simple example of a CAPM equilibrium.

Example 4.25 (Representative-Agent Equilibrium with HARA Utility)
Consider the agents $(C^i, \succ^i, e^i)$, $i = 1, \ldots, I$, *where* $\succ^i$ *is assumed to have an EU representation* (P, u^i). *We assume that* u^i *is HARA with coefficients* (α^i, β) *and therefore* $C^i = \{w : \alpha^i + \beta w > 0\}^K$. *Both the probability* P *and the coefficient* β *are common among all agents. We will construct a forward-market equilibrium in* J *assets, whose payoffs are the rows of the matrix* D, *under the assumption that the endowment of agent* i *takes the form*

$$e^i = a^i \mathbf{1} + b^{i\prime} D, \quad a^i \in \mathbb{R}, \quad b^i \in \mathbb{R}^J.$$

The set of feasible trades for agent i *is* $\Theta^i = \{\theta \in \mathbb{R}^J : e^i + \theta'(D - F) \in C^i\}$. *A* **forward-market equilibrium** *consists of a trade profile and a column vector of forward prices,*

$$(\theta^1, \ldots, \theta^I) \in \Theta^1 \times \cdots \times \Theta^I, \quad F \in \mathbb{R}^J,$$

such that each agent i *finds trade* θ^i *optimal given the forward prices* F *and markets clear:*

$$\mathbb{E}u^i(e^i + \theta^{i\prime}(D - F)) = \max_{\theta \in \Theta^i} \mathbb{E}u^i(e^i + \theta'(D - F)) \quad and \quad \sum_i \theta^i = 0.$$

Let $\alpha = \sum_i \alpha^i$, $a = \sum_i a^i$, $b = \sum_i b^i$ *and* $e = \sum_i e^i = a\mathbf{1} + b'D$. *The representative agent* $(C, \succ, e)$ *is endowed with the aggregate consumption plan* e *and has a preference* $\succ$ *with an EU representation* (P, u), *where* u *is in the HARA class with coefficients* (α, β). *An equilibrium is implied by the representative agent's marginal pricing at the aggregate consumption and the allocations described in Propositions 3.24 and 3.27. The resulting equilibrium prices and trades are given by*

$$F = \frac{1}{\mathbb{E}u'(e)} \mathbb{E}[u'(e)D], \quad b^i + \theta^i = \frac{\alpha^i + \beta(a^i + b^{i\prime}F)}{\alpha + \beta(a + b'F)} b, \quad i = 1, \ldots, I.$$

115

The case $\beta = -1$ corresponds to quadratic expected utility and results in a CAPM equilibrium that is consistent with the setting of Exercise 8 of Chapter 3.

4.6 SIMPLE PORTFOLIO CHOICE FOR SMALL RISKS

Smooth expected utility over small risks is particularly tractable, since it can be approximated by quadratic expected utility. An example of a small risk is a price change over a sufficiently short interval of time. This section utilizes this idea to derive a simple expression for a near-optimal portfolio. The single-period intuition introduced here extends recursively to multiperiod settings, where large risks are resolved continuously in small amounts and an agent can trade dynamically in response to small risk resolutions. Such a notion of continuous information is formalized in continuous-time models with information generated by Brownian motion.

Revisiting the context of Section 4.4, consider the problem of maximizing the function U of equation (4.17). The optimality conditions characterize an optimal portfolio only implicitly. For example, if u is differentiable, the optimal θ is computed as a solution to $\mathbb{E}[u'(x^\theta)Y] = 0$. If, however, u is a concave quadratic function (ignoring the utility monotonicity requirement and letting $\ell = -\infty$ for now), then $u'(x^\theta) = u'(w) + u''(w)(x^\theta - w)$ and therefore the optimal trade can be computed as

$$\theta^* = \frac{1}{A^u(w)} \frac{\mu}{\sigma^2}, \qquad (4.23)$$

where $\mu = \mathbb{E}Y$ and $\sigma^2 = \mathbb{E}Y^2$. Expression (4.23) is quite intuitive and generalizes easily to a formulation with multiple risky assets. Although quadratic utility has undesirable features (such as nonmonotonicity), in this section we argue that for any u that is sufficiently smooth so that it can be approximated by a quadratic function near w, the trade (4.23) is nearly optimal, provided Y represents a small risk. The argument reinforces the local risk-aversion interpretation of the coefficient of absolute risk aversion, and introduces an essential intuition that is behind tractable dynamic continuous-time models in which information is generated by Brownian motion.

We begin our analysis with a review of the requisite Taylor series approximation result. Given any n-times differentiable real-valued function f on some interval containing zero, we let $f^{(k)}$ denote the kth derivative of f, and we let f_n denote the n-degree polynomial that has the same value and first n derivatives at zero as f:

$$f(0) = f_n(0) \quad \text{and} \quad f^{(k)}(0) = f_n^{(k)}(0), \quad k = 1, \ldots, n. \tag{4.24}$$

While the general formula for f_n is no doubt familiar, we are going to use only

$$f_1(x) = f(0) + f'(0)x \quad \text{and} \quad f_2(x) = f(0) + f'(0)x + f''(0)\frac{x^2}{2}.$$

An estimate of the error $f - f_n$ is given below. We will need the result for $n \in \{1, 2\}$, but the lemma is as easy to state and prove as for a general positive integer n. For $x < 0$, the notation $(0, x)$ denotes the interval $(-x, 0)$.

Lemma 4.26. *Suppose that* $0 \in (a, b) \subseteq \mathbb{R}$ *and* $f : (a, b) \to \mathbb{R}$ *is* $n + 1$ *times differentiable. Then for any* $x \in (a, b)$,

$$f(x) = f_n(x) + f^{(n+1)}(x_{n+1})\frac{x^{n+1}}{(n+1)!} \quad \text{for some } x_{n+1} \in (0, x). \tag{4.25}$$

Proof. We define $C \in \mathbb{R}$ and $\varepsilon : (a, b) \to \mathbb{R}$ by

$$f(t) = f_n(t) + C\frac{t^{n+1}}{(n+1)!} + \varepsilon(t) \quad \text{and} \quad \varepsilon(x) = 0. \tag{4.26}$$

Letting $t = x$ determines C, which then determines $\varepsilon(t)$ for all $t \in (a, b)$. Since ε vanishes at 0 and x and is continuous on $[0, x]$, it must achieve a minimum or a maximum at some $x_1 \in (0, x)$, and therefore $\varepsilon^{(1)}(x_1) = 0$. We repeat the same argument n times, utilizing equations (4.24): $\varepsilon^{(1)}(0) = \varepsilon^{(1)}(x_1) = 0$ implies $\varepsilon^{(2)}(x_2) = 0$ for some $x_2 \in (0, x_1)$; $\ldots$; $\varepsilon^{(n)}(0) = \varepsilon^{(n)}(x_n) = 0$ implies $\varepsilon^{(n+1)}(x_{n+1}) = 0$ for some $x_{n+1} \in (0, x_n)$. Since $f^{(n+1)}(t) = C + \varepsilon^{(n+1)}(t)$, it follows that $C = f^{(n+1)}(x_{n+1})$. The proof is concluded by letting $t = x$ in (4.26). ∎

Returning to the setting of Section 4.4, we change the unit of time so that time one becomes time $h > 0$, and we write $Y(h)$ (instead of Y) for the net payoff of the single forward contract maturing at time h. Analogously, we let $\Theta(h)$ be the set of all $\theta \in \mathbb{R}$ such that $w\mathbf{1} + \theta Y(h)$ is valued in (ℓ, ∞).

The following restrictions on the agent's preferences and the payoffs $Y(h)$ are assumed throughout the rest of this section.

- Consumption is valued in (ℓ, ∞), where $\ell \in (-\infty, 1)$. The agent's preferences have the EU representation (P, u), where $u : (\ell, \infty) \rightarrow \mathbb{R}$ has a continuous third derivative.

- There exists a random variable B with $\mathbb{E}B = 0$ and $\text{var}[B] = 1$, scalars $\mu, \sigma \in \mathbb{R}$ and a function $\varepsilon_Y : \mathbb{R}_{++} \rightarrow \mathbb{R}^K$ such that

$$Y(h) = \mu h + \sigma B \sqrt{h} + \varepsilon_Y(h) \quad \text{and} \quad \lim_{h \downarrow 0} \frac{\varepsilon_Y(h)}{h} = 0. \qquad (4.27)$$

Therefore, for small h, the mean and variance of $Y(h)$ are approximately equal to μh and $\sigma^2 h$ respectively.

- The market is arbitrage-free and therefore $Y(h)^+, Y(h)^- \neq 0$ and $\Theta(h)$ is a bounded interval (since ℓ is finite).

The compensation function, $\upsilon : (\ell, \infty)^K \rightarrow (\ell, \infty)$, of any utility function with EU representation (P, u) is given by

$$\upsilon(c) = u^{-1} \mathbb{E} u(c).$$

For every $c \in (\ell, \infty)^K$, $\upsilon(c)$ is the certainty equivalent of c, in the sense that the agent is indifferent between $\upsilon(c)\mathbf{1}$ and c. We derive a quadratic approximation of the certainty equivalent value for payoffs generated by trading in the forward market.

Proposition 4.27. *Given the above restrictions, there exist some $\delta > 0$ and functions $\varepsilon : \Theta(h) \times [0, \delta] \rightarrow \mathbb{R}$, $h \in [0, \delta]$, such that*

$$\upsilon(w\mathbf{1} + \theta Y(h)) = w + \left(\theta \mu - \frac{1}{2} A^u(w)(\theta \sigma)^2\right)h + \varepsilon(\theta, h), \qquad (4.28)$$

for all $h \in [0, \delta]$ and $\theta \in \Theta(h)$, and

$$\limsup_{h \downarrow 0} \frac{1}{h} |\varepsilon(\theta, h)| = 0. \qquad (4.29)$$

Proof. Since $\lim_{h \to 0} Y(h) = 0$ and $\Theta(h)$ is bounded, there exist some $\delta > 0$ and some bounded interval $(a, b) \subseteq (\ell, \infty)$ containing w such that $w + \theta Y(h)$ is valued in (a, b) for all $\theta \in \Theta(h)$ and $h \in [0, \delta]$. For the remainder of this proof, we assume that $\theta \in \Theta(h)$ and $h \in [0, \delta]$.

Since the third derivative of u is continuous, it is bounded on $[a,b]$. By Lemma 4.26 with $f(x) = u(w+x)$ and $n = 2$,

$$\limsup_{h\downarrow 0} \frac{1}{\theta} \frac{1}{h} \left[u(w+\theta Y(h)) \right.$$

$$\left. - \left(u(w) + u'(w)\theta Y(h) + \frac{1}{2}u''(w)(\theta Y(h))^2 \right) \right] = 0.$$

Taking expectations and using (4.27), we find that

$$\mathbb{E}u(w+\theta Y(h))$$

$$= u(w) + u'(w)\left(\theta\mu - \frac{1}{2}A^u(w)(\theta\sigma)^2 \right) h + \varepsilon(\theta,h), \qquad (4.30)$$

where the function $\varepsilon : \Theta(h) \times [0,\delta] \to \mathbb{R}$ satisfies (4.29). Applying u^{-1} on both sides of (4.30), equation (4.28) follows by a first-order Taylor series approximation of u^{-1} around $u(w)$ (that is, we apply Lemma 4.26 with $f(x) = u^{-1}(u(w)+x)$ and $n = 1$). To compute the latter, we differentiate the identity $u^{-1}(u(w)) = w$ twice to conclude that

$$(u^{-1})'(u(w)) = \frac{1}{u'(w)} \quad \text{and} \quad (u^{-1})''(u(w)) = -\frac{u''(w)}{u'(w)^3}. \qquad \blacksquare$$

Finally, the fact that the above quadratic approximation is uniform in θ allows us to conclude the near optimality of the trade θ^* of equation (4.23), in the sense that the certainty equivalent loss from selecting θ^* rather than the optimal θ is small.

Proposition 4.28. *Under this section's restrictions, there exist some $\delta > 0$ and a function $\varepsilon : [0,\delta] \to \mathbb{R}_+$ such that*

$$\sup_{\theta\in\Theta(h)} \upsilon(w\mathbf{1}+\theta Y(h)) \le \upsilon(w\mathbf{1}+\theta^* Y(h)) + \varepsilon(h), \quad h \in [0,\delta],$$

and

$$\lim_{h\downarrow 0} \frac{\varepsilon(h)}{h} = 0.$$

119

Proof. By its definition, $\theta = \theta^*$ maximizes $\theta\mu - (1/2)A^u(w)(\theta\sigma)^2$. The result follows from the last proposition by taking the supremum over $\theta \in \Theta(h)$ on both sides of (4.28) and then using approximation (4.28) once again with $\theta = \theta^*$. ∎

4.7 STOCHASTIC DOMINANCE

Stochastic dominance is a dual notion to that of comparative risk aversion. Whereas the latter involves the comparison of preferences based on how they rank certain types of payoffs, stochastic dominance involves the comparison of payoffs based on how they are ranked by preferences within a certain class. Fixing an underlying probability P, in this section we introduce two examples of this idea, the first based on the class of expected utilities relative to P and the second based on the class of risk-averse expected utilities relative to P. A more general theory of stochastic orders is cited in the notes. This section makes use of some simple probability concepts that go beyond the finite state-space theory of Appendix B, although the reader familiar with the first four sections of the latter should have no trouble following.

For simplicity, we assume that the set of **payoffs** is $\mathbb{R}_{++}^K$. $\mathcal{U}$ denotes the set of all continuous increasing functions of the form $u : (0, \infty) \to \mathbb{R}$. Each $u \in \mathcal{U}$ is identified with an EU representation (P, u). Recall that the latter represents a risk-averse preference if and only if u is concave.

Definition 4.29. *The payoff x **first-order stochastically dominates** the payoff y if $\mathbb{E}u(x) \geq \mathbb{E}u(y)$ for every $u \in \mathcal{U}$. The payoff x **second-order stochastically dominates** y if $\mathbb{E}u(x) \geq \mathbb{E}u(y)$ for every concave $u \in \mathcal{U}$.*

Stochastic dominance relations are better understood by embedding the K states in a richer probability model. More concretely, we take the state space to be the unit square $\Omega = [0, 1] \times [0, 1]$, we define an **event** to be any subset of Ω with a well-defined area,[5] and we define the probability $P(A)$ of an event A to be the area of A. A **random variable** is any mapping of

---

[5] In the axiomatic setting of mainstream probability theory, which includes the axiom of choice and defines probabilities to be countably additive, it is well-known that a uniform probability measure on the set of all subsets of the unit square does not exist. The reader familiar with more advanced probability notions can take P to be Lebesgue measure on the Borel σ-algebra of the unit square. The more informal description given here suffices for our purposes.

the form $x : \Omega \to \mathbb{R}$ such that the set $\{x \in J\} = \{\omega \in \Omega : x(\omega) \in J\}$ is an event, for any interval J. A random variable is **simple** if its image is finite. The **cumulative distribution function** of a random variable x is the function $F_x : \mathbb{R} \to [0, 1]$ defined by $F_x(t) = P[x \le t]$. The random variables x and y are **equal in distribution**, denoted $x =_d y$, if $F_x = F_y$.

Let the random variables U_1 and U_2 be defined by

$$U_i(\omega_1, \omega_2) = \omega_i, \quad i = 1, 2.$$

It then follows that $P[U_1 \le a,\ U_2 \le b] = ab$ for all $a, b \in [0, 1]$ and therefore U_1 and U_2 are stochastically independent $[0, 1]$-uniform random variables. We can think of U_1 and U_2 as two random number generators. The first random number generator, U_1, will be used to simulate payoffs that are contingent on the K states, while the second random number generator, U_2, will be used to simulate noise. More formally, we embed the K states of the original model in the enlarged state space by identifying state $k \in \{1, \dots, K\}$ with the event $\{U_1 \in J_k\}$, where $J_k = [\sum_{l<k} P_l, \sum_{l \le k} P_l)$. Therefore, by construction, $P_k = P[U_1 \in J_k]$ for every state k. A **payoff** $x \in \mathbb{R}^K_{++}$ is identified with the simple random variable $f_x(U_1)$, where $f_x : [0, 1) \to \mathbb{R}_{++}$ is the step function defined by $f_x(t) = x_k$ for $t \in J_k$. The random variable U_2 will be used in Theorem 4.31 to represent a source of noise.

The following proposition characterizes first-order stochastic dominance in the current setting of random variables taking finitely many values. The result is also valid for general random variables, with essentially the same proof.

Proposition 4.30. *For any payoffs x, y, the following are equivalent:*

1. *x first-order stochastically dominates y.*

2. *$F_x(t) \le F_y(t)$ for all $t > 0$.*

3. *There exist functions $f, g : [0, 1) \to \mathbb{R}$ such that*

$$x =_d f(U_1), \quad y =_d g(U_1) \quad and \quad f \ge g.$$

Proof. ($1 \implies 2$) Given any $t > 0$, let $u(s) = 0$ if $s \le t$ and $u(s) = 1$ if $s > t$, and note that $\mathbb{E}u(z) = 1 - F_z(t)$ for any random variable z. Select a sequence $\{u_n\} \subseteq \mathcal{U}$ such that $\lim_{n \to \infty} u_n(s) = u(s)$ for all s. Condition 1 implies that $\mathbb{E}u_n(x) \ge \mathbb{E}u_n(y)$ for all n and therefore $\mathbb{E}u(x) \ge \mathbb{E}u(y)$, which is equivalent to $F_x(t) \le F_y(t)$.

(2 $\Longrightarrow$ 3) Given any cumulative distribution function F, define the function $F^{-1}(\alpha) = \sup\{t : F(t) < \alpha\}$, $\alpha \in [0, 1)$. Condition 3 is satisfied with $f = F_x^{-1}$ and $g = F_y^{-1}$.

(3 $\Longrightarrow$ 1) Immediate. ∎

Second-order stochastic dominance in the current context is characterized in the following theorem. Generalizations are cited in the notes.

Theorem 4.31. *For any payoffs x, y such that $\mathbb{E}x = \mathbb{E}y$, the following are equivalent:*

1. *x second-order stochastically dominates y.*
2. *$\int_0^t F_x(s)\,ds \leq \int_0^t F_y(s)\,ds$ for all $t > 0$.*
3. *$y =_d x + \varepsilon(x, U_2)$ for   some $\varepsilon : (0, \infty) \times [0, 1] \to \mathbb{R}$ such   that $\mathbb{E}\varepsilon(t, U_2) = 0$ for all $t \in (0, \infty)$.*
4. *There exists a random variable n such that*

$$y =_d x + n \quad \text{and} \quad \mathbb{E}[n \mid x] = 0.$$

Proof. Given any random variable x, we define $\phi_x(t) = \int_0^t F_x(\alpha)\,d\alpha$, which is a convex function. A **kink** of ϕ_x is a value t such that $\phi'_+(t) > \phi'_-(t)$. If x is simple, then ϕ_x is a piecewise linear function with a finite number of kinks. Moreover, an exercise shows that for any payoff x (which is simple and positive by definition) and any $m \in (0, \infty)$,

$$P[x > m] = 0 \implies \mathbb{E}x = \int_0^m P[x > \alpha]d\alpha = m - \phi_x(m). \quad (4.31)$$

Fixing two payoffs x, y such that $\mathbb{E}x = \mathbb{E}y$, we begin the main part of the proof.

(1 $\Longrightarrow$ 2) Given any $t > 0$, define the functions $u_\delta \in \mathcal{U}$ by

$$u_\delta(\alpha) = \min\{\alpha, t + \delta(\alpha - t)\}, \quad \delta \in [0, 1).$$

Condition 1 implies that $\mathbb{E}u_\delta(x) \geq \mathbb{E}u_\delta(y)$ for all $\delta \in (0, 1)$. Letting δ approach zero, it follows that $\mathbb{E}u_0(x) \geq \mathbb{E}u_0(y)$. Applying (4.31),

$$\mathbb{E}u_0(x) = \int_0^t P[u_0(x) > \alpha]\,d\alpha = \int_0^t P[x > \alpha]\,d\alpha = t - \phi_x(t).$$

Similarly, $\mathbb{E}u_0(y) = t - \phi_y(t)$ and therefore $\phi_x(t) \leq \phi_y(t)$.

(2 $\implies$ 3) We use the following terminology and notation. A **lottery** is a simple random variable of the form $f(U_2)$, for some $f : [0, 1) \to \mathbb{R}$. A lottery is represented by a finite set of the form $\{(p_i, \alpha_i) : i = 1, \ldots, n\} \subseteq \mathbb{R}_+ \times \mathbb{R}$, where $\sum_{i=1}^{n} p_i = 1$, with the corresponding function f defined by

$$f(t) = \alpha_i, \quad \text{for } t \in \left[\sum_{k<i} p_k, \sum_{k \leq i} p_k \right), \quad i = 1, \ldots, n.$$

In words, we say that the lottery pays out α_i with probability p_i.

Suppose $\phi_x \leq \phi_y$ and choose $m \in \mathbb{R}_+$ large enough so that $x, y \leq m1$. By equation (4.31), $\phi_x(m) = \phi_y(m)$. Let $[a, b]$ be a maximal closed subinterval of $[0, m]$ so that $\phi_x(t) < \phi_y(t)$ for $t \in (a, b)$ and $\phi_x(a) = \phi_y(a)$. Let k be the total number of kinks of ϕ_x and ϕ_y that belong to (a, b). If $k = 0$, then $y =_d x$. Suppose $k > 0$. Referring to Figure 4.3 for guidance, let α_1 be the first kink of ϕ_x to the right of a, and let α_2 be either the first kink of ϕ_x to the right of α_1 or b, whichever comes first. Note that $a < \alpha_1 < \alpha_2 \leq b$ and a is a kink of ϕ_y. Let β be the smallest kink of ϕ_y that is greater than a, and note that $\beta \in (a, b]$. Let $l(t)$ denote the line segment connecting the point $(a, \phi_x(a))$ to the point $(t, \phi_x(t))$. As t moves to the right from α_1 toward α_2, one of two things happens first. Either $l(t)$ hits the point $(\beta, \phi_y(\beta))$ for some $t \in (\alpha_1, \alpha_2)$, or t hits α_2 and $l(\alpha_2)$ is below the graph of ϕ_y. Let α be the value of t

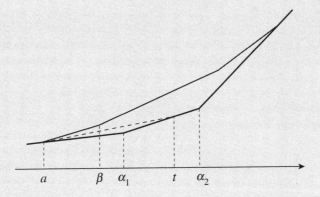

Figure 4.3 The upper line is the graph of ϕ_y; the lower line is the graph of ϕ_x. Both graphs are convex and piecewise linear. The dotted line is $l(t)$.

at which one of these two condition is met, let $q \in (0, 1)$ be such that $\alpha_1 = qa + (1 - q)\alpha$, and define the function $\delta^1 : (0, \infty) \times [0, 1] \to \mathbb{R}$ by letting $\delta^1(t, \cdot) = 0$ if $t \neq \alpha_1$ and letting $\delta^1(\alpha_1, U_2)$ be the lottery that is equal to $a - \alpha_1$ with probability q and $\alpha - \alpha_1$ with probability $1 - q$. By construction, $\mathbb{E}[\delta^1(t, U_2)] = 0$ for all t. Letting $x^1 = x + \delta^1(x, U_2)$, note that the graph of ϕ_{x^1} is the same as that of ϕ_x outside the interval $[a, \alpha]$, and it is the line segment $l(\alpha)$ on $[a, \alpha]$. The total number of kinks in the set $\{t : \phi_{x^1}(t) < \phi_y(t)\}$ is, therefore, one less than the total number of kinks in $\{t : \phi_x(t) < \phi_y(t)\}$. If $x^1 =_d y$, the proof is completed by letting $\varepsilon = \delta^1$. Otherwise, repeat the above construction with x^1 in place of x, and define δ^2 in terms of x^1 the way δ^1 was defined in terms of x. If $x^2 =_d y$, the proof is complete with $\varepsilon(t, U_2) = \delta^1(t, U_2) + \delta^2(t + \delta^1(t, U_2), U_2)$. Otherwise, repeat the pattern. Since there are finitely many kinks the process terminates after finitely many steps.

$(3 \implies 4)$ Set $n = \varepsilon(x, U_2)$.

$(4 \implies 1)$ If u is concave, we have

$$\mathbb{E}u(y) = \mathbb{E}u(x + n) = \mathbb{E}[\mathbb{E}[u(x + n) \mid x]] \leq \mathbb{E}u(\mathbb{E}[x + n \mid x]) = \mathbb{E}u(x).$$

The second equality follows by the law of iterated expectations in a somewhat more general form than Proposition B.17 (but with a straightforward proof). The inequality follows by Jensen's inequality for conditional expectations, whose proof is essentially the same as in Lemma 4.13. ∎

4.8 EXERCISES

1. (a) Verify the equivalence of condition (4.5) (resp. (4.6), (4.7)) to the CRRA (resp. IRRA, CARA) property.

    (b) Prove Propositions 4.4 and 4.6.

    (c) Define **decreasing absolute risk aversion (DARA)** analogously to the IRRA definition. Characterize DARA preferences analogously to Proposition 4.6 for the IRRA case. Finally, characterize all CRRA preferences that are DARA.

    (d) Provide definitions of **risk seeking** and **DRRA** (decreasing relative risk aversion) for preference analogous to those for risk aversion and IRRA, so that a CARA preference is DRRA if and only if it is risk seeking. Prove the last statement.

2. Prove the first part of Lemma 4.13 (Jensen's inequality) by an induction in the number of states, using directly the definition of concavity. Also explain why the lemma's second part implies the converse of the first part.

3. This exercise outlines an alternative proof of the implication ($3 \implies 1$) of Theorem 4.15. Suppose that $\succ$ is risk averse and show that u is concave by proving condition (4.12). Without loss of generality, assume $K = 2$, let $p = P_1 = 1 - P_2$ and define q by $p^{-1} + q^{-1} = 1$. Suppose condition (4.12) is violated and therefore there exists some $w_0 \in (\ell, \infty)$ and $x = (x_1, x_2) \in (\ell - w_0, \infty)^2$ such that $\mathbb{E}x < 0$ and $\mathbb{E}u(w_0 \mathbf{1} + x) > u(w_0)$. The proof will be completed by deriving a contradiction in the following steps.

(a) Assuming $x_1 > 0 > x_2$, let $\lambda = x_2/x_1$ and define μ by $\lambda^{-1} + \mu^{-1} = 1$. Verify that $\lambda < q < 0 < p < \mu < 1$.

(b) Argue that there exists some $h > 0$ such that $\mathbb{E}u(w\mathbf{1} + \phi x) \geq u(w)$ for all $w \in (w_0 - h, w_0 + h)$ and $\phi \in (0, 1)$.

(c) Define $f(\delta) = u(w_0 + \delta h) - u(w_0)$ and show that the condition of part (b) is equivalent to $q(f(\delta + \alpha) - f(\delta)) \leq f(\delta + \lambda\alpha) - f(\delta)$ for all $\delta \in (-1, 1)$ and $\alpha \in (0, x_1/h)$.

(d) For every positive integer n, use part (c) with $\delta = \mu^{n+1}$ and $\delta + \alpha = \mu^n$ to show that

$$\frac{p}{\mu} \times \frac{f(\mu^n)}{\mu^n} \geq \frac{f(\mu^{n+1})}{\mu^{n+1}} \geq 0.$$

(e) For every positive integer n, use part (c) with $\delta = -(1 - \mu)^{n+1}$ and $\delta + \lambda\alpha = -(1 - \mu)^n$ to show that

$$0 \leq \frac{1 - \lambda}{1 - q} \times \frac{-f(-(1 - \mu)^n)}{(1 - \mu)^n} \leq \frac{-f(-(1 - \mu)^{n+1})}{(1 - \mu)^{n+1}}.$$

(f) For any sufficiently large integer n, define the scalar α_n and the integer $m(n)$ by the conditions

$$\alpha_n = -\frac{1}{\lambda}(1 - \mu)^n \quad \text{and} \quad \mu^{m(n)+1} < \alpha_n \leq \mu^{m(n)}.$$

Use part (c) with $\delta = 0$ and $\alpha = \alpha_n$ to show that

$$\frac{f(\mu^{m(n)})}{\mu^{m(n)+1}} \geq \frac{f(\alpha_n)}{\alpha_n} \geq \frac{f(\lambda\alpha_n)}{q\alpha_n} = \frac{1}{|q|} \frac{-f(-(1-\mu)^n)}{(1-\mu)^n}.$$

Let $n \to \infty$ and use the last two parts to derive a contradiction.

4. Using your definition of **risk seeking** from Exercise 1, prove that a preference with EU representation (P, u) is risk seeking if and only if u is convex. Finally, define a preference to be **risk neutral** if and only if it is both risk seeking and risk averse, and conclude that a preference with EU representation (P, u) is risk neutral if and only if u is affine.

5. In the context of Section 4.4, use Proposition 4.19 to compare the optimal risky-asset positions of two versions of the same agent with different values of the endowment $w1$, assuming the agent has DARA preferences. Repeat for IARA, CARA, DRRA, IRRA and CRRA preferences.

6. Consider the single-period binomial model of Exercise 4 of Chapter 1. An agent can trade the single risky asset and the bond at time zero but consumes only at time one and has preferences that are represented by expected utility in the HARA class. Given a deterministic initial endowment, compute the agent's optimal portfolio.

7. (a) Suppose $A : (\ell, \infty) \to \mathbb{R}$ is any continuous function. Derive an expression for a function $\bar{u} : (\ell, \infty) \to \mathbb{R}$ such that $A^{\bar{u}} = A$, $\bar{u}(1) = 0$ and $\bar{u}'(1) = 1$. Show that if $u : (\ell, \infty) \to \mathbb{R}$ is any twice continuously differentiable increasing function such that $A^u = A$, then $u = a\bar{u} + b$ for some $a \in (0, \infty)$ and $b \in \mathbb{R}$.

(b) Consider a strictly positive probability P and a continuous function $A : (\ell, \infty) \to \mathbb{R}$. Then there exists a unique preference $\succ$ on $(\ell, \infty)^K$ that admits an EU representation of the form (P, u), where $A^u = A$. Conversely, suppose $\succ$ is any preference on $(\ell, \infty)^K$ that admits some twice-differentiable EU representation. Then there exist a unique strictly positive probability P and continuous function $A : (\ell, \infty) \to \mathbb{R}$ such that υ has an EU representation of the form (P, u), where $A^u = A$. Prove these claims.

8. This exercise gives local versions of the "only if" statements in the first two parts of Proposition 4.21.

(a) Suppose f and g are real-valued functions on some open interval around zero that satisfy $f(0) = g(0) = 0$, $g'(0) \neq 0$ and $0 = \max\{f :$ $g \leq 0\}$. Show that there exists some $\lambda \in \mathbb{R}_+$ such that $\lambda g(0) = 0$, $f'(0) = \lambda g'(0)$ and $f''(0) \leq \lambda g''(0)$. *Hints:* Use Theorem A.39. If $f''(0) > \lambda g''(0)$, the Lagrangian $f - \lambda g$ has a local strict minimum at zero, which contradicts $0 = \max\{f : g \leq 0\}$.

(b) Suppose the preference $\succ$ on $(\ell, \infty)^K$ has the EU representation (P, u), where $u \in C^2(\ell, \infty)$. Given any $w \in (\ell, \infty)$ and $x \in (\ell, \infty)^K$ such that $\mathbb{E}x, \mathbb{E}x^2 \neq 0$, use part (a) to show that $A^u(w) \geq 0$ if there exists an $\varepsilon \in (0, \infty)$ such that

$$\theta \in (-\varepsilon, +\varepsilon) \quad \text{and} \quad w\mathbf{1} \succ w\mathbf{1} + \theta x \quad \Longrightarrow \quad w\mathbf{1} \succ w\mathbf{1} + 2\theta x.$$

Hint: $f(\theta) = u(w) - \mathbb{E}[u(w + \theta x)]$, $g(\theta) = u(w) - \mathbb{E}[u(w + 2\theta x)]$.

(c) For $i \in \{1, 2\}$, suppose the preference $\succ^i$ on $(\ell, \infty)^K$ has the EU representation (P, u^i), where $u^i \in C^2(\ell, \infty)$. Given any $w \in (\ell, \infty)$ and $x \in (\ell, \infty)^K$ such that $\mathbb{E}x, \mathbb{E}x^2 \neq 0$, use part (a) to show that $A^{u^1}(w) \geq A^{u^2}(w)$ if there exists an $\varepsilon \in (0, \infty)$ such that

$$\theta \in (-\varepsilon, +\varepsilon) \quad \text{and} \quad w\mathbf{1} \succ^2 w\mathbf{1} + \theta x \quad \Longrightarrow \quad w\mathbf{1} \succ^1 w\mathbf{1} + \theta x.$$

Hint: $f(\theta) = u^2(w) - \mathbb{E}[u^2(w + \theta x)]$, $g(\theta) = u^1(w) - \mathbb{E}[u^1(w + \theta x)]$.

(d) Derive part (b) as a corollary of part (c).

9. Complete the proof of Proposition 4.21 by verifying equation (4.20) and providing the details for part (c). Finally, extend the result to include the characterization of IRRA, CARA and IARA.

10. Prove Propositions 4.22 and 4.24.

11. (a) Verify the equilibrium of Example 4.25. Is the equilibrium unique?

(b) Derive a CAPM beta-pricing condition for $\beta = -1$.

(c) Extend Example 4.25 by introducing time-zero consumption and risk-free borrowing and lending, assuming that agents have preferences of the form $U(c) = u(c_0) + \delta \mathbb{E}u(c_1)$, where u takes the same HARA functional forms as in Example 4.25.

12. The CAPM argument applies with an infinite number of states and a finite number of assets provided all random variables are restricted to have finite variance. In such a setting, suppose X is implemented by spot trading in J assets whose payoffs are normally distributed.

Show that in this case the assumption of mean-variance preferences over marketed cash flows follows from preference monotonicity with respect to first-order stochastic dominance. (The notes of Chapter 3 provide related references discussing a broader class of distributions that also generates mean-variance preferences.)

13. Prove that condition (4.31) holds for any positive payoff x and positive scalar m.

14. Assume that the number of states K is at least three and consider the increasing, concave, twice continuously differentiable functions $u_1, u_2 : \mathbb{R} \to \mathbb{R}$. We say that u_1 is **more risk averse** than u_2 if for any probability P, the preference on $\mathbb{R}^K$ with EU representation (P, u_1) is more risk averse than the preference with EU representation (P, u_2). We say that u_1 is **strongly more risk averse** than u_2 if, given any probability P and $x, y \in \mathbb{R}^K$ such that $\mathbb{E}x = \mathbb{E}y$ and x second-order stochastically dominates y,

$$[\mathbb{E}u_i(x - \theta_i \mathbf{1}) = \mathbb{E}u_i(y), \ \theta_i \in \mathbb{R}, \ i = 1, 2] \implies \theta_1 \geq \theta_2. \qquad (4.32)$$

The amount θ_i in (4.32) compensates for switching from the payoff x to the riskier payoff y.

(a) Show that if u_1 is strongly more risk averse than u_2, then u_1 is more risk averse than u_2.

(b) Show that u_1 is strongly more risk averse than u_2 if and only if

$$\frac{u_1'(\alpha)}{u_2'(\alpha)} \leq \frac{u_1''(\beta)}{u_2''(\beta)}, \quad \text{for all } \alpha, \beta \in (\ell, \infty),$$

if and only if $u_1 = \lambda u_2 + g$ for some $\lambda \in (0, \infty)$ and concave nonincreasing function $g : \mathbb{R} \to \mathbb{R}$.

Hint: To show that the first condition implies the second one, take x to be equal to a with probability p and b with probability $1 - p$. Choose y to be of the form $x + sn$, where $s \in \mathbb{R}$ and n equals zero on the event $\{x = a\}$. Define $\theta_i(s)$ to be the value θ_i in (4.32) as a function of the noise scale s. Argue that $\theta_1(s) - \theta_2(s)$ is minimized at $s = 0$ and consider the corresponding second-order necessary conditions of optimality.

(c) Specify an example of u_1 and u_2 so that u_1 is more risk averse than u_2, but u_1 is not strongly more risk averse than u_2.

4.9 NOTES

The axiomatic foundation of expected utility began with von Neumann and Morgenstern (1944) (see also Herstein and Milnor (1953) and Aumann (1962, 1964)), who considered preferences over objective probability distributions. Incorporating a subjective view of probability in the tradition of Ramsey (1926) and de Finetti (1937), Savage (1954) developed an axiomatic foundation for expected utility with a (nonatomic) probability that is uniquely determined by preferences over "acts," which Savage defined as mappings from states to consequences. Anscombe and Aumann (1963) offered an alternative foundation for subjective expected utility that utilizes objective probabilities to calibrate subjective beliefs. A highly readable account of these contributions is Kreps (1988). Another approach to expected utility with subjective probabilities builds on the additive representation theory discussed in the last chapter and is exemplified by the contributions of Luce and Krantz (1971), Wakker (1984, 1989) and Nakamura (1990). The axiomatization of Theorem 4.12 is based on Skiadas (1997) and is a variant of Wakker's approach.

As pointed out in Theorem 4.23 (which is Theorem 3.37 rephrased), under a minor regularity assumption, an expected utility representation results from an additive representation if scale or translation invariance is assumed, without the need of the elaborate structures normally required for a full theory of subjective expected utility. This class of preference along with the Gorman aggregation argument leads to the HARA class, whose background literature is discussed in last chapter's notes. The trades in the equilibrium of the HARA Example 4.25 are shown by DeMarzo and Skiadas (1998) to be part of a rational expectations equilibrium with asymmetrically informed agents, even if prices are only partially informative (which they can be).

This chapter's treatment of risk aversion builds on classic work by Arrow (1965, 1970), Pratt (1964) and Yaari (1969), although Definition 4.1 of absolute risk aversion is, to my knowledge, original, as is the part of Theorem 4.15 showing the equivalence of this notion of risk aversion to concavity in the context of expected utility. The alternative proof outlined in Exercise 3 is based on an idea that was suggested to me by Ioan Mirciov. The more standard definition of risk aversion as convexity of a preference order is well-known to correspond to utility concavity, a fact that is a consequence of a more general theory of quasiconcavity of additive functions.

129

A utility that represents a convex preference is known as quasiconcave. For expected utility, the equivalence of quasiconcavity and concavity is a special case of the following more general fact: If the function $f(x) = \sum_{i=1}^{n} f_i(x_i)$ is quasiconcave, where each f_i is a real-valued continuous function on some interval, then at most one of the f_i is not concave. This fact was proved by Yaari (1977), who credited Koopmans with a different proof, as well as Gorman for the twice-differentiable case (in both cases in unpublished papers). The result was further extended by Debreu and Koopmans (1982), Crouzeix and Lindberg (1986) and Monteiro (1999).

The theory of stochastic orders introduced in Section 4.7 goes back to Hardy, Littlewood and Pólya (1929, 1934), Blackwell (1951, 1953), Sherman (1951), Stein (1951) and Strassen (1965). The adoption of these methods in economic theory was strongly influenced by the papers of Rothschild and Stiglitz (1970, 1971, 1972), whose main characterization of increasing risk was, however, already known in the above cited literature. A modern overview of the field of stochastic orders can be found in the monograph of Müller and Stoyan (2002). The definition and characterization of "strongly more risk averse" in Exercise 14 is due to Ross (1981) (see also Machina and Neilson (1987)).

A large literature in psychology and economics has documented the descriptive failures of expected utility. Highly influential examples of this literature include Allais (1953), Ellsberg (1961), Kahneman and Tversky (1979) and Tversky and Kahneman (1981). Rabin (2000) related risk aversion toward moderate risks to large risks in thought-provoking ways. For example, he proved that any risk-averse expected-utility maximizing agent who turns down a 50-50 bet of losing $100 or gaining $105 given any reference wealth level less than $350,000 must necessarily also turn down a 50-50 bet of losing $4,000 and gaining $635,670 given an initial wealth of $340,000. The volumes edited by Kahneman and Tversky (2000) and Camerer, Loewenstein, and Rabin (2004) provide a good introduction to a related literature.

In Chapter 6 we will use expected utility as a building block in the formulation of recursive dynamic utility. While the limitations of expected utility are clearly relevant in the dynamic setting, how the discussion of static results applies in the dynamic setting is not always clear, and more research in that direction is needed. For example, information is often assumed to arrive in small amounts over short intervals of time, in which case expected utility is applied only over small risks, where its predictions can be argued are more robust. Machina (1982) discusses a related local interpretation of expected utility analysis. On the other hand, Skiadas (2008b) shows that the class of "divergence preferences" of Maccheroni, Marinacci, and Rustichini (2006), representing ambiguity aversion, is approximately consistent with expected utility for some types of small risk but not others. The notes of Chapter 6 provide references to the dynamic choice literature, as well as continuous-time models alluded to in Section 4.6. Further discussion of asset pricing theory in the expected utility framework can be found in the exposition of Gollier (2001).

PART TWO

DISCRETE DYNAMICS

CHAPTER FIVE

Dynamic Arbitrage Pricing

THIS CHAPTER presents a multiperiod extension of the arbitrage-pricing theory of Chapter 1. The formal structure of the set of traded cash flows, present-value functions and the fundamental theorems of asset pricing remains the same as in the single-period case. New to the multiperiod setting is the dynamic implementation of cash flows over time, with the important conclusion that given the possibility of frequent trading, a relatively small number of financial contracts can be used to span the uncertainty represented by a large number of states. The concept of dominant choice, introduced in Chapter 1, is extended to take into account dynamic consistency issues, with a main application being the optimal exercise and valuation of options. The chapter emphasizes arguments that extend readily in more general stochastic settings, based on the language and tools of martingale theory. Familiarity with Chapter 1 and Appendix B is assumed.

5.1 DYNAMIC MARKET AND PRESENT VALUE

We begin with the definition of a market and a present-value function in a multiperiod setting, in a way that will allow the direct reinterpretation of the fundamental theorems of asset pricing of Chapter 1. A market is introduced from the perspective of time-zero planning and is then related to the market as viewed from the perspective of every other informational spot.

5.1.1 Time-Zero Market and Present-Value Functions

Throughout Part II, we represent uncertainty and the arrival of information over time by the following primitives:

- A finite state space Ω.
- A finite set of **times** $\{0, 1, \dots, T\}$.
- A filtration $\{\mathcal{F}_t : t = 0, \dots, T\}$, where $\mathcal{F}_0 = \{\emptyset, \Omega\}$ and $\mathcal{F}_T = 2^\Omega$.

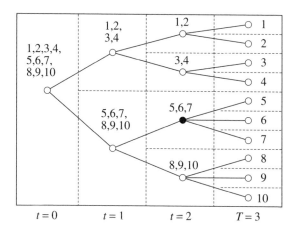

t = 0   t = 1   t = 2   T = 3

Figure 5.1 An example of a filtration, with $\Omega = \{1, 2, 3, 4, 5, 6, 7, 8, 9, 10\}$. The boxes above time t correspond to the partition generating $\mathcal{F}_t$. For example, the time-two partition is $\{\{1, 2\}, \{3, 4\}, \{5, 6, 7\}, \{8, 9, 10\}\}$. Every single box or circle is a spot. For example, the dark circle corresponds to the spot $(\{5, 6, 7\}, 2)$.

A **spot** is a pair (F, t), where t is a time and F is a member of the partition generating $\mathcal{F}_t$. The filtration $\{\mathcal{F}_t\}$ can equivalently be thought of as an information tree, as illustrated in the example of Figure 5.1 and further explained in Section B.5. We let $1 + K$ be the total number of spots. The stochastic model of Part I is obtained by letting $T = 1$.

From Section B.5, we recall that an **adapted process** is any function of the form $x : \Omega \times \{0, \dots, T\} \to \mathbb{R}$ such that x_t is $\mathcal{F}_t$-measurable for every time t. An adapted process can equivalently be viewed as an assignment of a scalar to each spot, and therefore the set of all adapted processes $\mathcal{L}$ can be identified with the Euclidean space $\mathbb{R}^{1+K}$. For any spot (F, t), we write $x(F, t)$ to denote the common value of $x(\omega, t)$ for all $\omega \in F$. For any subset S of $\Omega \times \{0, \dots, T\}$, we use the notation 1_S for the process defined by

$$1_S(\omega, t) = \begin{cases} 1, & \text{if } (\omega, t) \in S; \\ 0, & \text{otherwise.} \end{cases}$$

We define the market that an agent faces from the perspective of time zero, along with the associated notions of arbitrage and market completeness, just as in Chapter 1.

Definition 5.1. *A* **cash flow** *is any adapted process. A (time-zero)* **market** *is a linear subspace X of the set of cash flows $\mathcal{L}$. A cash flow c is an* *arbitrage if* $0 \neq c \geq 0$. *The market* X *is **arbitrage-free** if it contains no arbitrage. A cash flow* c *is **marketed** (at time zero) if there exists some* $w \in \mathbb{R}$ *such that* $c - w 1_{\Omega \times \{0\}} \in X$. *The market* X *is **complete** if every cash flow is marketed.*

We interpret a market X as a set of incremental cash flows that are the result of market transactions, which can now involve trading over time as information unfolds. The linearity of a market is a consequence of the implicit assumption of perfect competition and the lack of transaction costs or trading constraints (other than possible market incompleteness). We refer to the elements of a market X as the **traded cash flows**, or simply **trades**.

Fixing a reference market X, our definition of a corresponding time-zero present-value function is also identical to the single-period case.

Definition 5.2. *A (time-zero) **present-value function** is any linear function of the form* $\Pi_0 : \mathcal{L} \to \mathbb{R}$ *such that*

1. $\Pi_0(x) \leq 0$ *for every* $x \in X$.
2. $\Pi_0(c) > 0$ *for every arbitrage cash flow* c.
3. $\Pi_0(1_{\Omega \times \{0\}}) = 1$.

For any present-value function Π_0 and cash flow c, we interpret $\Pi_0(c)$ as the time-zero present value of c. A **state-price vector**, or **process**, is any p in $\mathbb{R}_{++}^{1+K}$ or $\mathcal{L}_{++}$ such that a present-value function Π_0 is defined by

$$\Pi_0(c) = \frac{p \cdot c}{p_0}, \quad c \in \mathcal{L}.$$

An **Arrow cash flow** is any cash flow of the form $1_{F \times \{t\}}$, where (F, t) is a spot. Any cash flow is a linear combination of the $1 + K$ Arrow cash flows, reflecting the identification of $\mathcal{L}$ and $\mathbb{R}^{1+K}$. A state-price process p satisfies, for any two spots (F, t) and (G, s),

$$\frac{p(F, t)}{p(G, s)} = \frac{\Pi_0(1_{F \times \{t\}})}{\Pi_0(1_{G \times \{s\}})},$$

revealing the interpretation of state prices as relative time-zero prices of Arrow cash flows. For the purposes of Part II, it is convenient to represent state prices in terms of state-price densities or equivalent martingale measures, which will be introduced in Section 5.3.

Given the identification of $\mathbb{R}^{1+K}$ with the set of cash flows, the fundamental theorems of asset pricing of Chapter 1 remain meaningful and valid in our new setting.

Theorem 5.3 (1st and 2nd Fundamental Theorems of Asset Pricing). *For any market X, a present-value function exists if and only if X is arbitrage-free, and is unique if and only if X is complete.*

5.1.2 Dynamic Market and Present-Value Functions

Most of the analysis of Part II is based on the simple notion of a market and present value introduced above. This leaves open a question of interpretation with regard to the market faced by an agent at every other spot of the information tree. We begin to address this question in this subsection with a notion of dynamic market. A main conclusion will be that under a dynamic consistency assumption, a time-zero present-value function also serves as a present-value function at every other spot. Moreover, given an additional liquidity assumption, the whole dynamic market is entirely determined by the time-zero market, and any present-value function at any given spot can be determined from a corresponding time-zero present-value function. These arguments justify our focus on the time-zero perspective while studying arbitrage pricing. The argument will be extended in the following chapter with regard to optimality and equilibrium via a notion of dynamic consistency of preferences.

We use the notation

$$\mathcal{L}_{F,t} = \{x \in \mathcal{L} : x = x1_{F \times \{t,\ldots,T\}}\},$$

which represents the set of adapted processes or cash flows that vanish outside the subtree rooted at spot (F, t).

Definition 5.4. *A **dynamic market** is a collection of the form*

$$\{X_{F,t} : (F, t) \text{ is a spot}\} \tag{5.1}$$

with the properties:

1. *(adaptedness and linearity) $X_{F,t}$ of a linear subspace of $\mathcal{L}_{F,t}$.*
2. *(dynamic consistency) For all spots (F, t) and (G, s),*

$$G \subseteq F \text{ and } s \geq t \implies X_{G,s} \subseteq X_{F,t}. \tag{5.2}$$

We think of $X_{F,t}$ as a set of incremental cash flows available to a market participant at spot (F, t) through trading over the information subtree rooted at (F, t). Such cash flows are naturally viewed as elements of $\mathcal{L}_{F,t}$. The linearity of $X_{F,t}$ is motivated just as for the time-zero market. To interpret the dynamic consistency condition, consider any spots (F, t) and (G, s) such that $G \subseteq F$ and $s \geq t$, meaning that (G, s) lies on the subtree rooted at spot (F, t). A trader at spot (F, t) can have any cash flow x in $X_{G,s}$ by making a contingent plan to carry out the transactions that result in x if (G, s) materializes. The trade x is therefore effectively also available to the agent at spot (F, t), resulting in the inclusion of condition (5.2).

We fix a reference dynamic market $\{X_{F,t}\}$ for the remainder of this section and we simplify the notation for the time-zero market by writing

$$X = X_{\Omega,0}.$$

A present-value function from the point of view of any given spot is defined analogously to a time-zero present-value function.

Definition 5.5. *A spot-(F, t) present-value function is any linear function of the form $\Pi_{F,t} : \mathcal{L}_{F,t} \to \mathbb{R}$ that satisfies*

1. *$\Pi_{F,t}(x) \leq 0$ for every $x \in X_{F,t}$.*
2. *$\Pi_{F,t}(c) > 0$ for any arbitrage c in $\mathcal{L}_{F,t}$.*
3. *$\Pi_{F,t}(1_{F \times \{t\}}) = 1$.*

The dynamic consistency of the market implies that for any time-zero present-value function Π_0 and any spot (F, t),

$$\Pi_{F,t}(c) = \frac{\Pi_0(c)}{\Pi_0(1_{F \times \{t\}})}, \quad c \in \mathcal{L}_{F,t}, \tag{5.3}$$

defines a spot-(F, t) present-value function $\Pi_{F,t}$. We refer to $\Pi_{F,t}$ as the spot-(F, t) present-value function that is **induced** by Π_0.

In the natural extension of our earlier terminology, for any spot (F, t), we say that $X_{F,t}$ is **arbitrage-free** if it contains no arbitrage; the cash flow c in $\mathcal{L}_{F,t}$ is **marketed at spot** (F, t) if there exists some $w \in \mathbb{R}$ such that $c - w1_{F \times \{t\}} \in X_{F,t}$; and $X_{F,t}$ is **complete** if every cash flow in $\mathcal{L}_{F,t}$ is marketed at (F, t). The fundamental theorems of asset pricing imply that a spot-(F, t) present-value function exists if and only if $X_{F,t}$ is arbitrage-free, and is unique if and only if $X_{F,t}$ is complete.

We say that the dynamic market $\{X_{F,t}\}$ is **arbitrage-free** if every $X_{F,t}$ is arbitrage-free, and **complete** if every $X_{F,t}$ is complete. Dynamic consistency implies that the time-zero market X is arbitrage-free if and only if the entire dynamic market $\{X_{F,t}\}$ is arbitrage-free, in which case, a time-zero present-value function Π_0 induces a spot-(F,t) present-value function, for every spot (F,t). The uniqueness of a time-zero present-value function does not, however, imply the uniqueness of another spot's present-value function. This is because completeness of the market X does not generally imply completeness of the dynamic market $\{X_{F,t}\}$. For example, X can be complete while $X_{F,t} = \{0\}$ for every spot (F,t) with $t > 0$. This issue relates to the following notion of "liquidity."

Definition 5.6. *The dynamic market $\{X_{F,t}\}$ is **liquid** if for any trade x in the time-zero market X and any spot (F,t), the cash flow $x1_{F \times \{t,...,T\}}$ is marketed at spot (F,t).*

The cash flow $x1_{F \times \{t,...,T\}}$ is marketed at spot (F,t) if and only if there exists some $y \in X_{F,t}$ such that $(x-y)1_{F \times \{t+1,...,T\}} = 0$. We can therefore think of the liquidity condition as stating that if an agent transacts at time zero in a way that results in a cash flow x, then at any spot the agent can trade in the market in a way that cancels out all future payments of the cash flow x. Liquidity can mean a variety of things in finance, but here it essentially means that a trader is able to liquidate any positions in the market at any spot.

Given liquidity, completeness of a dynamic market reduces to completeness of the time-zero market.

Proposition 5.7. *Assuming it is liquid, the dynamic market $\{X_{F,t}\}$ is complete if and only if the time-zero market X is complete.*

Proof. Suppose X is complete and (F,t) is any spot with $t > 0$. Given any $c \in \mathcal{L}_{F,t}$, let $w_0 \in \mathbb{R}$ and $x \in X$ be such that $c = w_0 1_{\Omega \times \{0\}} + x$, and let $y \in X_{F,t}$ be such that $(x-y)1_{F \times \{t+1,...,T\}} = 0$. It follows that $(c-y)1_{F \times \{t+1,...,T\}} = 0$. Since $c - y \in \mathcal{L}_{F,t}$, there exists $w \in \mathbb{R}$ such that $c = w1_{F \times \{t\}} + y$. This proves that $\{X_{F,t}\}$ is complete. The converse is immediate. ∎

A simplifying implication of liquidity is that assuming there is no arbitrage, the entire dynamic market $\{X_{F,t}\}$ is determined by the time-zero market X, and any present-value function at any spot is induced by some time-zero present-value function.

Proposition 5.8. *Suppose the dynamic market $\{X_{F,t}\}$ is liquid and arbitrage-free. Then the following conditions hold, for any spot (F, t):*

(a) $X_{F,t} = X \cap \mathcal{L}_{F,t}$.

(b) Given any spot-(F, t) present-value function $\Pi_{F,t}$, there exists some time-zero present-value function Π_0 that induces $\Pi_{F,t}$ by equation (5.3).

Proof. (a) By the definition of a dynamic market, $X_{F,t} \subseteq X \cap \mathcal{L}_{F,t}$. To show the reverse inclusion, suppose that $x \in X \cap \mathcal{L}_{F,t}$ and let $y \in X_{F,t}$ be such that $(x - y)1_{F \times \{t+1,\dots,T\}} = 0$. Since $x \in \mathcal{L}_{F,t}$, it follows that $x - y = (x - y)1_{F \times \{t\}} \in X$. Since X is arbitrage-free, $(x - y)1_{F \times \{t\}} = 0$ and therefore $x = y \in X_{F,t}$.

(b) For any spot (F, t) and any cash flow c, we use the notation $c^{F,t} = c - c1_{F \times \{t,\dots,T\}}$; that is, $c^{F,t}$ is the cash flow obtained from c by setting to zero every value of c on the subtree rooted at spot (F, t). Suppose $\Pi_{F,t}$ is a given spot-(F, t) present-value function, let $\tilde{\Pi}_0$ be an arbitrary time-zero present-value function, and define the function $\Pi_0 : \mathcal{L} \to \mathbb{R}$ by

$$\Pi_0(c) = \tilde{\Pi}_0(c^{F,t} + \Pi_{F,t}(c1_{F \times \{t,\dots,T\}})1_{F \times \{t\}}).$$

We will show that Π_0 is a time-zero present-value function, which completes the proof, since $\Pi_{F,t}$ is induced by Π_0. Linearity, positivity and normalization of Π_0 are immediate. We still must verify that Π_0 vanishes on X. Given any $x \in X$, let $y \in X_{F,t}$ be such that $(x - y)1_{F \times \{t+1,\dots,T\}} = 0$. The last condition implies that

$$\Pi_{F,t}((x - y)1_{F \times \{t,\dots,T\}})1_{F \times \{t\}} = (x - y)1_{F \times \{t,\dots,T\}}.$$

Therefore, $\Pi_0(x - y) = \tilde{\Pi}_0(x - y) = 0$ (since $x - y \in X$). Also, since $y \in \mathcal{L}_{F,t}$, $y^{F,t} = 0$; and since $y \in X_{F,t}$, $\Pi_{F,t}(y) = 0$. Therefore, $\Pi_0(y) = 0$. Finally, $\Pi_0(x) = \Pi_0(x - y) + \Pi_0(y) = 0$. ∎

The fact that a liquid, arbitrage-free dynamic market is entirely characterized by the time-zero market justifies our subsequent focus on the latter. In our approach, a time-zero market generalizes the notion of a single-period market of Part I. Alternatively, the results of Part I can be applied, for each spot $(F, t - 1)$, to the single-period market of all traded cash flows that vanish outside $F \times \{t - 1, t\}$, that is, spot $(F, t - 1)$ and its immediate successors. For example, the results of Chapter 2 can be applied in this manner, conditionally on any given nonterminal spot, relative to the one-period-ahead uncertainty. Given market liquidity, conditional single-period characterizations can be tied together recursively, forming the basis for alternative derivations of many of the results of Part II.

5.2 FINANCIAL CONTRACTS

Extending the single-period discussion of Section 1.5, this section introduces financial contracts that pay dividends and can be traded at every spot of the information tree. While in the single-period model portfolios are formed only at time zero, now they can be rebalanced at every spot, necessitating the notion of a trading strategy. A contract can be priced "by arbitrage" if it can be replicated by a trading strategy in other contracts with known prices.

5.2.1 Basic Arbitrage Restrictions and Trading Strategies

We begin with the definition of a simple type of (financial) contract. The trading of contracts is defined relative to a given reference market X that is fixed throughout.

Definition 5.9. *A* **contract** *is any pair,* (δ, V), *of adapted processes. The process* δ *is the contract's* **dividend process**, *while* V *is the contract's* **value process** *or* **cum-dividend price process**. *The contract's* **ex-dividend price process** *is* $S = V - \delta$. *The contract* (δ, V) *is* **traded at spot** (F, t) *if the market* X *contains the cash flow*

$$x = -V1_{F \times \{t\}} + \delta 1_{F \times \{t, \ldots, T-1\}} + V1_{F \times \{T\}}, \qquad (5.4)$$

in which case we refer to x *as the cash flow that is generated by* **buying** *the contract at spot* (F, t), *while* $-x$ *is generated by* **selling** *the contract at the same spot. The contract* (δ, V) *is* **traded** *if it is traded at every spot.*

The owner (long position) of the contract (δ, V) receives the dividend payment δ_t at time t. The contract's time-t value, V_t, represents, by convention, a cum-dividend price. If the contract is bought at time t, either the buyer pays the seller V_t and receives the time-t dividend δ_t, or the buyer pays the seller the ex-dividend price S_t and the time-t dividend goes to the seller.

Proposition 5.10. *Suppose the market is arbitrage-free and consider any two traded contracts,* (δ^1, V^1) *and* (δ^2, V^2)*, with the same terminal ex-dividend price, that is,*

$$S_T^1 = V_T^1 - \delta_T^1 = V_T^2 - \delta_T^2 = S_T^2.$$

Then $\delta^1 = \delta^2$ *if and only if* $V^1 = V^2$.

Proof. Suppose $\delta^1 = \delta^2$. Selling contract one and buying contract two at spot (F, t) results in a net cash flow $(V^1(F, t) - V^2(F, t))1_{F \times \{t\}}$. Since the market is arbitrage-free, $1_{F \times \{t\}} \notin X$ and therefore $V^1(F, t) = V^2(F, t)$.

Conversely, suppose $V^1 = V^2$. Since $S_T^1 = S_T^2$, we have $\delta_T^1 = \delta_T^2$. Assuming that we have shown that $\delta_u^1 = \delta_u^2$ for all $u > t$, we show that $\delta_t^1 = \delta_t^2$. Let (F, t) be any spot such that $\delta^1(F, t) > \delta^2(F, t)$. Buying contract one and selling contract two at spot (F, t) results in the net cash flow $(\delta^1(F, t) - \delta^2(F, t))1_{F \times \{t\}}$, contradicting the assumption that the market is arbitrage-free. This shows that $\delta_t^1 \leq \delta_t^2$. By symmetry, $\delta_t^1 = \delta_t^2$. ∎

Remark 5.11. *The first part of the proof also shows that if the two contracts are traded at the single spot* (F, t)*,* δ^1 *and* δ^2 *are equal on* $F \times \{t, \ldots, T\}$ *and* $S_T^1 = S_T^2$ *on* F*, then* $V^1(F, t) = V^2(F, t)$.

It is worth noting that the above conclusions can be dually derived in terms of a present-value function Π_0. Applying the restriction $\Pi_0(x) = 0$ to the cash flow of equation (5.4) shows that if (δ, V) is traded at spot (F, t), then

$$V(F, t) = \Pi_{F, t}(\delta 1_{F \times \{t, \ldots, T\}} + S1_{F \times \{T\}}), \tag{5.5}$$

where $\Pi_{F, t}$ is the spot-(F, t) present-value function induced by Π_0, as defined in (5.3). Proposition 5.10 and Remark 5.11 follow easily from this equation.

Default-free single-period borrowing or lending can be implemented by a special type of contract that we call a "money-market account." We recall, from Section B.5, that an adapted process x is **predictable** if the value x_t is $\mathcal{F}_{t-1}$-measurable for every time $t > 0$.

Definition 5.12. *A (default-free)* **money-market account** *is any contract* (δ, V) *whose value process* V *is predictable and strictly positive. The* **rate**

143

process r *of the money-market account* (δ, V) *with ex-dividend price process* $S = V - \delta$ *is defined by*

$$r_0 = 0 \quad and \quad 1 + r_t = \frac{V_t}{S_{t-1}}, \quad t = 1, \ldots, T. \tag{5.6}$$

A process r *is a* **short-rate process** *(of the market* X*) if there exists a traded money-market account with rate process* r.

By construction, a short-rate process is an element of the set $\mathcal{P}_0$ of all predictable processes that vanish at time zero.

Consider any traded contract (δ, V) and let $S = V - \delta$. Buying (δ, V) at spot $(F, t - 1)$ and selling it at each of its immediate successor spots generates the net cash flow

$$x = -S1_{F \times \{t-1\}} + V1_{F \times \{t\}}.$$

If the market is arbitrage-free and V is strictly positive, then necessarily S_{t-1} is strictly positive for every $t \in \{1, \ldots, T\}$. In particular, if (δ, V) is a money-market account, then its rate process r is well-defined and the above transactions implement single-period default-free lending at spot $(F, t - 1)$. The loan is default-free because the amount V_t paid back at time t is determined at time $t - 1$, a consequence of the key assumption that V is predictable.

Two money-market accounts that are traded in an arbitrage-free market must have a common rate process; otherwise, at any given nonterminal spot where one rate is higher than the other, an arbitrage can be created by borrowing at the lower rate and lending at a higher rate for one period. Based on the above arguments, we conclude:

Proposition 5.13. *Suppose the market is arbitrage-free and some money-market account is traded. Then the short-rate process* r *is unique and* $1 + r$ *is strictly positive.*

In applications, the market is typically assumed to be implemented by trading in a given set of contracts. To formalize this idea, we introduce J contracts, which are listed as rows of the matrix

$$(\delta, V) = \begin{pmatrix} \delta^1 & V^1 \\ \vdots & \vdots \\ \delta^J & V^J \end{pmatrix} \in \mathcal{L}^{J \times 2},$$

with corresponding J-dimensional **ex-dividend price process**

$$S = V - \delta.$$

We refer to (δ^j, V^j) as the jth contract of (δ, V). Throughout Part II, we use superscripts to index contracts (instead of the subscripts used in Part I) to avoid conflict with time subscripts.

Definition 5.14. *The **market implemented** by the J contracts (δ, V), denoted $X(\delta, V)$, is the intersection of all markets in which every contract of (δ, V) is traded. The contracts (δ, V) are **arbitrage-free** if $X(\delta, V)$ is arbitrage-free.*

Consider the set $X^0(\delta, V)$ of all cash flows generated by buying some contract at some spot; that is, $X^0(\delta, V)$ consists of every cash flow of the form

$$-V^j 1_{F \times \{t\}} + \delta^j 1_{F \times \{t,...,T-1\}} + V^j 1_{F \times \{T\}}, \tag{5.7}$$

where (F, t) is any spot and $j \in \{1, \ldots, J\}$. A market in which every contract of (δ, V) is traded is a linear space that contains $X^0(\delta, V)$. The smallest (relative to inclusion) such space is the linear span of $X^0(\delta, V)$, and therefore $X(\delta, V) = \text{span}(X^0(\delta, V))$. The weights used to form this linear span are conveniently represented as trading strategies.

Definition 5.15. *A **trading strategy** in the contracts (δ, V) is any element of $\mathcal{P}_0^J$, that is, any J-dimensional predictable process $\theta = (\theta^1, \ldots, \theta^J)'$ such that $\theta_0 = 0$. The trading strategy θ **generates** the cash flow x defined by*

$$x_t = \theta_t' V_t - \theta_{t+1}' S_t, \quad t = 0, 1, \ldots, T-1; \quad x_T = \theta_T' V_T. \tag{5.8}$$

Notationally, a trading strategy takes the form of a column vector θ, with its time-t value denoted θ_t. The random variable θ_t^j represents the number of shares of contract j held during period t, with a negative value indicating a short position. The vector θ_t is a **period-t portfolio**, whose value is selected at the beginning of period t, which is time $t-1$. Equation (5.8) is the **budget equation** corresponding to the trading strategy θ. One can think of x_t as the net of the time-t value $\theta_t' V_t$ of the period-t portfolio and the time-t cost $\theta_{t+1}' S_t$ of forming the period-$(t+1)$ portfolio. Since $\theta_0 = 0$, the budget equation implies that $x_0 = -\theta_1' S_0$, which is the initial payment required

145

to start the strategy. The final payment x_T equals the terminal portfolio's liquidation value.

Proposition 5.16. *The market $X(\delta, V)$ is the set of all cash flows that are generated by trading strategies in (δ, V).*

Proof. We use the fact that $X(\delta, V) = \text{span}(X^0(\delta, V))$, as discussed above. Suppose first there is only one contract $(J = 1)$. Let Y be the set of all cash flows that are generated by trading strategies in (δ, V). We call a trading strategy **basic** if it is of the form $1_{F \times \{t, \ldots, T\}}$ for some spot $(F, t - 1)$. Since $X^0(\delta, V)$ is the set of cash flows generated by basic trading strategies, $X(\delta, V) \subseteq Y$. For the converse inclusion, it suffices to verify that every trading strategy is the linear combination of basic strategies. Consider any θ in $\mathcal{P}_0$. Since $\theta = \sum_{t=1}^{T} \theta 1_{\Omega \times \{t\}}$, it suffices to show that $\theta 1_{\Omega \times \{t\}}$ is a linear combination of basic strategies for every time $t > 0$. Fixing $t > 0$, let $\mathcal{F}_{t-1}^0 = \{F_1, \ldots, F_n\}$. Since θ_t is $\mathcal{F}_{t-1}$-measurable, there exist scalars α_i such that $\theta_t = \sum_{i=1}^{n} \alpha_i 1_{F_i}$ and therefore $\theta 1_{\Omega \times \{t\}} = \sum_{i=1}^{n} \alpha_i 1_{F_i \times \{t\}}$. There remains to show that $1_{F \times \{t\}}$ is a linear combination of basic strategies, for any spot $(F, t - 1)$. This follows from the fact that

$$1_{F \times \{t\}} = 1_{F \times \{t, \ldots, T\}} - \sum_{i=0}^{d} 1_{G_i \times \{t+1, \ldots, T\}},$$

where $(G_0, t), \ldots, (G_d, t)$ are the immediate successor spots to $(F, t - 1)$.

We have proved the result for $J = 1$. The general case follows by noting that $Y = \sum_j Y_j$, where Y_j is the set of cash flows generated by trading in contract j only, and $X(\delta, V) = \sum_j \text{span}(X^0(\delta_j, V_j))$. ∎

5.2.2 Budget Equations and Synthetic Contracts

In this subsection we consider some formal manipulations of budget equations that are analytically useful as well as easily generalizable to continuous-time models in which the budget equation in the form (5.8) is meaningless. We use the process notation introduced in Section B.5. In particular, we note that $x_-(0) = x(0)$ and $x_-(t) = x(t-1)$ for $t > 0$; $\Delta x = x - x_-$; and that $x \bullet y$ is the process defined by $\Delta(x \bullet y) = x \Delta y$ and $(x \bullet y)_0 = 0$. We write $\mathbf{t}$ to denote the process that counts time, that is, $\mathbf{t}(t) = t$. Therefore, $(x \bullet \mathbf{t})(t) = \sum_{s=1}^{t} x_s$ for $t > 0$.

We continue to take as given the J contracts forming the rows of the matrix $(\delta, V) \in \mathcal{L}^{J \times 2}$. The corresponding J-dimensional **gain process** is defined by

$$G = V + \delta_- \bullet t.$$

For any times $u > t$, the increment $G_u^j - G_t^j$ represents the total gain (or loss if negative) resulting from purchasing the jth contract at time t and selling it at time u. If θ_t^j shares of the contract are held during period t, the incremental gain over the period is $\theta_t^j \Delta G_t^j$. Therefore, $(\theta' \bullet G)_t$ represents the total gain of the trading strategy θ up to time t.

Proposition 5.17. *The trading strategy θ generates the cash flow x if and only if*

$$\theta' V = \theta' \bullet G - x_- \bullet t, \qquad \theta_T' V_T = x_T. \tag{5.9}$$

Proof. Noting that $\Delta G_t = V_t - S_{t-1}$, the budget equation (5.8) can be equivalently stated as $\theta_T' V_T = x_T$ and $\Delta(\theta' V)_t = \theta_t' \Delta G_t - x_{t-1}$ for every $t > 0$, which is clearly equivalent to (5.9). ∎

A useful transformation of the budget equation results from a change of the unit of account at each spot. Suppose the process $\pi \in \mathcal{L}_{++}$ is such that $\pi(F, t)$ specifies a unit conversion ratio at spot (F, t). For any $z \in \mathcal{L}^J$, we write πz for the process in $\mathcal{L}^J$ whose value at spot (F, t) is

$$(\pi z)(F, t) = (\pi(F, t)z_1(F, t), \ldots, \pi(F, t)z_J(F, t))'.$$

After the units change implied by π, the contracts (δ, V) become contracts $(\pi \delta, \pi V)$. The corresponding gain process is denoted

$$G^\pi = \pi V + (\pi \delta)_- \bullet t.$$

Clearly, changing units should not affect the validity of a budget equation.[1]

Proposition 5.18. *For any $\pi \in \mathcal{L}_{++}$, the trading strategy θ generates the cash flow x if and only if*

$$\theta'(\pi V) = \theta' \bullet G^\pi - (\pi x)_- \bullet t \quad \text{and} \quad \theta_T'(\pi_T V_T) = \pi_T x_T. \tag{5.10}$$

---

[1] This change of units is often referred to in the literature as a "change of numeraire." In our context, the **numeraire** would be the contract $(0, \pi^{-1})$, which is a non-dividend-paying contract whose value process is identically equal to one under the new units.

Proof. Multiply equation (5.8) by π_t and use Proposition 5.17. ∎

Trading strategies in the contracts (δ, V) can be used to define new, synthetic contracts. We think of a synthetic contract generated by a trading strategy θ as a share in a fund following trading strategy θ.

Definition 5.19. *The trading strategy θ, generating the cash flow x, defines a **synthetic contract**, which is denoted $(\delta^\theta, V^\theta)$ and is defined by*

$$(\delta_0^\theta, V_0^\theta) = (\theta_1' \delta_0, \theta_1' V_0), \quad (\delta_T^\theta, V_T^\theta) = (\theta_T' \delta_T, \theta_T' V_T),$$
$$(\delta_t^\theta, V_t^\theta) = (x_t, \theta_t' V_t), \quad t = 1, \ldots, T - 1.$$

*A contract is **synthetic** in (δ, V) if it is of the form $(\delta^\theta, V^\theta)$ for some trading strategy θ. The trading strategy θ **replicates** the contract (δ^*, V^*) if $\delta^* = \delta^\theta$ and $V_T^* = \theta_T' V_T$.*

Consider any trading strategy θ and corresponding synthetic contract $(\delta^\theta, V^\theta)$. Then the ex-dividend price process $S^\theta = V^\theta - \delta^\theta$ satisfies

$$S_{t-1}^\theta = \theta_t' S_{t-1}, \quad t = 1, \ldots, T; \quad S_T^\theta = \theta_T' S_T. \tag{5.11}$$

The gain process of the contract $(\delta^\theta, V^\theta)$ is given by

$$G^\theta = V^\theta + \delta_-^\theta \bullet \mathbf{t} = V_0^\theta + \theta' \bullet G, \tag{5.12}$$

as can be seen by rearranging the budget equation (5.9). This transformation of gain processes is particularly useful when combined with a change of units. For any $\pi \in \mathcal{L}_{++}$, we note that the synthetic contract generated by the trading strategy θ in the contracts $(\pi\delta, \pi V)$ is equal to $(\pi\delta^\theta, \pi V^\theta)$ and therefore the corresponding gain process can be written as

$$G^{\theta\pi} = \pi V^\theta + (\pi\delta^\theta)_- \bullet \mathbf{t} = \pi_0 V_0^\theta + \theta' \bullet G^\pi. \tag{5.13}$$

Consider now the trading strategies $\theta_1, \ldots, \theta_m$ in the original contracts (δ, V) and let $\alpha \in \mathcal{P}_0^m$ be a trading strategy in the synthetic contracts

$$(\delta^{\theta_i}, V^{\theta_i}), \quad i = 1, \ldots, m,$$

generating the cash flow x. One can think of α as a trading strategy in m funds, where fund i follows trading strategy θ_i. The same cash flow x can be generated by the trading strategy $\theta = \sum_{i=1}^m \alpha_i \theta_i$ in the original contracts (δ, V). While this claim is rather obvious, it is worth reviewing the associated formal budget-equation manipulations. The budget equation corresponding to the trading strategy α in the synthetic contracts can be written as

$$\sum_{i=1}^{m} \alpha_i V^{\theta_i} = \sum_{i=1}^{m} \alpha_i \bullet G^{\theta_i} - x_- \bullet \mathbf{t}, \quad \sum_{i=1}^{m} \alpha_{iT} V_T^{\theta_i} = x_T.$$

At time zero, both sides of the first equation vanish. For any time $t > 0$, $V_t^{\theta_i} = \theta_{it}' V_t$ and $G_t^{\theta_i} = G_0^{\theta_i} + (\theta_i' \bullet G)_t$. Making these substitutions and noting that

$$\alpha_i \bullet (\theta_i' \bullet G) = (\alpha_i \theta_i)' \bullet G,$$

we obtain the budget equation (5.9) for $\theta = \sum_i \alpha_i \theta_i$. This argument implies:

Proposition 5.20. *Suppose the market X is implemented by contracts that are synthetic in (δ, V). Then $X \subseteq X(\delta, V)$. In particular, the market implemented by the contracts (δ, V) and any number of contracts that are synthetic in (δ, V) is $X(\delta, V)$.*

We have defined traded contracts and synthetic contracts. In an arbitrage-free market, the two notions are equivalent.

Proposition 5.21. *Every contract that is synthetic in (δ, V) is traded in $X(\delta, V)$. Conversely, if the contracts (δ, V) are arbitrage-free, any contract that is traded in $X(\delta, V)$ is synthetic in (δ, V).*

Proof. Since $X(\delta^*, V^*)$ is the smallest market in which (δ^*, V^*) is traded, (δ^*, V^*) is traded in $X(\delta, V)$ if and only if $X(\delta^*, V^*) \subseteq X(\delta, V)$. If (δ^*, V^*) is synthetic in (δ, V), the last proposition implies $X(\delta^*, V^*) \subseteq X(\delta, V)$. Conversely, suppose $X(\delta^*, V^*) \subseteq X(\delta, V)$ and let x be the cash flow generated by buying (δ^*, V^*) at time zero. Since $x \in X(\delta, V)$, there exists a trading strategy θ in (δ, V) that generates x, and therefore $\delta^* = \delta^\theta$ and $V_T^* = V_T^\theta$. Assuming (δ, V) is arbitrage-free, Proposition 5.10 implies $V^* = V^\theta$. ∎

The application of Proposition 5.10 in the last step of the preceding proof is worth highlighting. Suppose the market X is arbitrage-free, the contracts (δ, V) are traded in X, and (δ^*, V^*) is another contract that is

149

also traded in X. If (δ^*, V^*) is replicated by the trading strategy θ in (δ, V), then the synthetic contract $(\delta^\theta, V^\theta)$ is traded in X and therefore $V^* = V^\theta$. Proposition 5.10 also gives a converse: If there exists a trading strategy θ such that $V^* = V^\theta$, then θ replicates (δ^*, V^*). Finally, we note that the arbitrage-pricing method based on replication applies to all contracts if and only if the market is complete.

Proposition 5.22. *The contracts (δ, V) implement a complete market if and only if every contract can be replicated in (δ, V).*

5.3 Probabilistic Representations of Value

This section extends the representation of present-value functions through state-price densities or equivalent martingale measures to the multiperiod setting, with emphasis on a natural and important link to martingale theory.

We let Q denote the set of all strictly positive probability measures on 2^Ω. Given any P in Q, we write $\mathbb{E}^P$ for the corresponding expectation operator and we define the inner product

$$(x \mid y)^P = \mathbb{E}^P\left[\sum\nolimits_{t=0}^{T} x_t y_t\right], \quad x, y \in \mathcal{L}. \tag{5.14}$$

The notation for the conditional expectation under P given time-t information is simplified by writing $\mathbb{E}_t^P[x]$ or $\mathbb{E}_t^P x$ instead of $\mathbb{E}^P[x \mid \mathcal{F}_t]$. A P-**martingale** is a martingale relative to the probability P. In later sections, we omit the superscript P and simply say that a process is a martingale, where the reference probability P is unambiguous.

Throughout this section, we take as given a reference market X, relative to which state-price densities and equivalent martingale measures are defined.

5.3.1 State-Price Densities

As in the single-period case of Section 1.4, a state-price density can be defined as any adapted process π such that a state-price vector $p \in \mathbb{R}^{1+K}$ is well-defined by letting $p(F, t) = \pi(F, t)P(F)$ for every spot (F, t). We use an equivalent definition, which avoids reference to state-price vectors and can be interpreted in more general stochastic settings than the current finite-spot model.

Definition 5.23. *A state-price density process (SPD) with respect to the strictly positive probability P is any strictly positive adapted process π such that*

$$(\pi \mid x)^P \leq 0 \quad \text{for all } x \in X.$$

A probability-SPD pair is any (P, π) in $Q \times \mathcal{L}_{++}$ such that π is an SPD with respect to P. The present-value function $\Pi_0 : \mathcal{L} \to \mathbb{R}$ represented by the probability-SPD pair (P, π) is defined by

$$\Pi_0(c) = \frac{1}{\pi_0}(\pi \mid c)^P, \quad c \in \mathcal{L}. \tag{5.15}$$

It is immediate from the definitions that if (P, π) is a probability-SPD pair, then (5.15) defines a present-value function. Conversely, given any strictly positive probability, a present-value function is represented by a unique, up to positive scaling, SPD relative to the given probability.

Proposition 5.24. *Suppose Π_0 is a present-value function. For any $P \in Q$ and $\alpha \in (0, \infty)$, there exists a unique π in $\mathcal{L}_{++}$ such that $\pi_0 = \alpha$ and the pair (P, π) represents Π_0.*

Proof. For any P in Q, Proposition A.8 implies that there is a unique $\bar{\pi}$ in $\mathcal{L}$ such that $\Pi_0(c) = (\bar{\pi} \mid c)^P$ for all $c \in \mathcal{L}$. The strict positivity of Π_0 implies that of $\bar{\pi}$. The proposition follows by making the substitution $\bar{\pi} = \pi/\alpha$. ∎

Given the above observations, we can restate the fundamental theorems of asset pricing in terms of state-price densities: *For any P in Q, an SPD with respect to P exists if and only if X is arbitrage-free, and is unique up to positive scaling if and only if X is complete.*

To discuss the use of state-price densities in pricing contracts, we consider J contracts listed as rows of the matrix $(\delta, V) \in \mathcal{L}^{J \times 2}$.

Definition 5.25. *The pair (P, π) in $Q \times \mathcal{L}_{++}$ prices the contracts (δ, V) if*

$$V_t = \frac{1}{\pi_t}\mathbb{E}_t^P\left[\sum_{u=t}^{T-1} \pi_u \delta_u + \pi_T V_T\right], \quad t = 0, \ldots, T-1. \tag{5.16}$$

Equation (5.16) is another version of equation (5.5), which we saw is valid for any traded contract. We review the associated pricing argument directly in terms of state-price densities.

Proposition 5.26. *(a) A probability-SPD pair prices every traded contract.*

(b) Suppose the market is implemented by the contracts (δ, V). A pair (P, π) in $\mathcal{Q} \times \mathcal{L}_{++}$ is a probability-SPD pair if and only if (P, π) prices (δ, V).

Proof. As in Section 5.2.1, let $X^0(\delta, V)$ be the set of all cash flows of the form (5.7) and recall that $X(\delta, V)$ is the linear span of $X^0(\delta, V)$. It follows that a pair $(P, \pi) \in \mathcal{Q} \times \mathcal{L}_{++}$ is a probability-SPD pair relative to the market $X(\delta, V)$ if and only if $(\pi \mid x)^P = 0$ for every $x \in X^0(\delta, V)$, a condition that can be equivalently stated as: For every spot (F, t),

$$\mathbb{E}^P[\pi_t V_t 1_F] = \mathbb{E}^P\left[\left(\sum_{u=t}^{T-1} \pi_u \delta_u + \pi_T V_T\right) 1_F\right].$$

Since $\pi_t V_t$ is $\mathcal{F}_t$-measurable, Proposition B.16 implies the equivalence of the above condition to condition (5.16). Therefore, (P, π) is a probability-SPD pair relative to the market $X(\delta, V)$ if and only if (P, π) prices (δ, V). Both parts are corollaries of this fact. ∎

Some useful equivalent versions of the pricing condition (5.16) follow.

Proposition 5.27. *For any $(P, \pi) \in \mathcal{Q} \times \mathcal{L}_{++}$ and $(\delta, V) \in \mathcal{L}^{J \times 2}$, the following conditions are equivalent:*

1. *(P, π) prices the contracts (δ, V).*
2. *$G^\pi = \pi V + (\pi \delta)_- \bullet t$ is a P-martingale.*
3. *(δ, V) solves the backward (in time) recursion*

$$V_{t-1} = \delta_{t-1} + \frac{1}{\pi_{t-1}} \mathbb{E}_{t-1}^P[\pi_t V_t], \quad t = 1, \ldots, T. \tag{5.17}$$

Proof. Multiplying the pricing condition (5.16) by π_t and adding $\sum_{u=0}^{t-1} \pi_u \delta_u$ on both sides results in the condition $G_t^\pi = \mathbb{E}_t^P[G_T^\pi]$ for all t, which is a form of the martingale property of G^π. The latter can be restated in recursive form as $\mathbb{E}_{t-1}[\Delta G_t^\pi] = 0$, which can be rearranged to recursion (5.17). This establishes the equivalence of the three conditions. ∎

Remark 5.28. *The martingale characterization of pricing leads to an interpretation of the budget equation as the Doob decomposition of a trading strategy's value process following a change of units. Suppose that* $(P, \pi) \in \mathcal{Q} \times \mathcal{L}_{++}$ *prices the contracts* (δ, V) *and* θ *is a trading strategy in* (δ, V) *that generates the cash flow* x. *By Proposition 5.18,*

$$\pi \theta' V = \theta' \bullet G^\pi - (\pi x)_- \bullet \mathbf{t}. \tag{5.18}$$

Since θ *is predictable and* G^π *is a P-martingale,* $\theta' \bullet G^\pi$ *is P-martingale. The process* $(\pi x)_- \bullet \mathbf{t}$ *is predictable, and therefore equation* (5.18) *is the Doob decomposition of the process* $\pi \theta' V$.

The following can be viewed as a corollary of either one of the last two propositions.

Corollary 5.29. *Suppose the pair* (P, π) *in* $\mathcal{Q} \times \mathcal{L}_{++}$ *prices the contracts* (δ, V). *Then* (P, π) *also prices every synthetic contract in* (δ, V).

Proof. Suppose (P, π) prices (δ, V) and is therefore a probability-SPD pair relative to the market $X(\delta, V)$. Since every synthetic contract in (δ, V) is traded in $X(\delta, V)$, it must be priced by (P, π). Alternatively, we can can argue that for any trading strategy θ in (δ, V), $G^{\theta\pi} = \pi_0 V_0^\theta + \theta' \bullet G^\pi$ is a martingale if G^π is a martingale, and therefore (P, π) prices $(\delta^\theta, V^\theta)$ if it prices (δ, V). ∎

Using the recursive valuation formula (5.17) to price a unit of account delivered for sure at time t from the point of view of time $t - 1$ motivates the definition of a risk-free discount process.

Definition 5.30. *The* **risk-free discount process implied by the pair** (P, π) *in* $\mathcal{Q} \times \mathcal{L}_{++}$ *is the predictable process* ρ *defined by the recursion*

$$\rho_0 = 1 \quad and \quad \frac{\rho_t}{\rho_{t-1}} = \frac{\mathbb{E}_{t-1}^P[\pi_t]}{\pi_{t-1}}, \quad t = 1, \ldots, T. \tag{5.19}$$

If a money-market account is traded, the risk-free discount process is determined by the short-rate process.

153

Proposition 5.31. *Suppose* (P, π) *is a probability-SPD pair, r is a (necessarily unique) short-rate process and* ρ *is the risk-free discount process implied by* (P, π). *Then* ρ *can be computed in terms of r by*

$$\rho_0 = 1 \quad and \quad \rho_t = \prod_{u=1}^{t} \frac{1}{1 + r_u}, \quad t = 1, \dots, T; \quad (5.20)$$

and r can be computed in terms of ρ *by*

$$r = -\frac{\Delta\rho}{\rho}. \quad (5.21)$$

Proof. Suppose (δ, V) is a traded money-market account and $S = V - \delta$. Recall that V is predictable and $r \in \mathcal{P}_0$ is defined by $1 + r_t = V_t / S_{t-1}$ for $t > 0$. If (P, π) is a probability-SPD pair, then it prices (δ, V) and therefore recursion (5.17) holds. The latter can be restated as

$$S_{t-1} = \frac{1}{\pi_{t-1}} \mathbb{E}_{t-1}^{P} [\pi_t V_t] = V_t \frac{\mathbb{E}_{t-1}^{P} [\pi_t]}{\pi_{t-1}} = V_t \frac{\rho_t}{\rho_{t-1}}.$$

Rearranging, we obtain (5.21), which is easily seen to be a recursive version of (5.20). ∎

Whether a money-market account is traded or not, if ρ is the risk-free discount process implied by $(P, \pi) \in \mathcal{Q} \times \mathcal{L}_{++}$, for any contract (δ, V), recursion (5.17) can be rearranged to

$$V_{t-1} = \delta_{t-1} + \frac{\rho_t}{\rho_{t-1}} \mathbb{E}_{t-1}^{P} [V_t] + \operatorname{cov}_{t-1}^{P} \left[\frac{\pi_t}{\pi_{t-1}}, V_t \right], \quad (5.22)$$

where $\operatorname{cov}_{t-1}^{P}$ denotes conditional covariance given $\mathcal{F}_{t-1}$ relative to P. From the point of view of time $t - 1$, which is the beginning of period t, the conditional expectation term prices the predictable part of the end-of-period contract value $\mathbb{E}_{t-1}^{P} [V_t]$, while the conditional covariance part adjusts this valuation to account for the risk in the innovation $V_t - \mathbb{E}_{t-1}^{P} [V_t]$.

5.3.2 Equivalent Martingale Measures

We continue taking the reference market X as given and we define equivalent martingale measures in a way that generalizes the corresponding definition of Section 1.4.

Definition 5.32. *A (risk-free) **discount process** is any predictable strictly positive process ρ such that $\rho_0 = 1$. An **equivalent martingale measure**[2] **(EMM)** is any strictly positive probability Q with respect to which there exists a predictable SPD. An **EMM-discount pair** is any (Q, ρ) in $\mathcal{Q} \times \mathcal{P}$ such that ρ is both a discount process and an SPD with respect to Q.*

Suppose (Q, ρ) is an EMM-discount pair. Since (Q, ρ) is also a probability-SPD pair, our earlier results on pricing using state-price densities all apply, with several simplifications due to the predictability of ρ. The risk-free discount process implied by (Q, ρ) is ρ (Definition 5.30). If r is the rate process of a traded money-market account, then $r = -\Delta \rho / \rho$, and conversely ρ is determined by r as in Proposition 5.31. By Propositions 5.26 and 5.27, if the contracts (δ, V) are traded, they are priced by (Q, ρ), a condition that can be equivalently expressed either as the Q-martingale property of G^ρ, or by the recursive pricing equation

$$V_{t-1} = \delta_{t-1} + \frac{\rho_t}{\rho_{t-1}} \mathbb{E}^Q_{t-1}[V_t], \quad t = 1, \ldots, T. \tag{5.23}$$

While in recursion (5.22) risk adjustment is expressed by the conditional covariance term, in (5.23) risk adjustment is incorporated in the EMM Q.

A forward pricing interpretation of an EMM is essentially the same as in Chapter 1, applied conditionally at every node of the information tree. A more formal explanation follows.

Example 5.33 (EMM and Forward Pricing). *Suppose $(V - F, V - F)$ is a traded contract, where V is an adapted process and F is a predictable process. We interpret V_t as the time-t value of some asset and F_t as the time-$(t - 1)$ forward price of the asset for time-t delivery (assuming $t > 0$). Buying the contract at time $t - 1$ and selling it at time t results in the net cash flow x, where $x_u = 0$ for $u \neq t$ and $x_t = V_t - F_t$. From the perspective of time $t - 1$, the trade is equivalent to entering a forward contract for time-t delivery of the asset at the forward price F_t, whose value is determined at time $t - 1$. Pricing*

---

[2] The terms "equivalent" and "martingale measure" have their origin in probability theory. A probability (measure) Q is said to be **equivalent** to P if $Q(A) = 0 \iff P(A) = 0$ for every event A. In our setting, for any $P \in \mathcal{Q}$, the set of all equivalent-to-P probabilities on 2^Ω is $\mathcal{Q}$. A **martingale measure** is a probability relative to which a given set of processes is a set of martingales. In the current context, such a set is that of the properly discounted gain processes of all traded contracts, as discussed at the end of this section.

the contract $(V - F, V - F)$ *by an EMM-discount pair* (Q, ρ) *results in*

$$F_t = \mathbb{E}^Q_{t-1}[V_t], \quad t = 1, \ldots, T.$$

The conditional expectation $\mathbb{E}^Q_{t-1}$ *can therefore be viewed as a one-period-ahead forward pricing operator.*

According to Definition 5.23, an EMM-discount pair (Q, ρ) represents the present-value function

$$\Pi_0(x) = (\rho \mid x)^Q, \quad x \in \mathcal{L}.$$

Consider now any present-value function Π_0. We have seen that for any choice of the strictly positive probability P, there exists a unique SPD π relative to P such that $\pi_0 = 1$ and (P, π) represents Π_0. We will further show that a present-value function Π_0 has a unique EMM representation; that is, there exists a unique strictly positive probability Q such that the unique SPD ρ such that $\rho_0 = 1$ and (Q, ρ) represents Π_0 is predictable. To show this claim, we derive a formula that relates probability-SPD pairs to EMM-discount pairs representing the same present-value function, starting with two preliminary lemmas.

The first lemma establishes a multiplicative version of Doob's decomposition. $\mathcal{P}_{++}$ denotes the set of all strictly positive predictable processes and $\mathcal{M}^P$ denotes the set of all P-martingales.

Lemma 5.34. *For any* $(P, \pi) \in \mathcal{Q} \times \mathcal{L}_{++}$, π *admits a unique decomposition of the form*

$$\pi = \pi_0 \rho \xi; \quad \rho \in \mathcal{P}_{++}, \quad \xi \in \mathcal{M}^P, \quad \xi_0 = 1. \tag{5.24}$$

The process ρ *in this decomposition is the same as the risk-free discount process implied by* (P, π).

Proof. Let ρ be the risk-free discount process implied by (P, π) and let $\xi = (\pi_0 \rho)^{-1} \pi$. Applying equation (5.19), we find that $\xi \in \mathcal{M}^P$ and $\xi_0 = 1$, resulting in (5.24). Conversely, condition (5.24) implies (5.19), and therefore ρ must be the risk-free discount process implied by π. ∎

The second lemma we will need is a change-of-measure formula for the inner product $(\cdot \mid \cdot)^P$. Given any $P, Q \in \mathcal{Q}$, the **conditional density process** of Q with respect to P is defined by

$$\xi_t = \mathbb{E}_t^P\left[\frac{dQ}{dP}\right], \quad t = 0, 1, \ldots, T. \tag{5.25}$$

Our simplifying assumption $\mathcal{F}_T = 2^\Omega$ implies that $\xi_T = dQ/dP$. From Section B.8, we know that ξ is a strictly positive unit-mean martingale relative to P, whose value at any given spot can be thought of as the ratio of the likelihood of the path leading to that spot under Q to the likelihood of the same path under P.

Lemma 5.35. *For any $P, Q \in \mathcal{Q}$ and $x, y \in \mathcal{L}$, $(x \mid y)^Q = (\xi x \mid y)^P$.*

Proof. Using Proposition B.5 and basic properties of conditional expectations, we compute

$$\mathbb{E}^Q[x_t y_t] = \mathbb{E}^P \mathbb{E}_t^P\left[\frac{dQ}{dP} x_t y_t\right] = \mathbb{E}^P[\xi_t x_t y_t], \quad t = 0, \ldots, T.$$

Adding up over t gives the result. ∎

Conditions (5.24) and (5.25) relate a probability-SPD pair (P, π) to the unique EMM-discount pair (Q, ρ) defining the same present-value function as (P, π). The following proposition elaborates on this relationship.

Proposition 5.36. *(a) Suppose (P, π) is a probability-SPD pair that represents the present-value function Π_0 and implies the risk-free discount process ρ. Let the probability Q be defined by*

$$Q(F) = \mathbb{E}^P[\xi_T 1_F], \quad F \in \mathcal{F}_T, \quad where \quad \xi_T = \frac{1}{\rho_T}\frac{\pi_T}{\pi_0}. \tag{5.26}$$

Then (Q, ρ) is an EMM-discount pair representing Π_0, and $\xi_t = \mathbb{E}_t^P[\xi_T]$ defines the conditional density process of Q with respect to P.

(b) Suppose (Q, ρ) is an EMM-discount pair representing the present-value function Π_0. Given any strictly positive probability P and scalar $\pi_0 > 0$, let $\pi = \pi_0 \rho \xi$, where ξ is the conditional density process of Q with respect to P. Then (P, π) is probability-SPD pair that represents Π_0 and implies the risk-free discount process ρ.

Proof. (a) Applying Lemma 5.34, we let ρ and ξ be specified by the unique decomposition (5.24). Since ξ_T is strictly positive and

$\mathbb{E}^P \xi_T = 1$, there exists a unique strictly positive probability Q such that $dQ/dP = \xi_T$, given by (5.26). Since $\xi \in \mathcal{M}^P$, condition (5.25) follows. By Lemma 5.35,

$$(\rho \mid x)^Q = \frac{1}{\pi_0}(\pi \mid x)^P = \Pi_0(x), \quad x \in \mathcal{L}.$$

Therefore, (Q, ρ) is an EMM-discount pair representing Π_0.

(b) Follows similarly from Lemma 5.35. ∎

Corollary 5.37. *For any present-value function Π_0, there exists a unique probability Q in $\mathcal{Q}$ such that (Q, ρ) is an EMM-discount pair representing Π_0, for some (necessarily unique) discount process ρ.*

Corollary 5.38. *An EMM exists if and only if the market is arbitrage-free. An EMM-discount pair is unique if and only if the market is complete.*

We have mapped a state-price density with respect to the given probability P to an EMM-discount pair through a common present-value function. Alternatively, this mapping can be made in terms of the martingale property of the gain processes of a set of contracts that implement the market, after a suitable change of units. Suppose the market is implemented by the contracts $(\delta, V) \in \mathcal{L}^{J \times 2}$, $\pi \in \mathcal{L}$ is any strictly positive adapted process, $\rho \in \mathcal{P}$ is any discount process, and let

$$G^\pi = \pi V + (\pi \delta)_- \bullet \mathbf{t} \quad \text{and} \quad G^\rho = \rho V + (\rho \delta)_- \bullet \mathbf{t}.$$

For any $P, Q \in \mathcal{Q}$, Propositions 5.26 and 5.27 imply the equivalences:

$$\pi \text{ is an SPD relative to } P \quad \Longleftrightarrow \quad G^\pi \text{ is a } P\text{-martingale},$$
$$(Q, \rho) \text{ is an EMM-discount pair} \quad \Longleftrightarrow \quad G^\rho \text{ is a } Q\text{-martingale}.$$

In this context, Proposition 5.36 follows from Lemma 5.34 and Proposition B.49, which shows that given conditions (5.24) and (5.25),

$$G^\pi \text{ is a } P\text{-martingale} \quad \Longleftrightarrow \quad G^\rho \text{ is a } Q\text{-martingale}.$$

For example, suppose (Q, ρ) is an EMM-discount pair and a money-market account is traded. Then the Q-martingale G^ρ represents the gain process vector of the contracts (δ, V) taking as the unit of account the value of the contract $(0, 1/\rho)$, which is a traded money-market account paying no dividends.

5.4 DOMINANT CHOICE AND OPTION PRICING

This section extends the notion of dominant choice, introduced in Section 1.3, to the setting of a multiperiod liquid market and applies it to the formulation of an arbitrage theory of option pricing. We use the term "option" in a broad sense, as a set of cash flows that an agent can choose from in exercising the option, with the assumption that the option holder need not commit to a cash flow choice as uncertainty unfolds.

Throughout the section, we take as given a strictly positive probability P, relative to which state-price densities are defined. For simplicity, we write $\mathbb{E}$ instead of $\mathbb{E}^P$, and $(\cdot \mid \cdot)$ instead of $(\cdot \mid \cdot)^P$. We assume throughout that an agent can trade in the arbitrage-free liquid dynamic market $\{X_{F,t}\}$. The time-zero market is denoted $X = X_{\Omega,0}$. As shown in Proposition 5.8, the liquidity assumption implies that for any spot (F, t),

$$X_{F,t} = X \cap \mathcal{L}_{F,t}, \quad \text{where } \mathcal{L}_{F,t} = \{x 1_{F \times \{t,...,T\}} : x \in \mathcal{L}\}.$$

One can think of $X_{F,t}$ as the set of every cash flow that is generated by buying or selling at spot (F, t) some contract that is traded in X.

We define an option below as a set of cash flows $\mathcal{D}$, which we interpret as the set of cash flows that is available to the option holder at time zero. For any cash flow δ and spot (F, t), we define the notation

$$\mathcal{D}_{F,t}(\delta) = \{\delta^{\sharp} \in \mathcal{D} : \delta^{\sharp} 1_{F \times \{0,...,t-1\}} = \delta 1_{F \times \{0,...,t-1\}}\}, \quad (5.27)$$

which represents the set of cash flows in $\mathcal{D}$ that are equal to δ along the path on the information tree from time zero up to but not including spot (F, t). The latter restriction is null at time zero and therefore $\mathcal{D}_{\Omega,0} = \mathcal{D}$. Suppose the option holder selects the cash flow δ in $\mathcal{D}$ at time zero, but at spot (F, t) switches to the cash flow $\delta^{\sharp}$ in $\mathcal{D}_{F,t}(\delta)$. In effect, the option holder selects the cash flow $\delta + (\delta^{\sharp} - \delta)1_{F \times \{t,...,T\}}$, which is equal to $\delta^{\sharp}$ on the subtree rooted at (F, t) and is equal to δ otherwise. Since we assume the option holder does not have to commit at time zero, effectively this new cash flow is also available at time zero and should therefore be an element of $\mathcal{D}$. This consideration motivates the following formal definition of an option.

Definition 5.39. *An option is a set $\mathcal{D}$ of cash flows such that*

$$\delta \in \mathcal{D} \text{ and } \delta^\sharp \in \mathcal{D}_{F,t}(\delta) \implies \delta + (\delta^\sharp - \delta)1_{F \times \{t,\dots,T\}} \in \mathcal{D}, \qquad (5.28)$$

for every spot (F, t).

An American option is a special type of option, which we formally define as follows. Let $\mathcal{T}$ denote the set of all stopping times, that is, the set of all mappings of the form $\tau : \Omega \to \{0, 1, \dots, T\} \cup \{\infty\}$ such that $\{\tau \le t\} \in \mathcal{F}_t$ for every time t. For any $\tau \in \mathcal{T}$, we use the notation

$$[\tau] = \{(\omega, \tau(\omega)) : \omega \in \Omega, \ \tau(\omega) < \infty\}.$$

Therefore, $1_{[\tau]}$ denotes the process whose value at (ω, t) is one if $\tau(\omega) = t$ and zero otherwise. This definition implies that $1_{[\tau]}(\omega, t) = 0$ for all t if $\tau(\omega) = \infty$.

Definition 5.40. *An **American option** is an option of the form*

$$\mathcal{D} = \{Y1_{[\tau]} : \tau \in \mathcal{T}\},$$

*for some adapted process Y that we call the option's **payoff process**.*

5.4.1 Dominant Choice

In the single-period case, Propositions 1.12 and 1.14 characterize dominant cash flows as present-value-maximizing cash flows. These results would apply directly in the current context if we were to assume that the option owner must commit to a cash flow choice at time zero. We argue below that present-value maximization characterizes dominant choice even without the commitment assumption.

We fix a reference option $\mathcal{D}$ and we use the term "dominant" as short for "dominant in $\mathcal{D}$ given the liquid dynamic market $\{X_{F,t}\}$."

Definition 5.41. *The cash flow δ in $\mathcal{D}$ is **dominant at spot** (F, t) if, given any $\delta^\sharp$ in $\mathcal{D}_{F,t}(\delta)$, there exists some $x \in X_{F,t}$ such that*

$$\delta 1_{F \times \{t,\dots,T\}} + x \ge \delta^\sharp 1_{F \times \{t,\dots,T\}}.$$

*A cash flow in $\mathcal{D}$ is **dominant** if it is dominant at every spot.*

A dominant cash flow is an optimal choice out of $\mathcal{D}$ for any agent that does not dislike additional income and can trade in the dynamic market $\{X_{F,t}\}$.

Given a reference state-price density (SPD) π, we define, for every $\delta \in \mathcal{D}$ and spot (F, t), the (possibly infinite) value

$$J^\pi(\delta)(F, t) = \sup_{y \in \mathcal{D}_{F,t}(\delta)} \frac{1}{\pi(F, t)} \mathbb{E}\left[\sum_{u=t}^{T} \pi_u y_u \,\middle|\, F\right]. \qquad (5.29)$$

By the definition of the set $\mathcal{D}_{F,t}(\delta)$ in equation (5.27), the value $J^\pi(\delta)(F, t)$ depends on δ only through its restriction on $F \times \{0, \ldots, t-1\}$, representing the option's exercise history at spot (F, t). The values $J^\pi(\delta)(F, t)$ for every spot (F, t) define an entire adapted process $J^\pi(\delta)$ that is valued in $\mathbb{R} \cup \{+\infty\}$.

Theorem 5.42. *Given an arbitrage-free liquid dynamic market, the following conditions are equivalent, for any option $\mathcal{D}$ and cash flow δ^* in $\mathcal{D}$:*

1. *δ^* is dominant.*
2. *For any $\delta \in \mathcal{D}$, there exists some $x \in X$ such that $\delta^* + x \geq \delta$.*
3. *$\Pi_0(\delta^*) = \max_{\delta \in \mathcal{D}} \Pi_0(\delta)$ for every time-zero present-value function Π_0.*
4. *For every SPD π, the process $J^\pi(\delta^*)$ is finite-valued, the pair (P, π) prices the contract $(\delta^*, J^\pi(\delta^*))$, and $J_T^\pi(\delta^*) = \delta_T^*$.*

Proof. $(1 \implies 2)$ If δ^* is dominant, it is dominant at spot $(\Omega, 0)$.

$(2 \iff 3)$ This is Proposition 1.14.

$(3 \implies 4)$ Suppose there exists some SPD π such that for some spot (F, t) and cash flow $\delta \in \mathcal{D}_{F,t}(\delta^*)$,

$$\mathbb{E}\left[\sum_{u=t}^{T} \pi_u \delta_u \,\middle|\, F\right] > \mathbb{E}\left[\sum_{u=t}^{T} \pi_u \delta_u^* \,\middle|\, F\right].$$

Let $\delta^\sharp = \delta^* + (\delta - \delta^*)1_{F \times \{t,\ldots,T\}}$. Using basic properties of conditional expectations, it follows that $(\pi \mid \delta^\sharp) > (\pi \mid \delta^*)$. This proves that

$$J^\pi(\delta^*)(F, t) = \frac{1}{\pi(F, t)} \mathbb{E}\left[\sum_{u=t}^{T} \pi_u \delta_u^* \,\middle|\, F\right], \qquad (5.30)$$

for every spot (F, t), which is a restatement of condition 4.

$(4 \implies 1)$ Since the market is assumed liquid, Proposition 5.8(b) implies that any spot-(F, t) present-value function $\Pi_{F,t}$ can be

161

expressed as

$$\Pi_{F,t}(c) = \mathbb{E}\left[\sum_{u=t}^{T} \pi_u c_u \mid F\right], \quad c \in \mathcal{L}_{F,t}, \qquad (5.31)$$

for some SPD π relative to the time-zero market X. More constructively, suppose $\pi^\sharp$ is the unique process in $\mathcal{L}_{F,t}$ satisfying (5.31) with $\pi^\sharp$ in place of π, and let π^b be any SPD relative to X that is scaled so that $\pi^b(F, t) = 1$. The process $\pi = \pi^b + (\pi^\sharp - \pi^b)1_{F \times \{t,...,T\}}$ is an SPD relative to X satisfying (5.31), by the same argument used in the proof of Proposition 5.8(b).

We conclude that if (5.30) holds for every SPD π, then δ^* maximizes over $\mathcal{D}_{F,t}(\delta^*)$ any spot-(F, t) present-value function, and therefore δ^* is dominant at (F, t) by the argument of Proposition 1.14 applied to $X_{F,t}$. ∎

Corollary 5.43. *Given an arbitrage-free liquid dynamic market, suppose a money-market account is traded, with short-rate process r, and corresponding risk-free discount process ρ defined in (5.20). Then δ^* is dominant if and only if*

$$(\rho \mid \delta^*)^Q = \max\{(\rho \mid \delta)^Q : \delta \in \mathcal{D}\} \quad \text{for every EMM } Q.$$

Corollary 5.44. *Given a complete and arbitrage-free dynamic market, any compact option contains a dominant element.*

Let us now consider the special case in which $\mathcal{D}$ is an American option with payoff process Y. An **exercise policy** is any stopping time τ and is **dominant** if the cash flow $Y1_{[\tau]}$ is dominant. As in Section B.5, we adopt the convention $Y_\infty = 0$ and we define the random variable Y_τ, where τ is any stopping time, by $Y_\tau(\omega) = Y(\omega, \tau(\omega))$, $\omega \in \Omega$. For any SPD π,

$$(\pi \mid Y1_{[\tau]}) = \mathbb{E}[\pi_\tau Y_\tau], \quad \text{for all } \tau \in \mathcal{T},$$

and therefore the determination of a dominant exercise policy τ^* corresponds to the **optimal stopping problem**

$$\mathbb{E}[\pi_{\tau^*} Y_{\tau^*}] = \max_{\tau \in \mathcal{T}} \mathbb{E}[\pi_\tau Y_\tau]. \qquad (5.32)$$

Example 5.45 (American Call). *Given an underlying arbitrage-free liquid dynamic market, we assume that there is a traded money-market account and* *the short-rate process r takes nonnegative values. The corresponding discount process ρ, defined by $\rho_0 = 1$ and $\Delta\rho/\rho = -r$, has nonincreasing paths. Also assumed to be traded is the contract $(0, S)$, which we call the **stock**. As the notation indicates, the stock pays no dividends. We consider an **American call option** on the stock, with **strike price** $K \in \mathbb{R}$ and **maturity** T, formally defined as the American option with payoff process $Y = S - K$.*

Let τ^* be the exercise policy that requires waiting until maturity and then exercising the option if and only if the option is in the money. More formally,

$$\tau^*(\omega) = \begin{cases} T, & \text{if } S_T(\omega) > K; \\ \infty, & \text{otherwise.} \end{cases}$$

We argue that τ^* is dominant. Any other exercise policy τ is dominated by exercising at τ^* and adding the traded cash flow

$$x = (S - K)1_{[\tau]} + \left(K\frac{\rho_{\tau \wedge T}}{\rho_T} - S \right) 1_{[T \vee \tau]},$$

which is generated by the following trading strategy: On the event $\{\tau < T\}$, short the stock at time τ and at the same time invest the amount K in a money-market account, reinvesting all interest up to time T. Finally, liquidate all positions at time T. No trading is required on the event $\{\tau \geq T\}$. The cash flow $Y1_{[\tau]}$ is dominated by the cash flow $Y1_{[\tau^*]} + x$, since the difference $Y1_{[\tau^*]} + x - Y1_{[\tau]}$ vanishes at every nonterminal time and takes the terminal value

$$\left(\frac{\rho_{\tau \wedge T}}{\rho_T} - 1 \right) K + (K - S_T)^+ 1_{\{\tau < \infty\}} + (S_T - K)^+ 1_{\{\tau = \infty\}} \geq 0.$$

The first term represents the interest on the strike price saved by not exercising prior to maturity, the second term can be thought of as the insurance benefit of keeping the option alive up to maturity, and the last term represents the benefit of not letting the option expire unexercised in the money.

To illustrate Theorem 5.42, we consider a dual proof of the dominance of the exercise policy τ^*. Let $Y^\rho = \rho Y$. By Corollary 5.43, it suffices to verify that

$$\mathbb{E}^Q[Y_{\tau^*}^\rho] = \max_{\tau \in \mathcal{T}} \mathbb{E}^Q[Y_\tau^\rho] \quad \text{for every EMM } Q,$$

with the convention $Y_\infty^\rho = 0$. Clearly, the maximum cannot be achieved by an exercise policy that allows the option to expire unexercised on the event $\{Y_T > 0\}$ (in the money). It is therefore sufficient to show that $\mathbb{E}^Q[Y_{\tau^*}^\rho] \geq \mathbb{E}^Q[Y_\tau^\rho]$ for any EMM Q and stopping time τ such that $\tau \leq \tau^*$. Consider *any such stopping time τ and any EMM Q. Then $\rho_{\tau^* \wedge T} \leq \rho_{\tau \wedge T}$, since ρ has nonincreasing paths, and $\mathbb{E}^Q[\rho_{\tau^* \wedge T} S_{\tau^* \wedge T}] = \mathbb{E}^Q[\rho_{\tau \wedge T} S_{\tau \wedge T}]$, since ρS is a Q-martingale (see Proposition B.38). Therefore,*

$$\mathbb{E}^Q[Y^\rho_{\tau^* \wedge T}] \geq \mathbb{E}^Q[Y^\rho_{\tau \wedge T}]. \tag{5.33}$$

The assumption $\tau \leq \tau^*$ implies that $\{\tau = \infty\} \cap \{Y_T > 0\} = \emptyset$ and therefore

$$\mathbb{E}^Q[Y^\rho_{\tau \wedge T} 1_{\{\tau=\infty\}}] = \mathbb{E}^Q[Y^\rho_T 1_{\{\tau=\infty, Y_T<0\}}]$$
$$\geq \mathbb{E}^Q[Y^\rho_T 1_{\{Y_T<0\}}] = \mathbb{E}^Q[Y^\rho_{\tau^* \wedge T} 1_{\{\tau^*=\infty\}}].$$

Combining the last inequality with (5.33), we conclude

$$\mathbb{E}^Q[Y^\rho_{\tau^*}] = \mathbb{E}^Q[Y^\rho_{\tau^* \wedge T} 1_{\{\tau^*<\infty\}}] = \mathbb{E}^Q[Y^\rho_{\tau^* \wedge T}] - \mathbb{E}^Q[Y^\rho_{\tau^* \wedge T} 1_{\{\tau^*=\infty\}}]$$
$$\geq \mathbb{E}^Q[Y^\rho_{\tau \wedge T}] - \mathbb{E}^Q[Y^\rho_{\tau \wedge T} 1_{\{\tau=\infty\}}] = \mathbb{E}^Q[Y^\rho_\tau].$$

5.4.2 Recursive Value Maximization

In this subsection, we are concerned with a recursive characterization of dominant choice and associated option value, which is often a starting point of efficient computational methods. Fixing any reference $\pi \in \mathcal{L}_{++}$, we assume that the process $J^\pi(\delta)$ is defined by (5.29) and takes only finite values, for each $\delta \in \mathcal{D}$. These processes define a function $J^\pi : D \to \mathcal{L}$, which, by virtue of the option property (5.28), can equivalently be expressed as

$$J^\pi_t(\delta) = \sup_{y \in \mathcal{D}_t(\delta)} \mathbb{E}_t \left[\sum_{u=t}^T \frac{\pi_u}{\pi_t} y_u \right], \quad t = 0, \ldots, T, \quad \delta \in \mathcal{D}, \tag{5.34}$$

where

$$\mathcal{D}_t(\delta) = \{\delta^\sharp \in \mathcal{D} : \delta^\sharp_u = \delta_u \text{ for } u = 0, \ldots, t-1\}. \tag{5.35}$$

Moreover, J^π is an option value function in the following formal sense.

Definition 5.46. *An **option value function** is any mapping of the form J: $\mathcal{D} \to \mathcal{L}$ such that for any $\delta \in \mathcal{D}$ and spot (F, t), the value $J(\delta)(F, t)$ depends on δ only through the restriction of δ on $F \times \{0, \ldots, t-1\}$, that is,*

$$\delta^\sharp 1_{F \times \{0, \ldots, t-1\}} = \delta 1_{F \times \{0, \ldots, t-1\}} \implies J(\delta^\sharp)(F, t) = J(\delta)(F, t),$$

for every $\delta^\sharp \in \mathcal{D}$. In particular, $J_0 = J(\delta)(\Omega, 0)$ does not depend on δ.

The function J^{π} can be characterized recursively by a so-called **Bellman equation**, which in this context takes the form

$$J_t^{\pi}(\delta) = \sup_{y \in \mathcal{D}_t(\delta)} \left\{ y_t + \mathbb{E}_t \left[\frac{\pi_{t+1}}{\pi_t} J_{t+1}^{\pi}(y) \right] \right\}, \quad \delta \in \mathcal{D}; \quad J_{T+1}^{\pi} = 0. \quad (5.36)$$

For every time t, the Bellman equation computes the value of $J_t^{\pi}(\delta)$ for each $\delta \in \mathcal{D}$, given the value $J_{t+1}^{\pi}(y)$ for every $y \in \mathcal{D}$. As with expression (5.34), the supremum in the Bellman equation (5.36) can be computed at each time-t spot separately. Moreover, the supremum at spot (F, t) is effectively over the value of the single scalar $y(F, t)$, since, for any $y \in \mathcal{D}_t(\delta)$, the values $y_0, \ldots, y_{t-1}$ are fixed by δ, and the values $y_{t+1}, \ldots, y_T$ do not affect $J_{t+1}^{\pi}(y)$. The computational complexity associated with actually solving the Bellman equation can be reduced in Markovian models, discussed in this chapter's final section.

Lemma 5.47. *An option value function J^{π} solves the Bellman equation (5.36) if and only if it is given by (5.34).*

Proof. Suppose J^{π} is defined by (5.34). Using basic properties of conditional expectations and the key property (5.28) in the definition of an option, one can verify that

$$
\begin{aligned}
J_t^{\pi}(\delta) &= \sup_{y \in \mathcal{D}_t(\delta)} \left\{ y_t + \mathbb{E}_t \left[\frac{\pi_{t+1}}{\pi_t} \mathbb{E}_{t+1} \left[\sum_{u=t+1}^{T} \frac{\pi_u}{\pi_{t+1}} y_u \right] \right] \right\} \\
&= \sup_{y \in \mathcal{D}_t(\delta)} \left\{ y_t + \mathbb{E}_t \left[\frac{\pi_{t+1}}{\pi_t} \sup_{z \in \mathcal{D}_{t+1}(y)} \mathbb{E}_{t+1} \left[\sum_{u=t+1}^{T} \frac{\pi_u}{\pi_{t+1}} z_u \right] \right] \right\} \\
&= \sup_{y \in \mathcal{D}_t(\delta)} \left\{ y_t + \mathbb{E}_t \left[\frac{\pi_{t+1}}{\pi_t} J_{t+1}^{\pi}(y) \right] \right\}.
\end{aligned}
$$

Therefore, J^{π} solves the Bellman equation. The Bellman equation uniquely determines J_t^{π} given J_{t+1}^{π}. Since $J_{T+1}^{\pi} = 0$, a recursive argument shows that the solution to the Bellman equation is unique. ∎

Based on the last lemma, we have the following extension of Theorem 5.42.

Theorem 5.48. *Given an arbitrage-free liquid dynamic market and any option $\mathcal{D}$, a cash flow δ^* in $\mathcal{D}$ is dominant if and only if for every SPD π,* *there exists an option value function J^π satisfying, for every time t,*

$$J_t^\pi(\delta^*) = \max_{y \in \mathcal{D}_t(\delta^*)} \left\{ y_t + \mathbb{E}_t \left[\frac{\pi_{t+1}}{\pi_t} J_{t+1}^\pi(y) \right] \right\} = \delta_t^* + \mathbb{E}_t \left[\frac{\pi_{t+1}}{\pi_t} J_{t+1}^\pi(\delta^*) \right],$$

with the convention $J_{T+1}^\pi = 0$.

Proof. The result follows from the equivalence (1 $\Longleftrightarrow$ 4) of Theorem 5.42, the recursive characterization of Proposition 5.27 of the condition that (P, π) prices the contract $(\delta^*, J^\pi(\delta^*))$, and the last lemma. ∎

In the special case in which $\mathcal{D}$ is an American option with payoff process Y, the option value function J^π can be summarized by the process $V^* = J^\pi(0)$. For each time t,

$$V_t^* = \max \left\{ \mathbb{E}_t \left[\frac{\pi_\tau}{\pi_t} Y_\tau \right] : \tau \geq t, \ \tau \in \mathcal{T} \right\} \tag{5.37}$$

(with the usual convention, $Y_\infty = 0$) represents the time-t value of the American option, provided it has not been exercised prior to time t. At each spot (F, t), either the American option has been exercised prior to (F, t), in which case $J(\delta)(F, t) = 0$, or the option has not been exercised, in which case $J(\delta)(F, t) = V^*(F, t)$. As a consequence, the Bellman equation (5.36) simplifies to

$$V_t^* = \max \left\{ Y_t, \mathbb{E}_t \left[\frac{\pi_{t+1}}{\pi_t} V_{t+1}^* \right] \right\}, \quad V_{T+1}^* = 0. \tag{5.38}$$

A dominant exercise policy is defined in terms of V^* by

$$\tau^* = \min\{t : V_t^* = Y_t\}, \quad \text{where } \min \emptyset = \infty, \tag{5.39}$$

in which case

$$V_0^* = J_0^\pi = \frac{1}{\pi_0} \mathbb{E}[\pi_{\tau^*} Y_{\tau^*}]. \tag{5.40}$$

5.4.3 Arbitrage Pricing of Options

An option can be bought or sold. The buyer of an option pays a premium and chooses how to exercise the option. The seller or "writer" of the option is on the other side of this transaction and therefore receives a premium and is obligated to deliver the cash flow selected by the option buyer. Assuming the existence of a marketed dominant choice at time zero, as well as a dominant choice at every other spot given any exercise history, we will show that the premium that is consistent with the absence of arbitrage opportunities is the present value of a dominant cash flow. The only subtlety in this argument is that an arbitrageur that writes an option must be able to hedge potentially suboptimal cash flows selected by the option buyer.

We continue taking as given the arbitrage-free market X and an option $\mathcal{D}$, whose (time-zero) premium will be denoted by the scalar p_0. For notational simplicity, we consider the trading of the option $\mathcal{D}$ at time zero only. For any $\delta \in \mathcal{D}$, the trading of the option $\mathcal{D}_{F,t}(\delta)$ at spot (F, t) can be analyzed by applying the same arguments on the subtree rooted at (F, t). We analyze the buying and selling of an option separately, in order to account for the fact that only the owner decides how to exercise the option.

A lower bound on the premium p_0 is obtained by arguing that if p_0 is sufficiently low, then an arbitrage can be created by buying the option and selecting a dominant cash flow. A buyer of the option pays the premium p_0, can select any cash flow δ in $\mathcal{D}$ and can trade in the market X, thus generating a cash flow of the form

$$-p_0 1_{\Omega \times \{0\}} + \delta + x, \quad \delta \in \mathcal{D}, \quad x \in X. \tag{5.41}$$

Proposition 5.49. *Suppose the market is arbitrage-free and the cash flow $\delta^* \in \mathcal{D}$ is dominant and marketed, with present value p_0^*. Then there exists no arbitrage of the form (5.41) if and only if $p_0 \geq p_0^*$.*

Proof. Since δ^* is marketed and has present value p_0^*, we can write $\delta^* = p_0^* 1_{\Omega \times \{0\}} + x^*$ for some $x^* \in X$. If $p_0 < p_0^*$, then the cash flow

$$-p_0 1_{\Omega \times \{0\}} + \delta^* - x^* = (p_0^* - p) 1_{\Omega \times \{0\}}$$

is an arbitrage. Conversely, suppose $p_0 \geq p_0^*$ and let $c = -p_0 1_{\Omega \times \{0\}} + \delta + x$ for some $\delta \in \mathcal{D}$ and $x \in X$. The dominance of δ^* implies that $\delta^* + y \geq \delta$ for some $y \in X$. Therefore,

$$c \leq -p_0^* 1_{\Omega \times \{0\}} + (\delta^* + y) + x = x^* + x + y \in X.$$

Since X is arbitrage-free, c is not an arbitrage. ∎

The arbitrage of the above proof is not reversible, since the option writer cannot guarantee that the option buyer will select the dominant cash flow δ^*. After strengthening the assumption of Proposition 5.49, we will still be able, however, to argue that if $p_0 > p_0^*$, then an arbitrage is possible that involves writing the option, without knowledge of how the option buyer is

167

going to exercise the option. A key aspect of the arbitrageur's hedging strategy is that it can be implemented without knowledge of the future choices by the option holder. We formalize this type of informational restriction as follows.

Definition 5.50. *A $\mathcal{D}$-adapted strategy is a mapping h that assigns to each nonterminal spot (F, t) a function $h_{F,t} : \mathcal{D} \to X_{F,t}$ such that*

$$\delta 1_{F \times \{0,...,t\}} = \delta^{\sharp} 1_{F \times \{0,...,t\}} \implies h_{F,t}(\delta) = h_{F,t}(\delta^{\sharp}). \tag{5.42}$$

Given a $\mathcal{D}$-adapted strategy h, $h_{F,t}(\delta)$ selects a trade in $X_{F,t}$ as a function of the path of δ from time zero up to and including spot (F, t). In our application, we think of $h_{F,t}(\delta)$ as the incremental trade that the option writer must enter at spot (F, t) in order to hedge any future choices by the option buyer who has selected δ up to spot (F, t).

Given a $\mathcal{D}$-adapted strategy h, any $\delta \in \mathcal{D}$ and any time $t < T$, we define the function $h_t(\delta) : \Omega \to X$ by letting, for each spot (F, t),

$$h_t(\delta)(\omega) = h_{F,t}(\delta) \quad \text{for all } \omega \in F. \tag{5.43}$$

Following the strategy h implements the overall cash flow $\sum_{t=0}^{T-1} h_t(\delta)$. The option seller receives a premium p_0 at time zero and must deliver whatever cash flow δ in $\mathcal{D}$ is selected by the option buyer. If the option seller also follows the hedging strategy h, the resulting incremental cash flow is

$$p_0 1_{\Omega \times \{0\}} - \delta + \sum_{t=0}^{T-1} h_t(\delta). \tag{5.44}$$

In this case, the option seller would guarantee an arbitrage if (5.44) were an arbitrage cash flow for every choice $\delta \in \mathcal{D}$ by the option buyer. By excluding this type of arbitrage, we now derive an upper bound for the option premium, which together with the lower bound of Proposition 5.49 pins down the option premium as the present value of a dominant cash flow.

Proposition 5.51. *Suppose the market is arbitrage-free and there exists a cash flow δ^* in $\mathcal{D}$ that is both dominant and marketed, with present value p_0^*. Suppose further that given any $\delta \in \mathcal{D}$ and spot (F, t), there exists a cash flow $\delta^{F,t}$ in $\mathcal{D}_{F,t}(\delta)$ that is dominant at spot (F, t). Then the following two conditions are equivalent:*

1. *There exists no $\mathcal{D}$-adapted strategy h such that the cash flow (5.44) is an arbitrage for every $\delta \in \mathcal{D}$.*

2. $p_0 \leq p_0^*$.

Proof. $(2 \implies 1)$ This follows similarly to the "if" part of Proposition 5.49.

$(1 \implies 2)$ Suppose that $p_0 > p_0^*$. We will construct a $\mathcal{D}$-adapted strategy h such that the cash flow (5.44) is an arbitrage for every $\delta \in \mathcal{D}$.

We begin with some notation. For any set of times $\{t_1, \ldots, t_n\}$, we write

$$1_{[t_1, \ldots, t_n]} = 1_{\Omega \times \{t_1, \ldots, t_n\}}.$$

Given any reference $\delta \in \mathcal{D}$, we select $\delta^{F,t} \in \mathcal{D}_{F,t}(\delta)$ to be dominant at spot (F, t). Letting $\mathcal{F}_t^0 = \{F_1, \ldots, F_n\}$ denote the partition generating $\mathcal{F}_t$, we define

$$\delta^t = \sum_{i=1}^{n} \delta^{F_i, t} 1_{F_i \times \{0, \ldots, T\}} = \delta 1_{\{0, \ldots, t-1\}} + \sum_{i=1}^{n} \delta^{F_i, t} 1_{F_i \times \{t, \ldots, T\}}.$$

The option property (5.28) implies that $\delta^t \in \mathcal{D}_t(\delta)$.

Using the assumption that δ^* is dominant, we select some $x \in X$ such that $\delta^* + x \geq \delta^1$ and define

$$h_0(\delta) = -p_0^* 1_{[0]} + \delta^* + x.$$

Since the choice of x depends on δ only through the value δ_0, we can assume that $h_0(\delta)$ has the same property. At time zero the arbitrageur sells the option, receiving the premium p_0, buys the cash flow δ^* for a price p_0^* and enters the trade x, which together with δ^* dominates δ^1. Immediately after entering these trades and paying $\delta_0 = \delta_0^1$ to the option buyer, the arbitrageur is faced with the cash flow c^0, where

$$c^0 = p_0 1_{[0]} + h_0(\delta) - \delta 1_{[0]} \geq (p_0 - p_0^*) 1_{[0]} + \delta^1 1_{[1, \ldots, T]}.$$

We proceed inductively. Given any $t \in \{1, \ldots, T-1\}$, suppose that after all transactions up to and including time $t-1$ the arbitrageur faces an overall cash flow c^{t-1} such that

$$c^{t-1} \geq (p_0 - p_0^*) 1_{[0]} + \delta^t 1_{[t, \ldots, T]}.$$

For any spot (F, t), the dominance of $\delta^{F,t}$ at spot (F, t) implies that we can define the value $h_{F,t}(\delta) \in X_{F,t}$ so that

$$\delta^t 1_{F \times \{t, \ldots, T\}} + h_{F,t}(\delta) \geq \delta^{t+1} 1_{F \times \{t, \ldots, T\}}.$$

A key observation is that the arbitrageur can compute $\delta^{t+1} 1_{F \times \{t,...,T\}}$ and therefore $h_{F,t}(\delta)$, having observed only $\delta 1_{F \times \{0,...,t\}}$. At time t the arbitrageur enters the trade $h_t(\delta)$, defined in (5.43), and pays out δ_t to the option holder, resulting in the new cash flow c^t, where

$$c^t = c^{t-1} + h_t(\delta) - \delta 1_{[t]} \geq (p_0 - p_0^*) 1_{[0]} + \delta^{t+1} 1_{[t+1,...,T]}.$$

This completes the inductive step.

Finally, at time T the arbitrageur pays out δ_T to the option holder, resulting in the overall arbitrage cash flow

$$c^{T-1} - \delta 1_{[T]} \geq (p_0 - p_0^*) 1_{[0]}.$$

Iterating the recursive construction of the cash flows c^t shows that $c^{T-1} - \delta 1_{[T]}$ is equal to (5.44). Since the above construction of $h_{F,t}(\delta)$ depends on δ only through its restriction on $F \times \{0, \ldots, t\}$, we have defined an entire $\mathcal{D}$-adapted strategy h, resulting in an arbitrage of the form (5.44). ∎

5.5 STATE-PRICE DYNAMICS

This section introduces the modeling device of a dynamic martingale basis, which is essentially a spot-by-spot specification of a set of linear factors that span the single-period uncertainty ahead of each spot. A dynamic martingale basis is used in this section to interpret the dynamics of a state-price density in terms of conditional factor pricing, and in the following section to discuss the dynamic implementation of markets through contract trading. The language and notation introduced here extend directly to continuous-time settings, for example, to models with a Brownian filtration.

For expositional simplicity, we assume that the filtration $\{\mathcal{F}_t : t = 0, \ldots, T\}$ is uniform with spanning number $1 + d$ for some positive integer d, meaning that every nonterminal spot has $1 + d$ immediate successors. Unless otherwise stated, expectations, the martingale property and state-price densities are all relative to the underlying strictly positive probability P, which is fixed throughout. As in Appendix B, $\mathcal{M}_0$ denotes the set of zero-mean martingales, while $\mathcal{P}_0$ is the set of predictable processes that take the value zero at time zero.

By Theorem B.44, we can and do assume that the filtration $\{\mathcal{F}_t\}$ is generated by a d-dimensional zero-mean martingale $B = (B^1, \ldots, B^d)'$ such that

$$\mathbb{E}_{t-1}[\Delta B_t^i \Delta B_t^j] = \begin{cases} 1 & \text{if } i = j, \\ 0 & \text{if } i \neq j, \end{cases} \quad t \in \{1, \ldots, T\}, \qquad (5.45)$$

and any zero-mean martingale M can be uniquely expressed as $M = \beta' \bullet B$, where $\beta \in \mathcal{P}_0^d$. In the language of Section B.7, B is a **dynamic orthonormal basis** for $\mathcal{M}_0$.

The Doob decomposition of any adapted process $x \in \mathcal{L}^n$ (Proposition B.40) can be uniquely expressed as

$$x = x_0 + \mu^x \bullet \mathbf{t} + \sigma^x \bullet B, \quad \mu^x \in \mathcal{P}_0^n, \quad \sigma^x \in \mathcal{P}_0^{n \times d},$$

or, equivalently, as

$$\Delta x = \mu^x + \sigma^x \Delta B, \quad \mu^x \in \mathcal{P}_0^n, \quad \sigma^x \in \mathcal{P}_0^{n \times d}.$$

We call this the **predictable representation** or the **dynamics** of x. The predictable coefficients μ^x and σ^x can be computed as

$$\mu_t^x = \mathbb{E}_{t-1}[\Delta x_t] \quad \text{and} \quad \sigma_t^x = \mathbb{E}_{t-1}[\Delta x_t \Delta B_t'].$$

Note that since $x_{t-1} = \mathbb{E}_{t-1}[x_t] - \mu_t^x$ and $\sigma_t^x = \mathbb{E}_{t-1}[x_t \Delta B_t']$, any expression that determines μ_t^x as a function of σ_t^x is equivalent to a backward recursion on the information tree that computes x_{t-1} in terms of x_t.

In Section 5.3 we saw that a state-price density takes the form $\pi = \pi_0 \rho \xi$, where ρ is the discount process implied by π, and ξ is the conditional density process of the equivalent martingale measure associated with π. Here we are concerned with the dynamics of ρ and ξ relative to B, and the relationship of these dynamics to contract pricing.

From Section B.8, we review a one-to-one and onto mapping between the set

$$\mathcal{H} = \{\eta \in \mathcal{P}_0^d : 1 - \eta' \Delta B \in \mathcal{L}_{++}\} \qquad (5.46)$$

and the set $\mathcal{Q}$ of strictly positive probabilities.

Given any $Q \in \mathcal{Q}$, let ξ be its conditional density process, that is, $\xi_t = \mathbb{E}_t[dQ/dP]$. Since ξ is a martingale and ξ_- is predictable, the process $\xi_-^{-1} \bullet \xi$ is a zero-mean martingale and therefore admits the unique

171

predictable representation

$$\frac{1}{\xi_-} \bullet \xi = -\eta' \bullet B, \quad \eta \in \mathcal{P}_0^d. \tag{5.47}$$

The process η can be computed as

$$\eta_t = -\mathbb{E}_{t-1}\left[\frac{\xi_t}{\xi_{t-1}}\Delta B_t\right] = -\mathbb{E}_{t-1}^Q[\Delta B_t], \tag{5.48}$$

where the last equality follows from Lemma B.48. Equation (5.47) implies that $1 - \eta'\Delta B = \xi/\xi_-$ and therefore $\eta \in \mathcal{H}$.

Conversely, given any $\eta \in \mathcal{H}$, the unique process ξ that solves (5.47) and satisfies $\xi_0 = 1$ is the unit-mean martingale

$$\xi_t = \prod_{u=0}^{t}(1 - \eta_u'\Delta B_u), \quad t = 0, 1, \ldots, T, \tag{5.49}$$

which is expression (B.25) with $\ell = -\eta' \bullet B$. We define the probability P^η so that $dP^\eta/dP = \xi_T$ or, more explicitly,

$$P^\eta(F) = \mathbb{E}[\xi_T 1_F], \quad \text{for every event } F.$$

Since ξ is a martingale, $\xi_t = \mathbb{E}_t[\xi_T]$ and therefore ξ is the conditional density process of P^η. This argument establishes that $\eta \mapsto P^\eta$ is a one-to-one and onto mapping from $\mathcal{H}$ to $\mathcal{Q}$.

Girsanov's theorem in the current context states that for any $\eta \in \mathcal{H}$,

$$B^\eta = B + \eta \bullet \mathbf{t} \text{ is a } P^\eta\text{-martingale,}$$

a fact that follows immediately from (5.48) with $Q = P^\eta$.

We henceforth fix a strictly positive probability Q with conditional density process ξ and a strictly positive predictable process ρ with $\rho_0 = 1$. The processes $\eta \in \mathcal{H}$ and $r \in \mathcal{P}_0$ are defined by the equations

$$Q = P^\eta \quad \text{and} \quad r = -\frac{\Delta\rho}{\rho}. \tag{5.50}$$

The pair (η, r) provides a useful representation of (Q, ρ) interpreted as an EMM-discount pair, or the corresponding SPD $\pi = \pi_0\rho\xi$, whose dynamics can be written as

$$\frac{\Delta\pi}{\pi_-} = -\frac{1}{1+r}(r + \eta'\Delta B). \tag{5.51}$$

Consider any contract (δ, V), with ex-dividend price process $S = V - \delta$ and gain process

$$G = V + \delta_- \bullet \mathbf{t} = V_0 + \mu^G \bullet \mathbf{t} + \sigma^G \bullet B. \tag{5.52}$$

Proposition 5.52. *The pair (Q, ρ) prices the contract (δ, V) if and only if*

$$\mu^G = rS_- + \sigma^G \eta. \tag{5.53}$$

Proof. We recall that (Q, ρ) prices the contract (δ, V) if and only if

$$G^\rho = \rho V + (\rho\delta)_- \bullet \mathsf{t} \text{ is a } Q\text{-martingale.}$$

A direct calculation of ΔG^ρ shows that

$$G^\rho = (\rho(\mu^G - rS_- - \sigma^G \eta)) \bullet \mathsf{t} + (\rho\sigma^G) \bullet B^\eta.$$

Since $(\rho\sigma^G) \bullet B^\eta$ is a Q-martingale, it follows that G^ρ is a Q-martingale if and only if the predictable term of the last decomposition vanishes, a condition that is clearly equivalent to equation (5.53). ∎

Equation (5.53) corresponds to the linear factor pricing notion of Section 2.7, applied conditionally at each spot of the information tree for the one-period-ahead uncertainty. This connection becomes more transparent when formulated in terms of returns. We assume that S is nonzero at all nonterminal spots and we define the **cumulative return process** R and its dynamics by

$$\Delta R = \frac{\Delta G}{S_-} = \mu^R + \sigma^R \Delta B, \quad \mu^R \in \mathcal{P}_0, \quad \sigma^R \in \mathcal{P}_0^{1 \times d}. \tag{5.54}$$

The choice of an initial value R_0 is arbitrary. We note that η solves equation (5.53) if and only if

$$\mu^R - r = \sigma^R \eta. \tag{5.55}$$

The last condition is equivalent to R having the following predictable representation relative to B^η:

$$R = R_0 + r \bullet \mathsf{t} + \sigma^R \bullet B^\eta.$$

While B^η is a dynamic basis for the set of zero-mean martingales relative to Q, Proposition B.53 shows that B^η is generally not dynamically orthonormal under Q. Anticipating a subject that is beyond the scope of the current text, we note that in a limiting version of this model in which trading can occur infinitely often, B is Brownian motion and B^η is a dynamically orthonormal basis under Q, which is to say it is a Brownian motion under Q. Proposition B.53 provides a glimpse into why this happens: The risk-premium term of the conditional covariation formula goes to zero because

173

the length of every period goes to zero, while the three-way covariation, or conditional skewness, term goes to zero thanks to the central limit theorem.

5.6 MARKET IMPLEMENTATION

An arbitrage-pricing model typically begins with a specification of the dividends and price dynamics for a set of traded contracts and then uses such a specification to replicate and price synthetic contracts. In this section we introduce a general framework for this type of modeling and we use it to show that the number of contracts required to implement a complete market is equal to the filtration's spanning number.

We adopt last section's stochastic setting and we further assume that the market is implemented by the contracts

$$(\delta^0, V^0), (\delta^1, V^1), \dots, (\delta^J, V^J). \tag{5.56}$$

The contract (δ^0, V^0) is a money-market account with rate process $r \in \mathcal{P}_0$, ex-dividend price process $S^0 = V^0 - \delta^0$ and gain process $G^0 = V^0 + \delta^0_- \bullet \mathsf{t}$. For concreteness, and without loss in generality, we assume

$$S^0 = 1, \quad \delta^0 = r, \quad V^0 = 1 + r, \quad G^0 = 1 + r \bullet \mathsf{t}. \tag{5.57}$$

The corresponding discount process ρ is defined by

$$\rho_t = \prod_{u=1}^{t} \frac{1}{1 + r_u}, \quad t = 1, \dots, T; \quad \rho_0 = 1. \tag{5.58}$$

Let $(\delta, V) \in \mathcal{L}^{J \times 2}$ be the matrix whose rows are the remaining J contracts listed in (5.56). The corresponding vector of ex-dividend price processes is denoted $S = V - \delta$, while the corresponding gain process and its dynamics are denoted

$$G = V + \delta_- \bullet \mathsf{t} = V_0 + \mu^G \bullet \mathsf{t} + \sigma^G \bullet B, \quad \mu^G \in \mathcal{P}_0^J, \quad \sigma^G \in \mathcal{P}_0^{J \times d}. \tag{5.59}$$

A trading strategy in this context takes the form (θ^0, θ), where $\theta^0 \in \mathcal{P}_0$ is a trading strategy in the money-market account and $\theta \in \mathcal{P}_0^J$ is a trading strategy in the remaining J contracts (δ, V). We write $(\delta^\theta, V^\theta)$, rather than the more cumbersome $(\delta^{(\theta^0, \theta)}, V^{(\theta^0, \theta)})$, for the corresponding synthetic contract.

Definition 5.53. A **market-price-of-risk process** (relative to the market implemented by the contracts (5.56)) is any η in $\mathcal{P}_0^d$ such that

$$\mu^G = rS_- + \sigma^G \eta. \tag{5.60}$$

Proposition 5.54. A strictly positive probability Q is an EMM (relative to the market implemented by the contracts (5.56)) if and only if there exists a market-price-of-risk process η in $\mathcal{H}$ such that $Q = P^\eta$.

Proof. By Proposition 5.26, (Q, ρ) is an EMM-discount pair if and only if it prices all the contracts in (5.56). By the definition of ρ, the pair (Q, ρ) prices the money-market account, and therefore Q is an EMM if and only if (Q, ρ) prices the remaining J contracts, (δ, V). An application of Proposition 5.52 completes the proof. ∎

If the market is arbitrage-free, an EMM Q exists and Proposition 5.54 implies the existence of a market-price-of-risk process. The existence of a market-price-of-risk process η is not, however, sufficient to exclude all arbitrage opportunities; the additional restriction $\eta \in \mathcal{H}$ is required. The following characterization shows that the existence of a market-price-of risk process is equivalent to the absence of any arbitrage that is the result of trading the money-market account against a synthetic money-market account.

Proposition 5.55. A market-price-of-risk process exists if and only if every synthetic money-market account has r as its rate process.

Proof. A market-price-of-risk process exists if and only if

$$\text{for all } \theta \in \mathcal{P}_0^J, \quad \theta' \sigma^G = 0 \implies \theta'(\mu^G - rS_-) = 0. \tag{5.61}$$

The "only-if" part is immediate. Conversely, suppose (5.61) holds. We use an orthogonal decomposition at each spot to write $\mu^G - rS_- = \sigma^G \eta + \varepsilon$, for some $\eta \in \mathcal{P}_0^d$ and $\varepsilon \in \mathcal{P}_0^J$ such that $\varepsilon' \sigma^G = 0$ and therefore $\varepsilon'(\mu^G - rS_-) = 0$. Since $\varepsilon'(\mu^G - rS_-) = \varepsilon'\varepsilon$, it follows that $\varepsilon = 0$, proving (5.60).

Consider now any synthetic contract $(\delta^\theta, V^\theta)$. The corresponding ex-dividend price process S^θ and gain process G^θ satisfy

$$S_{t-1}^\theta = \theta_t^0 + \theta_t' S_{t-1}, \quad t = 1, \dots, T;$$
$$\Delta G^\theta = \theta^0 \Delta G^0 + \theta' \Delta G = \theta^0 r + \theta' \mu^G + \theta' \sigma^G \Delta B.$$

If $(\delta^\theta, V^\theta)$ is a money-market account, then S_-^θ is strictly positive and G^θ is predictable, which implies that $\theta' \sigma^G = 0$. If a market-price-of-risk process exists, then (5.61) implies that $\theta' \mu^G = r\theta' S_-$, and therefore the rate process of $(\delta^\theta, V^\theta)$ can be computed to be r. Conversely, suppose that every synthetic money-market account has r as its rate process. Given any $\theta \in \mathcal{P}_0^d$ such that $\theta' \sigma^G = 0$, we define θ^0 so that $S_{t-1}^\theta = \theta_t^0 + \theta_t' S_{t-1} = 1$ for $t > 0$. The rate process of $(\delta^\theta, V^\theta)$ is then equal to

$$r = \frac{\Delta G^\theta}{S_-^\theta} = \theta^0 r + \theta' \mu^G = (1 - \theta' S_-) r + \theta' \mu^G,$$

which implies that $\theta'(\mu^G - rS_-) = 0$, confirming (5.61). ∎

In the remainder of this section we assume that the market is arbitrage-free. Consider any traded contract (δ^*, V^*) and let $S^* = V^* - \delta^*$ and

$$G^* = V^* + \delta_-^* \bullet t$$
$$= V_0^* + \mu^* \bullet t + \sigma^* \bullet B, \quad \mu^* \in \mathcal{P}_0, \quad \sigma^* \in \mathcal{P}_0^{1 \times d}. \qquad (5.62)$$

By Proposition 5.21, we know that $(\delta^*, V^*) = (\delta^\theta, V^\theta)$ for some replicating trading strategy (θ^0, θ). In a typical application, the dividend process δ^* and the terminal value V_T^* (or S_T^*) are specified and we are interested in computing V^* and (θ^0, θ). The value process V^* can be computed by constructing a market-price-of-risk process η in $\mathcal{H}$. The restriction

$$\mu^* = rS_-^* + \sigma^* \eta$$

is equivalent to a backward recursion on the information tree that entirely determines the value process V^* as a function of δ^* and V_T^* (see Proposition 5.52). A replicating trading strategy is constructed as follows.

Proposition 5.56. *Suppose that the market (implemented by the contracts (5.56)) is arbitrage-free and (δ^*, V^*) is a traded contract with gain-process dynamics (5.62). For every $\theta \in \mathcal{P}_0^J$, there exists some $\theta^0 \in \mathcal{P}_0$ such that the trading strategy (θ^0, θ) replicates (δ^*, V^*) if and only if*

$$\sigma^* = \theta' \sigma^G. \qquad (5.63)$$

Finally, if the trading strategy (θ^0, θ) replicates (δ^*, V^*), then

$$\theta_t^0 = \frac{V_t^* - \theta_t' V_t}{1 + r_t}, \quad t = 1, \dots, T; \quad \theta_0^0 = 0. \qquad (5.64)$$

Proof. Consider any trading strategy (θ^0, θ). The corresponding budget equation in the form of Proposition 5.17 together with equation (5.62) imply that

$$V^* - \theta' V = \text{predictable term} + (\sigma^* - \theta' \sigma^G) \bullet B. \qquad (5.65)$$

If equation (5.63) holds, then $V^* - \theta' V$ is predictable and therefore equation (5.64) defines a predictable process θ^0. By construction of θ^0, $V_t^* = V_t^\theta$ for all $t > 0$. By Proposition 5.10, it follows that $(\delta^*, V^*) = (\delta^\theta, V^\theta)$. Conversely, if the trading strategy (θ^0, θ) replicates the contract (δ^*, V^*), then, again by Proposition 5.10,

$$V_t^* = \theta_t^0(1 + r_t) + \theta_t' V_t, \quad t = 1, \ldots, T,$$

which implies (5.64). Since θ^0 is predictable, so is $V^* - \theta' V$, and (5.63) follows from (5.65). ∎

Definition 5.57. *The contracts* (5.56) *are **dynamically independent** if every synthetic contract is generated by a unique trading strategy. A contract* (δ^*, V^*) *is **everywhere risky** if for every time* $t > 0$ *and every nonempty event* $F \in \mathcal{F}_t$, *the random variable* $V_t^* 1_F$ *is not* $\mathcal{F}_{t-1}$*-measurable.*

The replication condition (5.63) together with Propositions 5.22 and 5.10 imply the following characterizations.

Proposition 5.58. *Suppose the market is arbitrage-free and is implemented by the* $1 + J$ *contracts* (5.56).

(a) *The* $1 + J$ *contracts* (5.56) *are dynamically independent if and only if the columns of the* $J \times d$ *matrix* $\sigma^G(\omega, t)$ *are linearly independent for every* $(\omega, t) \in \Omega \times \{1, \ldots, T\}$.

(b) *The market is complete if and only if the rank of* $\sigma^G(\omega, t)$ *is* d *for all* $(\omega, t) \in \Omega \times \{1, \ldots, T\}$.

(c) *A contract* (δ^*, V^*) *with gain-process dynamics* (5.62) *is everywhere risky if and only if* $\sigma^*(\omega, t)$ *is nonzero for all* $(\omega, t) \in \Omega \times \{1, \ldots, T\}$.

Finally, we argue that every complete market on the given filtration can be implemented by $1 + d$ contracts. In contrast, if we were to implement a

177

complete market by forming portfolios at time zero only, as many contracts as there are non–time-zero spots would be required, a number that rises exponentially in T, if $d > 0$.

Theorem 5.59. *Suppose the underlying filtration is uniform with spanning number $1 + d$. An arbitrage-free market is complete if and only if it can be implemented by $1 + d$ dynamically independent contracts: one money-market account and d everywhere risky contracts.*

Proof. The "if" part is an immediate consequence of Proposition 5.58. Conversely, suppose the market X is complete and arbitrage-free, and let (Q, ρ) be the corresponding unique EMM-discount pair, with the corresponding processes $\eta \in \mathcal{H}$ and $r \in \mathcal{P}_0$ defined in (5.50). Market completeness implies that

$$X = \{x \in \mathcal{L} : (\rho \mid x)^Q = 0\},$$

and therefore a contract is traded (in X) if and only if it is priced by (Q, ρ). We define the money-market account (δ^0, V^0) by (5.57). By construction, (δ^0, V^0) is priced by (Q, ρ) and is therefore traded. We define the everywhere risky contracts $(\delta, V) \in \mathcal{L}^{d \times 2}$ by letting $V_t = B_t$ for $t > 0$, specifying the dividend process as

$$\delta_{t-1} = \frac{1}{1+r_t}(r_t V_{t-1} + \eta_t), \quad t = 1, \ldots, T, \quad \delta_T = V_T,$$

and finally letting $V_0 = (\rho \mid \delta)^Q$. Proposition 5.52 applies, with $\mu^G = \delta_-$ and σ_t^G equal to the d-by-d identity matrix for all $t > 0$, to confirm that (Q, ρ) prices the contracts in (δ, V), which are therefore traded. The market implemented by the contracts (δ^0, V^0) and (δ, V) is contained in X and is complete, and is therefore equal to X. ∎

5.7 MARKOVIAN PRICING

For any traded contract with a given dividend process and terminal value, the computation of the contract's time-zero value V_0 given a probability-SPD pair requires the solution of a backward recursion that begins with the known values at all terminal spots and proceeds backward at every spot of the information tree. The number of arithmetic operations required to compute V_0 using this recursion rises exponentially with the number of periods T, rendering the procedure impractical. In this section we discuss one way in which this problem is overcome in practical modeling through the assumption that all dividends and prices are driven by some underlying low-dimensional Markov process.

The setting is that of the last section, specialized by additional structure. The first new restriction we impose is that the dynamic orthonormal martingale basis B has **independent increments**, meaning that

$\Delta B_1, \ldots, \Delta B_T$ are stochastically independent random variables.

We assume that the market X is arbitrage-free and is implemented by the money-market account (δ^0, V^0) and the J contracts (δ, V), as specified in the last section, whose notation we continue to use. Dividend and value processes will be assumed to be specified in terms of the k-dimensional adapted process Z, which is defined in terms of a given initial value $Z_0 \in \mathbb{R}^k$ and the functions

$$\mu^Z : \{1, \ldots, T\} \times \mathbb{R}^k \to \mathbb{R}^k \quad \text{and} \quad \sigma^Z : \{1, \ldots, T\} \times \mathbb{R}^k \to \mathbb{R}^{k \times d},$$

by the recursion

$$\Delta Z_t = \mu^Z(t, Z_{t-1}) + \sigma^Z(t, Z_{t-1})\Delta B_t, \quad t = 1, \ldots, T. \tag{5.66}$$

By Proposition B.57, Z is a Markov process (relative to the probability P and the filtration $\{\mathcal{F}_t\}$).

For each time t, we let $\mathcal{N}_t$ denote the set of all possible values of Z_t:

$$\mathcal{N}_t = \{Z_t(\omega) : \omega \in \Omega\}.$$

One can think of $\bigcup_t \mathcal{N}_t$ as being the set of nodes of a tree that is recombining, in the sense that different paths on the information tree can lead to the same node. The number of nodes on the recombining tree becomes significantly smaller than the number of all spots as T increases. For any adapted process x, we abuse notation by writing $x_t = x(t, Z_t)$ to mean that there exists a function $x(t, \cdot) : \mathcal{N}_t \to \mathbb{R}$ such that $x(\omega, t) = x(t, Z(\omega, t))$ for all $\omega \in \Omega$ (or, equivalently, that x_t is $\sigma(Z_t)$-measurable). Similarly, if x is a predictable process, we write $x_t = x(t, Z_{t-1})$ to express the condition that there exists a function $x(t, \cdot) : \mathcal{N}_{t-1} \to \mathbb{R}$ such that $x(\omega, t) = x(t, Z(\omega, t-1))$ for all $\omega \in \Omega$ (a condition that is equivalent to the $\sigma(Z_{t-1})$-measurability of x_t).

With the above notational conventions, we assume throughout that

$$r_t = r(t, Z_{t-1}) \quad \text{and} \quad \delta_t = \delta(t, Z_t), \quad t = 1, \ldots, T. \tag{5.67}$$

Before stating analogous restrictions on prices, we show a lemma that helps clarify the content of these restrictions. The processes μ^G and σ^G in the lemma correspond to the predictable representation (5.59) of the gain process associated with the contracts (δ, V).

Lemma 5.60. *(a) Given the assumption* (5.67), $V_t = V(t, Z_t)$ *for every time* t *if and only if* $V_T = V(T, Z_T)$ *and* $\mu_t^G = \mu^G(t, Z_{t-1})$ *for every time* $t > 0$.

(b) Given the assumption that B *has independent increments,* $\sigma_t^G = \sigma^G(t, Z_{t-1})$ *for all* $t > 0$ *if* $V_t = V(t, Z_t)$ *for all* t.

Proof. (a) Suppose $V_t = V(t, Z_t)$ for all t. Using the Markov property of Z, we have

$$\mu_t^G = \mathbb{E}_{t-1}[\Delta G_t]$$
$$= \mathbb{E}[V_t \mid Z_{t-1}] - V(t-1, Z_{t-1}) + \delta(t-1, Z_{t-1})$$
$$= \mu^G(t, Z_{t-1}).$$

Conversely, suppose $V_T = V(T, Z_T)$ and $\mu_t^G = \mu^G(t, Z_{t-1})$ for all $t > 0$. A backward-in-time induction shows that $V_t = V(t, Z_t)$ for all t. The inductive step assumes that $V_t = V(t, Z_t)$, which implies that $\mathbb{E}_{t-1}[V_t] = \mathbb{E}_{t-1}[V_t \mid Z_{t-1}]$ and therefore

$$V_{t-1} = \mathbb{E}[V_t \mid Z_{t-1}] - \mu^G(t, Z_{t-1}) + \delta(t-1, Z_{t-1}) = V(t-1, Z_{t-1}).$$

(b) Using the dynamics (5.66) of Z, we compute

$$\sigma_t^G = \mathbb{E}_{t-1}[V_t \Delta B_t']$$
$$= \mathbb{E}_{t-1}\left[\sum_{z \in N_{t-1}} 1_{\{Z_{t-1}=z\}} V(t, z + \mu^Z(t, z) + \sigma^Z(t, z)\Delta B_t)\Delta B_t' \right]$$
$$= \sum_{z \in N_{t-1}} 1_{\{Z_{t-1}=z\}} \mathbb{E}[V(t, z + \mu^Z(t, z) + \sigma^Z(t, z)\Delta B_t)\Delta B_t']$$
$$= \sigma^G(t, Z_{t-1}).$$

In the third equation, $\mathbb{E}_{t-1}$ was replaced by the unconditional expectation $\mathbb{E}$, using the assumption that B has independent increments. ∎

We henceforth assume that in addition to (5.67), for all $t > 0$,

$$V_t = V(t, Z_t), \quad \mu_t^G = \mu^G(t, Z_{t-1}), \quad \sigma_t^G = \sigma^G(t, Z_{t-1}), \qquad (5.68)$$

and therefore $S_t = V_t - \delta_t = S(t, Z_t)$. A market-price-of-risk process in this context is any process η in $\mathcal{P}_0^d$ that satisfies

$$\mu^G(t, Z_{t-1}) = r(t, Z_{t-1}) S(t-1, Z_{t-1}) + \sigma^G(t, Z_{t-1}) \eta_t, \quad \text{all } t > 0. \quad (5.69)$$

We recall that for η to define an EMM, it must also be a member of the set $\mathcal{H}$; that is, $1 - \eta' \Delta B$ must be strictly positive.

Lemma 5.61. *In the above context, there exists a market-price-of-risk process η in $\mathcal{H}$ such that $\eta_t = (t, Z_{t-1})$ for every time $t > 0$.*

Proof. Since the market is arbitrage-free, there exists an EMM. By Proposition 5.54, there is a corresponding market-price-of-risk process $\tilde{\eta}$ such that $1 - \tilde{\eta}' \Delta B$ is a strictly positive process, although $\tilde{\eta}_t$ need not be $\sigma(Z_{t-1})$-measurable. Consider any time $t > 0$ and value $z \in \mathcal{N}_{t-1}$, and let $F_1, \ldots, F_n$ be the events of the partition generating $\mathcal{F}_{t-1}$ whose union is the event $\{Z_{t-1} = z\}$. Since $\tilde{\eta}$ is predictable, there exist corresponding scalars $\alpha_1, \ldots, \alpha_n$ such that $\tilde{\eta}(\omega, t) = \alpha_i$ for $\omega \in F_i$. Since $1 - \tilde{\eta}' \Delta B$ is assumed strictly positive and ΔB_t is stochastically independent of $\mathcal{F}_{t-1}$, we have

$$1 = P[1 - \alpha_i' \Delta B_t > 0 \mid F_i] = P[1 - \alpha_i' \Delta B_t > 0]$$
$$= P[1 - \alpha_i' \Delta B_t > 0 \mid Z_{t-1} = z], \quad i = 1, \ldots, n.$$

This argument shows that each $1 - \alpha_i' \Delta B_t$ is strictly positive on the event $\{Z_{t-1} = z\}$. Let $\mu = \mu^G - r S_-$. Since $\tilde{\eta}$ is a market-price-of-risk process, $\sigma^G(t, z) \alpha_i = \mu(t, z)$ for $i = 1, \ldots, n$. Therefore, if we select any value for $\eta(t, z)$ that lies in the convex hull of $\{\alpha_1, \ldots, \alpha_n\}$, we are guaranteed that $1 - \eta(t, z)' \Delta B > 0$ on $\{Z_{t-1} = z\}$ and $\sigma^G(t, z) \eta(t, z) = \mu(t, z)$. Repeating for every $z \in \mathcal{N}_{t-1}$ and every time $t > 0$, and letting $\eta_0 = 0$, we complete the construction of the required market-price-of-risk process η. ∎

Given the last lemma, we can and do assume that η is a market-price-of-risk process in $\mathcal{H}$ such that $\eta_t = (t, Z_{t-1})$ for $t > 0$. By Proposition 5.54, η defines an EMM $Q = P^\eta$, and by Proposition B.57, Z is a Markov process relative to Q (as well as P).

As in the last section, we consider a situation in which we are interested in pricing and replicating a traded contract, (δ^*, V^*), with given dividend process and terminal value that we now assume to be of the form

$$\delta_t^* = \delta^*(t, Z_t), \quad t = 0, \ldots, T-1; \quad V_T^* = V^*(T, Z_T).$$

A backward induction shows that the contract's value process satisfies $V_t^* = V^*(t, Z_t)$, for all t. The condition is valid for $t = T$ by assumption. The inductive step is obtained by pricing the contract recursively using the EMM Q and the Markov property of Z relative to Q:

$$V_{t-1}^* = \delta^*(t-1, Z_{t-1}) + \frac{\mathbb{E}^Q[V^*(t, Z_t) \mid Z_{t-1}]}{1 + r(t, Z_{t-1})} = V^*(t-1, Z_{t-1}).$$

Denoting the dynamics of the gain process $G^* = V^* - \delta_-^* \bullet t$ as in (5.62) and using Lemma 5.60, we conclude that

$$\mu_t^* = \mu(t, Z_{t-1}) \quad \text{and} \quad \sigma_t^* = \sigma^*(t, Z_{t-1}), \quad t = 1, \ldots, T.$$

Remark 5.62. *The first of these equations also follows from the second one and the fact that $\mu^* = rS_- + \sigma^*\eta$. The above argument also shows that an alternative modeling approach would have been to postulate (5.67) together with the assumptions $\eta_t = \eta(t, Z_{t-1})$ and $V_T = V(T, Z_T)$, in which case conditions (5.68) follow.*

Finally, we discuss the Markovian structure of a trading strategy that replicates the contract (δ^*, V^*). By Proposition 5.21, there exists a trading strategy (θ^0, θ) such that $(\delta^*, V^*) = (\delta^\theta, V^\theta)$. By Proposition 5.56, the trading strategy (θ^0, θ) replicates (δ^*, V^*) for some $\theta^0 \in \mathcal{P}_0$ if and only if

$$\sigma^*(t, Z_{t-1}) = \theta_t' \sigma^G(t, Z_{t-1}), \quad t = 1 \ldots, T, \tag{5.70}$$

in which case θ^0 is computed by setting the value of the value process of the replicating portfolio equal to V^*, resulting in equation (5.64). We claim that we can select the replicating trading strategy to satisfy

$$\theta_t^0 = \theta^0(t, Z_{t-1}) \quad \text{and} \quad \theta_t = \theta(t, Z_{t-1}), \quad t = 1, \ldots, T. \tag{5.71}$$

Clearly, there is a selection of θ that satisfies both (5.70) and (5.71). Rewriting equation (5.64) as

$$\theta_t^0(1 + r_t) = V_{t-1}^* + \Delta G_t^* - \delta_{t-1}^* - \theta_t'(V_{t-1} + \Delta G_t - \delta_{t-1}),$$

and using the dynamics of G and G^* with equation (5.70), we infer that θ^0 also satisfies (5.71), where the function $\theta^0(t, z)$ is computed as

$$\begin{aligned}
\theta^0(t, z)(1 + r(t, z)) &= V^*(t-1, z) + \mu^*(t, z) - \delta^*(t-1, z) \\
&\quad - \theta(t, z)'(V(t-1, z) + \mu^G(t, z) - \delta(t-1, z)).
\end{aligned}$$

5.8 EXERCISES

1. Use Proposition 5.27 to give an alternative proof of Proposition 5.10, based on the idea that if the contract $(\delta^1 - \delta^2, 0)$ is traded, then $G^\pi = (\pi\delta)_- \bullet t$ is a predictable zero-mean martingale.

2. Construct an example of contracts $(\delta, V) \in \mathcal{L}^{J \times 2}$ and a contract (δ^*, V^*) that is traded in $X(\delta, V)$ but is not a synthetic contract in (δ, V).

3. Prove Proposition 5.22.

4. Suppose $\{X_{F,t}\}$ is an arbitrage-free liquid dynamic market and $X = X_{\Omega,0}$ is implemented by trading in the J contracts (δ, V). For any spot (F, t), extend Definition 5.14 to apply from the perspective of spot (F, t), and prove that the same contracts (δ, V) implement $X_{F,t}$. Finally, give an example of an arbitrage-free nonliquid dynamic market that is implemented by a given set of contracts, but under trading constraints.

5. Suppose that the pair (P, π) in $\mathcal{Q} \times \mathcal{L}_{++}$ prices the contract (δ, V). Show that for any stopping time τ,

$$V_t = \frac{1}{\pi_t} \mathbb{E}_t \left[\sum_{u=t}^{\tau-1} \pi_u \delta_u + \pi_\tau V_\tau \right] \quad \text{on the event } \{\tau > t\}.$$

6. Consider a contract (δ, V) whose ex-dividend price process $S = V - \delta$ is nonzero at all nonterminal spots. Given any $\pi \in \mathcal{L}_{++}$, define the cumulative return processes R and R^π to satisfy

$$\Delta R = \frac{\Delta G}{S_-} \quad \text{and} \quad \Delta R^\pi = \frac{\Delta G^\pi}{(\pi S)_-}.$$

Suppose that $(P, \pi) \in \mathcal{Q} \times \mathcal{L}_{++}$ implies the risk-free discount process ρ, and $r = -\Delta\rho/\rho$. Show that the following conditions are equivalent:

- (P, π) prices (δ, V).

- R^π is a P-martingale.

- $\mathbb{E}_{t-1}^P[(\pi_t/\pi_{t-1})(1 + \Delta R_t)] = 1, \quad t = 1, \ldots, T.$

- $\mathbb{E}_{t-1}^P[\pi_t(\Delta R_t - r_t)] = 0, \quad t = 1, \ldots, T.$

Finally, explain how the above conditions simplify if $(P, \pi) = (Q, \rho)$ is an EMM-discount pair.

7. Show how the multiplicative decomposition of x in equation (5.24) can be computed in terms of the Doob decomposition (B.10), and conversely.

8. Given are an arbitrage-free market X and a probability $P \in \mathcal{Q}$.

(a) Show that $(\pi \mid x)^P = 0$ for every SPD π with respect to P if and only if $x \in X$. (This is the same as a part of Exercise 6 of Chapter 1.)

(b) Show that a contract is traded if and only if it is priced by every probability-SPD pair of the form (P, π).

(c) Suppose that a money-market account is traded, with short rate process r, and let ρ be the corresponding discount process defined by (5.20). Show that a contract is priced by (Q, ρ) for every EMM Q if and only if it is traded.

(d) State and prove a version of part (c) that does not assume the tradeability of a money-market account.

9. (Binomial Replication) Suppose $\Omega = \{0, 1\}^T$ and the filtration $\{\mathcal{F}_t\}$ is generated by the process N, defined recursively by

$$N_0 = 0; \quad \Delta N_t(\omega) = \omega_t, \quad \omega = (\omega_1, \ldots, \omega_T) \in \Omega, \quad t \in \{1, \ldots, T\}.$$

Note that $N_t(\omega)$ is the number of ones in $(\omega_1, \ldots, \omega_t)$. The market is implemented by two contracts. The first contract (δ^0, V^0) is a money-market account with a rate process identically equal to a given constant $r \in (-1, \infty)$. For concreteness, assume that $\delta^0 = r$ and $S^0 = V^0 - \delta^0 = 1$. The second contract (δ, V) has an ex-dividend price process $S = V - \delta$ that is specified by a given initial value $S_0 \in (0, \infty)$ and the recursion

$$\frac{S_t}{S_{t-1}} = (\Delta N_t)U + (1 - \Delta N_t)D, \quad t = 1, \ldots, T, \qquad (5.72)$$

for given constants $U, D \in (0, \infty)$, where $U > D$. The dividend process δ corresponds to a constant dividend yield $y \in (-1, \infty)$ and is formally defined by

$$\delta_t = yS_t, \quad t = 1, \ldots, T; \quad \delta_0 = 0. \qquad (5.73)$$

(a) Show that S generates the underlying filtration. List the set $\mathcal{N}_t$ of all possible values of S_t. The **recombining tree** is the set $\bigcup_{t=0}^{T} \mathcal{N}_t$, whose elements we call **nodes**. Provide a diagrammatic representation of the recombining tree, and explain how it relates to the information tree. What is the difference between a spot and a node? How many nodes are there and how many spots? How do these numbers increase with T? Compute the order of magnitude of these two numbers for $T = 100$.

(b) Show that the market is arbitrage-free if and only if

$$U(1 + y) > 1 + r > D(1 + y) > 0. \qquad (5.74)$$

Assume this condition is satisfied in the remainder of this exercise.

(c) Suppose that we wish to replicate a contract (δ^*, V^*) that, for simplicity, is assumed to pay no dividends ($\delta^* = 0$). Assume that the contract's price is given as $S_t^* = V_t^* = f_t(S_t)$, for some functions $f_t : \mathcal{N}_t \to (0, \infty)$ (whose computation is the topic of the next question). Suppose the trading strategy (θ^0, θ) in the contracts (δ^0, V^0) and (δ, V) replicates (δ^*, V^*). Show that

$$\theta_t^0 = g_t(S_{t-1}) \quad \text{and} \quad \theta_t = h_t(S_{t-1}), \quad t = 1, \ldots, T.$$

where the functions $g_t, h_t : \mathcal{N}_{t-1} \to \mathbb{R}$ are given by

$$g_t(s) = \frac{Uf_t(sD) - Df_t(sU)}{(1+r)(U-D)}, \quad h_t(s) = \frac{f_t(sU) - f_t(sD)}{(1+y)(sU - sD)}.$$

10. (Binomial Pricing) Consider the binomial model of Exercise 9 and define the constant

$$q = \frac{(1+r)/(1+y) - D}{U - D}. \qquad (5.75)$$

(a) Show that the model is arbitrage-free if and only if $q \in (0,1)$. Assume this condition is satisfied in the remainder of this exercise.

(b) Suppose Q is any strictly positive probability and ρ is the deterministic discount process defined by $\rho_t = (1+r)^{-t}$. Show that (Q, ρ) is an EMM-discount pair if and only if it prices the contract (δ, V). Use this fact to argue that Q is an EMM if and only if, under the probability Q, the random variables $\Delta N_1, \ldots, \Delta N_T$ are stochastically independent, with $Q(\Delta N_t = 1) = 1 - Q(\Delta N_t = 0) = q$, in which case

$$Q(\omega) = \mathbb{E}\left[\prod_{t=1}^{T} 1_{\{\Delta N_t = \omega_t\}}\right] = \prod_{t=1}^{T} \mathbb{E}[1_{\{\Delta N_t = \omega_t\}}]$$
$$= q^{N_T(\omega)}(1-q)^{T-N_T(\omega)}, \quad \omega \in \Omega. \tag{5.76}$$

Explain why each of the above equations is valid.

(c) Explain why part (b) implies market completeness.

(d) Consider the European option (δ^*, V^*), a contract that is specified in terms of the **payoff** function $f_T : \mathcal{N}_T \to \mathbb{R}$ by

$$S_T^* = f_T(S_T) \quad \text{and} \quad \delta^* = 0.$$

For example, setting $f_T(S_T) = (S_T - K)^+$ for some positive constant K corresponds to a **European call option** on the contract (δ, V). Compute the option value process using the EMM Q, and use the Markov property of S relative to Q to show that

$$S_t^* = \frac{\mathbb{E}^Q[f_T(S_T) \mid S_t]}{(1+r)^{T-t}} = f_t(S_t),$$

where the functions $f_t : \mathcal{N}_t \to (0, \infty)$ are computed recursively, starting with the known terminal function f_T and proceeding backward in time:

$$f_{t-1}(s) = \frac{qf_t(sU) + (1-q)f_t(sD)}{1+r}, \quad s \in \mathcal{N}_{t-1}. \tag{5.77}$$

Explain why S is a Markov process relative to Q. Finally, compute the number of operations required to compute f_0 using recursion (5.77), and compare this number to the number of spots.

(e) Show how to price an American call option with payoff process $S - K$, recursively on the binomial tree. Construct a simple example in which exercising the option prior to maturity is optimal. Would such an example contradict the conclusion of Example 5.45?

11. (a) Show that an American option (Definition 5.40) is an option (Definition 5.39).

    (b) Show that condition (5.28) in the definition of an option is required for the validity of Theorem 5.42, by providing a counterexample to Corollary 5.44 in its absence.

    (c) Verify the consistency of the two expressions for $J^{\pi}(\delta)$ in (5.29) and in (5.34).

    (d) Provide a more detailed proof for Lemma 5.47, highlighting the role of condition (5.28) in the argument.

12. Prove that the exercise policy τ^* defined by (5.39) is the smallest dominant exercise policy; that is, prove that τ^* is dominant and any other dominant exercise policy τ satisfies $\tau \geq \tau^*$. Is there a greatest dominant exercise policy? If so, give a characterization of such a policy that is analogous to (5.39).

13. (Submartingales and American Call) A process x is a **submartingale** if it is adapted and $\mathbb{E}_{t-1}[\Delta x_t] \geq 0$ for every $t > 0$.

    (a) Show that a process is a submartingale if and only if it is the sum of a zero-mean martingale and a nondecreasing predictable process. The latter is known as the **Doob decomposition** of the submartingale. Show that the Doob decomposition of a submartingale is unique.

    (b) Use Jensen's inequality (Lemma 4.13) to verify that if x is a submartingale and $f : \mathbb{R} \to \mathbb{R}$ is a nondecreasing convex function, then $f(x)$ is also a submartingale.

    (c) Consider the setting of Example 5.45, of an American call on a stock that pays no dividends, and give yet another proof of the optimality of not exercising prior to maturity, along the following lines. First, argue that we can assume that the option's payoff process is $Y = (S - K)^+$ (instead of $Y = S - K$, as assumed in Example 5.45). Use parts (a) and (b) to show that ρY is a submartingale, and then part (a) again to show that $\mathbb{E}[\rho_T Y_T] \geq \mathbb{E}[\rho_\tau Y_\tau]$ for every stopping time τ.

14. (Snell Envelope) Suppose y is an adapted process. The **Snell envelope** of the process y is the process υ defined recursively by

$$\upsilon_{t-1} = \max\{y_{t-1}, \mathbb{E}_{t-1}[\upsilon_t]\}, \quad t = 1, \ldots, T; \quad \upsilon_T = y_T. \quad (5.78)$$

187

(a) In a deterministic setting, assume $T = 16$ and

$$y_t = \frac{1}{1+t} \cos\left(\frac{\pi}{2}t\right).$$

Plot the Snell envelope of y.

(b) Again in a deterministic setting, prove that the Snell envelope of y is the smallest nonincreasing function that is greater than or equal to y at every time.

(c) In the stochastic setting, suppose υ is the Snell envelope of the adapted process y and define, for every time t,

$$\upsilon_t^* = \max\{\mathbb{E}_t[y_{\tau \wedge T}] : \tau \geq t, \tau \in \mathcal{T}\},$$
$$\tau^*(t) = \min\{u : u \geq t, \upsilon_u = y_u\}.$$

Show that $\upsilon_t^* = \upsilon_t = \mathbb{E}_t[y_{\tau^*(t)}]$ for every time t, and that if τ is a stopping time such that $\tau \geq t$ and $\upsilon_t = \mathbb{E}_t[x_\tau]$, then $\tau^*(t) \leq \tau$.

(d) A process x is a **supermartingale** if $-x$ is a submartingale, as defined in Exercise 13, whose characterization you can use here. Prove that the Snell envelope υ of y is a supermartingale such that $\upsilon \geq y$ and is the least supermartingale with this property (that is, if $\tilde{\upsilon}$ is a supermartingale and $\tilde{\upsilon} \geq y$, then $\tilde{\upsilon} \geq \upsilon$).

(e) Explain how the above results apply to the pricing of American options given a complete market.

15. (Dual Characterization of Optimal Stopping) Let υ be the Snell envelope of the adapted process y, as defined in the last exercise, whose characterization can be used here.

(a) Show that

$$\upsilon_0 = \max_{\tau \in \mathcal{T}} \mathbb{E}[y_{\tau \wedge T}] = \min_{M \in \mathcal{M}_0} \mathbb{E}[\max_t (y_t - M_t)],$$

where $\mathcal{M}_0$ is the set of zero-mean martingales. You can use the fact, shown in Exercise 13, that every supermartingale can be (uniquely) decomposed into a sum of a zero-mean martingale and a nonincreasing predictable process. *Hint:* The minimum is achieved by the martingale part of the Doob decomposition of υ (defined analogously to Exercise 13).

(b) Based on Lemma 5.34, derive a multiplicative Doob decomposition result for positive supermartingales. Using this result, state and prove a multiplicative version of part (a), assuming υ is strictly positive.

16. Assume an underlying arbitrage-free liquid dynamic market $\{X_{F,t}\}$ and let $\mathcal{D}$ be an option. The cash flow $\delta \in \mathcal{D}$ is **dominant at time** t if it is dominant at every time-t spot. The cash flow δ is **marketed at time** t if for any time-t spot (F, t), there exists a scalar $\Pi_{F,t}(\delta)$ such that

$$-\Pi_{F,t}(\delta)1_{F\times\{t\}} + \delta 1_{F\times\{t,\dots,T\}} \in X_{F,t}.$$

Since the market is arbitrage-free, the scalar $\Pi_{F,t}(\delta)$ is unique, defining the spot-(F, t) present value of δ. The values $\Pi_{F,t}(\delta)$ define an adapted process $\Pi(\delta)$, whose time-t value $\Pi_t(\delta)$ is the time-t present value of δ.

(a) Suppose the following condition is valid.

Condition 5.63. *For every $\delta \in \mathcal{D}$ and time t, there exists a cash flow δ^t in $\mathcal{D}_t(\delta)$ that is dominant and marketed at time t as well as at time $t - 1$ if $t > 0$.*

Let p_0^* be the time-zero present value of a marketed dominant cash flow, and suppose the option $\mathcal{D}$ can be sold (or written) for a premium p_0. Show that if $p_0 > p_0^*$, then there exists an arbitrage of the form (5.44), where

$$h_t(\delta) = (-\Pi(\delta^{t+1}) + \delta)1_{[t]} + \Pi(\delta^{t+1})1_{[t+1]}, \quad t < T.$$

Show that the above equation defines a $\mathcal{D}$-adapted strategy h.

(b) Use the results of Exercise 8 to show that Condition 5.63 is equivalent to the existence of an option value function J with the following properties: Given any $\delta \in \mathcal{D}$ and time t, there exists some $\delta^t \in \mathcal{D}_t(\delta)$ such that

$$J_t(\delta) = J_t^\pi(\delta) = \mathbb{E}_t\left[\sum_{u=t}^{T} \frac{\pi_u}{\pi_t}\delta_u^t\right] \quad \text{for every SPD } \pi,$$

and the value $\mathbb{E}_{t-1}[(\pi_t/\pi_{t-1})J_t(\delta)]$ is the same for every SPD π and time $t > 0$. Explain how J relates to $\Pi(\delta)$ and to the arbitrage of part (a). Finally, use J to relate the arbitrage cash flow of part (a) to the Bellman equation.

17. Explain how the computational complexity of the Bellman equation (5.36) for option pricing can be reduced in the Markovian

189

setting of Section B.9, under a suitable Markovian structure of the option.

18. (Binomial Martingale Basis and Market Price of Risk) Consider the binomial model of Exercises 9 and 10, and postulate an underlying probability P that is defined in terms of the constant $p \in (0, 1)$ by

$$P(\{\omega\}) = p^{N_T(\omega)}(1 - p)^{T - N_T(\omega)}, \quad \omega \in \Omega.$$

The process B is defined recursively by

$$B_0 = 0, \quad \Delta B_t = (\Delta N_t)\sqrt{\frac{1 - p}{p}} - (1 - \Delta N_t)\sqrt{\frac{p}{1 - p}}, \quad t = 1, \ldots, T.$$

(a) Verify that B is dynamic orthonormal basis under P, and compute the coefficients α and β so that

$$\frac{\Delta S}{S_-} = \alpha + \beta \Delta B.$$

(b) Suppose the cumulative return process R of the risky contract (δ, V) follows the dynamics (5.54). Argue that the probability $Q = P^\eta$, where $\eta \in \mathcal{H}$, is an EMM if and only if

$$\eta = \frac{\mu^R - r}{\sigma^R}.$$

Assuming the constant dividend-yield specification (5.73), show that

$$\mu^R = \alpha + y(1 + \alpha) \quad \text{and} \quad \sigma^R = (1 + y)\beta,$$

and compute η in terms of the parameters p and q, as defined in (5.75).

(c) Suppose η is given as in part (b) and therefore $Q = P^\eta$ is an EMM. Show that

$$1 - \eta \Delta B = \frac{q}{p}\Delta N + \frac{1 - q}{1 - p}(1 - \Delta N),$$

and that the conditional density process $\xi_t = \mathbb{E}_t[dQ/dP]$ is given by

$$\xi_t = \left(\frac{q}{p}\right)^{N_t}\left(\frac{1 - q}{1 - p}\right)^{t - N_t}.$$

Finally, compute $Q(\{\omega\}) = \mathbb{E}^P[1_{\{\omega\}}\xi_T]$ to recover the EMM formula (5.76).

(d) With η specified as above, show directly (that is, without using Proposition B.53) that

$$\mathbb{E}^Q_{t-1}[(\Delta B^\eta)^2] = 1 - \eta^2 - \eta\mathbb{E}^P_{t-1}[\Delta B^3].$$

Parameterize the discrete time model by the number of periods and a given terminal time T. Calibrate η by assuming that the mean and variance of ΔR are proportional to time. Assuming ΔB is symmetrically distributed, show that the above expression, properly scaled, converges to one as the number of periods goes to infinity.

19. (a) In the context of Section 5.6, suppose $\tilde{B}$ is another orthonormal dynamic basis. How should the replication formulas of Proposition 5.56 and the market-price-of-risk property be modified if the martingale basis B is replaced by $\tilde{B}$?

(b) How should Proposition 5.56 be modified if there is no traded money-market account?

20. Given the dynamic market $\{X_{F,t}\}$, define a **dynamic linear valuation rule** to be an assignment of a linear functional $\Pi_{F,t} : \mathcal{L}_{F,t} \to \mathbb{R}$ to each spot (F, t) such that $\Pi_{F,t}(1_{F\times\{t\}}) = 1$ and $\Pi_{F,t}(x) \leq 0$ for any $x \in X_{F,t}$. Note that unlike a present-value function, $\Pi_{F,t}$ is not required to assign a positive value to every arbitrage. The dynamic linear valuation rule $\{\Pi_{F,t}\}$ is defined to be **consistent** if it satisfies condition (5.3), where $\Pi_0 = \Pi_{\Omega\times\{0\}}$. The dynamic market $\{X_{F,t}\}$ satisfies the **law of one price** if $1_{F\times\{t\}} \notin X_{F,t}$ for every spot (F, t). A reinterpretation of Exercise 9 of Chapter 1 shows that a dynamic linear valuation rule exists if and only if the dynamic market satisfies the law of one price.

(a) Construct an example of a dynamic market that satisfies the law of one price, but admits no consistent dynamic linear valuation rule.

(b) Prove that a consistent dynamic linear valuation rule exists if and only if $1_{F\times\{t\}} \notin X_{\Omega,0}$ for every spot (F, t).

21. This exercise examines the state-price dynamics for a market with trading constraints and a possibly nonlinear budget equation. The formal setting is that of Section 5.5. The money-market account (δ^0, V^0) and the J contracts (δ, V) are as in Section 5.6, whose notation we adopt here. The market X will be assumed to be implemented by these contracts, but in a generalized sense; X is no longer assumed to be a linear subspace, as a consequence of a more general budget

equation to be specified shortly. A trading strategy takes the form (θ^0, θ), where θ^0 is a trading strategy in the money-market account and θ is a trading strategy in the J contracts. The **ex-dividend value process** S^θ associated with the trading strategy (θ^0, θ) is defined by

$$S_{t-1}^\theta = \theta_t^0 + \theta_t' S_{t-1}, \quad t > 0; \quad S_T^\theta = \theta_T^0 + \theta_T' S_T.$$

One can think of S^θ as the ex-dividend price process of a synthetic contract defined by (θ^0, θ), given the more general budget equation that follows.

For every spot $(F, t-1)$, we postulate a nonempty set $D(F, t) \subseteq \mathbb{R}^{1+J}$ of allowable portfolios and a function $f(F, t, \cdot) : D(F, t) \to \mathbb{R}$. We also define

$$D(\omega, t) = D(F, t) \quad \text{and} \quad f(\omega, t, \cdot) = f(F, t, \cdot) \quad \text{for all } \omega \in F.$$

The trading strategy (θ^0, θ) is **feasible** if

$$(S^\theta(\omega, t-1), \theta(\omega, t)) \in D(\omega, t) \text{ for all } \omega \in \Omega \text{ and } t \in \{1, \ldots, T\},$$

a condition that we henceforth abbreviate to $(S_-^\theta, \theta) \in D$. Similarly, we state the budget equation by writing $f(S_-^\theta, \theta)$ for the process that takes the value $f(\omega, t, S^\theta(\omega, t-1), \theta(\omega, t))$ at (ω, t). A **consumption plan** is any cash flow. A feasible trading strategy (θ^0, θ) **finances** the consumption plan c if the following **budget equation** is satisfied:

$$S^\theta = w + (f(S_-^\theta, \theta) - c) \bullet \mathbf{t} + \theta'\sigma^G \bullet B.$$

The consumption plan c is **feasible** if it is financed by some feasible trading strategy.

We consider an agent whose status quo plan is to follow the feasible trading strategy (θ^{*0}, θ^*), which finances the consumption plan c^*. The corresponding ex-dividend value process is denoted $S^* = S^{\theta^*}$. The agent's market is defined as

$$X = \{x : c^* + x \text{ is a feasible consumption plan}\}.$$

A process $\pi \in \mathcal{L}_{++}$ is a **state-price density** (SPD) if

$$x \in X \implies (\pi \mid x) \leq 0.$$

This notion of state pricing is used in the following chapter to characterize the optimality of the consumption plan c^*. Fixing a reference process $\pi \in \mathcal{L}_{++}$, we define the predictable processes $\zeta \in \mathcal{P}_0$ and $\eta \in \mathcal{P}_0^d$ by

$$\frac{\Delta \pi}{\pi_-} = -\frac{1}{1+\zeta}(\zeta + \eta' \Delta B).$$

We are interested in restrictions on (ζ, η) that imply that π is SPD.

(a) Provide expressions that compute ζ and η in terms of π and B.

(b) Consider a feasible incremental trading strategy (θ^0, θ) financing the incremental cash flow $x \in X$. In other words, the trading strategy $(\theta^{*0} + \theta^0, \theta^* + \theta)$ is feasible and finances the consumption plan $c^* + x$. Show that

$$(\pi \mid x) = (\pi \mid f(S_-^* + S_-^\theta, \theta^* + \theta) - f(S_-^*, \theta^*) - S_-^\theta \zeta - \theta' \sigma^G \eta).$$

Then use this fact to show that $\pi \in \mathcal{L}_{++}$ is an SPD if

$$(\zeta, \sigma^G \eta) \in \partial f(S_-^*, \theta^*). \tag{5.79}$$

(c) Explain how condition (5.79) applies in the following contexts:

- A market with no trading constraints and a linear budget equation as in the main part of this chapter.

- A market with short-sale constraints.

- A market in which the single-period default-free rate is higher for borrowing than for lending.

- A market with margin requirements similar to those of Exercise 17 of Chapter 1.

5.9 NOTES

The classic references on arbitrage pricing theory introduced in the notes of Chapter 1 are clearly also directly relevant to this chapter. Exercises 10 and 18 are based on the binomial pricing model of Cox, Ross and Rubinstein (1979), Rendleman and Bartter (1979) and Sharpe (1978). The whole chapter can be viewed as a generalization of the binomial model, from an advanced perspective that anticipates the continuous-time theory surveyed by Duffie (2001). Merton (1973b) began the systematic study of arbitrage pricing of options, showing, among other results, the main conclusion of Example 5.45. The optimal stopping problem associated with the risk-neutral valuation of American options has been mathematically studied mainly in continuous-time settings in a large literature, starting with McKean (1965) and Bensoussan (1984) (see also Karatzas (1988)). The arbitrage argument of Section 5.4.3 extends a corresponding discussion offered by Duffie (2001) by making the weaker assumption of the existence of a marketed dominant choice in place of full market completeness, by adopting a broader definition of an option, and by formalizing the notion of hedging strategies by an option writer that can be contingent on (potentially suboptimal) decisions by the option buyer. Exercise 14 is based on a well-known theory of discrete-time optimal stopping, an exposition of which is given by Chow, Robbins and Siegmund (1991). Exercise 15 is based on Rogers (2002), Haugh and Kogan (2004) and Jamshidian (2003). Exercise 21 is a discrete version of an argument in Schroder and Skiadas (2008).

CHAPTER SIX

Dynamic Optimality and Equilibrium

GIVEN DYNAMICALLY consistent preferences, the theory of Chapter 3 applies in the setting of a multiperiod finite information tree through the same identification of the set of cash flows used in the last chapter to reinterpret the fundamental theorems of asset pricing. Besides elaborating on this observation, this chapter develops a theory of recursive utility that achieves a certain separation of the generally intertwined notions of risk aversion and preferences over deterministic consumption. Recursive utility is used to obtain expressions for equilibrium state prices, as well as solutions to models of optimal lifetime consumption and portfolio choice. The themes of scale invariance and translation invariance, introduced in Chapter 3 in the context of representative-agent pricing, also play an important simplifying role in this chapter. Familiarity with Chapters 3 and 5, as well as Appendix B, is assumed.

6.1 DYNAMIC UTILITY

We continue with last chapter's uncertainty model, consisting of the finite state space Ω, the time set $\{0, \ldots, T\}$ and the filtration $\{\mathcal{F}_t : t = 0, \ldots, T\}$, where $\mathcal{F}_0 = \{\Omega, \emptyset\}$ and $\mathcal{F}_T = 2^{\Omega}$. There are $1 + K$ spots on the filtration. We recall that $\mathcal{L}$ denotes the set of all adapted processes and $\mathcal{L}_{F,t} = \{x 1_{F \times \{t, \ldots, T\}} : x \in \mathcal{L}\}$ for any spot (F, t). A **consumption plan** is any cash flow, that is, any adapted process. We call a consumption plan, or any other stochastic process, **deterministic** if its value depends only on the time argument.

The analysis of Chapter 3 can be reinterpreted in this context once we identify the set of cash flows with $\mathbb{R}^{1+K}$. New to the multiperiod setting is the possibility that an agent optimally selects a consumption plan c at time zero, yet the same agent has an incentive to trade away from c at some later spot. We exclude this possibility by assuming dynamically consistent preferences. Suppose that at spot (F, t) an agent prefers to add to a consumption plan c the incremental cash flow x in $\mathcal{L}_{F,t}$. Dynamic consistency requires that the agent also prefers the plan $c + x$ over c at time zero. This requirement parallels the dynamic consistency restriction we imposed on a dynamic market in Definition 5.4; any (contingent) trade available at some spot is also available at time zero. As a consequence, an agent with dynamically consistent preferences that finds a plan optimal given a dynamic market at time zero also finds the same plan optimal at every other spot. The reduction of optimality at every spot to optimality at time zero makes meaningful the application of the results of Chapter 3 in a multiperiod setting.

While the discussion thus far applies in great generality, we now introduce further simplifying structure that will be assumed throughout this chapter. As in Section 3.5, we consider a consumption set of the form

$$C = (\ell, \infty)^{1+K} \quad \text{for some } \ell \in [-\infty, 1), \tag{6.1}$$

typically, $\ell = -\infty$ or 0. We equivalently think of elements of C as adapted processes that are valued in (ℓ, ∞). Since $\ell < 1$, the consumption set C includes the cash flow identically equal to one, which we denote $\mathbf{1}$.

For simplicity, we assume that preferences are independent of past or unrealized consumption, meaning that an agent's preferences at a spot (F, t) are independent of the agent's consumption at any spot outside the tree rooted at (F, t). This assumption is made part of the definition of a dynamic utility below.

Definition 6.1. *A spot-(F, t) **utility** on the consumption set C is any continuous function of the form $U_{F,t} : C \to \mathbb{R}$ that satisfies*

1. *(irrelevance of past or unrealized consumption) For every $c, \tilde{c} \in C$,*

$$c \mathbf{1}_{F \times \{t,\dots,T\}} = \tilde{c} \mathbf{1}_{F \times \{t,\dots,T\}} \implies U_{F,t}(c) = U_{F,t}(\tilde{c}).$$

2. *(monotonicity) For every $c \in C$ and $x \in \mathcal{L}_{F,t}$, if x is an arbitrage cash flow, then $U_{F,t}(c + x) > U_{F,t}(c)$.*

*A **dynamic utility** on the consumption set C is a function of the form $U : C \to \mathcal{L}$ such that for any spot (F, t), a spot-(F, t) utility $U_{F,t} : C \to \mathbb{R}$ is well-defined by letting $U_{F,t}(c) = U(c)(F, t)$, $c \in C$.*

We interpret the condition $U_{F,t}(a) > U_{F,t}(b)$ as stating that at spot (F, t), the agent prefers to continue with plan a rather than plan b, whereas $U_{F,t}(a) = U_{F,t}(b)$ indicates indifference between the two plans, again from the perspective of spot (F, t). The assumption of the irrelevance of past or unrealized consumption states that the value $U_{F,t}(c)$ depends on c only through its restriction on the subtree rooted at (F, t). Given this assumption, we extend the notation by writing

$$U_{F,t}(c1_{F \times \{t,\ldots,T\}}) = U_{F,t}(c), \quad c \in C, \quad \text{even if } 0 \notin (\ell, \infty).$$

Given a dynamic utility U, we refer to $U(c)$ as the **utility process** of the consumption plan c, and we write either $U(c)(F, t)$ or $U_{F,t}(c)$ for its value at spot (F, t). We also write $U_t(c)$, rather than $U(c)_t$, for the time-t value of $U(c)$.

The dynamic consistency assumption described earlier translates to the following condition, which will be imposed on every dynamic utility U in this chapter.

A1 (Dynamic Consistency). For any spot (F, t) and $c, c + x \in C$,

$$x \in \mathcal{L}_{F,t} \text{ and } U_{F,t}(c + x) > U_{F,t}(c) \quad \text{implies} \quad U_0(c + x) > U_0(c). \quad (6.2)$$

By virtue of the assumed continuity and monotonicity of utilities, condition A1 is equivalent to an apparently stronger version.

Lemma 6.2. *The dynamic consistency condition A1 is satisfied if and only if for any spot (F, t), $c \in C$ and $x \in \mathcal{L}_{F,t}$ such that $c + x \in C$,*

$$U_{F,t}(c + x) \geq U_{F,t}(c) \quad \Longleftrightarrow \quad U_0(c + x) \geq U_0(c).$$

Proof. We show the "only if" part; the converse is immediate. Suppose A1 is satisfied and consider any $c, c + x \in C$ with $x \in \mathcal{L}_{F,t}$. If $U_{F,t}(c + x) \geq U_{F,t}(c)$, then, by the monotonicity of utility, $U_{F,t}(c + x + \varepsilon 1) > U_{F,t}(c)$ for every $\varepsilon > 0$ and therefore $U_0(c + x + \varepsilon 1) > U_0(c)$ for every $\varepsilon > 0$. Letting ε go to zero, we conclude that $U_0(c + x) \geq U_0(c)$. If $U_{F,t}(c) > U_{F,t}(c + x)$, then applying (6.2) with $c + x$ in place of c and $-x$ in place of x, we obtain $U_0(c) > U_0(c + x)$. Therefore, $U_0(c + x) \geq U_0(c)$ implies $U_{F,t}(c + x) \geq U_{F,t}(c)$. ∎

Time-zero optimality of c given a market X means that there exists no $x \in X$ such that $U_0(c + x) > U_0(c)$. The above dynamic consistency assumption on U guarantees that if a plan c is optimal at time zero, then the agent will not strictly prefer to deviate from c at a later spot (F, t),

197

given any dynamic market that is consistent with X, since there can be no $x \in X \cap \mathcal{L}_{F,t}$ such that $U_{F,t}(c + x) > U_{F,t}(c)$. Moreover, if the agent were to switch at spot (F, t) from c to $c + x$ for some $x \in X \cap \mathcal{L}_{F,t}$ such that $U_{F,t}(c + x) = U_{F,t}(c)$, Lemma 6.2 implies that it would also be the case that $U_0(c + x) = U_0(c)$, and therefore $c + x$ would also be optimal from the perspective of time zero.

We list two more assumptions that will be imposed on every dynamic utility, U, in this chapter.

A2 (Irrelevance of Current Consumption for Risk Aversion). For any nonterminal spot (F, t) with immediate successor spots $(F_0, t + 1), \ldots,$ $(F_d, t + 1)$, any vector $z \in (\ell, \infty)^{1+d}$ and any scalars $x, y, \bar{z} \in (\ell, \infty)$,

$$U_{F,t}\left(x 1_{F \times \{t\}} + \sum\nolimits_{i=0}^{d} z_i 1_{F_i \times \{t+1, \ldots, T\}}\right) = U_{F,t}\left(x 1_{F \times \{t\}} + \bar{z} 1_{F \times \{t+1, \ldots, T\}}\right)$$

implies

$$U_{F,t}\left(y 1_{F \times \{t\}} + \sum\nolimits_{i=0}^{d} z_i 1_{F_i \times \{t+1, \ldots, T\}}\right) = U_{F,t}\left(y 1_{F \times \{t\}} + \bar{z} 1_{F \times \{t+1, \ldots, T\}}\right).$$

To interpret the above condition, we think of the consumption level $\bar{z}$ as a conditional certainty equivalent of the contingent consumption levels $z_0, \ldots, z_d$ from the perspective of the single-period uncertainty at spot (F, t). Assumption A2 requires that the value of such a certainty equivalent $\bar{z}$ does not depend on the amount consumed at spot (F, t). In this sense, risk aversion relative to the single-period uncertainty following spot (F, t) is not dependent on consumption at spot (F, t).

A3 (State Independence of Time Preferences). For any time $t < T$, spots (F, t) and (G, t) and scalars $x, y, z \in (\ell, \infty)$, $U_{F,t}(x 1_{F \times \{t\}} + y 1_{F \times \{t+1, \ldots, T\}}) = U_{F,t}(z 1_{F \times \{t, \ldots, T\}})$ implies $U_{G,t}(x 1_{G \times \{t\}} + y 1_{G \times \{t+1, \ldots, T\}}) = U_{G,t}(z 1_{G \times \{t, \ldots, T\}})$.

The last assumption requires that if an agent is indifferent between the deterministic consumption streams $(x, y, \ldots, y)$ and $(z, z, \ldots, z)$ condition-ally on the realization of some time-t spot, the same indifference holds conditionally on the realization of any other time-t spot.

Extending Definition 3.28, we say that two dynamic utilities $U, \bar{U} :$ $C \to \mathcal{L}$ are **ordinally equivalent** if they represent the same preference at every spot or, equivalently, if there exist (strictly) increasing functions

$\varphi_{F,t} : \mathbb{R} \to \mathbb{R}$ such that $U_{F,t} = \varphi_{F,t} \circ \bar{U}_{F,t}$ for every spot (F, t). Assumptions A1, A2 and A3 are **ordinal properties**, in the sense that they hold for a dynamic utility U if and only if they hold for every dynamic utility that is ordinally equivalent to U.

It will be convenient to select ordinally equivalent versions of utilities that are normalized to correspond to the notion of a compensation function of Section 3.5 at every spot. We call a dynamic utility U on the consumption set $(\ell, \infty)^{1+K}$ **normalized** if

$$U(\alpha \mathbf{1}) = \alpha \mathbf{1} \quad \text{for every } \alpha \in (\ell, \infty).$$

With the obvious extension of the language introduced in Section 3.5, the normalized version of a spot-(F, t) utility $U_{F,t}$ is the compensation function of the preference represented by $U_{F,t}$.

Finally, we note that although assumptions A1, A2 and A3 were stated as restrictions on a dynamic utility U, they can equivalently be thought of as ordinal restrictions on a single time-zero utility $U_0 : C \to \mathbb{R}$, by letting, for any spot (F, t),

$$U_{F,t}(c) = U_0(\mathbf{1} + (c-\mathbf{1})\mathbf{1}_{F \times \{t,\dots,T\}}), \quad c \in C.$$

Dynamic consistency (via Lemma 6.2) and the assumed irrelevance of past or unrealized consumption imply that any dynamic utility that is consistent with U_0 is ordinally equivalent to the dynamic utility just defined.

6.2 EXPECTED DISCOUNTED UTILITY

A common type of dynamic utility in the literature is expected discounted utility, whose additive structure provides certain tractability advantages and satisfies last section's assumptions A1–A3. We will argue, however, that expected discounted utility is severely limited as a joint representation of time preferences and risk aversion. This limitation motivates the introduction of recursive utility in the following section.

We fix a reference consumption set C of the form (6.1) and an underlying probability P, with corresponding expectation operator $\mathbb{E}$. **Expected discounted utility** is a dynamic utility $U : C \to \mathcal{L}$ with the representation

$$U_t(c) = \mathbb{E}_t\left[\sum_{s=t}^{T} \frac{D_s}{D_t} u_s(c_s)\right], \quad t = 0, \dots, T, \quad c \in C, \quad (6.3)$$

for some continuous and increasing functions $u_t : (\ell, \infty) \to \mathbb{R}$, $t = 0, \ldots,$ T, and a strictly positive deterministic process[1] D. Confirmation of the validity of conditions A1–A3 is straightforward in this case. In particular, dynamic consistency means that dynamic optimality is characterized as optimality relative to the time-zero utility $U_0 : C \to \mathbb{R}$. The latter takes the additive form of Examples 3.40 and 3.50, which illustrate some tractability advantages of utility additivity. The following example is a first indication of the limitations of expected discounted utility in modeling risk aversion.

Example 6.3. *Suppose the filtration is generated by a process b such that $b_0 = 0$ and the random variables $b_1, \ldots, b_T$ are stochastically independent, with*

$$P[b_t = 0] = P[b_t = 1] = \frac{1}{2}, \quad t = 1, \ldots, T.$$

The consumption plan a is defined in terms of b as

$$a_0 = 0, \quad a_1 = a_2 = \cdots = a_T = b_1.$$

We can think of b as a consumption plan that at the end of each period takes the value one or zero depending on the outcome of a coin toss. Following the first period, a is repeatedly one or zero depending only on the outcome of the first coin toss. From the perspective of time zero, both a and b have an expected payoff of $1/2$ at the end of each period, but plan a is riskier than b, in the sense that it pays out all or nothing based on a single coin toss. If the utility $U_0 : C \to \mathbb{R}$ takes the expected discounted form (6.3), for deterministic D, then

$$U_0(a) = \sum_{t=0}^{T} \frac{D_t}{D_0} \frac{u_t(1) + u_t(0)}{2} = U_0(b).$$

In other words, if we restricted ourselves to expected discounted utility, we would be unable to model an agent who is not indifferent between a and b.

The normalized version, $\bar{U}$, of the dynamic utility (6.3) is

$$\bar{U}_t(c) = \varphi_t^{-1}(U_t(c)), \quad \text{where} \quad \varphi_t(\alpha) = \sum_{s=t}^{T} \frac{D_s}{D_t} u_s(\alpha), \quad \alpha \in (\ell, \infty).$$

---

[1] By passing to the ordinally equivalent utility DU, it can be assumed without loss in generality that $D = 1$. Example 6.4 gives a case where a nonconstant D allows the functions u_t to be time-independent.

In anticipation of our discussion of recursive utility, we note that the process $\bar{U}(c)$ can be computed recursively backward in time as

$$\bar{U}_t(c) = f(t, c_t, \varphi_{t+1}^{-1}(\mathbb{E}_t[\varphi_{t+1}(\bar{U}_{t+1}(c))])), \quad \bar{U}_T(c) = c_T, \quad (6.4)$$

where the function $f : \{0, \dots, T-1\} \times (\ell, \infty)^2 \to (\ell, \infty)$ is defined by

$$f(t, x, y) = \varphi_t^{-1}\left(u_t(x) + \frac{D_{t+1}}{D_t}\varphi_{t+1}(y)\right). \quad (6.5)$$

Example 6.4. *Suppose that for some constant $\beta \in (0, 1)$,*

$$D_t = \beta^t \quad \text{for} \quad t < T \quad \text{and} \quad D_T = \frac{\beta^T}{1-\beta} = \beta^T + \beta^{T+1} + \cdots$$

Suppose also that $u_0 = \cdots = u_T = u$. Time-zero expected discounted utility in this case takes the form

$$U_0(c) = \mathbb{E}\left[\sum_{t=0}^{T-1} \beta^t u(c_t) + \frac{\beta^T}{1-\beta}u(c_T)\right].$$

In the corresponding recursive representation (6.4), $\varphi_t = (1 - \beta)^{-1}u$ for $t < T$, $\varphi_T = u$ and

$$f(t, x, y) = u^{-1}((1 - \beta)u(x) + \beta u(y)). \quad (6.6)$$

Recursion (6.4) suggests that the functions φ_t relate to risk aversion, since, from the perspective of time t, the uncertain continuation utility $\bar{U}_{t+1}(c)$ is reduced to the conditional certainty equivalent

$$\varphi_{t+1}^{-1}(\mathbb{E}_t[\varphi_{t+1}(\bar{U}_{t+1}(c))]).$$

From the expected utility analysis of Theorem 4.14, we know that the above expression, viewed as a utility function over time-$(t + 1)$ payoffs at each time-t spot, represents more risk-averse preferences the more concave φ_{t+1} is. On the other hand, preferences over deterministic plans are entirely determined by the function f, since, for a deterministic consumption plan c, the process $\bar{U}(c)$ is also deterministic and solves the recursion $\bar{U}_t(c) = f(t, c_t, \bar{U}_{t+1}(c))$. The main limitation of expected discounted utility relates to the fact that the risk-aversion functions φ_t are also used in specifying the function f in (6.5). More to the point, we argue that any two agents whose preferences are represented by expected discounted utility relative to a common probability must have identical preferences as long as they have identical preferences over deterministic consumption plans.

201

We call two dynamic utilities, U^1 and U^2, over the common consumption set C, **ordinally equivalent over deterministic plans** if

$$a, b \text{ deterministic } \implies [U^1_{F,t}(a) > U^1_{F,t}(b)$$
$$\iff U^2_{F,t}(a) > U^2_{F,t}(b)], \qquad (6.7)$$

for every $a, b \in C$ and spot (F, t). By Lemma 6.2, if the dynamic utilities U^1 and U^2 are dynamically consistent (that is, they satisfy A1), then they are ordinally equivalent over deterministic plans if and only if the time-zero utilities U^1_0 and U^2_0 have the same property, in the sense that (6.7) holds for $(F, t) = (\Omega, 0)$.

Proposition 6.5. *For each $i \in \{1, 2\}$, suppose $U^i : C \to \mathcal{L}$ is an expected discounted utility with representation*

$$U^i_t(c) = \mathbb{E}_t \left[\sum_{s=t}^T \frac{D^i_s}{D^i_t} u^i_s(c_s) \right], \qquad c \in C.$$

If U^1 and U^2 are ordinally equivalent over deterministic plans, then they are ordinally equivalent.

Proof. The uniqueness statement of Theorem 3.36, applied to the restriction of U^i_0 on the set of deterministic plans, implies that $D^1 u^1 = a D^2 u^2 + b$ for some $a \in \mathbb{R}_{++}$ and deterministic process b. ∎

6.3 RECURSIVE UTILITY

We saw in Proposition 6.5 that for an agent maximizing expected discounted utility under a given probability, attitude toward risk is entirely determined by the agent's preferences over deterministic plans. Recursive utility overcomes this limitation by retaining a backward recursion of the type (6.4), but without the ad hoc relationship (6.5) required for additivity. In this section we define recursive utility and we show that a dynamic utility is recursive utility if and only if it satisfies conditions A1–A3. In the following section we will see how a recursive utility can be made more or less risk averse without changing its ranking of deterministic consumption plans.

We fix a reference consumption set $C = (\ell, \infty)^{1+K}$, where $\ell \in [-\infty, 1)$, on which we will define recursive utility. For this purpose, we introduce some preliminary notation and terminology. We assume throughout that utilities are normalized and we therefore make normalization part of the definitions that follow. We will define a recursive utility U so that for any deterministic consumption plan c in C, the utility process $U(c)$ is also deterministic and is computed backward in time by the recursion

$$U_t(c) = f(t, c_t, U_{t+1}(c)), \quad U_T(c) = c_T, \quad (c \text{ deterministic}) \quad (6.8)$$

where the function f is an aggregator, in the following formal sense.

Definition 6.6. *An **aggregator** is a function of the form $f : \{0, \ldots, T-1\} \times (\ell, \infty)^2 \to (\ell, \infty)$, whose sections $f(t, \cdot) : (\ell, \infty)^2 \to (\ell, \infty)$ are increasing continuous functions that satisfy*

$$f(t, \alpha, \alpha) = \alpha \quad \text{for every} \quad \alpha \in (\ell, \infty). \quad (6.9)$$

For a nondeterministic consumption plan c, the backward recursion (6.8) defining recursive utility will be modified by collapsing $U_{t+1}(c)$ to its conditional certainty equivalent, $\upsilon_t(U_{t+1}(c))$, given time-t information. The notion of a conditional certainty equivalent is defined formally below, using the notation

$$L_t = \{z : z \text{ is an } (\ell, \infty)\text{-valued } \mathcal{F}_t\text{-measurable random variable}\}.$$

Definition 6.7. *A **conditional certainty equivalent** (**conditional CE**) is a mapping υ that assigns to every time $t \in \{0, \ldots, T-1\}$ a continuous function of the form $\upsilon_t : L_{t+1} \to L_t$ such that*

$$\upsilon_t(\alpha 1) = \alpha \quad \text{for every} \quad \alpha \in (\ell, \infty), \quad (6.10)$$

and for every $x, y \in L_{t+1}$ and spot (F, t),

$$x 1_F = y 1_F \implies \upsilon_t(x) 1_F = \upsilon_t(y) 1_F, \quad \text{and}$$
$$x 1_F \geq y 1_F \neq x 1_F \implies \upsilon_t(x) 1_F > \upsilon_t(y) 1_F.$$

The last two conditions mean that for any $z \in L_{t+1}$, the value $\upsilon_t(z)$ at spot (F, t), which we denote $\upsilon_{F,t}(z)$, is an increasing function of the restriction of z on F. Given this fact, we extend the notation by writing

$$\upsilon_{F,t}(z 1_F) = \upsilon_{F,t}(z), \quad z \in L_{t+1}, \quad \text{even if } 0 \notin (\ell, \infty).$$

If $(F_0, t+1), \ldots, (F_d, t+1)$ denote the immediate successor spots of (F, t), then the value $\upsilon_{F,t}(z)$ depends on z through the vector $(z_0, \ldots, z_d) \in (\ell, \infty)^{1+d}$, where $z 1_F = \sum_{i=0}^{d} z_i 1_{F_i}$, and therefore one can equivalently

203

think of $\upsilon_{F,t}$ as a continuous increasing function from $(\ell, \infty)^{1+d}$ to (ℓ, ∞) satisfying $\upsilon_{F,t}(\alpha \mathbf{1}) = \alpha$ for all $\alpha \in (\ell, \infty)$.

Definition 6.8. **Recursive utility** *is any dynamic utility* $U : C \to \mathcal{L}$ *for which there exists a pair of an aggregator* f *and a conditional CE* υ *such that for every* $c \in C$, *the process* $U(c)$ *is computed by the backward recursion*

$$U_t(c) = f(t, c_t, \upsilon_t(U_{t+1}(c))), \quad t = 0, \ldots, T-1; \quad U_T(c) = c_T. \quad (6.11)$$

Kreps-Porteus utility *is any recursive utility whose conditional CE is of the form*

$$\upsilon_t(\cdot) = u^{-1}(\mathbb{E}_t[u(\cdot)]), \quad (6.12)$$

for some increasing and continuous function $u : (\ell, \infty) \to \mathbb{R}$ *and expectation operator* $\mathbb{E}$ *relative to some strictly positive probability* P.

We can equivalently express the recursive step in (6.11) as

$$U_{F,t}(c) = f\left(t, c(F, t), \upsilon_{F,t}\left(\sum_{i=0}^{d} U_{F_i, t+1}(c)1_{F_i}\right)\right), \quad (6.13)$$

where $(F_0, t+1), \ldots, (F_d, t+1)$ are the immediate successor spots of (F, t). The recursive step first collapses the $1 + d$ utility values $U_{F_i, t+1}(c)$ to a single spot-(F, t) certainty equivalent and then combines the latter with the spot-(F, t) consumption to compute the spot-(F, t) utility value. The recursion begins with the terminal values $U_T(c) = c_T$, implied by normalization, and proceeds backward on the information tree to determine the entire adapted process $U(c)$. For Kreps-Porteus utility, which will be assumed in our later applications, the conditional CE term in (6.13) takes the form

$$\upsilon_{F,t}\left(\sum_{i=0}^{d} U_{F_i, t+1}(c)1_{F_i}\right) = u^{-1}\left(\sum_{i=0}^{d} u(U_{F_i, t+1}(c))P[F_i \mid F]\right).$$

A characterization of recursive utility follows (with a variant given in Exercise 1). As explained at the end of Section 6.1, this characterization can be expressed entirely in terms of ordinal properties of the time-zero utility U_0. An ordinal characterization of Kreps-Porteus utility can be obtained by combining the following construction with the expected-utility characterization of Section 4.2.

Proposition 6.9. *A normalized dynamic utility* U *is recursive utility if and only if it satisfies conditions* A1, A2 *and* A3.

Proof. We assume that U is a normalized dynamic utility satisfying A1–A3 and we construct a recursive representation of U. The converse claim is immediate.

Step 1 (construction of the aggregator). For any time $t < T$, we fix an arbitrary reference spot (F, t), and we define the increasing continuous function $f(t, \cdot) : (\ell, \infty)^2 \to \mathbb{R}$ by letting, for any $x, y \in (\ell, \infty)$,

$$f(t, x, y) = U_{F,t}(f(t, x, y)\mathbf{1}) = U_{F,t}(x\mathbf{1}_{F \times \{t\}} + y\mathbf{1}_{F \times \{t+1, \ldots, T\}}), \quad (6.14)$$

where the first equality follows from the assumption that U is normalized. By assumption A3, the above construction does not depend on the choice of the reference time-t spot (F, t). The monotonicity and continuity of $U_{F,t}$ implies the respective properties for $f(t, \cdot)$, while the assumption that U is normalized implies that $f(t, x, x) = x$ for all $x \in (\ell, \infty)$. Therefore, f is an aggregator.

Step 2 (construction of the conditional CE). Given any nonterminal spot (F, t) and vector $z \in L_{t+1}$, we construct the conditional CE value $v_{F,t}(z)$ as follows. Let $(F_0, t+1), \ldots, (F_d, t+1)$ be the immediate successor spots of (F, t), and let $z_{\max} = \max_i z_i$ and $z_{\min} = \min_i z_i$. Fixing any $x \in (\ell, \infty)$, utility monotonicity and the aggregator construction in (6.14) imply that

$$f(t, x, z_{\max}) \geq U_{F,t}\left(x\mathbf{1}_{F \times \{t\}} + \sum_{i=0}^{d} z_i \mathbf{1}_{F_i \times \{t+1, \ldots, T\}}\right) \geq f(t, x, z_{\min}).$$

Using the fact that $f(t, x, \cdot)$ is increasing and continuous, we define $v_{F,t}(z)$ as the unique value such that

$$f(t, x, v_{F,t}(z)) = U_{F,t}\left(x\mathbf{1}_{F \times \{t\}} + \sum_{i=0}^{d} z_i \mathbf{1}_{F_i \times \{t+1, \ldots, T\}}\right). \quad (6.15)$$

Assumption A2 with equations (6.14) imply that the value $v_{F,t}(z)$ does not depend on the choice of x. The normalization, continuity and monotonicity properties of $v_{F,t}$ follow from the respective properties of the aggregator f and the utility $U_{F,t}$.

Step 3 (verification of recursiveness). Given any consumption plan c in C, we verify recursion (6.11). Consider a nonterminal spot (F, t)

with immediate successor spots $(F_0, t+1), \ldots, (F_d, t+1)$, and let

$$x_i = U_{F_i, t+1}(c) 1_{F_i \times \{t+1, \ldots, T\}} - c 1_{F_i \times \{t+1, \ldots, T\}}, \quad i = 0, \ldots, d.$$

Adding x_i to c replaces the values of c on the subtree rooted at $(F_i, t+1)$ with the constant value $U_{F_i, t+1}(c)$. We show inductively that

$$U_{F,t}(c) = U_{F,t}\left(c + \sum_{i=0}^{k} x_i\right), \quad k = 0, 1, \ldots, d. \tag{6.16}$$

The root of the induction is the identity $U_{F,t}(c) = U_{F,t}(c)$. For the inductive step, we assume that $U_{F,t}(c) = U_{F,t}(b)$, where $b = c + \sum_{i=0}^{k-1} x_i$, with $b = c$ for $k = 0$. The utility normalization implies that $U_{F_k, t+1}(c) = U_{F_k, t+1}(c + x_k)$. Since c equals b on the subtree rooted at $(F_k, t+1)$, we also have $U_{F_k, t+1}(b) = U_{F_k, t+1}(b + x_k)$. By Lemma 6.2, the last condition implies $U_0(b) = U_0(b + x_k)$, which in turn implies that $U_{F,t}(b) = U_{F,t}(b + x_k)$. The last equation combined with the inductive hypothesis gives $U_{F,t}(c) = U_{F,t}(b + x_k)$, proving (6.16).

Equation (6.16) for $k = d$, combined with equation (6.15), results in recursion (6.13), which is a restatement of (6.11). ∎

6.4 BASIC PROPERTIES OF RECURSIVE UTILITY

This section establishes some basic properties of recursive utility. The first subsection discusses comparative risk aversion, showing how, unlike expected discounted utility, recursive utility can be made more or less risk averse without changing the utility values for deterministic plans. The second subsection computes the gradient of a smooth recursive utility. The third and last subsection gives a result on the (strict) concavity of recursive utility.

6.4.1 Comparative Risk Aversion

To discuss how recursive utility overcomes the limitation of expected discounted utility stated in Proposition 6.5, we introduce a notion of comparative risk aversion. We will not attempt to compare risk aversion for utilities that do not agree on the ranking of deterministic plans, since in this case a preference for smoothing across spots may not admit a satisfactory decomposition as time preferences and attitudes toward risk. We therefore consider two dynamic utilities, U^1 and U^2, on a common consumption set C, that are ordinally equivalent over deterministic plans. We say that U^1 is **more risk averse** than U^2 if for every $b, c \in C$ and spot (F, t),

$$b \text{ deterministic} \implies [U^2_{F,t}(b) > U^2_{F,t}(c) \implies U^1_{F,t}(b) > U^1_{F,t}(c)]. \quad (6.17)$$

An application of Lemma 6.2 shows that provided U^1 and U^2 are dynamically consistent (in that they satisfy A1), U^1 is more risk averse than U^2 if and only if the time-zero utility U^1_0 is more risk averse than the time-zero utility U^2_0, in the sense that (6.17) is satisfied for $(F, t) = (\Omega, 0)$ only.

One can easily check that if U^1 and U^2 are recursive utilities, then they are ordinally equivalent over deterministic plans if and only if they share the same aggregator. Given a common aggregator, comparative risk aversion is characterized in terms of the conditional CE as follows.

Proposition 6.10. *Suppose that for each $i \in \{1, 2\}$, $U^i : C \to \mathcal{L}$ is a recursive utility with aggregator f (common to both utilities) and conditional CE υ^i. Then U^1 is more risk averse than U^2 if and only if*

$$\upsilon^1_{F,t} \leq \upsilon^2_{F,t} \quad \text{for every nonterminal spot } (F, t). \quad (6.18)$$

Suppose further that each U^i is Kreps-Porteus utility, with conditional CE $\upsilon^i_t = u_i^{-1} \mathbb{E}_t u_i$. Then U^1 is more risk averse than U^2 if and only if there exists a concave function $\phi : \{u_2(x) : x \in (\ell, \infty)\} \to \mathbb{R}$ such that $u_1 = \phi \circ u_2$.

Proof. Since the aggregator f is common to the two utilities, $U^1(b) = U^2(b)$ for any deterministic plan b in C. Given this observation and the normalization $U^i(\alpha 1) = \alpha 1$ for any $\alpha \in (\ell, \infty)$, it follows that U^1 is more risk averse than U^2 if and only if $U^1(c) \leq U^2(c)$ for every $c \in C$.

Suppose condition (6.18) is satisfied. Given any c, we argue by a backward induction that $U^1(c) \leq U^2(c)$. At the terminal time, we have $U^1_T(c) = U^2_T(c) = c_T$. For the inductive step, we assume that $U^1_{t+1}(c) \leq U^2_{t+1}(c)$, and we use the utility recursion and condition (6.18) to infer

$$U^1_t(c) = f(t, c_t, \upsilon^1_t(U^1_{t+1})) \leq f(t, c_t, \upsilon^1_t(U^2_{t+1}))$$
$$\leq f(t, c_t, \upsilon^2_t(U^2_{t+1})) = U^2_t(c).$$

Conversely, suppose $U^1 \leq U^2$ and consider any spot (F, t) with immediate successor spots $(F_i, t+1)$, $i = 0, \ldots, d$. Given any vector

$z \in (\ell, \infty)^{1+d}$, let c be the consumption plan that is equal to z_i on $F_i \times \{t+1, \ldots, T\}$ for $i = 0, \ldots, d$ and is equal to one at every other spot. Noting that $U_{F_i, t+1}(c) = z_i$, the utility recursion implies that $U_{F,t}^i(c) = f(t, 1, v_{F,t}^i(z))$ and therefore $v_{F,t}^1(z) \leq v_{F,t}^2(z)$. This proves condition (6.18).

Finally, the claim for the case of Kreps-Porteus utility follows by combining Proposition 4.4 and Theorem 4.14 to characterize condition (6.18). ∎

6.4.2 Utility Gradient Density

As noted earlier, because of our assumption of dynamically consistent markets and preferences, the optimality and equilibrium theory of Chapter 3 applies wholesale to this chapter's setting. The relationship between utility gradients and individual or allocational optimality discussed in the last two sections of Chapter 3 motivates this section's remaining results: the computation of the utility gradient of recursive utility, and a proposition providing sufficient conditions for the (strict) concavity of recursive utility. These results will be used in later sections, in conjunction with scale- or translation-invariance structure, to formulate a more detailed theory of equilibrium state pricing and optimal consumption and portfolio choice.

We take as given a strictly positive probability P, with expectation operator $\mathbb{E}$, and we consider a normalized dynamic utility U on the consumption set $C = (\ell, \infty)^{1+K}$, where $\ell \in [-\infty, 1)$. We define the gradient density of U_0 to correspond to the gradient of U_0 (as defined in Section A.9) relative to the inner product

$$(x \mid y) = \mathbb{E}\left[\sum_{t=0}^{T} x_t y_t\right], \quad x, y \in \mathcal{L}.$$

Definition 6.11. *A **gradient density** of the time-zero utility U_0 at $c \in C$ is an adapted process π such that*

$$\lim_{\alpha \downarrow 0} \frac{U_0(c + \alpha x) - U_0(c)}{\alpha} = (\pi \mid x), \quad \text{for all } x \in \mathcal{L}.$$

In the notation of Chapter 3, $\nabla U_0(c)$ denotes the gradient of U_0 at c relative to the Euclidean inner product. For any spot (F, t), the quantity $\pi(F, t)P(F)$ is the partial derivative of U_0 at c with respect to consumption at spot (F, t), and therefore

$$\nabla U_0(c) \cdot x = (\pi \mid x), \quad x \in \mathcal{L}.$$

Taking a reference market as given, it follows that $\nabla U_0(c)$ is a state-price vector if and only if π is a state-price density (SPD). Based on these observations, the results of the last two sections of Chapter 3 can be restated in a straightforward manner in terms of utility gradient densities. For example, Proposition 3.39 becomes:

Proposition 6.12. *Given any $c \in C$, suppose that the gradient density π of U_0 at c exists and is strictly positive. If c is optimal, then π is an SPD. Conversely, if U is concave and π is an SPD, then c is optimal.*

Assuming that U is recursive utility with (sufficiently smooth) aggregator f and conditional CE υ, we wish to derive a formula for the utility gradient density in terms of the pair (f, υ). For this purpose, we define the derivative of the conditional CE υ. We let $L(\mathcal{F}_t)$ denote the set of all $\mathcal{F}_t$-measurable random variables.

Definition 6.13. *The **derivative** of the conditional CE υ is a mapping κ that assigns to each pair of a time $t \in \{1, \ldots, T\}$ and (ℓ, ∞)-valued random variable $z \in L(\mathcal{F}_t)$ a random variable $\kappa_t(z) \in L(\mathcal{F}_t)$ with the following property: Given any $\varepsilon > 0$, there exists some $\delta > 0$ such that for every $h \in L(\mathcal{F}_t)$,*

$$\mathbb{E}_{t-1}[h^2] < \delta \implies \left| \upsilon_{t-1}(z+h) - \upsilon_{t-1}(z) - \mathbb{E}_{t-1}[\kappa_t(z)h] \right| < \varepsilon \sqrt{\mathbb{E}_{t-1}[h^2]}.$$

To express the derivative κ more concretely, consider any spot $(F, t-1)$ with immediate successor spots $(F_0, t), \ldots, (F_d, t)$, and let $\kappa_{F_i, t}(z)$ be the value of $\kappa_t(z)$ at spot (F_i, t). Viewing $\upsilon_{F, t-1}$ as a real-valued function on $(\ell, \infty)^{1+d}$, the vector $(\kappa_{F_i, t}(z)P[F_i \mid F])_{i=0,\ldots,d}$ is the derivative of $\upsilon_{F, t-1}$ at z in the usual sense. In particular, $\kappa_{F_i, t}(z)P[F_i \mid F]$ is the partial derivative of $\upsilon_{F, t-1}$ at z with respect to the value of z on the event F_i :

$$\kappa_{F_i, t}(z)P[F_i \mid F] = \frac{\partial \upsilon_{F, t-1}(\sum_{i=0}^{d} z_i 1_{F_i})}{\partial z_i}, \quad (z_0, \ldots, z_d) \in (\ell, \infty)^{1+d}.$$

Conversely, if the above partial derivatives exist and are continuous, then the conditional CE derivative exists.

Example 6.14. *Suppose the conditional CE υ takes the form $\upsilon_t = u^{-1} \mathbb{E}_t u$ for some continuously differentiable function $u : (\ell, \infty) \to \mathbb{R}$, with u' denoting* *its derivative. Then the derivative κ of υ exists and is given by*

$$\kappa_t(z) = \frac{u'(z)}{u'(\upsilon_{t-1}(z))}.$$

The gradient density of a recursive utility is computed in the following proposition, where f_c and f_υ denote the partial derivatives of the aggregator f with respect to its consumption and conditional CE arguments, respectively.

Proposition 6.15. *Suppose $U : C \to \mathcal{L}$ is a recursive utility with aggregator f and conditional CE υ. Suppose also that $f(t, \cdot)$ is differentiable for every time $t < T$ and υ has derivative κ. Given any reference plan $c \in C$, let the processes λ and $\mathcal{E}$ be defined by*

$$\lambda_t = f_c(t, c_t, \upsilon_t(U_{t+1}(c))), \quad t < T, \quad \lambda_T = 1, \tag{6.19}$$

$$\mathcal{E}_t = \prod_{s=1}^{t} f_\upsilon(s-1, c_{s-1}, \upsilon_{s-1}(U_s(c))) \, \kappa_s(U_s(c)), \quad t > 0, \quad \mathcal{E}_0 = 1. \tag{6.20}$$

Then for any adapted process x and time t,

$$\lim_{\alpha \downarrow 0} \frac{U_t(c + \alpha x) - U_t(c)}{\alpha} = \mathbb{E}_t \left[\sum_{s=t}^{T} \frac{\mathcal{E}_s}{\mathcal{E}_t} \lambda_s x_s \right]. \tag{6.21}$$

In particular, the process $\pi = \mathcal{E}\lambda$ is the gradient density of U_0 at c.

Proof. Fixing any $x \in \mathbb{R}^{1+K}$, we define the notation

$$\phi_t(\alpha) = U_t(c + \alpha x), \quad \text{for all sufficiently small } \alpha \in \mathbb{R}.$$

The left-hand side in (6.21) defines the derivative $\phi_t'(0)$. Differentiating at $\alpha = 0$ the utility recursion

$$\phi_t(\alpha) = f(t, c_t + \alpha x_t, \upsilon_t(\phi_{t+1}(\alpha)))$$

and using the chain rule of differentiation yields

$$\phi_t'(0) = \lambda_t x_t + f_\upsilon(t, c_t, \upsilon_t(U_{t+1}(c))) \, \mathbb{E}_t[\kappa_{t+1}(\phi_{t+1}(0)) \, \phi_{t+1}'(0)].$$

This is a linear backward recursion for $\phi_t'(0)$, starting with the terminal value $\phi_T'(0) = x_T$. Letting $V_t = \phi_t'(0)$ and $\delta_t = \lambda_t x_t$, the recursion can be restated as

$$V_t = \delta_t + \frac{1}{\mathcal{E}_t} E_t[\mathcal{E}_{t+1} V_{t+1}].$$

By Proposition 5.27, the pair $(P, \mathcal{E})$ prices the contract (δ, V) (in the sense of Definition 5.25), a condition that can be restated as equation (6.21). ∎

Remark 6.16. *The process* λ *defined in* (6.19) *can be interpreted as a marginal-value-of-wealth process. Suppose, for simplicity, that U is concave and therefore the utility gradient density* π *at c is strictly positive. (These conditions will be satisfied in our applications.) Consider the family of problems*

$$J_0(\delta) = \max\left\{ U_0(c + x) : \frac{1}{\pi_0}(\pi \mid x) \le \delta, \ c + x \in C \right\}, \quad \delta \in \mathbb{R}.$$

Our assumptions imply that $J_0(0) = U_0(c)$. *We interpret the latter as the optimal utility level of an agent who initially finds the consumption plan c optimal given the complete market that is orthogonal to* π. *Suppose now that this agent is incrementally endowed with the cash flow* $\delta 1_{\Omega \times \{0\}}$, *where* δ *is a small scalar. If the agent were to reoptimize given the new time-zero wealth, then the agent would achieve the optimal utility level* $J_0(\delta)$. *By Proposition 3.41, we can approximate the value increment* $J_0(\delta) - J_0(0)$ *with the amount*

$$J_0'(0)\,\delta = (\pi \mid \delta 1_{\Omega \times \{0\}}) = \lambda_0\,\delta,$$

where we have used the utility gradient density formula $\pi = \mathcal{E}\lambda$ *and the fact that* $\mathcal{E}_0 = 1$. *In this sense,* λ_0 *represents the time-zero marginal value of wealth. The same argument can be applied with any other spot* (F, t) *in place of time zero, using the conditional gradient density calculation* (6.21), *to obtain an interpretation of* $\lambda(F, t)$ *as the marginal value of spot-*(F, t) *wealth from the perspective of spot* (F, t).

6.4.3 Concavity

In using Proposition 6.12 to verify optimality, we need a way of verifying the concavity of recursive utility in terms of properties of the aggregator and conditional CE. We conclude this section with such a result that is sufficient for our later applications. In fact, in the equilibrium pricing and optimal consumption/portfolio theory to follow, we are going to assume strict concavity of the utility, which will imply the uniqueness of an optimum. We therefore state the proposition below in terms of strict concavity, although the result and its proof remain valid if the "strict" qualification is dropped.

A real-valued function F on some convex set is **strictly concave** if for any x, y in the domain of F,

$$x \neq y \text{ and } p \in (0, 1) \quad \text{implies}$$
$$F(px + (1-p)y) > pF(x) + (1-p)F(y).$$

A dynamic utility U is **strictly concave** if $U_{F,t}$ is strictly concave as a function on $C \cap \mathcal{L}_{F,t}$ for every nonterminal spot (F, t). An aggregator f is **strictly concave** if the function $f(t, \cdot) : (\ell, \infty)^2 \to \mathbb{R}$ is strictly concave for every time $t < T$. A conditional CE υ is **strictly concave** if $\upsilon_{F,t}$ is a strictly concave function for every nonterminal spot (F, t).

Proposition 6.17. *Suppose U is recursive utility with aggregator f and conditional CE υ. If f and υ are strictly concave, then U is strictly concave.*

Proof. Given any plans c^0, c^1 in the domain of U and any $p \in (0, 1)$, let $c^p = pc^1 + (1-p)c^0$. We first show by a backward recursion that for every time $t > 0$,

$$U_t(c^p) \geq pU_t(c^1) + (1-p)U_t(c^0). \tag{6.22}$$

By the utility normalization, (6.22) holds as an equality for $t = T$. For the recursive step, we show (6.22) for any $t < T$, assuming that it is valid with $t + 1$ in place of t:

$$U_t(c^p) = f(t, c_t^p, \upsilon_t(U_{t+1}(c^p)))$$
$$\geq f(t, c_t^p, \upsilon_t(pU_{t+1}(c^1) + (1-p)U_{t+1}(c^0)))$$
$$\geq f(t, c_t^p, p\upsilon_t(U_{t+1}(c^1)) + (1-p)\upsilon_t(U_{t+1}(c^0)))$$
$$\geq pU_t(c^1) + (1-p)U_t(c^0).$$

This proves that U is concave, given only the concavity of f and υ. To verify strict concavity of U_0, suppose further that $c^0 \neq c^1$. Then at some spot along the above backward recursion, at least one of the last two inequalities is strict, since either the conditional CE or the aggregator is applied to a convex combination of nonequal arguments. This strict inequality then propagates backward to time zero, confirming that $U_0(c^p) > p U_0(c^1) + (1-p) U_0(c^0)$. The same argument applies on the subtree rooted at any nonterminal spot (F, t), implying that $U_{F,t}$ is also strictly concave. ∎

6.5 SCALE / TRANSLATION INVARIANCE

This section characterizes scale- or translation-invariant Kreps-Porteus utility, which will play a central role in the theory of equilibrium pricing and optimal consumption/portfolio choice to follow. We will show that a (normalized) recursive utility is scale invariant if and only if both its aggregator and conditional CE are homogeneous of degree one. As a consequence, the conditional CE of a scale-invariant Kreps-Porteus utility must be of a power or logarithmic form. Analogous results hold for translation-invariant recursive utility, with quasilinearity with respect to **1** taking the role of homogeneity of degree one, and the conditional CE in the Kreps-Porteus case assuming an exponential form.

In the interest of readability, we write c to denote either a consumption plan or a scalar dummy variable representing a consumption value. Similarly, v can denote either a conditional CE or a dummy variable representing a conditional CE value. Given an aggregator $f(t, c, v)$, we write f_c and f_v to denote the partial derivatives of f with respect to c and v, respectively. Finally, we assume that Ω contains at least two states.

6.5.1 Scale-Invariant Kreps-Porteus Utility

We consider a dynamic utility U on the consumption set

$$C = \mathcal{L}_{++} = (0, \infty)^{1+K}.$$

We define U to be **scale invariant (SI)** if for any spot (F, t), the corresponding utility $U_{F,t} : C \to \mathbb{R}$ represents an SI preference (Definition 3.22). Assuming dynamic consistency (A1), U is SI if and only if the time-zero utility U_0 represents an SI preference. From the discussion of Section 3.5.1, we know that if U is also assumed to be normalized, then U

is SI if and only if it is **homogeneous of degree one**, meaning that for any spot (F, t) and plan c,

$$U_{F,t}(sc) = sU_{F,t}(c), \quad \text{for all } s \in (0, \infty).$$

Since we have made normalization part of the definition of recursive utility, the terms "scale invariant" and "homogeneous of degree one" are synonymous when applied to recursive utility.

In the following proposition, we characterize every SI Kreps-Porteus utility, given only a minor regularity assumption. Its proof first characterizes every SI recursive utility as one whose aggregator and conditional CE are homogeneous of degree one. For Kreps-Porteus utility, the conditional CE takes the form $v_t = u^{-1}\mathbb{E}_t u$ for a function $u : (0, \infty) \to \mathbb{R}$, in which case (under minor regularity on u) v is homogeneous of degree one if and only if u takes a power or logarithmic form. We call the function $\tilde{u} : (0, \infty) \to \mathbb{R}$ a **positive affine transformation** of the function $u : (0, \infty) \to \mathbb{R}$ if there exist constants $a \in (0, \infty)$ and $b \in \mathbb{R}$ such that $\tilde{u} = au + b$, in which case it is clear that $v_t = \tilde{u}^{-1}\mathbb{E}_t\tilde{u}$. Conversely, by Theorem 4.10, if $u^{-1}\mathbb{E}_t u = \tilde{u}^{-1}\mathbb{E}_t\tilde{u}$, then $\tilde{u}$ is a positive affine transformation of u.

Proposition 6.18. *Suppose U is a Kreps-Porteus utility on the consumption set $\mathcal{L}_{++}$ with aggregator f and conditional CE $v_t = u^{-1}\mathbb{E}_t u$, where the function $u : (0, \infty) \to \mathbb{R}$ is continuously differentiable on some (arbitrarily small) interval. Then U is homogeneous of degree one if and only if the following two conditions are satisfied:*

1. *The aggregator f is homogeneous of degree one; that is, there exists a function $g : \{0, \ldots, T-1\} \times (0, \infty) \to (0, \infty)$ such that*

$$f(t, c, v) = vg\left(t, \frac{c}{v}\right), \quad \text{for all } c, v \in (0, \infty). \quad (6.23)$$

2. *There exists a constant $\gamma \in \mathbb{R}$ such that u is given, up to a positive affine transformation, by*

$$u(x) = \frac{x^{1-\gamma} - 1}{1 - \gamma} \quad (\text{where } u(x) = \log(x) \text{ if } \gamma = 1). \quad (6.24)$$

Proof. Sufficiency of the above conditions for homogeneity is immediate. Conversely, suppose U is homogeneous of degree one. Equation (6.14) implies that f must also be homogeneous of degree one.

Similarly, we show that the conditional CE is homogeneous of degree one; that is, for every spot (F, t) with immediate successors $(F_0, t+1), \ldots, (F_d, t+1)$ and any $z \in (0, \infty)^{1+d}$,

$$\upsilon_{F,t}(sz) = s\upsilon_{F,t}(z), \quad s \in (0, \infty). \tag{6.25}$$

The argument in Step 2 of the proof of Proposition 6.9 characterizes $\upsilon_{F,t}(z)$ as the unique solution to

$$U_{F,t}(x1_{F\times\{t\}} + \upsilon_{F,t}(z)1_{F\times\{t+1,\ldots,T\}})$$
$$= U_{F,t}\left(x1_{F\times\{t\}} + \sum\nolimits_{i=0}^{d} z_i 1_{F_i\times\{t+1,\ldots,T\}}\right).$$

Recall that by A2, the validity of the preceding equation is independent of the choice of the spot-(F, t) consumption x. Multiplying through by s, the homogeneity of U results in

$$U_{F,t}(sx1_{F\times\{t\}} + s\upsilon_{F,t}(z)1_{F\times\{t+1,\ldots,T\}})$$
$$= U_{F,t}\left(sx1_{F\times\{t\}} + \sum\nolimits_{i=1}^{d} sz_i 1_{F_i\times\{t+1,\ldots,T\}}\right),$$

which implies (6.25).

The homogeneity of f and υ characterizes homogeneous recursive utility in general. In the Kreps-Porteus case considered here, an application of Theorem 3.37 (as restated in Theorem 4.23) results in the specific parameterization of the conditional CE. ∎

In the above representation of SI Kreps-Porteus utility, we refer to g as a **proportional aggregator** and to γ as a **coefficient of relative risk aversion**. Specializing our earlier discussion on comparative risk aversion for recursive utility, we note that for an SI recursive utility U, a proportional aggregator determines and is determined by preferences over deterministic consumption plans. Given the proportional aggregator g, the utility U is more risk averse the higher the value of γ.

Scale invariance narrows the functional form of the conditional CE of Kreps-Porteus utility to a single-parameter family, but places a much weaker restriction on the form of the proportional aggregator g. Any continuous increasing $g(t, \cdot) : (0, \infty) \to (0, \infty)$ satisfying $g(t, 1) = 1$ define an aggregator through (6.23), provided the latter is increasing in the CE argument. Assuming differentiability, the last restriction is equivalent to the requirement that the elasticity functions $d \log g(t, x)/d \log x$ are valued in

$(0, 1)$. A common parameterization of the proportional aggregator is given in the following example, which includes expected discounted power or logarithmic utility as a special case.

Example 6.19 (Epstein-Zin-Weil Utility). *The Epstein-Zin-Weil specification of Kreps-Porteus utility postulates the conditional CE* $v_t = u^{-1}\mathbb{E}_t u$, *where* $u : (0, \infty) \to \mathbb{R}$ *is given by (6.24) for some scalar* γ, *and the aggregator*

$$f(t, c, v) = v^{-1}((1 - \beta)v(c) + \beta v(v)), \quad \text{where } v(x) = \frac{x^{1-\delta} - 1}{1 - \delta},$$

for some $\beta \in (0, 1)$ *and* $\delta \in \mathbb{R}$ *(with* $v(x) = \log(x)$ *if* $\delta = 1$*). A simple calculation shows that this aggregator is of the homogeneous form (6.23), with proportional aggregator*

$$g(t, x) = \begin{cases} ((1 - \beta)x^{1-\delta} + \beta)^{1/(1-\delta)}, & \text{if } \delta \neq 1; \\ x^{1-\beta}, & \text{if } \delta = 1. \end{cases}$$

(Note that $x^{1-\beta}$ *is the limit of* $((1 - \beta)x^{1-\delta} + \beta)^{1/(1-\delta)}$ *as* $\delta \to 1$*.) If* $\gamma = \delta$, *then the above specification reduces to the expected discounted utility of Example 6.4, with u given in (6.24). The parameters* (β, δ) *are determined by the utility of deterministic plans. On the other hand, given* (β, δ), *increasing* γ *increases risk aversion. The fact that additivity requires that* $\gamma = \delta$ *illustrates once again the ad hoc restriction on risk aversion imposed by additivity. The constant* $1/\delta$ *in the Epstein-Zin-Weil specification is known in the literature as the **elasticity of intertemporal substitution (EIS)**, reflecting a calculation that is discussed in Exercise 5.*

The following result refines Proposition 6.17 for the case of SI Kreps-Porteus utility.

Proposition 6.20. *Suppose U is scale-invariant Kreps-Porteus utility with proportional aggregator g and coefficient of relative risk aversion* γ. *If g is strictly concave and* $\gamma > 0$, *then U is strictly concave.*

Proof. By Proposition 6.17, strict concavity of U follows if we show strict concavity of the corresponding aggregator f and conditional CE v, defined in (6.23) and (6.24), respectively.

Strict concavity of the aggregator. Suppose g is strictly concave and consider any pair of distinct points (c^1, v^1) and (c^2, v^2) in $(0, \infty)^2$. For any time $t < T$, strict concavity of $g(t, \cdot)$ implies

$$g\left(t, \frac{c^1 + c^2}{v^1 + v^2}\right) > \frac{v^1}{v^1 + v^2} g\left(t, \frac{c^1}{v^1}\right) + \frac{v^2}{v^1 + v^2} g\left(t, \frac{c^2}{v^2}\right).$$

Multiplying through by $v^1 + v^2$ shows that

$$f(t, c^1 + c^2, v^1 + v^2) > f(t, c^1, v^1) + f(t, c^2, v^2).$$

Since $f(t, \cdot)$ is homogeneous of degree one, $f(t, \cdot)$ is strictly concave, by an argument that is similar to that used to prove the part $(2 \implies 3)$ of Lemma 3.32.

Strict concavity of the conditional CE. Suppose $\gamma > 0$ and let u be defined in (6.24). A minor modification of an argument used in the proof of Lemma 3.32 shows that for any nonterminal spot (F, t), the strict concavity of the function

$$v_{F,t}(\cdot) = u^{-1}\mathbb{E}[u(\cdot) \mid F]$$

is implied by the condition

$$x \neq y \quad \text{and} \quad v_{F,t}(x) = v_{F,t}(y) \implies$$
$$v_{F,t}(px + (1-p)y) > v_{F,t}(x), \quad \text{for all } p \in (0, 1).$$

The above condition is an immediate consequence of the fact that u is increasing and strict concave. ∎

6.5.2 Translation-Invariant Kreps-Porteus Utility

The characterization of translation invariance for recursive utility is analogous to that of scale invariance and is in fact isomorphic to it in a sense to be made precise in the proof of Proposition 6.21. Consider a dynamic utility U on the consumption set $C = \mathcal{L} = \mathbb{R}^{1+K}$. We define U to be **translation invariant (TI)** if for any spot (F, t), the corresponding utility $U_{F,t} : C \to \mathbb{R}$ represents a TI preference. By dynamic consistency, U is TI if and only if the time-zero utility $U_0 : C \to \mathbb{R}$ represents a TI preference. From the discussion of Section 3.5.1, we know that if U is also assumed to be normalized, then U is TI if and only if it is **quasilinear with respect to 1**, meaning that for any spot (F, t), $U_{F,t}(c + \theta \mathbf{1}) = U_{F,t}(c) + \theta$ for all $\theta \in \mathbb{R}$ and $c \in C$. In particular, the terms "translation invariant" and "quasilinear with respect to $\mathbf{1}$" are synonymous when applied to recursive utility. The

217

following proposition characterizes every TI Kreps-Porteus utility, given only a minor regularity assumption.

Proposition 6.21. *Suppose U is a Kreps-Porteus utility on the consumption set $\mathcal{L}$ with aggregator f and conditional CE $\upsilon_t = u^{-1}\mathbb{E}_t u$, where the function $u : \mathbb{R} \to \mathbb{R}$ is continuously differentiable on some (arbitrarily small) interval. Then U is quasilinear with respect to $\mathbf{1}$ if and only if the following two conditions are satisfied:*

1. *The aggregator f is quasilinear with respect to $(1, 1)$; that is, there exists a function $g : \{0, \dots, T - 1\} \times \mathbb{R} \to \mathbb{R}$ such that*

$$f(t, c, \upsilon) = \upsilon + g(t, c - \upsilon), \quad \text{for all } c, \upsilon \in \mathbb{R}. \qquad (6.26)$$

2. *There exists a constant $\gamma \in \mathbb{R}$ such that u is given, up to a positive affine transformation, by*

$$u(x) = \frac{1 - \exp(-\gamma x)}{\gamma} \quad \text{(where } u(x) = x \text{ if } \gamma = 0). \qquad (6.27)$$

Proof. Define the utility $\tilde{U} : \mathcal{L}_{++} \to (0, \infty)$ by

$$\tilde{U}(\tilde{c}) = \exp U(\log \tilde{c}).$$

Since U is quasilinear with respect to $\mathbf{1}$ if and only if $\tilde{U}$ is homogeneous of degree one, the proposition follows by applying Proposition 6.18 to $\tilde{U}$. ∎

In the above representation of TI Kreps-Porteus utility, we refer to g as an **absolute aggregator** and to γ as a **coefficient of absolute risk aversion**. The absolute aggregator determines and is determined by preferences over deterministic consumption plans, while increasing γ makes the utility more risk averse. Any continuous increasing $g(t, \cdot) : \mathbb{R} \to \mathbb{R}$ satisfying $g(t, 0) = 0$ define an aggregator through (6.26), provided the latter is increasing in the CE argument. Assuming differentiability, the last restriction means that the derivatives $g'(t, \cdot)$ are valued in $(0, 1)$.

Example 6.22 (Recursive Exponential Utility). *This example formulates the TI analog of Epstein-Zin-Weil utility, which includes as a special case expected discounted exponential utility. We postulate the conditional CE $\upsilon_t = u^{-1}\mathbb{E}_t u$, where $u : (0, \infty) \to \mathbb{R}$ is given by (6.27) for some scalar γ, and* *the aggregator*

$$f(t, c, \upsilon) = \nu^{-1}((1 - \beta)\nu(c) + \beta\nu(\upsilon)), \quad \text{where } \nu(x) = \frac{1 - \exp(-\delta x)}{\delta},$$

for some $\beta \in (0, 1)$ and $\delta \in \mathbb{R}$ (with $\nu(x) = x$ if $\delta = 0$). A simple calculation shows that this aggregator is of the quasilinear form (6.26), with absolute aggregator

$$g(t, x) = \begin{cases} -\delta^{-1} \log((1 - \beta)\exp(-\delta x) + \beta), & \text{if } \delta \neq 0; \\ (1 - \beta)x, & \text{if } \delta = 0. \end{cases}$$

(Note that $(1 - \beta)x$ is the limit of $-\delta^{-1}\log((1 - \beta)\exp(-\delta x) + \beta)$ as $\delta \to 0$.) If $\gamma = \delta$, then the above specification reduces to the expected discounted utility of Example 6.4, with u given in (6.27). The parameters (β, δ) are determined by the utility of deterministic plans. For fixed (β, δ), increasing γ increases risk aversion.

We conclude with the analog of Proposition 6.20 for the TI case. The simple proof is left as an exercise.

Proposition 6.23. *Suppose U is translation-invariant Kreps utility with absolute aggregator g and coefficient of absolute risk aversion γ. If g is strictly concave and $\gamma > 0$, then U is strictly concave.*

6.6 EQUILIBRIUM PRICING

In Section 6.4.2 we established a formula for the gradient density of recursive utility, which, by virtue of Proposition 6.12, expresses an equilibrium state-price density (SPD) in terms of an agent's preferences and equilibrium consumption plan. In this section we specialize the recursive utility gradient density formula to scale-invariant (SI) or translation-invariant (TI) Kreps-Porteus utility. These utility forms are consistent with the representative-agent pricing arguments of Section 3.4, resulting in equilibrium SPD expressions in terms of aggregate consumption and market prices: the market return in the SI case and the price of a traded annuity in the TI case. While the section's analysis is motivated by equilibrium pricing interpretations, it is important to note that it consists of nothing more than manipulations of the recursive utility gradient density expression of Proposition 6.15. The analysis will also be a key tool in the following section's theory of optimal consumption and portfolio choice.

6.6.1 Intertemporal Marginal Rate of Substitution

Throughout this section, we assume that U is Kreps-Porteus utility with aggregator f and conditional CE

$$\upsilon_t(\,\cdot\,) = u^{-1}(\mathbb{E}_t[u(\,\cdot\,)]), \qquad (6.28)$$

satisfying the smoothness assumptions of Proposition 6.15. As usual, u' denotes the derivative of u, while f_c and f_υ denote the partial derivatives of f with respect to its consumption and conditional CE arguments, respectively.

We study the form of the utility gradient density π at a reference consumption plan c that is fixed throughout the section. In the context of equilibrium pricing, we interpret c either as a given agent's optimal consumption plan or, assuming a representative-agent pricing argument applies, as the economy's aggregate consumption. For simplicity, we abuse the notation by writing

$$U_t = U_t(c) \quad \text{and} \quad \upsilon_t = \upsilon_t(U_{t+1}(c)).$$

Therefore, U denotes the utility process of c and not the entire dynamic utility, which we will denote $U(\,\cdot\,)$ to avoid confusion. Similarly, the value υ_t should not be confused with the time-t conditional CE as the function defined in equation (6.28).

A key role in what follows is played by the process λ, defined by

$$\lambda_t = f_c(t, c_t, \upsilon_t), \quad t < T, \quad \lambda_T = 1. \qquad (6.29)$$

As noted in Remark 6.16, λ can be thought of as a marginal-value-of-wealth process.

Combining the expressions for the utility gradient density π of Proposition 6.15 and the derivative of the conditional CE (6.28) of Example 6.14, we compute the ratio

$$\frac{\pi_t}{\pi_{t-1}} = f_\upsilon(t-1, c_{t-1}, \upsilon_{t-1}) \frac{u'(U_t)}{u'(\upsilon_{t-1})} \frac{\lambda_t}{\lambda_{t-1}}, \qquad (6.30)$$

known as the **intertemporal marginal rate of substitution (IMRS)**. In equilibrium, the IMRS for all periods determines a unique, up to positive scaling, SPD π and therefore a unique present-value function.

In equilibrium, the IMRS places recursive restrictions on any traded (or synthetic) contract (δ, V):

$$V_{t-1} = \delta_{t-1} + \mathbb{E}_{t-1}\left[\frac{\pi_t}{\pi_{t-1}} V_t\right],$$

as shown in Propositions 5.26 and 5.27. Assuming the corresponding ex-dividend price process, $S = V - \delta$, does not vanish at any nonterminal spot, the above recursion can equivalently be stated as a traded-return restriction:

$$\mathbb{E}_{t-1}\left[\frac{\pi_t}{\pi_{t-1}}\frac{V_t}{S_{t-1}}\right] = 1.$$

With this observation, we can apply single-period results from Part I, conditionally at every nonterminal spot, to derive equilibrium restrictions on the IMRS. Notably, assuming the market structure of Section 5.6, Example 2.27 and Proposition 1.23 can be adapted to establish a conditional Hansen-Jagannathan lower bound on the conditional standard deviation of the IMRS.

In the following two subsections we develop specialized versions of the IMRS expression (6.30) by further assuming that U is SI or TI.

6.6.2 State Pricing with SI Kreps-Porteus Utility

We begin with the case of SI Kreps-Porteus utility, which, as noted in Example 6.19, includes Epstein-Zin-Weil utility, which in turn nests expected discounted power or logarithmic utility. We will express the IMRS of equation (6.30) as a function of the rate of change of wealth and the consumption-to-wealth ratio. In the representative-agent construction these two quantities correspond to the market return and dividend yield, by which we mean the return and dividend yield of a traded contract whose dividend process is proportional to the aggregate endowment. In fact, such a pricing relationship will be derived under the special assumption that the elasticity of the proportional aggregator is an invertible function. The assumption is satisfied in the parametric case of Epstein-Zin-Weil utility with nonunit EIS, but is not a consequence of scale invariance. Another special case is that of a unit coefficient of relative risk aversion, in which case the IMRS will be shown to be the inverse of the market return, for any proportional aggregator.

The following utility structure is assumed throughout this subsection.

Condition 6.24. *The (normalized) dynamic utility $U(\cdot)$ on the consumption set $\mathcal{L}_{++} = (0,\infty)^{1+K}$ is an SI Kreps-Porteus utility with proportional aggregator g and coefficient of relative risk aversion $\gamma > 0$. For every time $t < T$, the function $g_t = g(t,\cdot)$ is differentiable and its derivative g'_t is strictly decreasing and maps $(0,\infty)$ onto $(0,\infty)$.*

The recursion for the utility process $U = U(c)$ can be expressed as

$$U_t = v_t g_t\left(\frac{c_t}{v_t}\right), \qquad U_T = c_T, \tag{6.31}$$

where

$$v_t = \begin{cases} (\mathbb{E}_t[U_{t+1}^{1-\gamma}])^{1/(1-\gamma)}, & \text{if } \gamma \neq 1; \\ \exp \mathbb{E}_t[\log U_{t+1}], & \text{if } \gamma = 1. \end{cases}$$

Condition 6.24 implies that g_t is strictly increasing and strictly concave, and its derivative $g_t' : (0, \infty) \to (0, \infty)$ is invertible. We let $\mathcal{I}_t : (0, \infty) \to (0, \infty)$ denote the inverse function of g_t', defined implicitly by

$$g_t'(\mathcal{I}_t(y)) = y, \quad y \in (0, \infty). \tag{6.32}$$

The **convex dual** of g_t is the function $g_t^* : (0, \infty) \to (0, \infty)$ defined by

$$g_t^*(y) = \max_{x \in (0,\infty)} (g_t(x) - xy) = g_t(\mathcal{I}_t(y)) - \mathcal{I}_t(y)y, \quad y \in (0, \infty). \tag{6.33}$$

The definition of λ in (6.29) and the aggregator specification $f(t, c, v) = v g_t(c/v)$ imply the relationships

$$\lambda_t = g_t'\left(\frac{c_t}{v_t}\right), \quad \frac{c_t}{v_t} = \mathcal{I}_t(\lambda_t), \quad f_v(t, c_t, v_t) = g_t^*(\lambda_t). \tag{6.34}$$

A graphical representation of these quantities is given in Figure 6.1. The last equation in (6.34) and the definition of u in (6.24) reduce the IMRS expression (6.30) to

$$\frac{\pi_t}{\pi_{t-1}} = g_{t-1}^*(\lambda_{t-1}) \frac{\lambda_t}{\lambda_{t-1}} \left(\frac{U_t}{v_{t-1}}\right)^{-\gamma}. \tag{6.35}$$

Our goal is to relate the IMRS to what, in the representative-agent pricing context, is the market return and dividend yield. For this purpose, we define the key processes

$$W_t = \mathbb{E}_t\left[\sum_{s=t}^{T} \frac{\pi_s}{\pi_t} c_s\right], \quad M_t = \frac{W_t}{W_{t-1} - c_{t-1}}, \quad \varrho_t = \frac{c_t}{W_t}. \tag{6.36}$$

If π is an SPD, W_t is the time-t present value of the consumption plan c. Assuming the latter is marketed, W_t is the time-t wealth required to finance the consumption plan c from time t on; in other words, (c, W) is a traded contract. M_t represents the period-t gross return of this contract and ϱ_t its time-t dividend yield. In the representative-agent pricing context,

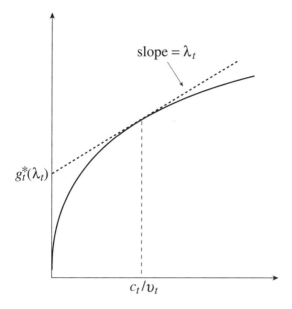

Figure 6.1 The curved line is the graph of g_t. The value $g_t^*(\lambda_t)$ is the intercept with the vertical axis of the line of slope λ_t that is tangent to the graph of g_t.

c is the aggregate endowment, and M_t and ϱ_t are the market return and dividend yield.

We proceed with three preliminary lemmas involving the above quantities. To motivate the first lemma, it is helpful to consider it in a context in which c is a marketed optimal consumption plan. Because of the homogeneity of the agent's budget constraint and utility function, scaling up the agent's wealth at an optimum scales up proportionately the agent's consumption and utility, while preserving optimality. Recalling the interpretation of λ in Remark 6.16 as a marginal-value-of-wealth process, this argument suggests the following key relationship between utility and wealth, which we prove directly as a consequence of utility homogeneity, without reference to a market.

Lemma 6.25. $U = \lambda W$.

Proof. By the homogeneity of U,

$$U_t(c) = \frac{U_t(c + \alpha c) - U_t(c)}{\alpha}, \quad \alpha > 0.$$

223

Letting $\alpha \downarrow 0$ and using Proposition 6.15, we obtain

$$U_t(c) = \mathbb{E}_t\left[\sum_{s=t}^{T} \frac{\mathcal{E}_s}{\mathcal{E}_t}\lambda_s c_s\right] = \lambda_t \mathbb{E}_t\left[\sum_{s=t}^{T} \frac{\pi_s}{\pi_t}c_s\right] = \lambda_t W_t.$$

∎

Our second lemma transforms the IMRS expression (6.35) to a form that in the representative-agent pricing context is more closely related to the market return and has as a corollary the interesting fact that in the case of unit relative risk aversion the IMRS is the inverse of the market return.

Lemma 6.26. *Under Condition 6.24,*

$$\frac{\pi_t}{\pi_{t-1}} = \frac{1}{M_t}\left(\frac{U_t}{v_{t-1}}\right)^{1-\gamma}.$$

Proof. Using the definition (6.33) of g^*, equations (6.34), the utility recursion (6.31) and last lemma's identity $U = \lambda W$, we have

$$g_{t-1}^*(\lambda_{t-1}) = \frac{U_{t-1}}{v_{t-1}} - \frac{c_{t-1}}{v_{t-1}}\lambda_{t-1} = (W_{t-1} - c_{t-1})\frac{\lambda_{t-1}}{v_{t-1}},$$

and therefore

$$g_{t-1}^*(\lambda_{t-1})\frac{\lambda_t}{\lambda_{t-1}} = \frac{W_{t-1} - c_{t-1}}{W_t}\frac{\lambda_t W_t}{v_{t-1}} = \frac{1}{M_t}\frac{U_t}{v_{t-1}}.$$

Substituting into the IMRS expression (6.35) completes the proof. ∎

Corollary 6.27 (IMRS with Unit Coefficient of Relative Risk Aversion). *If $\gamma = 1$, then*

$$\frac{\pi_t}{\pi_{t-1}} = \frac{1}{M_t}.$$

Our third lemma relates the consumption-to-wealth ratio ϱ_t to the marginal value of wealth λ_t in terms of the **elasticity** of the proportional aggregator g_t, which we define as the function

$$h_t(x) = \frac{d\log g_t(x)}{d\log x} = \frac{xg_t'(x)}{g_t(x)}, \quad x \in (0, \infty).$$

Lemma 6.28. *For every time $t < T$,*

$$\varrho_t = h_t\left(\frac{c_t}{\upsilon_t}\right) = h_t(\mathcal{I}_t(\lambda_t)).$$

Proof. Letting $x_t = c_t/\upsilon_t = \mathcal{I}_t(\lambda_t)$, we use Lemma 6.25 and the utility recursion (6.31) to compute

$$\varrho_t = \frac{c_t}{W_t} = \frac{c_t \lambda_t}{U_t} = \frac{c_t g_t'(x_t)}{\upsilon_t g_t(x_t)} = \frac{x_t g_t'(x_t)}{g_t(x_t)} = h_t(x_t). \tag{6.37}$$

∎

For $\gamma \neq 1$, will we will express the IMRS entirely in terms of M and ϱ, under the following restriction on the elasticity of the proportional aggregator, which is satisfied by any Epstein-Zin-Weil utility with nonunit EIS.

Condition 6.29. *For every time $t < T$, the elasticity function h_t is either strictly increasing or strictly decreasing.*

Let $J_t = \{h_t(x) : x \in (0, \infty)\}$. Since h_t is continuous, Condition 6.29 is equivalent to the invertibility of the function $h_t : (0, \infty) \to J_t$. We let $\mathcal{J}_t : J_t \to (0, \infty)$ denote the inverse function of h_t, defined implicitly by

$$h_t(\mathcal{J}_t(y)) = y. \tag{6.38}$$

The reason for assuming Condition 6.29 is that it allows us to apply Lemma 6.28 to compute λ as a function of ϱ :

$$\lambda_t = g_t'(\mathcal{J}_t(\varrho_t)). \tag{6.39}$$

This subsection's main result follows.

Theorem 6.30 (Pricing with SI Kreps-Porteus Utility). *Under Conditions 6.24 and 6.29, the IMRS is given by*

$$\frac{\pi_t}{\pi_{t-1}} = \left(\frac{1}{M_t}\right)^\gamma \left(\frac{1 - \varrho_{t-1}}{\varrho_{t-1}} \mathcal{J}_{t-1}(\varrho_{t-1}) g_t'(\mathcal{J}_t(\varrho_t))\right)^{1-\gamma}.$$

For $\gamma = 1$, the above IMRS expression is valid without assuming Condition 6.29.

225

Proof. We use the identities $U = \lambda W$ and $\lambda = g'(c/v)$ to compute the ratio

$$\frac{U_t}{v_{t-1}} = \frac{\lambda_t W_t}{c_{t-1}/\mathcal{I}_{t-1}(\lambda_{t-1})} = M_t \frac{1 - \varrho_{t-1}}{\varrho_{t-1}} \mathcal{I}_{t-1}(\lambda_{t-1})\lambda_t.$$

Substituting into the IMRS expression of Lemma 6.26, we obtain

$$\frac{\pi_t}{\pi_{t-1}} = \left(\frac{1}{M_t}\right)^\gamma \left(\frac{1 - \varrho_{t-1}}{\varrho_{t-1}} \mathcal{I}_{t-1}(\lambda_{t-1})\lambda_t\right)^{1-\gamma}.$$

Substituting expression (6.39) for λ proves the result for $\gamma \neq 1$. For $\gamma = 1$, Corollary 6.27 applies. ∎

Example 6.31 (Pricing with Epstein-Zin-Weil Utility). *We specialize the above setting by assuming that the proportional aggregator takes the Epstein-Zin-Weil form of Example 6.19 for some $\delta \in (0, \infty)$, where δ^{-1} is the EIS. Expected discounted power or logarithmic utility is obtained if $\gamma = \delta$. Assuming a nonunit EIS, direct computation shows that*

$$\mathcal{J}_t(\varrho) = \left(\frac{\beta}{1 - \beta} \frac{\varrho}{1 - \varrho}\right)^{1/(1-\delta)}, \qquad \delta \neq 1.$$

Substituting in the IMRS expression of Theorem 6.30 and simplifying results in

$$\frac{\pi_t}{\pi_{t-1}} = \left(\frac{1}{M_t}\right)^{1-\phi} \left(\beta\left(\frac{c_t}{c_{t-1}}\right)^{-\delta}\right)^\phi, \quad where\ \phi = \frac{1-\gamma}{1-\delta}, \quad \delta \neq 1. \quad (6.40)$$

An interpretation of the parameter ϕ is given in Exercise 7. For expected discounted power utility, the above IMRS expression simplifies to

$$\frac{\pi_t}{\pi_{t-1}} = \beta\left(\frac{c_t}{c_{t-1}}\right)^{-\gamma}, \qquad assuming\ \gamma = \delta \neq 1.$$

For unit EIS, the proportional aggregator has constant elasticity equal to $1 - \beta$ and therefore, by Lemma 6.28 and the definition of M, we have

$$\varrho_{t-1} = 1 - \beta \quad and \quad M_t = \frac{1}{\beta}\frac{c_t}{c_{t-1}}, \qquad assuming\ \delta = 1.$$

While Condition 6.29 is violated for unit EIS, in the special case of expected discounted logarithmic utility Corollary 6.27 applies to conclude that

$$\frac{\pi_t}{\pi_{t-1}} = \frac{1}{M_t} = \beta\left(\frac{c_t}{c_{t-1}}\right)^{-1}, \qquad assuming\ \gamma = \delta = 1.$$

6.6.3 State Pricing with TI Kreps-Porteus Utility

In this subsection, we specialize the IMRS expression (6.30) to the case of TI Kreps-Porteus utility, which, as noted in Example 6.22, includes expected discounted exponential utility. The class of preferences considered is consistent with the aggregation argument of Proposition 3.27, allowing a representative-agent pricing interpretation of the results. In the following section, we will use these calculations as a key step in analyzing optimal consumption/portfolio choice under TI Kreps-Porteus utility and a nontradeable income stream.

The following utility structure is assumed throughout this subsection.

Condition 6.32. *The (normalized) dynamic utility $U(\cdot)$ on the consumption set $\mathcal{L} = \mathbb{R}^{1+K}$ is a TI Kreps-Porteus utility with absolute aggregator g and coefficient of absolute risk aversion $\gamma > 0$. For every time $t < T$, the function $g_t = g(t, \cdot)$ is differentiable and its derivative g_t' is strictly decreasing and maps $\mathbb{R}$ onto $(0, 1)$.*

The recursion determining the utility process $U = U(c)$ is

$$U_t = v_t + g_t(c_t - v_t), \quad U_T = c_T, \tag{6.41}$$

where

$$v_t = -\frac{1}{\gamma} \log \mathbb{E}_t \exp(-\gamma U_{t+1}).$$

The utility quasilinearity allows us to express the process λ, defined in (6.29), in terms of the process

$$V_t^0 = \mathbb{E}_t \left[\sum_{s=t}^{T} \frac{\pi_s}{\pi_t} \right]. \tag{6.42}$$

Lemma 6.33. $\lambda = 1/V^0$.

Proof. Since $U_t(c + \theta 1) = U_t(c) + \theta$ for every $\theta \in \mathbb{R}$, we have

$$\frac{U_t(c + \theta 1) - U_t(c)}{\theta} = 1.$$

Letting θ go to zero and using Lemma 6.15, it follows that

$$1 = \mathbb{E}_t \left[\sum_{s=t}^{T} \frac{\mathcal{E}_s}{\mathcal{E}_t} \lambda_s \right] = \lambda_t \mathbb{E}_t \left[\sum_{s=t}^{T} \frac{\pi_s}{\pi_t} \right] = \lambda_t V_t^0.$$

∎

If π is an SPD, the process V^0 corresponds to the cum-dividend price process of a traded **annuity,** by which we mean a contract with dividend process 1. Recalling the interpretation of λ in Remark 6.16 as a marginal-value-of-wealth process, the relationship $\lambda = 1/V^0$ can be explained as follows. Suppose the agent finds the consumption plan c optimal, can trade in the annuity and is presented with a small additional time-t wealth δ. After reoptimizing, to first order, the agent's additional time-t utility value is $\lambda_t\delta$. Since the agent has TI preferences, however, all of the amount δ can be invested in the annuity while preserving optimality. By the quasilinearity of the utility function, the additional utility value is equal to the number of annuity shares purchased, δ/V_t^0. Matching the two ways of measuring the utility increment results in $\lambda_t = 1/V_t^0$.

We conclude with the main result, expressing the IMRS π_t/π_{t-1} in terms of V_{t-1}^0, V_t^0 and the consumption increment $c_t - c_{t-1}$, which in the representative-agent pricing interpretation of Proposition 3.27 is the period-t increment in the aggregate consumption. Condition 6.32 implies that g_t is strictly increasing and strictly concave, and that the function $g_t' : \mathbb{R} \to (0, 1)$ is invertible. We let $\mathcal{I}_t : (0, 1) \to \mathbb{R}$ denote the inverse function of g_t', defined implicitly by (6.32).

Proposition 6.34 (Pricing with TI Kreps-Porteus Utility). *Under Condition 6.32, the IMRS is given by*

$$\frac{\pi_t}{\pi_{t-1}} = \frac{V_{t-1}^0 - 1}{V_t^0} \exp[-\gamma(k_t + c_t - c_{t-1})],$$

where V^0 is defined in (6.42) and

$$k_t = g_t(\mathcal{I}_t(1/V_t^0)) - \mathcal{I}_t(1/V_t^0) + \mathcal{I}_{t-1}(1/V_{t-1}^0).$$

Proof. The TI aggregator form $f(t, c, v) = v + g_t(c - v)$ implies that

$$\lambda_t = g_t'(c_t - v_t) \quad \text{and} \quad f_v(t, c_t, v_t) = 1 - \lambda_t.$$

Given these expressions and the exponential form (6.27) of u, the IMRS expression (6.30) becomes

$$\frac{\pi_t}{\pi_{t-1}} = (1 - \lambda_{t-1})\frac{\lambda_t}{\lambda_{t-1}} \exp(-\gamma(U_t - v_{t-1})). \tag{6.43}$$

We use the identity $c_t - v_t = \mathcal{I}_t(\lambda_t)$ and the utility recursion (6.41) to compute

$$U_t - v_{t-1} = g_t(c_t - v_t) + \Delta v_t = g_t(\mathcal{I}_t(\lambda_t)) + \Delta(c_t - \mathcal{I}_t(\lambda_t)).$$

Substituting this expression in (6.43) and using Lemma 6.33, we obtain the claimed expression for the IMRS. ∎

Example 6.35 (Pricing with Recursive Exponential Utility). *Consider the utility specification of Example 6.22 with $\gamma, \delta > 0$; expected discounted utility is obtained if $\gamma = \delta$. In this case, the period-t IMRS can be expressed in terms of the consumption increment Δc_t and the annuity gross return*

$$A_t = \frac{V_t^0}{V_{t-1}^0 - 1}.$$

Indeed, direct calculation shows that

$$\mathcal{I}_t(\lambda) = -\frac{1}{\delta} \log\left(\frac{\beta}{1-\beta} \frac{\lambda}{1-\lambda} \right),$$

resulting in the IMRS expression

$$\frac{\pi_t}{\pi_{t-1}} = \left(\frac{1}{A_t}\right)^{1-\phi} \left(\beta \exp(-\delta \Delta c_t) \right)^{\phi}, \quad where \ \phi = \frac{\gamma}{\delta}.$$

An interpretation of the parameter ϕ is given in Exercise 7. In the case of expected discounted exponential utility, $\phi = 1$ and therefore the IMRS is determined solely by the consumption increment.

6.7 OPTIMAL CONSUMPTION AND PORTFOLIO CHOICE

This section analyzes the problem of optimal consumption and portfolio choice for an agent who maximizes recursive utility and can trade in a given set of contracts. For purposes of tractability, we will focus on two formulations. The first, scale-invariant (SI) formulation assumes that the agent maximizes SI Kreps-Porteus utility and that the agent's endowment is marketed. The second, translation-invariant (TI) formulation allows for a possibly nonmarketed endowment and assumes that the agent maximizes TI Kreps-Porteus utility, and that there is a traded annuity. In both cases, we will see that the solution reduces on a single backward recursion on the information tree.

6.7.1 Generalities

We begin with some general definitions and discussion, which will be later specialized to the SI and TI formulations. We consider an agent with a dynamic utility $U(\cdot)$ on a consumption set C and an endowment e. The agent can use an arbitrage-free market X to trade into any consumption plan in C of the form $e + x$, where $x \in X$. Dynamic consistency allows us to focus entirely on optimality from the perspective of time zero. A consumption plan c is **feasible** if $c \in C$ and $c = e + x$ for some $x \in X$. A feasible consumption plan c is **optimal** if $U_0(c) \geq U_0(\tilde{c})$ for any other feasible consumption plan $\tilde{c}$.

By the linearity of the market, optimality of a feasible consumption plan c is equivalent to the condition

$$x \in X \text{ and } c + x \in C \quad \text{implies} \quad U_0(c + x) \leq U_0(c).$$

We will verify optimality using the following special case of Proposition 6.12.

Lemma 6.36. *Suppose the time-zero utility function $U_0 : C \to \mathbb{R}$ is concave, $c \in C$ is a feasible consumption plan and π is both a gradient density of U_0 at c and a state-price density. Then c is optimal.*

Proof. For any $x \in X$ such that $c + x \in C$, the gradient inequality and the SPD property of π imply $U_0(c + x) \leq U_0(c) + (\pi \mid x) = U_0(c)$. ∎

In the SI and TI formulations, we will show constructively that there exists a feasible consumption plan c such that the utility gradient density at c is also an SPD, thus proving existence of an optimum. Strict concavity of the utility will imply the uniqueness of the optimum.

To discuss optimal portfolios, we assume throughout this section that the market X is implemented by the dynamically independent (Definition 5.57) contracts

$$(\delta^0, V^0), (\delta^1, V^1), \ldots, (\delta^J, V^J),$$

with corresponding ex-dividend price and gain processes

$$S^j = V^j - \delta^j, \quad G^j = V^j + \delta^j_- \bullet \mathbf{t}, \quad j = 0, 1, \ldots, J.$$

Contract zero will be a money-market account in the SI formulation and an annuity in the TI formulation. For the remaining contracts, $1 \ldots J$, we use the column vector notation

$$\delta = (\delta^1, \ldots, \delta^J)', \quad V = (V^1, \ldots, V^J)',$$

and analogously for S and G.

A trading strategy $(\theta^0, \theta) \in \mathcal{P}_0 \times \mathcal{P}_0^J$ **finances** the consumption plan c if it generates the cash flow $c - e$ and is **optimal** if it finances an optimal consumption plan. Recalling Proposition 5.18, we note that (θ^0, θ) finances the consumption plan c if and only if it satisfies the **budget equation**

$$\theta^0 V^0 + \theta' V = \theta^0 \bullet G^0 + \theta' \bullet G - (c - e)_- \bullet t, \quad \theta_T^0 V_T^0 + \theta_T' V_T = c_T - e_T.$$

The feasibility and optimality conditions for the agent's problem consist of the budget equation, the utility recursion and the SPD property of the utility gradient density. The three conditions form a coupled system of forward and backward recursions on the information tree. This system uncouples in the SI and TI formulations, effectively reducing to a single backward recursion.

To present a unified definition of wealth in the SI and TI formulations, we assume throughout that the agent's endowment is given by

$$e = w1_{\Omega \times \{0\}} + y.$$

We interpret the scalar w as an endowed initial financial wealth and the cash flow y as an exogenous income stream. Since y_0 need not be zero, this decomposition of e is mathematically arbitrary, but it does matter for how we define financial wealth.

Definition 6.37. *The (financial) **wealth process** W **generated** by the trading strategy (θ^0, θ) is defined by*

$$W_0 = w \quad and \quad W_t = \theta_t^0 V_t^0 + \theta_t' V_t \quad for\ t = 1, \ldots, T. \tag{6.44}$$

Suppose the trading strategy (θ^0, θ) finances the consumption plan c and generates the wealth process W. Then W_t is the time-t cum-dividend price of a traded (synthetic) contract with dividend process $c - y$, and therefore W_t is the time-t present value of the payment stream $c_t - y_t, \ldots, c_T - y_T$. The wealth W_t is financial in the sense that it does not include the value of the income stream y. In the SI formulation we are going to let $y = 0$, making the notation W_t consistent with equation (6.36), provided π is an SPD. In the TI formulation we are going to let $w = 0$, making W_t the time-t present value of the payments $c_t - e_t, \ldots, c_T - e_T$. Because of these assumptions, we will have no further use for the income-stream notation y.

6.7.2 Scale-Invariant Formulation

As in Section 6.6.2, we consider an agent with (sufficiently regular) SI Kreps-Porteus utility, Epstein-Zin-Weil utility being an example. SI preferences are in most contexts more realistic than TI preferences, as they allow risk aversion to scale with wealth. On the other hand, in order to maintain a scale-invariant structure in the market, we assume that the agent's endowment is marketed with present value $w \in (0, \infty)$. Given this assumption, we lose no generality in assuming that the agent's endowment is $e = w 1_{\Omega \times \{0\}}$, implying that any original endowed income stream has already been converted in the market to a single time-zero payment. With this convention, the agent enters each spot with some financial wealth and no future endowed income, and makes a decision on how to allocate this wealth among immediate consumption and available investment opportunities. Although not necessary, it is simpler in this context to work with returns and trading strategies described as wealth allocations, which is the choice we make below. We also assume that the market allows single-period default-free borrowing and lending (but see Exercise 17).

The following assumptions and notation are in place throughout this subsection.

SI Formulation. *The agent's preferences over the consumption set $\mathcal{L}_{++}$ are represented by the SI Kreps-Porteus utility $U(\cdot)$, with a proportional aggregator g restricted as in Condition 6.24 and a coefficient of relative risk aversion $\gamma \in (0, \infty)$. The agent's endowment is $e = w 1_{\Omega \times \{0\}}, w \in (0, \infty)$. For every contract j, the lagged ex-dividend price process S_-^j is strictly positive. Contract zero is a money-market account with short-rate process $r = \Delta G^0 / S_-^0$. The vector of risky-asset **excess returns** is denoted*

$$\tilde{r} = (\tilde{r}^1, \ldots, \tilde{r}^J)', \quad \text{where} \quad \tilde{r}^j = \frac{\Delta G^j}{S_-^j} - r.$$

In the current context, the SPD property can be stated entirely in terms of excess returns and the short-rate process r.

Lemma 6.38. *A process $\pi \in \mathcal{L}_{++}$ is an SPD if and only if it satisfies*

$$\mathbb{E}_{t-1}\left[\frac{\pi_t}{\pi_{t-1}}\tilde{r}_t\right] = 0 \quad \text{and} \quad \mathbb{E}_{t-1}\left[\frac{\pi_t}{\pi_{t-1}}\right] = \frac{1}{1 + r_t}. \tag{6.45}$$

Proof. Immediate from Propositions 5.26 and 5.27. ∎

To reformulate the problem in terms of allocations, suppose the agent follows the trading strategy (θ^0, θ), which finances the consumption plan c and generates the wealth process W. We will describe the agent's wealth allocation in terms of the ratios

$$\varrho = \frac{c}{W} \quad \text{and} \quad \psi^j = \frac{\theta^j S_-^j}{W_- - c_-}, \quad j = 1, \ldots, J, \qquad (6.46)$$

using the vector notation $\psi = (\psi^1, \ldots, \psi^J)'$.

At the beginning of period t, the agent allocates the proportion ϱ_{t-1} of the wealth W_{t-1} to immediate consumption and invests the remaining amount $(1 - \varrho_{t-1})W_{t-1}$ in the $1 + J$ contracts, with proportion ψ_t^j going to contract $j \in \{1, \ldots, J\}$ and the remaining proportion $1 - \sum_{j=1}^{J} \psi_t^j$ going to the money-market account. The end-of-period wealth W_t is the result of this investment and is therefore given as

$$W_t = W_{t-1}(1 - \varrho_{t-1})(1 + r_t + \psi_t' \tilde{r}_t), \quad W_0 = w. \qquad (6.47)$$

A simple calculation verifies that (6.47) is implied by the budget equation. Conversely, given any pair $(\varrho, \psi) \in \mathcal{L}_{++} \times \mathcal{P}_0^J$ such that $\varrho_T = 1$ and process $W \in \mathcal{L}_{++}$ solving (6.47), a corresponding consumption plan c and financing trading trading strategy (θ^0, θ) are uniquely determined by equations (6.44) and (6.46). These observations allow us to equivalently define optimality directly in terms of allocations, resulting in a more parsimonious formulation.

Definition 6.39. *A **consumption policy** is any strictly positive adapted process ϱ such that $\varrho_T = 1$. A **trading policy** is any process*

$$\psi = (\psi^1, \ldots, \psi^J)' \in \mathcal{P}_0^J.$$

*An **allocation policy** is a pair (ϱ, ψ) of a consumption policy and a trading policy. A **wealth process** is any strictly positive adapted process. The allocation policy (ϱ, ψ) **generates** the wealth process W if recursion (6.47) is satisfied, in which case the allocation policy (ϱ, ψ) is said to **finance** the consumption plan*

$$c = \varrho W.$$

*An allocation policy is **optimal** if it finances an optimal consumption plan.*

Using the notation and results of Section 6.6.2, we will show that the determination of an optimal allocation policy reduces to a single backward recursion that jointly determines the optimal trading policy ψ and the marginal-value-of-wealth process λ. It is a good exercise at this point to try to simplify the optimality conditions (consisting of the wealth dynamics, the utility recursion and the SPD property of the utility gradient density) using the key relationships $U = \lambda W$ and $\varrho = h(\mathcal{I}(\lambda))$ (with $h_T = 1$) from Section 6.6.2. Our analysis proceeds in the opposite direction, first describing the recursion determining (λ, ψ), and then verifying optimality and uniqueness of the constructed solution.

The backward recursion for (λ, ψ) begins at the terminal time, where we set $\lambda_T = 1$. For each time $t > 0$, the recursive step assumes λ_t is known and computes the pair (ψ_t, λ_{t-1}). Recalling that $L(\mathcal{F}_t)$ denotes the set of every $\mathcal{F}_t$-measurable random variable, we define the set

$$\Psi_t = \{\psi_t \in L(\mathcal{F}_{t-1})^J : 1 + r_t + \psi_t' \tilde{r}_t \text{ is strictly positive}\}. \tag{6.48}$$

The allocation ψ_t will be characterized as the unique element of Ψ_t that satisfies

$$\mathbb{E}_{t-1}[\lambda_t^{1-\gamma}(1 + r_t + \psi_t' \tilde{r}_t)^{-\gamma} \tilde{r}_t] = 0. \tag{6.49}$$

This equation can be recognized as a necessary and sufficient optimality condition for the maximization problem

$$\max_{\psi_t \in \Psi_t} \mathbb{E}_{t-1}\left[\lambda_t^{1-\gamma} \frac{(1 + r_t + \psi_t' \tilde{r}_t)^{1-\gamma} - 1}{1 - \gamma}\right], \tag{6.50}$$

which is in fact a family of noninteracting maximization problems—one for every time-$(t - 1)$ spot. Let us introduce the strictly positive probability $Q(t)$ with density

$$\frac{dQ(t)}{dP} = \frac{\lambda_t^{1-\gamma}}{\mathbb{E}[\lambda_t^{1-\gamma}]}.$$

By the change-of-measure formula of Proposition B.24, problem (6.50) is equivalent to

$$\max_{\psi_t \in \Psi_t} \mathbb{E}_{t-1}^{Q(t)}\left[\frac{(1 + r_t + \psi_t' \tilde{r}_t)^{1-\gamma} - 1}{1 - \gamma}\right]. \tag{6.51}$$

At each time-$(t - 1)$ spot, (6.51) computes the optimal allocation by maximizing a conditional expected power or logarithmic utility of the period-t portfolio return under the new probability $Q(t)$, which fully captures the problem's dynamic aspect. The existence of a maximum is guaranteed by the following lemma (whose proof is similar to that of Proposition 3.38).

Lemma 6.40. *Given any strictly positive λ_t in $L(\mathcal{F}_t)$, there exists a unique ψ_t in Ψ_t such that equation (6.49) is satisfied.*

Proof. Given the above discussion, it suffices to show existence and uniqueness of a maximum for problem (6.51). Uniqueness follows by the strict concavity of the objective and the assumption of dynamically independent contracts. To show the existence of a maximum, we let A_t denote the set of every random variable of the form $1 + r_t + \psi_t' \tilde{r}_t$ for some $\psi_t \in L(\mathcal{F}_{t-1})^J$. In particular, $1 + r_t \in A_t$. We proceed with slightly different arguments for the cases $\gamma < 1$ and $\gamma \geq 1$. Suppose first that $\gamma \geq 1$. Given any SPD π, we let B_t denote the set of every $\mathbb{R}_{++}$-valued $\mathcal{F}_t$-measurable random variable z_t such that

$$\mathbb{E}_{t-1}^{Q(t)}\left[\frac{z_t^{1-\gamma} - 1}{1 - \gamma}\right] \geq \frac{(1 + r_t)^{1-\gamma} - 1}{1 - \gamma} \quad \text{and} \quad \mathbb{E}_{t-1}\left[\frac{\pi_t}{\pi_{t-1}} z_t\right] = 1.$$

By Lemma 6.38, $\mathbb{E}_{t-1}[(\pi_t/\pi_{t-1})z_t] = 1$ for every $z_t \in A_t$, and therefore problem (6.51) is equivalent to the constrained problem

$$\max_{z_t \in A_t \cap B_t} \mathbb{E}_{t-1}^{Q(t)}\left[\frac{z_t^{1-\gamma} - 1}{1 - \gamma}\right]. \tag{6.52}$$

The set A_t is closed and the set B_t is compact. Therefore, $A_t \cap B_t$ is compact, and the existence of the maximum follows by the usual continuity-compactness argument. Finally, suppose $\gamma \in (0, 1)$, in which case B_t as defined above is not compact. We instead define B_t to be the set of every $\mathbb{R}_+$-valued random variable z_t such that $\mathbb{E}_{t-1}[(\pi_t/\pi_{t-1})z_t] = 1$. Arguing as above, we conclude that (6.52) has a solution, which is also a solution to problem (6.51), except that now we have to additionally verify that the optimizing value of z_t is strictly positive. This last claim follows from the fact that the marginal value $z_t^{-\gamma}$ becomes infinite at zero, and therefore a sufficiently small deviation away from zero is always improving. The formalization of this argument is left as an exercise. ∎

The recursive step is completed in Theorem 6.42 below, with an implicit rule for computing λ_{t-1} in terms of the pair (λ_t, ψ_t) that is based on the following lemma.

Lemma 6.41. *Given any time $t < T$ and $z \in (0, \infty)$, there exists a unique $y \in (0, \infty)$ such that*

$$\frac{y}{g_t^*(y)} = z.$$

Proof. We give a graphical argument, leaving a formal proof as an exercise. Referring to Figure 6.1, we see that as the slope of the tangent line decreases, the intercept with the vertical axis increases, and therefore g_t^* is a (strictly) decreasing function. Letting the tangent line's slope go to zero, we observe that

$$g_t^*(0+) = g_t(\infty) > g_t(1) = 1.$$

Consider now the graph of g_t^* on the plane and, for any given $z \in (0, \infty)$, the line $L = \{(\lambda, \lambda/z) : \lambda \in (0, \infty)\}$. The graph of g_t^* is downward sloping, it is above L near the vertical axis and therefore crosses L at exactly one point, which defines the unique $y \in (0, \infty)$ such that $z = y/g_t^*(y)$. ∎

Theorem 6.42. *The SI formulation admits a unique solution. The optimal consumption plan c, optimal utility process $U(c)$, optimal allocation policy (ϱ, ψ) and corresponding wealth process W can be computed in the following steps.*

1. *Determine the process $\lambda \in \mathcal{L}_{++}$ and the trading policy ψ by a backward recursion, starting with $\lambda_T = 1$. For the recursive step, suppose λ_t is known. First compute ψ_t as the unique element of the set Ψ_t (defined in (6.48)) that solves (6.49) (or, equivalently, solves (6.51)). Then advance the recursion by computing λ_{t-1} as the unique solution to*

$$\frac{\lambda_{t-1}}{g_{t-1}^*(\lambda_{t-1})} = \upsilon_{t-1}\big(\lambda_t(1 + r_t + \psi_t' \tilde{r}_t)\big), \tag{6.53}$$

where υ_{t-1} is the conditional CE corresponding to expected utility with constant coefficient of relative risk aversion γ.

2. *The optimal consumption policy is given in terms of the process* λ *by*

$$\varrho_t = h_t(\mathcal{I}_t(\lambda_t)), \quad t < T, \quad \varrho_T = 1, \tag{6.54}$$

where h_t *is the elasticity of the proportional aggregator* g_t, *and* $\mathcal{I}_t$ *is the inverse function of* g_t'.

3. *Given the optimal allocation policy* (ϱ, ψ), *compute the wealth process* W *by solving the forward recursion* (6.47). *The optimal consumption plan is* $c = \varrho W$ *and its utility process is* $U(c) = \lambda W$.

Proof. Lemmas 6.40 and 6.41 ensure that the theorem's recursion is well-defined. By Proposition 6.20, the utility is strictly concave, and therefore an optimal consumption plan, if it exists, is unique. A corresponding optimal trading strategy is also unique, since the $1 + J$ contracts implementing the market have been assumed to be dynamically independent. There remains to verify that the proposed solution is indeed feasible and optimal. We have already seen that the budget equation is equivalent to (6.47), which is valid by construction. We verify the utility recursion and the state-price density property of the utility gradient density. Optimality then follows by Lemma 6.36.

Verification of the utility recursion. Defining $U = \lambda W$, we are to show that $U = U(c)$. We have $U_T = \lambda_T W_T = c_T$, since $\lambda_T = 1$ and $\varrho_T = 1$. Let us now verify the utility recursion

$$U_{t-1} = v_{t-1}(U_t)\, g_{t-1}\!\left(\frac{c_{t-1}}{v_{t-1}(U_t)}\right). \tag{6.55}$$

Equation (6.54) implies

$$1 - \varrho_t = \frac{g_t^*(\lambda_t)}{g_t(\mathcal{I}_t(\lambda_t))}, \quad t < T. \tag{6.56}$$

Then the wealth dynamics (6.47) and the identity $U = \lambda W$ imply that

$$v_{t-1}\big(\lambda_t(1 + r_t + \psi_t'\tilde{r}_t)\big) = v_{t-1}\!\left(\frac{\lambda_t W_t}{W_{t-1}(1 - \varrho_{t-1})}\right)$$

$$= \frac{\lambda_{t-1}}{g_{t-1}^*(\lambda_{t-1})} \frac{g_{t-1}(\mathcal{I}_{t-1}(\lambda_{t-1}))}{U_{t-1}} v_{t-1}(U_t).$$

Substituting this expression into the recursion (6.53) for λ results in

$$U_{t-1} = v_{t-1}(U_t)\, g_{t-1}(\mathcal{I}_{t-1}(\lambda_{t-1})). \tag{6.57}$$

Expanding (6.54) using the definition of h and the identity $U = \lambda W$, we have

$$c_{t-1} = \varrho_{t-1} W_{t-1} = \frac{\mathcal{I}_{t-1}(\lambda_{t-1}) U_{t-1}}{g_{t-1}(\mathcal{I}_{t-1}(\lambda_{t-1}))} = \mathcal{I}_{t-1}(\lambda_{t-1}) v_{t-1}(U_t).$$

The last expression for c_{t-1} together with (6.57) proves (6.55).

Verification of the SPD property of the utility gradient density. Using equation (6.57), the identity $U = \lambda W$, the budget equation and expression (6.56), we compute

$$\frac{U_t}{v_{t-1}(U_t)} = g_{t-1}(\mathcal{I}_{t-1}(\lambda_{t-1})) \frac{U_t}{U_{t-1}} = g_{t-1}(\mathcal{I}_{t-1}(\lambda_{t-1})) \frac{\lambda_t}{\lambda_{t-1}} \frac{W_t}{W_{t-1}}$$

$$= g_{t-1}^*(\lambda_{t-1}) \frac{\lambda_t}{\lambda_{t-1}} (1 + r_t + \psi_t' \tilde{r}_t).$$

Combining the above with IMRS expression (6.35), we obtain

$$\frac{\pi_t}{\pi_{t-1}} = \left(g_{t-1}^*(\lambda_{t-1}) \frac{\lambda_t}{\lambda_{t-1}} \right)^{1-\gamma} (1 + r_t + \psi_t' \tilde{r}_t)^{-\gamma}.$$

Let us now verify the two state-pricing conditions of Lemma 6.38. Given the above expression for π_t / π_{t-1}, it is easy to check that the first equation in (6.45) is equivalent to equation (6.49) used to define ψ_t. There remains to verify the second equation in (6.45), which can be equivalently stated as

$$\mathbb{E}_{t-1}[\lambda_t^{1-\gamma}(1 + r_t + \psi_t' \tilde{r}_t)^{-\gamma}(1 + r_t)] = \left(\frac{\lambda_{t-1}}{g_{t-1}^*(\lambda_{t-1})} \right)^{1-\gamma}. \qquad (6.58)$$

Premultiplying equation (6.49) with ψ_t', we have

$$\mathbb{E}_{t-1}[\lambda_t^{1-\gamma}(1 + r_t + \psi_t' \tilde{r}_t)^{-\gamma} \psi_t' \tilde{r}_t] = 0. \qquad (6.59)$$

Therefore, equation (6.58) to be verified can equivalently be stated as

$$\mathbb{E}_{t-1}[\lambda_t^{1-\gamma}(1 + r_t + \psi_t' \tilde{r}_t)^{1-\gamma}] = \left(\frac{\lambda_{t-1}}{g_{t-1}^*(\lambda_{t-1})} \right)^{1-\gamma}.$$

This equation is trivially true if $\gamma = 1$ and is the same as recursion (6.53) for λ if $\gamma \neq 1$. ∎

We conclude with some special cases in which aspects of the solution to the SI formulation are significantly simplified.

Example 6.43 (Unit EIS). *Suppose the utility takes the Epstein-Zin-Weil form of Example 6.19 with unit EIS ($\delta = 1$). Then $h_t = 1 - \beta$, which is a constant. Therefore, the optimal consumption-to-wealth ratio is also a constant, $\varrho_t = 1 - \beta$, for any coefficient of relative risk aversion γ and any specification of the market. The case $\gamma = 1$ corresponds to expected discounted logarithmic utility.*

Example 6.44 (Unit CRRA). *In this example we do not restrict the proportional aggregator, but we assume a unit coefficient of relative risk aversion ($\gamma = 1$). In this case, the factor $\lambda_t^{1-\gamma}$ in (6.50) becomes equal to one, and therefore the determination of the time-t optimal portfolio weights is the same as for a myopic agent who at every spot maximizes the conditional expected logarithmic utility of single-period returns.*

Example 6.45. *We assume that the short-rate process r is deterministic and the vector of period-t excess returns $\tilde{r}_t$ is stochastically independent of $\mathcal{F}_{t-1}$, for every $t > 0$. In this case, a backward induction shows that the marginal-value-of-wealth process λ at the optimum is deterministic. As a consequence, the optimal allocation policy (ϱ, ψ) is also deterministic, with the optimal time-t portfolio weights determined as the solution to the myopic problem*

$$\max_{\psi_t} \mathbb{E}\left[\frac{(1 + r_t + \psi_t'\tilde{r}_t)^{1-\gamma} - 1}{1 - \gamma}\right],$$

where the maximization is over all $\psi_t \in \mathbb{R}^J$ such that $1 + r_t + \psi_t'\tilde{r}_t$ is strictly positive.

Example 6.46 (Markovian Formulation). *Suppose the contracts implementing the market have the Markovian structure of Section 5.7, which is defined in terms of an underlying martingale basis with stochastically independent increments. In this case, the process λ and the optimal allocation policy can be expressed as functions of the Markov state:*

$$\lambda_t = \lambda(t, Z_t), \quad \varrho_t = \varrho(t, Z_t) \quad \text{and} \quad \psi_t = \psi(t, Z_{t-1}),$$

where we have followed the notational convention of Section 5.7. Analogously to the arbitrage-pricing application of Section 5.7, the significance of the Markovian formulation is that the recursive formula determining ψ_t and λ_{t-1} in terms of λ_t need be evaluated only for every possible value of the Markov state Z_{t-1} rather than every time-$(t-1)$ spot.

6.7.3 Translation-Invariant Formulation

As in Section 6.6.3, we consider an agent with (sufficiently regular) translation-invariant (TI) Kreps-Porteus utility, an example of which is expected discounted exponential utility. In contrast to the SI formulation, we now allow the generality of a nonmarketed income stream. On the market side, we assume that there is a traded annuity, which we define as a contract with unit dividend process. More precisely, we adopt the following assumptions and notation throughout.

TI Formulation. *The agent's preferences over the consumption set $\mathcal{L}$ are represented by the TI Kreps-Porteus utility $U(\cdot)$, with an absolute aggregator g restricted as in Condition 6.32 and a coefficient of absolute risk aversion $\gamma \in (0, \infty)$. Contract zero, which we refer to as the* **annuity**, *satisfies*

$$\delta^0 = 1 \quad and \quad V_T^0 = 1.$$

We use the notation

$$Y_t = \frac{V_t}{V_t^0} - \frac{S_{t-1}}{S_{t-1}^0}, \quad t = 1, \ldots, T.$$

Remark 6.47. *To interpret Y_t, consider any portfolio $(\alpha^0, \alpha) \in L(\mathcal{F}_{t-1})^{1+J}$ that has zero time-$(t-1)$ ex-dividend value, that is,*

$$\alpha^0 S_{t-1}^0 + \alpha' S_{t-1} = 0.$$

Then

$$\alpha' Y_t = \frac{\alpha^0 V_t^0 + \alpha' V_t}{V_t^0}$$

is the time-t cum-dividend value of this portfolio, taking the annuity value as the unit of account.

Besides the above assumption on contract zero, we impose no further restrictions on the market structure described in Section 6.7.1. The time-t annuity value V_t^0 represents the time-t present value of the dividend process $\mathbf{1}$ and is therefore given by equation (6.42), for any SPD π. It follows that S_t^0 and $V_t^0 = S_t^0 + 1$ are strictly positive random variables, for every time $t < T$.

Example 6.48. *Suppose there is a traded money-market account with a deterministic short-rate process r and corresponding risk-free discount* *process*

$$\rho_t = \prod_{s=1}^{t} \frac{1}{1+r_s}, \quad \rho_0 = 1.$$

If Q is any EMM, then the traded annuity can be priced as

$$V_t^0 = \frac{1}{\rho_t} \mathbb{E}_t^Q \sum_{s=t}^{T} \rho_s = \frac{1}{\rho_t} \sum_{s=t}^{T} \rho_s,$$

and therefore V^0 is also a deterministic processes.

The following lemma provides a useful characterization of state-price densities, given the assumed tradeability of the annuity. The second equation in (6.60) recursively prices the annuity, while the first equation in (6.60) prices the remaining contracts relative to the annuity.

Lemma 6.49. *The process $\pi \in \mathcal{L}_{++}$ is an SPD if and only if*

$$\mathbb{E}_{t-1}\left[\frac{\pi_t V_t^0}{\pi_{t-1} S_{t-1}^0} Y_t \right] = 0 \quad \text{and} \quad \mathbb{E}_{t-1}\left[\frac{\pi_t V_t^0}{\pi_{t-1} S_{t-1}^0} \right] = 1. \tag{6.60}$$

Proof. By Proposition 5.26, (P, π) is a probability-SPD pair if and only if it prices the $1 + J$ contracts generating the market. By Proposition 5.27 and the strict positivity of S_-^0 and V^0, it follows that π is an SPD if and only if

$$\frac{S_{t-1}^j}{S_{t-1}^0} = \mathbb{E}_{t-1}\left[\frac{\pi_t V_t^0}{\pi_{t-1} S_{t-1}^0} \frac{V_t^j}{V_t^0} \right], \quad j = 0, \ldots, J. \tag{6.61}$$

Setting $j = 0$ results in the second equation of (6.60). The latter together with equation (6.61) for $j = 1, \ldots, J$ implies the first equation of (6.60). This proves the "only if" part of the lemma. Conversely, (6.60) clearly implies (6.61) and therefore that π is an SPD. ∎

Unlike the SI formulation, in the TI formulation consumption, prices and financial wealth can take zero or negative values. In particular, returns and wealth proportions need not be well-defined, and for this reason we go back to working with trading strategies expressed in numbers of shares. We adopt the convention that there is zero initial financial wealth, that is, $w = 0$ in equation (6.44), and therefore the (financial) wealth process

241

associated with the trading strategy $(\theta^0, \theta) \in P_0 \times P_0^J$ is given as

$$W = \theta^0 V^0 + \theta' V. \tag{6.62}$$

We recall that W_t is the time-t present value of the cash flow $c - e$, where c is the consumption plan financed by (θ^0, θ).

The key to uncoupling the forward-backward recursion of the optimality conditions is the translation-invariance property of preferences and the tradeability of the annuity. The basic idea is that if at any spot the agent has optimally selected a consumption plan and a trading strategy, then, by translation invariance, the agent can invest any additional financial wealth in the annuity, consuming all resulting incremental dividends while preserving optimality.

Arguing informally for now, let $(\bar{\theta}_t^0, \theta_t)$ be the optimal period-t portfolio for a hypothetical version of the agent who at time $t - 1$ has zero financial wealth, and let $\bar{U}_{t-1}$ denote the hypothetical agent's optimal utility level at the beginning of the period. Incrementally to $(\bar{\theta}_t^0, \theta_t)$, the original agent can optimally invest all of the time-$(t - 1)$ financial wealth in the annuity, thus purchasing W_{t-1}/V_{t-1}^0 shares of the annuity, and can optimally consume the resulting incremental cash flow. Since the utility is quasilinear with respect to $\mathbf{1}$, the resulting optimal portfolio (θ_t^0, θ_t) and utility level U_{t-1} must satisfy

$$\theta_t^0 = \bar{\theta}_t^0 + \frac{W_{t-1}}{V_{t-1}^0} \quad \text{and} \quad U_{t-1} = \bar{U}_{t-1} + \frac{W_{t-1}}{V_{t-1}^0}. \tag{6.63}$$

If at time $t - 1$ the hypothetical agent optimally consumes $\bar{c}_{t-1}$, the original agent consumes $c_{t-1} = \bar{c}_{t-1} + W_{t-1}/V_{t-1}^0$. Given zero financial wealth at time $t - 1$, the hypothetical agent's budget requires that the consumption $\bar{c}_{t-1}$ and the ex-dividend portfolio value $\bar{S}_{t-1} = \bar{\theta}_t^0 S_{t-1}^0 + \theta_t' S_{t-1}$ add up to the endowment e_{t-1} and therefore

$$\bar{S}_{t-1} = e_{t-1} - c_{t-1} + \frac{W_{t-1}}{V_{t-1}^0}. \tag{6.64}$$

At this point, it is a good exercise to use the above insights to transform the optimality conditions to an algorithm based on a backward recursion for computing $\bar{U}$ and $(\bar{\theta}^0, \theta)$ on the information tree. As for the SI formulation, we proceed in the opposite direction, first specifying a proposed solution and then verifying its optimality and uniqueness.

We will establish a backward recursion stipulating that θ_t is determined in terms of $\bar{U}_t$ as the unique element of $L(\mathcal{F}_{t-1})^J$ that satisfies

$$\mathbb{E}_{t-1}[\exp(-\gamma(\bar{U}_t + \theta_t' Y_t)) Y_t] = 0. \qquad (6.65)$$

This equation can be recognized as a sufficient and necessary optimality condition for the following family of single-period maximization problems (one for every time-$(t-1)$ spot):

$$\max_{\theta_t \in L(\mathcal{F}_{t-1})^J} \mathbb{E}_{t-1}[-\exp(-\gamma(\bar{U}_t + \theta_t' Y_t))]. \qquad (6.66)$$

Analogously to the SI analysis, the factor involving $\bar{U}_t$ can be absorbed in the expectation by introducing the new probability $Q(t)$, defined by its density:

$$\frac{dQ(t)}{dP} = \frac{\exp(-\gamma \bar{U}_t)}{\mathbb{E}[\exp(-\gamma \bar{U}_t)]}.$$

By the change-of-measure formula of Proposition B.24, problem (6.66) can be restated as

$$\max_{\theta_t \in L(\mathcal{F}_{t-1})^J} \mathbb{E}_{t-1}^{Q(t)}[-\exp(-\gamma \theta_t' Y_t)]. \qquad (6.67)$$

By Remark 6.47, we can interpret the above as the period-t problem of a myopic agent with prior $Q(t)$, who at the beginning of the period has zero wealth and selects a portfolio to maximize the expected exponential utility of the end-of-period value relative to the annuity, that is, taking the annuity cum-dividend price as the unit of account.

Lemma 6.50. *Given any $\mathcal{F}_t$-measurable random variable $\bar{U}_t$, there exists a unique J-dimensional $\mathcal{F}_{t-1}$-measurable random variable θ_t that satisfies (6.65).*

Proof. The argument is similar to that used in Lemma 6.40. Given our earlier discussion, it suffices to show existence and uniqueness of a maximum for problem (6.67). Let A_t be the set of every random variable of the form $\theta_t' Y_t$ for some $\theta_t \in L(\mathcal{F}_{t-1})^J$, and let π be any SPD. Let also B_t be the set of every strictly positive $\mathcal{F}_t$-measurable random variable z_t such that

$$\mathbb{E}_{t-1}^{Q(t)}[-\exp(-\gamma z_t)] \geq -1 \quad \text{and} \quad \mathbb{E}_{t-1}\left[\frac{\pi_t V_t^0}{\pi_{t-1} S_{t-1}^0} - z_t\right] = 0.$$

By Lemma 6.49, the last equation is satisfied by every $z_t \in A_t$, while the above inequality is satisfied by $0 \in A_t$. Therefore, the maximization problem (6.51) is equivalent to the constrained problem

$$\max_{z_t \in A_t \cap B_t} \mathbb{E}_{t-1}^{Q(t)}[-\exp(-\gamma z_t)].$$

The set A_t is closed and the set B_t is compact. Therefore, $A_t \cap B_t$ is compact, and the existence of the maximum follows by the usual continuity-compactness argument.

By the strict concavity of the objective function, the value $\theta_t' Y_t$ is unique at the optimum. The assumption of dynamically independent contracts (δ^j, V^j) then implies that the optimal θ_t is unique. To show this claim it suffices to show that given any $\phi_t \in L(\mathcal{F}_{t-1})^J$, $\phi_t' Y_t = 0$ implies $\phi_t = 0$. On the event $\{\phi_t' S_{t-1} \neq 0\}$, $\phi_t' Y_t = 0$ implies $\phi_t' V_t / \phi_t' S_{t-1} = V_t^0 / S_{t-1}^0$, meaning that a unit of account invested in the annuity yields identical payoff as the same unit invested in the portfolio $(0, \phi_t)$, which does not include the annuity, contradicting the assumption of dynamically independent contracts. Therefore, $\phi_t' Y_t = 0$ implies that $\phi_t' V_t = \phi_t' S_{t-1} = 0$, which, by the dynamic independence of the contracts (δ, V), implies that $\phi_t = 0$. ∎

Based on the above insights and the utility gradient density calculation of Proposition 6.34, we show a solution method in the following main result.

Theorem 6.51. *The TI formulation admits a unique solution. The optimal consumption plan c, optimal utility process $U = U(c)$, optimal trading strategy (θ^0, θ) and corresponding financial wealth process W can be computed in the following steps, using the abbreviated notation*

$$g_t = g_t(\mathcal{I}_t(1/V_t^0)) \quad \text{and} \quad \mathcal{I}_t = \mathcal{I}_t(1/V_t^0),$$

where $\mathcal{I}_t(\cdot)$ is the inverse function of $g_t'(\cdot)$.

1. *Determine the processes $\bar{U} \in \mathcal{L}, \bar{\theta}^0 \in \mathcal{P}_0$ and $\theta \in \mathcal{P}_0^J$ by a backward recursion, starting with $\bar{U}_T = e_T$. For the recursive step, suppose*

$\bar{U}_t$ is given. First compute θ_t as the unique $\mathcal{F}_{t-1}$-measurable J-dimensional random variable that satisfies (6.65) (or, equivalently, solves (6.67)). Then define

$$\bar{S}_{t-1} = \frac{S^0_{t-1}}{V^0_{t-1}}(e_{t-1} - \mathcal{I}_{t-1} - v_{t-1}(\bar{U}_t + \theta'_t Y_t)),$$

where v_{t-1} is the conditional CE corresponding to expected utility with constant coefficient of absolute risk aversion γ. Finally, set the value $\bar{\theta}^0_t$ and advance the recursion by computing $\bar{U}_{t-1}$ using the equations

$$\bar{S}_{t-1} = \bar{\theta}^0_t S^0_{t-1} + \theta'_t S_{t-1},$$
$$\bar{U}_{t-1} = e_{t-1} + g_{t-1} - \mathcal{I}_{t-1} - \bar{S}_{t-1}. \tag{6.68}$$

2. Compute the wealth process W through the forward recursion

$$\frac{W_t}{V^0_t} = \frac{W_{t-1}}{V^0_{t-1}} + \bar{\theta}^0_t + \frac{\theta'_t V_t}{V^0_t}, \quad W_0 = 0. \tag{6.69}$$

3. Compute the optimal consumption plan by

$$c_t = \bar{U}_t - g_t + \mathcal{I}_t + \frac{W_t}{V^0_t}, \quad t < T; \quad c_T = e_T + W_T. \tag{6.70}$$

Finally, compute θ^0 and U using (6.63), with the terminal value $U_T = c_T$.

Proof. Because of Lemma 6.50, the theorem's algorithm produces a well-defined candidate solution. If there is an optimal consumption plan, it is necessarily unique since the time-zero utility function is strictly concave. Moreover, a unique trading strategy finances the optimal consumption plan, since we have assumed that the contracts (δ^j, V^j) are dynamically independent. The proof will, therefore, be complete if we verify that the proposed solution is indeed feasible and optimal. To do so, we verify the utility recursion showing that $U(c) = U$, the SPD property of the gradient density at c and finally the budget equation showing that (θ^0, θ) generates the wealth process W and finances c.

Verification of the utility recursion. Since $U_T = c_T$ by construction, to show that $U = U(c)$, we have to confirm the utility recursion

$$U_{t-1} = v_{t-1}(U_t) + g_{t-1}(c_{t-1} - v_{t-1}(U_t)). \tag{6.71}$$

245

We begin with the identity

$$U_t = \bar{U}_t + \frac{W_t}{V_t^0}, \quad t = 0, \ldots, T,$$

which is (6.63) for $t < T$ and is satisfied for $t = T$, since $\bar{U}_T = e_T$, $V_T^0 = 1$ and $c_T = e_T + W_T$. Using the recursion for W in (6.69), the definition of Y and the fact that $\bar{S}_{t-1} = \bar{\theta}_t^0 S_{t-1}^0 + \theta_t' S_{t-1}$, it follows that

$$U_t = \bar{U}_t + \frac{W_{t-1}}{V_{t-1}^0} + \bar{\theta}_t^0 + \frac{\theta_t' V_t}{V_t^0} = \bar{U}_t + \theta_t' Y_t + \frac{W_{t-1}}{V_{t-1}^0} + \frac{\bar{S}_{t-1}}{S_{t-1}^0}. \quad (6.72)$$

The definition of $\bar{S}_{t-1}$ and the fact that $V_{t-1}^0 = S_{t-1}^0 + 1$ imply

$$\frac{\bar{S}_{t-1}}{S_{t-1}^0} = -\bar{S}_{t-1} + e_{t-1} - \mathcal{I}_{t-1} - v_{t-1}(\bar{U}_t + \theta_t' Y_t). \quad (6.73)$$

Putting together (6.72) and (6.73) to compute $v_{t-1}(U_t)$ and using (6.68), we obtain

$$v_{t-1}(U_t) = \frac{W_{t-1}}{V_{t-1}^0} - \bar{S}_{t-1} + e_{t-1} - \mathcal{I}_{t-1} = \bar{U}_{t-1} + \frac{W_{t-1}}{V_{t-1}^0} - g_{t-1}.$$

The last expression for $v_{t-1}(U_t)$ results in $U_{t-1} = v_{t-1}(U_t) + g_{t-1}(\mathcal{I}_{t-1})$ when combined with (6.63) and $\mathcal{I}_{t-1} = c_{t-1} - v_{t-1}(U_t)$ when combined with (6.70). The last two equations together prove the utility recursion (6.71).

Verification of the SPD property of the utility gradient density. Let π be the utility gradient density at c. We use the IMRS expression (6.43) with $\lambda = 1/V^0$ (see Proposition 6.34) and the identity $U_{t-1} = v_{t-1}(U_t) + g_{t-1}$, shown above, to obtain

$$\frac{\pi_t V_t^0}{\pi_{t-1} S_{t-1}^0} = \exp(-\gamma(U_t - v_{t-1}(U_t)))$$

$$= \exp(-\gamma(\Delta U_t + g_{t-1})). \quad (6.74)$$

We prove that π is an SPD by verifying that the above ratio satisfies the restrictions of Lemma 6.49.

Using the first equation of (6.74), we note that

$$\mathbb{E}_{t-1}\left[\frac{\pi_t V_t^0}{\pi_{t-1} S_{t-1}^0}\right] = 1 \iff v_{t-1}(U_t) = -\frac{1}{\gamma}\log \mathbb{E}_{t-1}\exp(-\gamma U_t).$$

Therefore, the second marginal pricing condition of Lemma 6.49 follows from the conditional CE specification.

To verify the first marginal pricing condition of Lemma 6.49, we use the second equation of (6.74) to note that

$$\mathbb{E}_{t-1}\left[\frac{\pi_t V_t^0}{\pi_{t-1} S_{t-1}^0} Y_t\right] = 0 \iff \mathbb{E}_{t-1}[\exp(-\gamma \Delta U_t)Y_t] = 0$$

$$\iff \mathbb{E}_{t-1}[\exp(-\gamma(\bar{U}_t + \theta_t' Y_t))Y_t] = 0,$$

where the second equivalence follows from (6.72), which implies that $\Delta U_t - (\bar{U}_t + \theta_t' Y_t)$ is $\mathcal{F}_{t-1}$-measurable. The last equation is valid by the construction of θ_t in (6.65), and the proof that π is an SPD is complete.

Verification of the budget equation. The second equation in (6.68) and the consumption expression (6.70) together imply that $\bar{S}_{t-1}$ satisfies (6.64). The expression for θ^0 in (6.63), the wealth recursion (6.69) and the definition of $\bar{\theta}^0$ in (6.68) imply that

$$W_t = \theta_t^0 V_t^0 + \theta_t' V_t \quad \text{and} \quad \bar{S}_{t-1} = (\theta_t^0 S_{t-1}^0 + \theta_t' S_{t-1}) - \frac{W_{t-1}}{V_{t-1}^0} S_{t-1}^0.$$

Combining the above with (6.64) and using the expression for c_T in (6.70) results in the budget equation expressing the fact that the trading strategy (θ^0, θ) generates the incremental cash flow $c - e$:

$$c_{t-1} - e_{t-1} = \theta_{t-1}^0 V_{t-1}^0 + \theta_{t-1}' V_{t-1} - (\theta_t^0 S_{t-1}^0 + \theta_t' S_{t-1}),$$

with the terminal condition $c_T - e_T = \theta_T^0 V_T^0 + \theta_T' V_T.$ ∎

We conclude with a special case in which the process $\bar{U}$ is deterministic. The discussion of a Markovian TI formulation is analogous to that of Example 6.46 and is left to the reader.

Example 6.52. *As in the last example, we assume that the short-rate process r is deterministic. We also assume that the endowment e is deterministic and Y_t is stochastically independent of $\mathcal{F}_{t-1}$ for each time $t > 0$. In this case, a backward induction shows that the process $\bar{U}$ is deterministic. As a consequence,* *the optimal consumption plan in* (6.70) *is an affine function of financial wealth with deterministic coefficients, and the optimal trading strategy is also deterministic. The optimal time-t portfolio θ_t is determined by solving the myopic problem*

$$\max_{\theta_t \in \mathbb{R}^J} \mathbb{E}[-\exp(-\gamma \theta_t' Y_t)].$$

6.8 EXERCISES

1. (a) Consider the following two conditions:

   A1* For any $c, c + x \in C$ and spot (F, t), if spot $(G, t+1)$ is an immediate successor of (F, t) and $x \in \mathcal{L}_{G,t+1}$, then

   $$U_{G,t+1}(c + x) \geq U_{G,t+1}(c) \quad \Longleftrightarrow \quad U_{F,t}(c + x) \geq U_{F,t}(c).$$

   A1° For any $c, c + x \in C$ and nonterminal spot (F, t), if $(G, t+1)$ is an immediate successor of (F, t) and $x \in \mathcal{L}_{G,t+1}$, then

   $$U_{G,t+1}(c + x) = U_{G,t+1}(c) \quad \Longrightarrow \quad U_{F,t}(c + x) = U_{F,t}(c).$$

   Show that A1 $\Longleftrightarrow$ A1* $\Longrightarrow$ A1°.

   (b) Show that a normalized dynamic utility U is recursive utility if and only if it satisfies A1°, A2 and A3. Only explain what part of the proof of Proposition 6.9 needs to be modified and how.

2. Suppose U is recursive utility on the consumption set $C = (\ell, \infty)^{1+K}$, with aggregator f and conditional CE υ. Suppose also that for every spot (F, t), $I_{F,t} \subseteq \mathbb{R}$ is a real interval and $h_{F,t} : (\ell, \infty) \to I_{F,t}$ is an increasing continuous onto (and hence invertible) function. Define the ordinally equivalent dynamic utility function $\tilde{U}$ by letting $\tilde{U}_{F,t} = h_{F,t} \circ U_{F,t}$ for every spot (F, t). Derive a recursive representation for $\tilde{U}$, providing formulas for the corresponding aggregator (which is now not necessarily normalized) and conditional CE. Finally, specialize these formulas to the case of a Kreps-Porteus representation.

3. Prove that any two (normalized) recursive utilities are ordinally equivalent over deterministic plans if and only if they have the same aggregator.

4. In Proposition 6.15, replace the assumption that $f(t, \cdot)$ is differentiable with the assumption that $f(t, \cdot)$ is concave, with superdiffer-

ential $\partial f(t, \cdot)$. Give a variant of the formulas of Proposition 6.15 that define a supergradient density of the time-zero utility, that is, an adapted process π such that $U_0(c + x) \leq U_0(c) + (\pi \mid x)$ for all $c, c + x \in C$.

5. (Elasticity of Intertemporal Substitution) Suppose U is a scale-invariant recursive utility with a smooth aggregator f. Show that the elasticity of intertemporal substitution (EIS) is well-defined by

$$\text{EIS} = \frac{d \log(c/\upsilon)}{d \log(f_c(t, c, \upsilon)/f_\upsilon(t, c, \upsilon))}.$$

Express the EIS in terms of the proportional aggregator corresponding to f, and verify that $\text{EIS} = 1/\delta$ in the Epstein-Zin-Weil specification of Example 6.31. What is an economic interpretation of the EIS? Is the above expression well-defined without the scale-invariance assumption? What would be an extension of the EIS definition to non–scale-invariant settings that is consistent with the given economic interpretation?

6. (a) Prove Proposition 6.23.

(b) We saw in Section 3.5.1 that for SI or TI utility concavity is an ordinal property. Show that strict concavity of SI or TI utility is also an ordinal property. Use these facts to verify that for SI or TI recursive utility, (strict) concavity of the entire dynamic utility is equivalent to that of the corresponding time-zero utility.

7. (Preferences for the Timing of Resolution of Uncertainty) In this book preferences are defined over consumption plans taking the information tree (filtration) as given. In settings in which the information structure is not fixed, it is natural to consider preferences not only over consumption but also over information. In particular, an agent may have preferences for earlier or later resolution of uncertainty about future consumption. In the context of Example 6.3, given the consumption plan b, an agent with preferences for early resolution of uncertainty would prefer to have all T coin tosses announced at time zero, rather than wait to find out the outcome of the tth coin toss at time t. References to a related literature can be found in the endnotes.

More formally, let C be a consumption set and let Φ be the set of every filtration $\{\mathcal{F}_t : 0, \dots, T\}$ satisfying $\mathcal{F}_0 = \{\Omega, \emptyset\}$ and $\mathcal{F}_T = 2^\Omega$. We consider a (nonnormalized) utility function $V_0(\cdot)$ over the set of all pairs $(c, \{\mathcal{F}_t\}) \in C \times \Phi$ such that c is adapted to $\{\mathcal{F}_t\}$. Taking as primitive an underlying probability with expectation operator $\mathbb{E}$ and the functions $F_t : \mathbb{R}^2 \to \mathbb{R}, t = 0, \ldots, T-1$, and $F_T : \mathbb{R} \to \mathbb{R}$, we assume that $V_0(c, \{\mathcal{F}_t\})$ is the initial value of the process V that solves the backward recursion

$$V_t = F_t(c_t, \mathbb{E}[V_{t+1} \mid \mathcal{F}_t]), \quad t = 0, \ldots, T-1; \quad V_T = F_T(c_T).$$

We say that the utility function $V_0(\cdot)$ expresses preferences for earlier resolution of uncertainty if for any $(c, \{\mathcal{F}_t^1\})$ and $(c, \{\mathcal{F}_t^2\})$ in its domain,

$$\mathcal{F}_t^1 \subseteq \mathcal{F}_t^2 \text{ for all } t \quad \text{implies} \quad V_0(c, \{\mathcal{F}_t^1\}) \leq V_0(c, \{\mathcal{F}_t^2\}).$$

Preferences for late resolution of uncertainty are defined analogously, with the last inequality reversed.

(a) Use Jensen's inequality (Lemma 4.13) to show that if the function F_t is convex (resp. concave) in its second (utility) argument for every $t < T$, then $V_0(\cdot)$ expresses preferences for earlier (resp. later) resolution of uncertainty. What does expected discounted utility imply for preferences over information?

(b) Relate the parameter ϕ of Examples 6.31 and 6.35 to preferences for the timing of resolution of uncertainty. *Hint:* Use Proposition 3.33.

8. Consider the setting of Section 5.6 and assume that the $1+J$ contracts implementing the market (one of which is a money-market account) are dynamically independent. Explain how Example 2.27 and Proposition 1.23 can be adapted to such a setting to compute a conditional Hansen-Jagannathan lower bound on the conditional standard deviation of the IMRS.

9. Perform the calculations required to show the IMRS expressions of Examples 6.31 and 6.35. Also provide direct calculations from first principles for the subcases corresponding to expected discounted utility.

10. In the context of Section 6.6.2, prove the alternative IMRS expression

$$\frac{\pi_t}{\pi_{t-1}} = \left(\frac{1}{M_t}\right)^\gamma \left(g_{t-1}^*(\lambda_{t-1})\frac{\lambda_t}{\lambda_{t-1}}\right)^{1-\gamma}.$$

11. (a) Using the normalization $g_t(1) = 1$, verify that the proportional aggregator g_t can be recovered from its elasticity function h_t by the equation

$$g_t(x) = \exp\left(\int_1^x \frac{h_t(z)}{z}dz\right), \quad x \in (0,\infty).$$

(b) Construct an example of a proportional aggregator whose corresponding elasticity function is not monotone (and as a consequence the construction of Proposition 6.30 does not apply).

12. Suppose the conditional CE υ has derivative κ. Show that if υ is homogeneous of degree one, then $\upsilon_{t-1}(U_t) = \mathbb{E}_{t-1}[\kappa_t(U_t)U_t]$.

13. Give a rigorous version of the proof of Lemma 6.41.

14. Prove the compactness of the set B_t in the proof of Lemmas 6.40 and 6.50, and formalize the argument at the end of the proof of Lemma 6.40 showing the strict positivity of the solution in the case $\gamma \in (0,1)$.

15. Prove that the conditions used in the solution method of Theorem 6.42 are necessary for optimality by arguing directly from the utility recursion, the wealth dynamics and the state-price density property of the utility gradient density at the optimal consumption plan.

16. (a) Consider the SI formulation of the optimal consumption and portfolio selection problem of Section 6.7.2. Simplify Theorem 6.42 under the additional assumption that the market is complete. In particular, derive a backward recursion for λ that is formulated without reference to the optimal trading policy ψ.

(b) Consider the TI formulation of the optimal consumption and portfolio selection problem of Section 6.7.3. Simplify Theorem 6.51 under the additional assumption that the market is complete. In particular, derive a backward recursion for $\bar{U}$ that is formulated without reference to the optimal trading strategy θ.

17. Prove a version of Theorem 6.42 without the assumption that the market allows default-free single-period borrowing and lending.

18. Prove that the conditions used in the solution method of Theorem 6.51 are necessary for optimality by arguing directly from the utility recursion, the wealth dynamics and the state-price density property of the utility gradient density at the optimal consumption plan. How are $\bar{\theta}^0$, $\bar{U}$ and $\bar{S}$ defined in terms of the optimal solution?

19. (a) Another approach to proving Theorem 6.42 is through dynamic programming, introduced in Section 5.4.2 in the context of option pricing. Let $J : (0, \infty) \to \mathcal{L}$ be the problem's **value** function, defined by the requirement that for any spot (F, t) and wealth level $w \in (0, \infty)$, $J(w)(F, t)$ is the optimal utility value for an agent at spot (F, t) with wealth w. Give a more rigorous definition of J and show that it satisfies the following **Bellman equation**:

$$J_{t-1}(w) = \max_{\varrho_{t-1}, \psi_t} f_{t-1}(\varrho_{t-1}w, \upsilon_{t-1}(J_t(w^{\varrho_{t-1}, \psi_t}))),$$

where

$$w^{\varrho_{t-1}, \psi_t} = w(1 - \varrho_{t-1})(1 + r_t + \psi_t' \tilde{r}_t),$$

explaining the sets over which ϱ_{t-1} and ψ_t are chosen. Argue that in the SI formulation, $J(w) = \lambda w$ for some positive adapted process λ, and use the Bellman equation to give another proof of Theorem 6.42.

(b) In the context of the TI formulation of Section 6.7.3, formulate an analogous argument to that of part (a), thus providing an alternative proof of Theorem 6.51 based on a Bellman equation.

20. Explain how the solution algorithms of Sections 6.7.2 and 6.7.3 simplify computationally under the assumption that the market has the Markovian structure of Section 5.7.

21. For the SI and TI solutions of Sections 6.7.2 and 6.7.3, apply the approximation method of Section 4.6 to derive simplified expressions for the optimal trading strategy (or policy in the SI case) that are analogous to expression (4.23). State all your assumptions clearly, utilizing an underlying dynamically orthonormal martingale basis that generates the filtration.

6.9 NOTES

Dynamic competitive equilibrium arguments in asset pricing are a natural outgrowth of the classical competitive equilibrium theory discussed in the notes of Chapter 3. In the tradition of the static CAPM, dynamic asset pricing models seek to establish empirically testable implications by imposing special assumptions on the primitives. Early models assume expected discounted utility, (effectively) complete markets and often specific parameterizations of endowment dynamics. Influential contributions of this type include Merton (1973a), Rubinstein (1976), Lucas (1978), Breeden (1979) (see also Duffie and Zame (1989)) and Cox, Ingersoll and Ross (1985). Our reinterpretation of static markets equilibrium in a dynamic setting is conceptually similar to the approach taken by Duffie and Huang (1985).

An early discussion of the issue of the dynamic consistency of preferences is given by Strotz (1957). Recursive utility goes back to Koopmans (1960) for the deterministic case and Kreps and Porteus (1978), Selden (1978), Johnsen and Donaldson (1985), Chew and Epstein (1989) and Epstein and Zin (1989) for the stochastic case. More recent decision-theoretic foundations for recursive utility include Skiadas (1998), Wang (2003), Hayashi (2005) and Klibanoff and Ozdenoren (2007). Kreps and Porteus (1978) first introduced preferences for the timing of resolution of uncertainty in the context of recursive utility. The formalism of Exercise 7 is based on Skiadas (1998), where preferences are defined over pairs of consumption plans and filtrations, with preference for early or late resolution of uncertainty corresponding to utility monotonicity with respect to the filtration argument. (An asset pricing illustration of the effect is given by Duffie, Schroder and Skiadas (1997).)

Recursive utility entered asset pricing theory mainly through the contributions of Epstein and Zin (1991), Giovannini and Weil (1989) and Weil (1989, 1990), whose arguments were motivated by the "equity-premium puzzle" of Mehra and Prescott (1985) (see Singleton (2006) and Constantinides (2002) for broad perspectives on empirical issues in asset pricing, including the equity-premium puzzle). These authors introduced the Epstein-Zin-Weil parametric case of Kreps-Porteus utility of Example 6.19 and based their analysis on the IMRS expression (6.40). A more recent application of this formula is given by Bansal and Yaron (2004), again addressing the equity-premium puzzle. Beyond the above parametric cases, this chapter's asset pricing theory for scale- or translation-invariant Kreps-Porteus recursive utility is, to my knowledge, original.

Motivated by the significance of continuous-time models in finance, Duffie and Epstein (1992b) formulated a continuous-time version of sufficiently smooth recursive utility (with the infinite-horizon case treated in Duffie, Epstein and Skiadas (1992)). The Duffie-Epstein analysis requires technical (Lipschitz-growth) restrictions on the utility aggregator that exclude the continuous-time version of Epstein-Zin-Weil utility. A theory of existence, uniqueness and basic properties for the latter is developed by Schroder and Skiadas (1999) (see also Skiadas (2003) for another interpretation of the same utility). Asset-pricing applications with Duffie-Epstein utility include Duffie and Epstein (1992a), Obstfeld (1994) and more recently Bhamra, Kühn and Strebulaev (2007) and Chen (2007). The utility gradient of Duffie-Epstein utility, which gives a formula for equilibrium state-price densities, is computed in Duffie and Skiadas (1994). The existence and efficiency of competitive equilibrium with Duffie-Epstein utility is the topic of Duffie, Geoffard and Skiadas (1994), with a dual characterization of efficient allocations given by Dumas, Uppal and Wang (2000). A generalized form of continuous-time recursive utility appears in Lazrak and Quenez (2003) and Schroder and Skiadas (2003, 2005, 2008). Skiadas (2008a,b) presents arguments for the use of such utilities in modeling various notions of risk or ambiguity aversion.

The modern theory of optimal lifetime consumption and portfolio choice was first formulated in continuous time in seminal papers by Merton (1969, 1971), assuming expected discounted utility. Merton's methodology is that of the Hamilton-Jacobi-Bellman equation of optimal control theory, modern expositions of which are given by Fleming and Soner (1993) and Yong and Zhou (1999). Svensson (1989) and Obstfeld (1994) are early, heuristic extensions of the Merton analysis that assume continuous-time recursive utility. The Merton solution was derived using the state-price density property of marginal utilities at the optimum by Karatzas, Lehoczky and Shreve (1987) and Cox and Huang (1989), whose arguments relied on utility additivity. The approach was generalized to include continuous-time recursive utilities in Duffie and Skiadas (1994), El Karoui, Peng and Quenez (2001) and Schroder and Skiadas (1999, 2003, 2005, 2008). Exercise 19 (which is a discrete version of the approach of Section 4.6 of Schroder and Skiadas 2003) indicates that the same results can be obtained by dynamic programming arguments, without introducing auxiliary Markovian dynamics. Bhamra and Uppal (2006) use dynamic programming to solve a discrete-time optimal consumption/portfolio choice problem with Epstein-Zin-Weil utility. This chapter's discrete-time optimal solutions for the more general scale- or translation-invariant formulations are, to my knowledge, original. Some further references to a large literature on optimal consumption/portfolio choice can be found in Skiadas (2008a).

Not discussed in this chapter is a class of utilities with so-called habit formation, representing preferences that can depend on past consumption. Such utilities have been extensively used in asset pricing theory, following the early contributions of Pollak (1970), Ryder and Heal (1973),

Sundaresan (1989) and Constantinides (1990) (see also Chapman (1998)). Detemple and Zapatero (1991) and Ingersoll (1992) analyze optimal lifetime consumption-portfolio choice with habit formation. Duffie and Skiadas (1994) computed the utility gradient for a general class of utilities that combine recursivity with habit formation. Schroder and Skiadas (2002) showed that for a linear habit formation formulation, which includes the case considered by Constantinides (1990), consumption and state prices can be redefined in a mechanical way that formally eliminates the habit dependence. The method is used, for example, to transform known optimal consumption/portfolio policies for recursive utility to corresponding solutions that combine recursive utility with habit formation. A decision-theoretic foundation for utilities with habit formation was recently formulated by Rozen (2008). Another strand of the literature, exemplified by Abel (1990) and Campbell and Cochrane (1999) (see also Chen, Cosimano and Himonas (2007)), considers utilities with external habits, representing preferences that depend on other agents' past consumption.

Finally, it should be emphasized that this text and the literature reviewed in the notes forms only a selective introduction to the theory of competitive equilibrium asset pricing, with emphasis on mature topics. Essential topics that have not been discussed, to name just a few, include equilibrium models with agent heterogeneity, incomplete markets with wealth effects, other trading constraints, durables, transaction costs and behavioral models that seek consistency with empirical evidence on human behavior from psychology.

PART THREE

MATHEMATICAL BACKGROUND

Optimization Principles

THIS APPENDIX presents a self-contained overview of the convex optimization theory used in this text. While the presentation here is limited to the finite-dimensional case, the theory generalizes to infinite-dimensional spaces, which arise in asset-pricing models with infinitely many states.

A.1 VECTOR SPACE

A (real) **vector** or **linear space** is a set X of elements, called **vectors** or **points**, together with two operations, **addition** and **multiplication by scalars**, that satisfy the following conditions, for all vectors x, y, z and real numbers α, β :

1. To (x, y) addition assigns a unique element of X denoted $x + y$, and to (α, x) multiplication by scalars assigns a unique element of X denoted αx.
2. $x + y = y + x$, $x + (y + z) = (x + y) + z$ and $\alpha(\beta x) = (\alpha\beta)x$.
3. $\alpha(x + y) = \alpha x + \alpha y$ and $(\alpha + \beta)x = \alpha x + \beta x$.
4. $0 + x = x$ and $1x = x$, where 0 is an element of X called the **zero vector.**
5. There exists a vector $-x$ such that $x + (-x) = 0$.

The zero vector is unique, and given any vector x, the vector $-x$ is unique. We write $x - y = x + (-y)$.

Although the term "vector space X" is common, it should be emphasized that a vector space specification includes not only a set of vectors but also the rules for adding vectors and multiplying by scalars. Two examples of a vector space X follow.

Example A.1. $X = \mathbb{R}^d$ is the usual d-dimensional Euclidean space. Vector addition and multiplication by scalars are defined coordinatewise: $(\alpha x + y)_i = \alpha x_i + y_i$ for any scalar α, vectors x, y and coordinate i.

Example A.2. Given an underlying probability space, $X = L_2$ is the set of all random variables of finite variance, with the usual rules for adding and scaling random variables.

A subset L of the vector space X is a **linear** (or **vector**) **subspace** if it is a vector space itself or, equivalently, if for all x, y in L and any real α, $x + y$ and αx are also elements of L. The linear subspace **generated** or **spanned** by a set of vectors S, denoted span(S), is the intersection of all linear subspaces that include S. Alternatively, the span of a set can be constructed from within. For a finite set of vectors $S = \{x_1, \ldots, x_n\}$, the set span(S), also denoted span($x_1, \ldots, x_n$), consists of all linear combinations of the form $\alpha_1 x_1 + \cdots + \alpha_n x_n$, where $\alpha_1, \ldots, \alpha_n \in \mathbb{R}$. For any set of vectors S, span(S) = $\bigcup\{\text{span}(F) : F \text{ is a finite subset of } S\}$.

A set of vectors S is **linearly independent** if every $x \in \text{span}(S)$ has a unique representation of the form $x = \alpha_1 x_1 + \cdots + \alpha_n x_n$, for some $\alpha_1, \ldots, \alpha_n \in \mathbb{R}$ and $x_1, \ldots, x_n \in S$. It follows easily that the set of vectors S is linearly independent if and only if for any $x_1, \ldots, x_n \in S$ and $\alpha_1, \ldots, \alpha_n \in \mathbb{R}$,

$$\alpha_1 x_1 + \cdots + \alpha_n x_n = 0 \quad \text{implies} \quad \alpha_1 = \cdots = \alpha_n = 0.$$

A **basis** of X is a linearly independent set of vectors S that generates X, that is, span(S) = X. A vector space is **finite dimensional** if it has a finite basis and **infinite dimensional** otherwise. Example A.2 with an infinite underlying probability space is an instance of an infinite-dimensional vector space. As noted in the introduction, this appendix is limited to the finite-dimensional case. Every basis of a finite-dimensional vector space has the same number of elements, called the space's **dimension**. The vector space $X = \{0\}$ has, by definition, dimension zero.

We henceforth assume that X is a finite-dimensional vector space of dimension d. We represent a basis $\{e_1, \ldots, e_d\}$ of X as a column matrix $e = (e_1, \ldots, e_d)'$. For any $x \in X$, we let x^e denote the column vector in $\mathbb{R}^d$ that **represents** x relative to the basis e, that is,

$$x = x^{e\prime} e = e' x^e = \sum_{i=1}^{d} x_i^e e_i.$$

A **functional** is any function of the form $f : X \to \mathbb{R}$. A functional f is **linear** if

$$f(\alpha x + \beta y) = \alpha f(x) + \beta f(y), \quad x, y \in X, \quad \alpha, \beta \in \mathbb{R}.$$

Given the basis $e = (e_1, \ldots, e_d)'$ and a linear functional f, we use the notation

$$f(e) = (f(e_1), \ldots, f(e_d))'$$

for the column vector that lists the values that f assigns to the basis elements. The vector $f(e)$ determines the entire function f, since

$$f(x) = f(e)'x^e = x^{e'}f(e), \quad x \in X.$$

A set $C \subseteq X$ is **convex** if $x, y \in C$ implies $\alpha x + (1 - \alpha)y \in C$ for all $\alpha \in (0, 1)$. The function $f : D \to \mathbb{R}$, where $D \subseteq X$, is **convex** if D is a convex set and

$$f(\alpha x + (1 - \alpha)y) \le \alpha f(x) + (1 - \alpha)f(y), \quad \alpha \in (0, 1), \quad x, y \in D.$$

The function f is **concave** if $-f$ is convex. A set $C \subseteq X$ is a **cone** if $x \in C$ and $\alpha \in \mathbb{R}_+$ implies $\alpha x \in C$. One can easily check that a cone C is convex if and only if $x, y \in C$ implies $x + y \in C$, and that a convex cone C is a linear subspace if and only if $x \in C$ implies $-x \in C$.

An important type of convex set is a linear manifold. Given a subset S of X and a vector x, we write $x + S = S + x = \{x + s : s \in S\}$ to denote the **translation** of S by x. A subset M of X is a **linear manifold** if some translation of M is a linear subspace. The **dimension** of a linear manifold M is that of the linear subspace to which M translates. An exercise shows:

Proposition A.3. *The set $M \subseteq X$ is a linear manifold if and only if $x, y \in M$ and $\alpha \in \mathbb{R}$ implies $\alpha x + (1 - \alpha)y \in M$.*

A.2 INNER PRODUCT

A widely applicable form of optimization involves projections. Informally, the projection of a point x onto a convex set S is the point of S that is closest to x. The simplest nontrivial instance of this problem is the case in which S is a line. Suppose that $S = \mathrm{span}(y)$ and y has unit "length." The scalar α such that αy is the projection of x onto S is the inner product of x and y, denoted $(y \mid x)$. Note that the functional $(y \mid \cdot)$ is linear. Defining

$(\alpha y \mid x) = \alpha(y \mid x)$ for all $\alpha \in \mathbb{R}$, it is not hard to see that the function $(\cdot \mid \cdot)$ is bilinear (linear in each argument), symmetric $((x \mid y) = (y \mid x))$ and positive definite $((x \mid x) > 0$ for $x \neq 0)$. With this geometric motivation, we take the notion of an inner product as a primitive object satisfying certain axioms.

Definition A.4. *A (real)* **inner product** $(\cdot \mid \cdot)$ *on the vector space X is a mapping that assigns to each $(x, y) \in X \times X$ a real number, denoted $(x \mid y)$, and satisfies, for all $x, y, z \in X$ and $\alpha \in \mathbb{R}$,*

1. $(x + y \mid z) = (x \mid z) + (y \mid z)$ *and* $(\alpha x \mid y) = \alpha(x \mid y)$.
2. $(x \mid y) = (y \mid x)$.
3. $(x \mid x) \geq 0$, *with equality holding if and only if $x = 0$.*

An **inner product space** *is a vector space X together with an inner product $(\cdot \mid \cdot)$ on X.*

Example A.5. *Suppose $X = \mathbb{R}^d$ and Q is a positive definite symmetric matrix. Then the quadratic form $(x \mid y) = x'Qy$ defines an inner product on X.*

Example A.6. *Suppose X is the set of all random variables on some finite probability space in which every state has positive probability. Then $(x \mid y) = \mathbb{E}[xy]$ defines an inner product. If Y is a subspace of X that does not contain the constant random variables, then $(x \mid y) = \mathrm{cov}[x, y] = \mathbb{E}[xy] - \mathbb{E}x\mathbb{E}y$ defines an inner product on Y but not on X (why?).*

We henceforth take as given a finite-dimensional inner product space $(X, (\cdot \mid \cdot))$.

It will be convenient to extend the inner product notation to matrices of vectors, using the usual matrix addition and multiplication rules. In particular, given a column matrix of vectors $e = (e_1, \ldots, e_d)'$ and any vector x, we write

$$
(e \mid x) = \begin{pmatrix} (e_1 \mid x) \\ (e_2 \mid x) \\ \vdots \\ (e_d \mid x) \end{pmatrix}, \quad (e \mid e') = \begin{pmatrix} (e_1 \mid e_1) & (e_1 \mid e_2) & \cdots & (e_1 \mid e_d) \\ (e_2 \mid e_1) & (e_2 \mid e_2) & \cdots & (e_2 \mid e_d) \\ \vdots & \vdots & \ddots & \vdots \\ (e_d \mid e_1) & (e_d \mid e_2) & \cdots & (e_d \mid e_d) \end{pmatrix}.
$$

The matrix $(e \mid e')$ is known as the **Gram matrix** of e and plays a crucial role in the computation of projections, starting with the computation of inner products.

Proposition A.7. *Given any basis* $e = (e_1, \ldots, e_d)'$ *of X, the Gram matrix* $(e \mid e')$ *is symmetric and positive definite, and*

$$(x \mid y) = x^{e'}(e \mid e')y^e, \quad x, y \in X.$$

Proof. Using the bilinearity of the inner product, we compute

$$(x \mid y) = (x^{e'}e \mid e'y^e) = x^{e'}(e \mid e'y^e) = x^{e'}(e \mid e')y^e.$$

The symmetry of the inner product implies that $(e \mid e')$ is a symmetric matrix. For any column vector $\alpha \in \mathbb{R}^d$, $\alpha'(e \mid e')\alpha = (\alpha'e \mid \alpha'e)$. By the positive definiteness of the inner product it follows that $\alpha'(e \mid e')\alpha \geq 0$, with equality holding if and only if $\alpha'e = 0$. Since e is a basis, $\alpha'e = 0$ if and only if $\alpha = 0$. This proves that $(e \mid e')$ is a positive definite matrix. ∎

Two vectors x and y are **orthogonal** if $(x \mid y) = 0$. A set of vectors is **orthogonal** if its elements are pairwise orthogonal. A basis e is **orthonormal** if it is orthogonal and normalized so that $(e_i \mid e_i) = 1$ for every i. We note that the basis e is orthonormal if and only if the Gram matrix $(e \mid e')$ is the identity matrix. In Section A.6 we show that every finite-dimensional vector space has an orthonormal basis, and therefore an inner product in a finite-dimensional space can always be represented as the usual Euclidean inner product.

A **Riesz representation** of the linear functional $f : X \to \mathbb{R}$ is a vector $y \in X$ such that $f(x) = (y \mid x)$ for all $x \in X$.

Proposition A.8. *Suppose $e = (e_1, \ldots, e_d)'$ is a basis of X, f is a linear functional and $f(e) = (f(e_1), \ldots, f(e_d))'$. Then a Riesz representation of f exists, is unique and is given by*

$$e'(e \mid e')^{-1}f(e).$$

Proof. For any $x = x^{e'}e$ and $y = e'y^e$, $f(x) = x^{e'}f(e)$ and $(x \mid y) = x^{e'}(e \mid e')y^e$. The vector $y = e'y^e$ is therefore a Riesz representation of

263

f if and only if $x^{e'}f(e) = x^{e'}(e \mid e')y^e$ for all $x^e \in \mathbb{R}^d$. The last condition is equivalent to $y^e = (e \mid e')^{-1}f(e)$. ∎

A.3 NORM

A **norm** (on the vector space X) is a function of the form $\| \cdot \| : X \to \mathbb{R}$ that satisfies the following properties for all $x, y \in X$:

1. (triangle inequality) $\|x + y\| \leq \|x\| + \|y\|$.
2. $\|\alpha x\| = |\alpha| \|x\|$ for all $\alpha \in \mathbb{R}$.
3. $\|x\| \geq 0$, with equality holding if and only if $x = 0$.

Here $\|x\|$ represents the value that the norm $\| \cdot \|$ assigns to x, referred to simply as the **norm of** x. The **norm induced** by an inner product $(\cdot \mid \cdot)$ is defined by

$$\|x\| = \sqrt{(x \mid x)}, \quad x \in X. \tag{A.1}$$

We think of $\|x\|$ as the length of x, in the sense used in our earlier informal motivation of inner products.

We defined the orthogonality of the vectors x and y by the condition $(x \mid y) = 0$. Orthogonality can also be characterized entirely in terms of norms.

Proposition A.9 (Pythagorean Identity). *For any $x, y \in X$, x is orthogonal to y if and only if*

$$\|x + y\|^2 = \|x\|^2 + \|y\|^2.$$

Proof. The claim follows from the computation

$$\|x + y\|^2 = (x + y \mid x + y) = (x \mid x) + (y \mid y) + 2(x \mid y)$$
$$= \|x\|^2 + \|y\|^2 + 2(x \mid y).$$

∎

Proposition A.10. *Given the inner product* $(\cdot \mid \cdot)$, *equation* $(A.1)$ *defines a norm* $\|\cdot\|$ *that satisfies the **Cauchy-Schwarz inequality***

$$|(x \mid y)| \leq \|x\|\|y\|, \quad x, y \in X,$$

with equality holding if and only if $x = \alpha y$ *for some* $\alpha \in \mathbb{R}$ *or* $y = 0$.

Proof. The Cauchy-Schwarz inequality holds trivially as an equality if either x or y is zero. Suppose x and y are nonzero, and let $\hat{x} = x/\|x\|$ and $\hat{y} = y/\|y\|$. Visualizing the vector $(\hat{x} \mid \hat{y})\hat{y}$ as the projection of $\hat{x}$ on the line spanned by $\hat{y}$, we note that $\hat{x} - (\hat{x} \mid \hat{y})\hat{y}$ is orthogonal to $(\hat{x} \mid \hat{y})\hat{y}$. Indeed,

$$(\hat{x} - (\hat{x} \mid \hat{y})\hat{y} \mid \hat{y}) = (\hat{x} \mid \hat{y}) - (\hat{x} \mid \hat{y})(\hat{y} \mid \hat{y}) = 0.$$

The Pythagorean identity then implies that

$$0 \leq \|\hat{x} - (\hat{x} \mid \hat{y})\hat{y}\|^2 = 1 - (\hat{x} \mid \hat{y})^2,$$

which implies the Cauchy-Schwarz inequality. Equality holds if and only if $\hat{x} = (\hat{x} \mid \hat{y})\hat{y}$, a condition that is equivalent to $x = \alpha y$ for some scalar α. We still must verify that $\|\cdot\|$ is a norm. We use the Cauchy-Schwarz inequality to show the triangle inequality:

$$\begin{aligned}\|x+y\|^2 &= \|x\|^2 + 2(x \mid y) + \|y\|^2 \\ &\leq \|x\|^2 + 2\|x\|\|y\| + \|y\|^2 = (\|x\| + \|y\|)^2.\end{aligned}$$

The remaining norm properties are immediate from the definitions. ∎

Remark A.11. *For another perspective on the Cauchy-Schwarz inequality, suppose x and y are linearly independent and let $e = (x, y)'$. Since the Gram matrix $(e \mid e')$ is positive definite, it has a positive determinant:* $\|x\|^2\|y\|^2 - (x \mid y)^2 > 0$.

Every norm we use in this text is induced by some inner product. Not every norm can be induced by an inner product, however. For example, a norm that is not translation invariant cannot be induced by an inner product.

A.4 CONTINUITY

The following topological definitions and notation will be of frequent use. Given any $r > 0$ and $x \in X$, the **open ball** with center x and radius r is denoted

$$B(x;r) = \{y \in X : \|y - x\| < r\}.$$

Let S be any subset of X. The **interior** of S is the set

$$S^0 = \{x : B(x;\varepsilon) \subset S \text{ for some } \varepsilon > 0\},$$

the **closure** of S is the set

$$\bar{S} = \{x : B(x;\varepsilon) \cap S \neq \emptyset \text{ for all } \varepsilon > 0\},$$

and the **boundary** of S is the set $\bar{S} \setminus S^0$. The set S is **open** if $S = S^0$ and is **closed** if $S = \bar{S}$. We list some properties of open and closed sets that can be easily confirmed. S is closed if and only if $X \setminus S$ is open. The empty set and X are both open and closed. Finite unions of closed sets are closed, and finite intersections of open sets are open. Arbitrary intersections of closed sets are closed, and arbitrary unions of open sets are open. The closure of a set is the intersection of all its closed supersets. The interior of a set is the union of all its open subsets.

A function $f : D \to \mathbb{R}$, where $D \subseteq X$, is **continuous at** $x \in D$ if given any $\varepsilon > 0$, there exists some $\delta > 0$ (depending on ε) such that $y \in D \cap B(x;\delta)$ implies $|f(y) - f(x)| < \varepsilon$. The function f is **continuous** if it is continuous at every point of its domain D. It is not hard to show that f is continuous if and only if the inverse image of every open set is open.

Proposition A.12. *If X is finite dimensional, then every linear functional is continuous.*

Proof. By Proposition A.8, a linear functional f has a Riesz representation y, that is, $f(x) = (y \mid x)$ for all $x \in X$. Continuity of f then follows from the Cauchy-Schwarz inequality. ∎

Remark A.13. *In an infinite-dimensional space, a linear functional need not be continuous. Details can be found in standard references cited in the notes.*

Topological properties can also be usefully characterized in terms of sequences. The sequence $\{x_n : n = 1, 2, \ldots\}$ of vectors **converges** to the **limit**

x if the sequence $\{\|x - x_n\| : n = 1, 2, \ldots\}$ converges to zero. It then follows that a vector x is a closure point of the set S if and only if there exists a sequence in S that converges to x. Therefore, S is closed if and only if every convergent sequence in S converges to a limit in S. The function $f : D \to \mathbb{R}$ is continuous at $x \in D$ if and only if for any sequence $\{x_n\} \subseteq D$ converging to x, the sequence $\{f(x_n)\}$ converges to $f(x)$. In finite dimensions, convergence corresponds to coordinatewise convergence, and therefore all inner products define the same notion of convergence, the same open and closed sets, and the same continuous functions.

Proposition A.14. *Suppose* $e = (e_1, \ldots, e_d)'$ *is a basis of* X. *The sequence* $\{x_n : n = 1, 2, \ldots\}$ *converges to* x *if and only if* $\{x_{ni}^e : n = 1, 2, \ldots\}$ *converges to* x_i^e *for all* $i \in \{1, \ldots, d\}$.

In a finite-dimensional space, a concave (or convex) function on an open domain is continuous. The remainder of this section proves this fact and can be skipped without loss of continuity.

Lemma A.15. *Suppose that* D *is a convex open subset of* X, $f : D \to \mathbb{R}$ *is a concave function, and* x *is any point in* D. *If there exists some ball* $B(x; r) \subseteq D$ *on which* f *is bounded below, then* f *is continuous at* x.

Proof. Suppose $f(y) \geq b$ for all $y \in B(x; r) \subseteq D$. Fixing any y such that $0 < \|y - x\| \leq r$, let

$$\phi(\alpha) = f\left(x + \alpha \frac{y - x}{\|y - x\|}\right), \quad \alpha \in [-r, r].$$

The function $\phi : [-r, r] \to \mathbb{R}$ is concave and bounded below by b. Therefore,

$$\frac{\phi(0) - b}{r} \geq \frac{\phi(0) - \phi(-r)}{r} \geq \frac{\phi(\|y - x\|) - \phi(0)}{\|y - x\|}$$

$$\geq \frac{\phi(r) - \phi(0)}{r} \geq \frac{b - \phi(0)}{r}.$$

(The three middle quantities represent slopes that decrease from left to right since ϕ is concave.) This proves that

$$|f(y) - f(x)| \leq \frac{f(x) - b}{r} \|y - x\|, \quad y \in B(x; r),$$

from which continuity of f at x if immediate. ∎

267

The preceding proof and lemma (as well as its converse, which we do not need here) are valid without the assumption that X is finite dimensional. Below, we use the assumption that X is finite dimensional to verify the local boundedness condition.

Theorem A.16. *Suppose that X is finite dimensional, D is an open convex set, and $f : D \to \mathbb{R}$ is concave. Then f is continuous.*

Proof. Suppose first that $X = \mathbb{R}^d$ with the standard Euclidean inner product. Let us call a **box** a set of the form $[\alpha, \beta] = \{x \in X : x_i \in [\alpha_i, \beta_i], \ i = 1, \ldots, d\}$, where $\alpha, \beta \in \mathbb{R}^d$ and $\alpha_i < \beta_i$ for all i. We fix any $x \in D$ and show that f is continuous at x. Using the assumption that D is open, an exercise shows that there exists a box $[\alpha, \beta]$ that is included in D and contains x in its interior. Since f is concave, it is minimized over $[\alpha, \beta]$ at some **extreme** point of $[\alpha, \beta]$, that is, a point x such that $x_i \in \{\alpha_i, \beta_i\}$ for all i. To see why, take any $x \in [\alpha, \beta]$ and any $k \in \{1, \ldots, d\}$, and define the points x^α and x^β by $x_i^\alpha = x_i = x_i^\beta$ for $i \neq k$, $x_k^\alpha = \alpha_k$ and $x_k^\beta = \beta_k$. Then for some $\rho \in [0, 1]$, $x = \rho x^\alpha + (1 - \rho)x^\beta$. Concavity implies $\min\{f(x^\alpha), f(x^\beta)\} \leq f(x)$. We can therefore replace x by one of x^α or x^β without increasing its value under f. Repeating this process for all coordinates shows that for every $x \in [\alpha, \beta]$, there exists some extreme point $\bar{x}$ of $[\alpha, \beta]$ such that $f(x) \geq f(\bar{x})$. Since $[\alpha, \beta]$ has only finitely many extreme points, f is bounded below on $[\alpha, \beta]$. Continuity of f at x follows from the last lemma.

If X is an arbitrary finite-dimensional space, we can use an ortho-normal basis e (whose existence is shown in Section A.6). We can then identify each element $x \in X$ with its basis representation $x^e \in \mathbb{R}^d$ and apply the above argument. ∎

A.5 Compactness

This section shows that a continuous function achieves a maximum and a minimum over any compact set. The arguments presented are special to the finite-dimensional case.

A subset S of a normed space is **compact** if every sequence in S has a subsequence that converges to a vector in S. The set S is **bounded** if there exists a constant that bounds from above the norm of each vector in S.

Proposition A.17. *A subset of the finite-dimensional vector space X is compact if and only if it is closed and bounded.*

Proof. "only if" If a set S is unbounded, then for every integer n, there exists some $s_n \in S$ such that $\|s_n\| > n$. The sequence $\{s_n\}$ has no convergent subsequence, and therefore S is not compact. Closure of a compact set is immediate from the definitions.
"if" By Proposition A.14, it suffices to consider the case in which the ambient normed space is a Euclidean space $\mathbb{R}^d$. Let $\{s(n) : n = 1, 2, \ldots\}$ be a sequence in a closed bounded subset S of $\mathbb{R}^d$. Then the first coordinate sequence $\{s_1(n)\}$ lies in some bounded interval I. Select a half-interval I_1 of I that contains infinitely many points of $\{s_1(n)\}$, and let $s_1(n_1)$ be one of these points. Then select a half-interval I^2 of I^1 that contains infinitely many points of the sequence $\{s_1(n) : n > n_1\}$, and let $s_1(n_2)$ be one of these points. Continuing in this manner, we obtain a nested sequence of intervals $\{I_n\}$ whose length shrinks to zero and a corresponding subsequence $\{s_1(n_i) : i = 1, 2, \ldots\}$ with $s_1(n_i) \in I_i$ for all i. Clearly, the subsequence $\{s_1(n_i)\}$ is Cauchy and therefore convergent. Repeating the argument we can extract a further subsequence for the second coordinate, then the third, and so on. This process generates a convergent subsequence of $\{s(n)\}$ whose limit point must be in S, since S is assumed closed. ∎

Proposition A.18. *Suppose that S is a compact subset of X and the function $f : S \to \mathbb{R}$ is continuous. Then there exist $s^*, s_* \in S$ such that*

$$f(s^*) \geq f(s) \geq f(s_*), \quad \text{for all } s \in S.$$

Proof. Let $\{s_n\}$ be a sequence such that $\lim_n f(s_n) = \sup f$. By the compactness of S, there exists a subsequence of $\{s_n\}$ converging to some $s^* \in S$. Since f is continuous, $f(s^*) = \sup f$ and therefore $f(s^*) \geq f(s)$ for all $s \in S$. The same argument applied to $-f$ completes the proof. ∎

Proposition A.19. *Suppose X is finite dimensional, A and B are closed subsets of X and at least one of them is bounded. Then there exists a pair $(\bar{a}, \bar{b}) \in A \times B$ such that $\|a - b\| \geq \|\bar{a} - \bar{b}\|$ for all $(a, b) \in A \times B$.*

Proof. Suppose A is bounded, and therefore we can select $r > 0$ large enough so that $A \subseteq B\,(0;r)$ and $B \cap B\,(0;r) \neq \emptyset$. Clearly, a closest pair $(\bar{a}, \bar{b}) \in A \times B$ exists if and only if it exists under the additional constraint $\bar{b} \in B(0;r)$. We therefore replace B with $B \cap B\,(0;r)$ and assume that both A and B are compact. Consider now the space $X \times X$ with the norm $\|(x, y)\| = \|x\| + \|y\|$. An exercise shows that $A \times B$ is a compact subset of $X \times X$, and the mapping $f : A \times B \to \mathbb{R}$ defined by $f(a, b) = \|a - b\|$ is convex and continuous. Therefore, f is minimized at some $(\bar{a}, \bar{b}) \in A \times B$. ∎

Finally, it is worth noting that Proposition A.18 applies with any underlying norm (not necessarily induced by an inner product), and it implies the topological equivalence of all norms on a finite-dimensional space, in the following sense. If $\| \cdot \|$ is a norm on the finite-dimensional vector space X, then any other norm $\| \cdot \|_*$ on X is convex and therefore continuous on the open ball $B(0; 2)$ (relative to $\| \cdot \|$). Since $B(0; 2)$ contains the closure of $B(0; 1)$, a compact set, it follows that $\| \cdot \|_*$ is bounded on $B(0; 1)$, and therefore there exists a constant K such that $\|x\|_* \leq K \|x\|$ for all $x \in X$. The argument also applies with the roles of $\| \cdot \|_*$ and $\| \cdot \|$ interchanged. In conclusion, all norms in finite dimensions define the same open sets and the same notion of convergence. This generalizes an analogous conclusion drawn earlier from Proposition A.14 in terms of inner products. The situation is very different in infinite-dimensional spaces, where the unit closed ball is not compact and different norms can define different topologies.

A.6 PROJECTIONS

Projections were introduced informally in motivating inner products. We now define projections formally and we use inner products to provide a dual characterization of projections on convex sets.

Definition A.20. Let S be any subset of X. The vector x_S is a **projection** of x on the set S if $x_S \in S$ and $\|x - s\| \geq \|x - x_S\|$ for all $s \in S$. The vector $z \in X$ **supports** the set S at $\bar{s} \in S$ if $(z \mid s - \bar{s}) \geq 0$ for all $s \in S$.

The inequality $(z \mid s - \bar{s}) \geq 0$ can be visualized as the requirement that the vectors z and $s - \bar{s}$ form an acute angle. The following central result (which does not use the assumption that X is finite dimensional) character-izes the projection of a point x onto a convex set S. The main idea is geo-metrically quite intuitive: A point x_S in S is the projection on S of a point x outside S if and only if for any $s \in S$ the vectors $x_S - x$ and $s - x_S$ form an acute angle.

Theorem A.21 (Projection Theorem). *Suppose S is a convex subset of X and $x, y \in X$.*

(a) *The vector x_S is a projection of x on S if and only if $x_S \in S$ and $x_S - x$ supports S at x_S.*

(b) *If x_S and y_S are projections on S of x and y, respectively, then*

$$\|x_S - y_S\| \leq \|x - y\|.$$

(c) *There exists at most one projection of x on S.*

Proof. (a) Suppose $x_S - x$ supports S at $x_S \in S$. Then for any $s \in S$,

$$\|x - s\|^2 = \|x - x_S\|^2 + \|s - x_S\|^2 + 2(x_S - x \mid s - x_S) \geq \|x - x_S\|^2,$$

proving that x_S is a projection of x on S. Conversely, suppose x_S is a projection of x on S. Given any nonzero $s \in S$ and $\alpha \in (0, 1)$, we define $x_\alpha = x_S + \alpha(s - x_S) \in S$. Then

$$2(x_S - x \mid s - x_S) = -\alpha \|s - x_S\|^2 + \frac{1}{\alpha}(\|x - x_\alpha\|^2 - \|x - x_S\|^2)$$
$$\geq -\alpha \|s - x_S\|^2.$$

Letting α approach zero, we conclude that $(x_S - x \mid s - x_S) \geq 0$.

(b) Let $\delta = y - x$ and $\delta_S = y_S - x_S$. By part (a), we have $(x_S - x \mid \delta_S) \geq 0$ and $(y - y_S \mid \delta_S) \geq 0$. Adding the two inequalities, we obtain $(\delta - \delta_S \mid \delta_S) \geq 0$. Finally,

$$\|\delta\|^2 = \|\delta - \delta_S\|^2 + \|\delta_S\|^2 + 2(\delta - \delta_S \mid \delta_S) \geq \|\delta_S\|^2.$$

(c) Apply part (b) with $x = y$. ∎

Theorem A.21 does not address the question of existence of a projection. For example, on the real line, the projection of zero on the convex set $(1, 2)$ does not exist. Given the assumption that X is finite dimensional, Proposition A.19 implies that the projection of any point x in X on any

271

closed subset of X exists. For infinite-dimensional X, an existence theory can be based on the notion of completeness (that is, any Cauchy sequence in S must converge to an element of S). Details are given in the references cited in the notes.

The remainder of this section is on the important special case of projections on linear manifolds. A vector x is **orthogonal** to a linear manifold M if for any $m_1, m_2 \in M$, x is orthogonal to $m_1 - m_2$. The linear subspace of all vectors that are orthogonal to a linear manifold M is the **orthogonal to M subspace**, denoted $M^{\perp}$. We note that a vector supports a linear manifold at some point if and only if it is orthogonal to the manifold. The definition of orthogonality to a linear manifold M implies that $M^{\perp} = (x + M)^{\perp}$ for every $x \in X$.

Specializing the projection theorem, we have:

Corollary A.22 (Orthogonal Projections). *Suppose M is a linear manifold in X and $x \in X$. A vector x_M is the projection of x on M if and only if $x_M \in M$ and $x - x_M \in M^{\perp}$.*

Projections to finite-dimensional subspaces and their orthogonal complements exist and can be expressed by simple formulas in terms of a given basis. (The following proposition and its proof remain valid for an infinite-dimensional ambient space X.)

Proposition A.23. *Suppose that $e = (e_1, \dots, e_k)'$ is a column matrix of linearly independent vectors in X, and let $M = \operatorname{span}(e_1, \dots, e_k)$. Given any $x \in X$, the vector*

$$x_M = e'(e \mid e')^{-1}(e \mid x) \tag{A.2}$$

is the projection of x on M, and $x - x_M$ is the projection of x on

$$M^{\perp} = \{y \in X : (e \mid y) = 0\}.$$

Finally, $M^{\perp\perp} = M$.

Proof. Writing $x_M = e'x_M^e \in M$, where $x_M^e = (e \mid e')^{-1}(e \mid x)$, for any $y = y^{e'}e \in M$, we have

$$(y \mid x_M) = y^{e'}(e \mid e')x_M^e = y^{e'}(e \mid e')(e \mid e')^{-1}(e \mid x) = (y \mid x).$$

This shows that $(x - x_M \mid y) = 0$ for all $y \in M$, confirming that x_M is the projection of x on M. It is immediate that $M \subseteq M^{\perp\perp}$. Therefore, $x - (x - x_M) = x_M \in M^{\perp\perp}$ and $x - x_M \in M^{\perp}$, implying that $x - x_M$ is the projection of x on $M^{\perp}$. Finally, we show that $M^{\perp\perp} \subseteq M$. Given any $x \in M^{\perp\perp}$, we can write $x = x_M + n$, where $x_M \in M$ and $n = x - x_M \in M^{\perp}$. Then $(x \mid n) = (x_M \mid n) + (n \mid n)$. Noting that $(x \mid n) = (x_M \mid n) = 0$, it follows that $(n \mid n) = 0$ and therefore $x = x_M \in M$. ∎

Corollary A.24. *Suppose that $e = (e_1, \ldots, e_k)'$ is a column matrix of linearly independent vectors in X, and $N = \{y \in X : (e \mid y) = \alpha\}$ for some column vector $\alpha \in \mathbb{R}^k$. Then $N^{\perp} = \mathrm{span}(e_1, \ldots, e_k)$, and the projection of x on N exists and is given by*

$$x_N = x - e'(e \mid e')^{-1}((e \mid x) - \alpha).$$

Corollary A.25. *Suppose M is a finite-dimensional linear manifold in X. Then every vector $x \in X$ has a unique decomposition of the form $x = m + n$, where $m \in M$ and $n \in M^{\perp}$.*

Formula (A.2) is the same as the Riesz representation expression of Proposition A.8 with $f(y) = (x \mid y)$. The reason should be clear given the following general relationship between orthogonal projections and Riesz representations (whose proof is immediate from the definitions).

Proposition A.26. *Suppose that $f(y) = (x \mid y)$ for all $y \in X$ and f_M is the restriction of f on the linear subspace M. The vector x_M is the Riesz representation of f_M in M if and only if it is the projection of x on M.*

If M has a finite orthogonal basis e, then $(e \mid e')$ is diagonal and formula (A.2) for the projection of x on M reduces to

$$x_M = \sum_{i=1}^{k} \frac{(x \mid e_i)}{(e_i \mid e_i)} e_i.$$

This equation can be used to recursively define an orthogonal basis for any finite-dimensional linear space X, a process known as **Gram-Schmidt orthogonalization**. We start with any element $e_1 \in X$. Assuming we have constructed k orthogonal elements $e_1, \ldots, e_k$ of X such that $M = \mathrm{span}(e_1, \ldots, e_k) \neq X$, we select any $x \in X \setminus M$ and define $e_{k+1} = x - x_M$, where x_M is the projection of x on M, given by the above formula. If X is d-dimensional, the recursive construction terminates for $k = d$. Normalizing the resulting orthogonal basis proves:

Proposition A.27. *Every finite-dimensional inner product space has an orthonormal basis.*

A.7 SUPPORTING HYPERPLANES

A **hyperplane** H is a linear manifold whose orthogonal subspace is of dimension one and can therefore be expressed as $H = \{x : (y \mid x) = \alpha\}$ for some scalar α and some nonzero vector y that is orthogonal to H. According to Definition A.20, the vector y supports the set $S \subseteq X$ at $\bar{s} \in S$ if and only if $(y \mid s) \geq (y \mid \bar{s})$ for all $s \in S$. Letting $\alpha = (y \mid \bar{s})$, this can be visualized as the condition that S is included in the half-space $\{x : (y \mid x) \geq \alpha\}$ on the one side of H, while touching H at $\bar{s}$. The following is an extension of Definition A.20 that does not require $\bar{s}$ to be an element of S.

Definition A.28. *The vector $y \in X$ supports the set S at $\bar{s} \in X$ if*

$$(y \mid \bar{s}) = \inf\{(y \mid s) : s \in S\}. \tag{A.3}$$

The following theorem and its corollary are valid only in the current context of a finite-dimensional inner product space X (see Exercise 15).

Theorem A.29 (Supporting Hyperplane Theorem). *Suppose S is a convex subset of X and the vector x is not in the interior of S. Then there exists a nonzero vector y such that $(y \mid x) \leq (y \mid s)$ for all $s \in S$. If x is on the boundary of S, then y supports S at x.*

Proof. Since x is not interior, we can construct a sequence $\{x_n : n = 1, 2, \ldots\}$ of vectors such that $x_n \notin \bar{S}$ for all n and $x_n \to x$ as $n \to \infty$. For each n, let $\bar{s}_n$ be the projection of x_n on $\bar{S}$ and define $y_n = (\bar{s}_n - x_n)/\|\bar{s}_n - x_n\|$. The dual characterization of projections gives $(y_n \mid \bar{s}_n) \leq (y_n \mid s)$ for all $s \in S$. By part (b) of Theorem A.21, the sequence $\{\bar{s}_n\}$ converges to the projection $\bar{s}$ of x on $\bar{S}$. The sequence $\{y_n\}$ lies in the closed unit ball, which is compact, and therefore we can extract a subsequence $\{y_{n_k}\}$ that converges to some vector y of unit norm. By the continuity of inner products (see Exercise 2), we conclude that $(y \mid \bar{s}) \leq (y \mid s)$ for all $s \in S$. If x is on the boundary of S, then $x = \bar{s}$ is the limit of some sequence $\{s_n\}$ in S. Therefore, $\{(y \mid s_n)\}$ converges to $(y \mid \bar{s})$, implying (A.3). If x is not on the boundary of S, then $\{y_n\}$ converges to $y = (\bar{s} - x)/\|\bar{s} - x\|$. Since $(y \mid \bar{s} - x) > 0$, it follows that $(y \mid x) < (y \mid \bar{s}) \leq (y \mid s)$ for all $s \in S$. $\blacksquare$

Corollary A.30 (Separating Hyperplane Theorem). *Suppose A and B are convex subsets of X. If $A \cap B \neq \emptyset$, then there exists a nonzero vector $y \in X$ such that*

$$\inf_{a \in A} (y \mid a) \geq \sup_{b \in B} (y \mid b). \tag{A.4}$$

Proof. Let $S = A - B = \{a - b : a \in A, b \in B\}$. Since $A \cap B \neq \emptyset$, zero is not in S. By the supporting hyperplane theorem, there exists a nonzero $y \in X$ such that $(y \mid s) \geq 0$ for all $s \in S$ and therefore $(y \mid a) \geq (y \mid b)$ for every $a \in A$ and $b \in B$. $\blacksquare$

We use supporting hyperplanes to discuss superdifferentials. Given a function $f : D \to \mathbb{R}$, where $D \subseteq X$, the vector y is a **supergradient** of f at $\hat{x} \in D$ if it satisfies the **gradient inequality**:

$$f(x) - f(\hat{x}) \leq (y \mid x - \hat{x}) \quad \text{for all } x \in D.$$

The **superdifferential** of f at $\hat{x}$, denoted $\partial f(\hat{x})$, is the set of all supergradients of f at $\hat{x}$. The supergradient property can be visualized as a support condition in the space $X \times \mathbb{R}$ with the inner product

$$((x_1, \alpha_1) \mid (x_2, \alpha_2)) = (x_1 \mid x_2) + \alpha_1 \alpha_2.$$

The **subgraph** of f is defined and denoted by

$$\mathrm{sub}(f) = \{(x, \alpha) \in D \times \mathbb{R} : \alpha \leq f(x)\}.$$

The following geometric representation of supergradients is immediate from the definitions:

$$y \in \partial f(\hat{x}) \quad \Longleftrightarrow \quad (y, -1) \text{ supports } \mathrm{sub}(f) \text{ at } (\hat{x}, f(\hat{x})).$$

Proposition A.31. *A concave real-valued function has a nonempty superdifferential at every interior point of its domain.*

Proof. Suppose the function $f : D \to \mathbb{R}$ is concave and $\hat{x}$ is in the interior of D. By the supporting hyperplane theorem, sub(f) is supported by some nonzero $(y, -\beta) \in X \times \mathbb{R}$ at $(\hat{x}, f(\hat{x}))$:

$$(y \mid \hat{x}) - \beta f(\hat{x}) = \min\{(y \mid x) - \beta\alpha : \alpha \leq f(x),\ x \in D,\ \alpha \in \mathbb{R}\}.$$

Since the left-hand side is finite, it follows that $\beta \geq 0$. If $\beta = 0$, then y supports D at $\hat{x}$, which contradicts the assumption that $\hat{x}$ is an interior point of D. Therefore, $\beta > 0$ and $y/\beta \in \partial f(\hat{x})$. ∎

A.8 GLOBAL OPTIMALITY CONDITIONS

We take as given the set $C \subseteq X$, and the functions $U : C \to \mathbb{R}$ and $G : C \to \mathbb{R}^n$, for some positive integer n. For each $\delta \in \mathbb{R}^n$, we consider the constrained optimization problem

$$J(\delta) = \sup\{U(x) : G(x) \leq \delta,\ x \in C\}. \tag{P_δ}$$

With the convention inf $\emptyset = -\infty$, this defines a function of the form $J : \mathbb{R}^n \to [-\infty, +\infty]$, which is clearly monotone: $\delta_1 \geq \delta_2 \implies J(\delta_1) \geq J(\delta_2)$. We will characterize the solution to the problem (P_0). Since problem (P_δ) is the same as problem (P_0) with $G - \delta$ in place of G, this covers the general case. The key to understanding (P_0), however, is to consider the entire function J.

Associated with problem (P_0) is the **Lagrangian**

$$\mathcal{L}(x, \lambda) = U(x) - \lambda \cdot G(x), \quad x \in C, \quad \lambda \in \mathbb{R}^n,$$

where the dot denotes the Euclidean inner product in $\mathbb{R}^n$. The parameter λ will be referred to as a **Lagrange multiplier**. Assuming $J(0)$ is finite, we extend our earlier definition (for finite-valued functions) by defining the **superdifferential** of J at zero to be the set

$$\partial J(0) = \{\lambda \in \mathbb{R}^n : J(\delta) - J(0) \leq \lambda \cdot \delta \text{ for all } \delta \in \mathbb{R}^n\}.$$

The monotonicity of J implies that $\partial J(0) \subseteq \mathbb{R}^n_+$. Indeed, if $\lambda \in \partial J(0)$, then $0 \leq J(\delta) - J(0) \leq \lambda \cdot \delta$ for all $\delta \geq 0$ and therefore $\lambda \geq 0$. The following relationship between the Lagrangian and the superdifferential of J at zero is key.

Lemma A.32. *Suppose that $J(0)$ is finite. Then for any $\lambda \in \mathbb{R}^n_+$,*

$$\lambda \in \partial J(0) \quad \Longleftrightarrow \quad J(0) = \sup\{\mathcal{L}(x, \lambda) : x \in C\}.$$

Proof. In the space $\mathbb{R}^n \times \mathbb{R}$ with the Euclidean inner product, $\lambda \in \partial J(0)$ if and only if $(\lambda, -1)$ supports at $(0, J(0))$ (in the sense of Definition A.28) the set

$$S_1 = \{(\delta, \upsilon) \in \mathbb{R}^n \times \mathbb{R} : \upsilon < J(\delta)\}.$$

Similarly, $J(0) = \sup\{\mathcal{L}(x, \lambda) : x \in C\}$ if and only if $(\lambda, -1)$ supports at $(0, J(0))$ the set

$$S_2 = \{(\delta, \upsilon) \in \mathbb{R}^n \times \mathbb{R} : G(x) \leq \delta \text{ and } \upsilon < U(x) \text{ for some } x \in C\}.$$

The proof is concluded by noting that $S_1 = S_2$. ∎

Lemma A.32 does not assume that an optimum is achieved. If a maximum does exist, the argument can be extended to obtain the following global optimality conditions for problem (P_0).

Theorem A.33. *Suppose that $c \in C$, $G(c) \leq 0$ and $\lambda \in \mathbb{R}^n$. Then the following two conditions are equivalent:*

1. $U(c) = J(0)$ *and* $\lambda \in \partial J(0)$.
2. $\mathcal{L}(c, \lambda) = \max_{x \in C} \mathcal{L}(x, \lambda)$, $\quad \lambda \cdot G(c) = 0$, $\quad \lambda \geq 0$.

Proof. $(1 \Longrightarrow 2)$ Suppose condition 1 holds. We noted that $\lambda \in \partial J(0)$ implies $\lambda \geq 0$. By the last lemma, $U(c) = \sup\{\mathcal{L}(x, \lambda) : x \in C\}$. Since $G(c) \leq 0$, we also have $\mathcal{L}(c, \lambda) \geq U(c)$, and therefore the last inequality is an equality, proving that $\lambda \cdot G(c) = 0$.

$(2 \Longrightarrow 1)$ Condition 2 implies that $U(c) = \mathcal{L}(c, \lambda) \geq \mathcal{L}(x, \lambda) \geq U(x)$ for any x such that $G(x) \leq 0$. Therefore, $U(c) = J(0)$, and condition 1 follows by the last lemma. ∎

Remark A.34. *(a) Given the inequalities $G(c) \leq 0$ and $\lambda \geq 0$, the restriction $\lambda \cdot G(c) = 0$ is known as* **complimentary slackness**, *since it is equivalent to $G(c)_i < 0 \implies \lambda_i = 0$, for every coordinate i. Intuitively, a constraint can have a positive price only if it is binding.*

(b) Condition 2 of Theorem A.33 is sometimes equivalently stated as a **saddle-point condition:** $\mathcal{L}(\cdot, \lambda)$ *is maximized over C at c, and $\mathcal{L}(c, \cdot)$ is minimized over $\mathbb{R}^n_+$ at λ.*

Assuming the existence of a maximum, the above global optimality conditions are applicable if and only if $\partial J(0)$ is nonempty. A set of convexity-based sufficient conditions for this to be true are given below. Besides convexity, the key assumption is the so-called **Slater condition:**

There exists $x \in C$ such that $G(x)_i < 0$ for all $i \in \{1, \ldots, n\}$. (A.5)

Proposition A.35. *Suppose that C, $-U$ and G are convex, $J(0)$ is finite and the Slater condition $(A.5)$ holds. Then $\partial J(0) \neq \emptyset$.*

Proof. One can easily verify that sub(J) is concave and has $(0, J(0))$ on its boundary. By the supporting hyperplane theorem, sub(J) is supported at $(0, J(0))$ by some nonzero $(\lambda, -\alpha)$, and therefore $\upsilon \leq J(\delta)$ implies $-\alpha J(0) \leq \lambda \cdot \delta - \alpha \upsilon$ for all $\delta \in \mathbb{R}^n$. If $\alpha < 0$, then one obtains a contradiction with $\delta = 0$. The Slater condition guarantees that $J(\delta) > -\infty$ for all δ sufficiently close to zero, and therefore $\alpha \neq 0$. The only possibility is $\alpha > 0$, in which case $\lambda/\alpha \in \partial J(0)$. ∎

A.9 Local Optimality Conditions

In this section we develop local optimality conditions, exploiting the fact that small feasible perturbations near an optimum cannot improve the optimization's objective. We begin with some requisite differentiability notions.

Given any function $f : D \to \mathbb{R}$, any $x \in D$, and any $h \in X$ such that $x + \alpha h \in D$ for every sufficiently small positive scalar α, the **directional derivative of f at x in the direction h** is defined and denoted by

$$f'(x; h) = \lim_{\alpha \downarrow 0} \frac{f(x + \alpha h) - f(x)}{\alpha}.$$

Remark A.36.   *If D is an interval of real numbers, we write $f'_+(x) = f'(x; 1)$ for the **right derivative** of f at x, and $f'_-(x) = -f'(x; -1)$ for the **left derivative** of f at x.*

We relate the notion of a directional derivative to that of a superdifferential by noting that for a concave function f, the projection of any supergradient of f at x on a line through x lies in an interval defined by the left and right derivatives of f at x in the direction of this line.

Proposition A.37.   *Suppose that the function $f : D \to \mathbb{R}$ is concave and $y \in \partial f(x)$ for some $x \in D$. Suppose $h \in X$ is such that $x + \alpha h \in D$ for all sufficiently small scalars α. Then*

$$\infty > -f'(x; -h) \geq y'h \geq f'(x; h) > -\infty.$$

The gradient of a function $f : D \to \mathbb{R}$, where $D \subseteq X$, is said to exist at a point x in the interior of D if the directional derivative $f'(x; h)$ exists for every $h \in X$ and the functional $f'(x; \cdot)$ is linear. In this case, the Riesz representation of the linear functional $f'(x; \cdot)$ is the **gradient** of f at x, denoted $\nabla f(x)$. Therefore, when it exists, the gradient $\nabla f(x)$ is characterized by the restriction

$$f'(x; h) = (\nabla f(x) \mid h), \quad \text{for all } h \in X.$$

Proposition A.37 implies that if the gradient $\nabla f(x)$ exists and the superdifferential of f at x is nonempty, then $\partial f(x) = \{\nabla f(x)\}$.

The following local optimality conditions under linear constraints are sufficient for most of this text's applications.

Proposition A.38.   *Consider a function $U : D \to \mathbb{R}$, where $D \subseteq X$, a finite set of linearly independent vectors $\{e_1, \ldots, e_k\} \subseteq X$ and the linear manifold*

$$M = \{x \in X : (e_i \mid x) = \alpha_i, \ i = 1, \ldots, k\}, \quad \text{where } \alpha \in \mathbb{R}^k.$$

Suppose that the gradient of U at $c \in D^0 \cap M$ exists. Then

$$U(c) = \max_{x \in D \cap M} U(x) \quad \text{implies} \quad \nabla U(c) = \sum_{i=1}^{k} \lambda_i e_i \text{ for some } \lambda \in \mathbb{R}^k.$$

The converse implication is also valid if U is assumed to be concave.

279

Proof. Suppose $U(c) = \max\{U(x) : x \in D \cap M\}$ and consider any vector h in the linear subspace

$$L = M - c = \{x \in X : (e_i \mid x) = 0,\ i = 1,\ldots,k\}.$$

Setting to zero the derivative at zero of $U(c + sh)$ as a function of s results in the orthogonality condition $(\nabla U(c) \mid h) = 0$. Therefore, $\nabla U(c) \in L^\perp$. By Proposition A.23, $L^\perp = M^\perp = \mathrm{span}(e_1,\ldots,e_k)$ and therefore $\nabla U(c)$ is a linear combination of the e_i. Conversely, suppose U is concave and $\nabla U(c) \in \mathrm{span}(e_1,\ldots,e_k)$. Consider any $x \in D \cap M$, and let $h = x - c \in L$. Using the gradient inequality and the fact that $\nabla U(c)$ is orthogonal to h, we conclude $U(x) \leq U(c) + (\nabla U(c) \mid h) = U(c)$. ∎

Finally, we derive the **Kuhn-Tucker optimality conditions** for last section's problem (P_0).

Theorem A.39. *Suppose that $c \in C^0$ solves problem $(P_0) : U(c) = J(0)$ and $G(c) \leq 0$. Suppose also that the gradients of U and G at c exist, and that*

$$\text{for some } h \in X,\ G_i(c) + (\nabla G_i(c) \mid h) < 0 \text{ for all } i. \tag{A.6}$$

Then there exists some $\lambda \in \mathbb{R}^n$ such that

$$\nabla U(c) = \lambda \cdot \nabla G(c), \quad \lambda \cdot G(c) = 0, \quad \lambda \geq 0.$$

Proof. An exercise shows that optimality of c implies that for any $h \in X$,

$$G_i(c) + (\nabla G_i(c) \mid h) < 0 \text{ for all } i \quad \Longrightarrow \quad (\nabla U(c) \mid h) \leq 0.$$

The following two convex subsets of $\mathbb{R}^n \times \mathbb{R}$ are therefore nonintersecting:

$A = \{(\delta, \upsilon) : \delta_i < 0 \text{ for all } i, \text{ and } \upsilon > 0\},$

$B = \{(\delta, \upsilon) : \text{for some } h \in X,$

$$\delta \geq G(c) + (\nabla G(c) \mid h) \text{ and } \upsilon \leq (\nabla U(c) \mid h)\}.$$

By the separating hyperplane theorem (Corollary A.30), there exists nonzero $(-\lambda, \alpha) \in \mathbb{R}^n \times \mathbb{R}$ that separates A and B, and therefore

$$\delta \leq 0 \text{ and } \upsilon \geq 0 \quad \Longrightarrow \quad -\lambda \cdot \delta + \alpha \upsilon \geq 0, \quad \text{(A.7)}$$

$$-\lambda \cdot [G(c) + (\nabla G(c) \mid h)] + \alpha(\nabla U(c) \mid h) \leq 0 \quad \text{for all } h \in X. \quad \text{(A.8)}$$

Condition (A.7) implies that $\alpha \geq 0$ and $\lambda \geq 0$. If $\alpha = 0$, assumption (A.6) is violated (why?). After proper scaling, we can therefore assume that $\alpha = 1$, and the Kuhn-Tucker conditions follow from condition (A.8) and the inequalities $\lambda \geq 0$ and $G(c) \leq 0$. ∎

A.10 EXERCISES

1. Prove Proposition A.3.

2. (a) Show that in any inner product space, $x_n \to x$ and $y_n \to y$ as $n \to \infty$ implies $(x_n \mid y_n) \to (x \mid y)$ as $n \to \infty$.

   (b) Prove Proposition A.14.

3. (a) Given any $x, y \in X$ and inner product $(\cdot \mid \cdot)$, show the **parallelogram identity**:

$$\|x + y\|^2 + \|x - y\|^2 = 2\|x\|^2 + 2\|y\|^2.$$

   Interpret this equation geometrically to justify its name.

   (b) Verify the equations in the proof of Theorem A.21.

4. Give an alternative proof of the necessity of the support condition in Theorem A.21(a) that utilizes the fact that the quadratic $f(\alpha) = \|x - x_\alpha\|^2$ is minimized at zero and therefore the right derivative of f at zero must be nonnegative. Also draw a diagram that makes it obvious that if the angle between $s - x_S$ and $x_S - x$ is wider than a right angle, then there exists some $\alpha \in (0, 1)$ such that $\|x - x_\alpha\| < \|x - x_S\|$.

5. (a) Show that the vector y supports the set S at some vector $\bar{s}$ if and only if y supports $\bar{S}$ at $\bar{s}$. (Note that it is not assumed that $\bar{s}$ is in S, and therefore Definition A.28 is required.)

   (b) Show that the closure of a convex set is convex, and conclude that, in finite dimensions, projections on the closure of a convex set always exist.

6. Give a simple direct proof to Corollary A.22.

7. Suppose L is a linear subspace of the finite-dimensional vector space X. Show that there exists a basis $\{e_1, \ldots, e_d\}$ of X such that $L = \operatorname{span}(e_1, \ldots, e_k)$ for some $k \leq d$. Using this fact, show that every linear manifold in X is closed, thus proving the existence of projections on linear manifolds in finite dimensions.

8. (a) State the projection expression of Proposition A.23 in common matrix notation, assuming that the underlying space is $X = \mathbb{R}^d$ with the Euclidean inner product $(x \mid y) = \sum_{i=1}^{n} x_i y_i$.

   (b) Prove Corollaries A.24 and A.25.

9. Prove Proposition A.26, and derive the projection expression of Proposition A.23 as a corollary of Proposition A.8.

10. Suppose P is a linear operator on the inner product space $(X, (\cdot \mid \cdot))$, that is, a function of the form $P : X \to X$ such that $P(\alpha x + \beta y) = \alpha P(x) + \beta P(y)$ for all $\alpha, \beta \in \mathbb{R}$ and $x, y \in X$. P is a **projection operator** if there exists a linear subspace L such that Px is the projection of x on L for all $x \in X$. The operator P is **idempotent** if $P^2 = P$. Finally, P is **self-adjoint** if $(Px \mid y) = (x \mid Py)$ for all $x, y \in X$.

    (a) Prove that P is a projection operator if and only if P is both idempotent and self-adjoint.

    (b) Apply part (a) to show that a matrix $A \in \mathbb{R}^{n \times n}$ is idempotent $(A^2 = A)$ and symmetric $(A' = A)$ if and only if there exists a full-rank matrix B such that $A = B'(BB')^{-1}B$.

11. (a) Suppose X, Y and Z are vector spaces, and $f : X \to Y$ and $g : X \to Z$ are linear functions such that $g(x) = 0$ implies $f(x) = 0$ for all $x \in X$. Show that $L = \{g(x) : x \in X\}$ is a linear subspace of Z, and that there exists a linear function $h : L \to Y$ such that $f = h \circ g$.

    (b) Suppose $f, g_1, \ldots, g_n$ are linear functionals on X such that $g_1(x) = \cdots = g_n(x) = 0$ implies $f(x) = 0$, for all $x \in X$. Show that $f = \sum_{i=1}^{n} \lambda_i g_i$ for some $\lambda \in \mathbb{R}^n$.

12. Use a projection argument to solve the problem

$$\min\{x'Qx : Ax = b, \ x \in \mathbb{R}^{n \times 1}\},$$

where $Q \in \mathbb{R}^{n \times n}$ is positive definite and symmetric, $A \in \mathbb{R}^{m \times n}$ is full rank and $b \in \mathbb{R}^m$ is in the range of A.

13. Consider the problem of finding a vector x of minimum norm satisfying $(x \mid y_i) \geq \alpha_i$, $i = 1, \ldots, n$, where the vectors $y_1, \ldots, y_n$ are linearly independent. Use projection arguments to show that the problem has a unique solution and to characterize the solution as a system of (in)equalities.

14. Suppose that the random vector $y = (y_1, \ldots, y_n)'$ is generated by the model $y = A\beta + \varepsilon$, where $A \in \mathbb{R}^{n \times m}$ is a known matrix, $\beta \in \mathbb{R}^m$ is an unknown vector, and ε is an unobservable zero-mean random vector, valued in $\mathbb{R}^n$, with variance-covariance matrix $\mathbb{E}[\varepsilon\varepsilon'] = \Sigma$, assumed to be positive definite. We are interested in a **linear estimator** of the parameter β, that is, an estimator of the form $\hat{\beta} = By$, for some $B \in \mathbb{R}^{m \times n}$. The linear estimator represented by B is **unbiased** if $BA = I$, since then $\mathbb{E}\hat{\beta} = \beta$ for every choice of β. Using projection theory, determine the unbiased linear estimator that minimizes the variance of $\hat{\beta} - \beta$.

15. Suppose $X = l_2$, the space of square summable sequences, with the inner product $(x \mid y) = \sum_{n=1}^{\infty} x(n)y(n)$. Let S be the positive cone of X, that is, the set of all $x \in X$ such that $x(n) \geq 0$ for all n. Show that $S = \bar{S}$ and $S^0 = \emptyset$. Finally, consider any $\bar{s} \in S$ such that $\bar{s}(n) > 0$ for all n, and show that the only vector y such that $(y \mid s) \geq (y \mid \bar{s})$ for all $s \in S$ is the zero vector.

16. Provide a geometric explanation of complementary slackness (defined in Remark A.34), based on a support condition relative to the set sub(J) in $\mathbb{R}^n \times \mathbb{R}$.

17. In the context of Section A.8, suppose that U and G are continuous. Is J necessarily continuous at an interior point of its effective domain (that is, the set where J is finite)? Provide a proof or a counterexample.

18. Suppose that $f : X \to \mathbb{R}$ is concave.
    (a) Show that $f'(x; h_1 + h_2) \geq f'(x; h_1) + f'(x; h_2)$ for every $h_1, h_2 \in X$ for which the above directional derivatives exist.
    (b) Show that if $f'(x; h)$ exists for all $h \in X$, then the function $f'(x; \cdot)$ is linear.

19. Prove the opening claim of the proof of Theorem A.39. Also, provide a set of convexity-based sufficient conditions for the Kuhn-Tucker conditions of Theorem A.39 to imply optimality, and prove your claim.

283

A.11 NOTES

Textbook accounts of this material, and much more, include Bertsekas (2003) and Boyd and Vandenberghe (2004), while a classic monograph on finite-dimensional convex analysis is Rockafellar (1970). Infinite-dimensional extensions of the theory can be found in Luenberger (1969), Ekeland and Témam (1999) and Zeidler (1985).

Discrete Stochastic Analysis

THIS APPENDIX provides a self-contained exposition of stochastic analysis principles specialized to the case of finitely many states and time periods. The material is prerequisite for Part II and assumes familiarity with the projection theory of Appendix A. A main pedagogical objective is the development of essential intuition behind concepts that apply to more general stochastic settings.

B.1 EVENTS, RANDOM VARIABLES, EXPECTATION

Given throughout this appendix is a finite set Ω, called the **state space**. An **event** is any subset of Ω (including the empty set). The set of all events is therefore 2^Ω (the set of all subsets of Ω). For events A, B, we use standard notation for the **union** $A \cup B = \{\omega : \omega \in A \text{ or } \omega \in B\}$, the **intersection** $A \cap B = \{\omega : \omega \in A \text{ and } \omega \in B\}$, the **set difference** $A \setminus B = \{\omega : \omega \in A \text{ and } \omega \notin B\}$ and the **complement** $A^c = \Omega \setminus A$. A **partition** is any set $\{A_1, \ldots, A_n\}$ of nonempty events whose union is Ω such that $A_i \cap A_j = \emptyset$ if $i \neq j$.

A **random variable** is any function of the form $x : \Omega \to \mathbb{R}$, that is, any element of $\mathbb{R}^\Omega$. We regard $\mathbb{R}^\Omega$ as a vector space with addition and multiplication by scalars defined state by state: For any $x, y \in \mathbb{R}^\Omega$ and $\alpha \in \mathbb{R}$, the random variable $x + \alpha y$ is defined by $(x + \alpha y)(\omega) = x(\omega) + \alpha y(\omega)$, $\omega \in \Omega$. We also define multiplication of random variables, again state by state: For any $x, y \in \mathbb{R}^\Omega$, the random variable xy is defined by $(xy)(\omega) = x(\omega)y(\omega)$, $\omega \in \Omega$.

As is common in probability theory, we identify a scalar $\alpha \in \mathbb{R}$ with the random variable that is identically equal to α. For example, if $x \in \mathbb{R}^\Omega$ and $\alpha \in \mathbb{R}$, then $x + \alpha$ is the random variable defined by $(x + \alpha)(\omega) = x(\omega) + \alpha$, $\omega \in \Omega$. The event of all $\omega \in \Omega$ for which a property $p(\omega)$ is true is denoted $\{p\}$. For example, given any random variable x, scalar α and set $S \subseteq \mathbb{R}$, we write $\{x \leq \alpha\} = \{\omega \in \Omega : x(\omega) \leq \alpha\}$, $\{x = \alpha\} = \{\omega \in \Omega : x(\omega) = \alpha\}$ and $\{x \in S\} = \{\omega : x(\omega) \in S\}$.

The **indicator function** of a set $S \subseteq \Omega$, denoted 1_S, is the random variable

$$1_S(\omega) = \begin{cases} 1, & \text{if } \omega \in S; \\ 0, & \text{if } \omega \notin S. \end{cases}$$

Every random variable x has a unique representation of the form

$$x = \sum_{i=1}^{m} \beta_i 1_{B_i}, \quad \text{where} \tag{B.1}$$

$\beta_i \in \mathbb{R}, \quad \beta_1 < \beta_2 < \cdots < \beta_m$ and $\{B_1, \ldots, B_m\}$ is a partition.

We refer to (B.1) as the **canonical representation** of x.

A **probability (measure)** on the finite state space Ω is a function of the form $P : 2^\Omega \to [0, 1]$ that is normalized so that $P(\Omega) = 1$ and is **additive**:

$$A \cap B = \emptyset \quad \implies \quad P(A \cup B) = P(A) + P(B).$$

The probability P is **strictly positive** if $P(A) > 0$ for every nonempty event A. There is a one-to-one correspondence between probability measures on Ω and elements of the simplex

$$\left\{ p \in \mathbb{R}_+^\Omega : \sum\nolimits_{\omega \in \Omega} p(\omega) = 1 \right\}.$$

Given a simplex element p, a corresponding probability measure P is defined by

$$P(A) = \sum\nolimits_{\omega \in A} p(\omega), \quad A \subseteq \Omega. \tag{B.2}$$

Conversely, a probability P defines the simplex element $p(\omega) = P(\{\omega\})$, $\omega \in \Omega$, satisfying (B.2).

We henceforth fix a reference strictly positive probability P on Ω.

Definition B.1. *For any random variable x with canonical representation* (B.1), *the **expectation** or **mean** of x (relative to the probability P) is*

$$\mathbb{E}[x] = \sum_{i=1}^{m} \beta_i P(B_i).$$

The function $\mathbb{E} : \mathbb{R}^\Omega \to \mathbb{R}$ *so defined is the **expectation operator** relative to P.*

Following common probabilistic notation, we often omit excessive parentheses, writing, for example,

$$\mathbb{E}x = \mathbb{E}[x], \quad \mathbb{E}\sum\nolimits_i x_i = \mathbb{E}\left[\sum\nolimits_i x_i\right], \quad P[x \le \alpha] = P(\{x \le \alpha\}).$$

Lemma B.2.   *Suppose $x = \sum_{i=1}^{n} \alpha_i 1_{A_i}$ for some partition $\{A_1, \ldots, A_n\}$ and (not necessarily distinct) scalars $\alpha_1, \ldots, \alpha_n$. Then $\mathbb{E}x = \sum_{i=1}^{n} \alpha_i P(A_i)$.*

Proof.   We use induction in the number of partition elements n. For $n = 1$ the result is immediate. We now show it holds for some $n > 1$, given that it is true for partitions with $n - 1$ elements. Suppose $x = \sum_{i=1}^{n} \alpha_i 1_{A_i}$. If all the α_i are distinct, then a permutation of the terms in the sum results in the canonical representation of x, and the claim follows from the expectation definition. If at least two of the α_i are the same, say $\alpha_1 = \alpha_2 = \alpha$, then $x = \alpha 1_{A_1 \cup A_2} + \sum_{i=3}^{n} \alpha_i 1_{A_i}$ and therefore, by the inductive hypothesis and additivity of P,

$$\mathbb{E}x = \alpha P(A_1 \cup A_2) + \sum_{i=3}^{n} \alpha_i P(A_i) = \sum_{i=1}^{n} \alpha_i P(A_i).$$

∎

The following characterization of expectations is essentially a corollary of the last lemma.

Proposition B.3.   *The expectation operator $\mathbb{E}$ is a linear functional on $\mathbb{R}^{\Omega}$ such that $\mathbb{E}x \geq 0$ if $x \geq 0$, and $\mathbb{E}1_{\Omega} = 1$. Conversely, a linear functional $\mathbb{E}$ on $\mathbb{R}^{\Omega}$ with these properties is an expectation operator relative to the probability P defined by $P(A) = \mathbb{E}[1_A]$.*

For any random variable x, we use the notation $\hat{x} = x - \mathbb{E}x$ for the **innovation** of x. Any random variable x can be uniquely decomposed as the sum of a scalar and a zero-mean random variable, by writing $x = \mathbb{E}x + \hat{x}$. The **covariance** of two random variables x, y is denoted and defined by

$$\text{cov}[x, y] = \mathbb{E}[\hat{x}\hat{y}] = \mathbb{E}[xy] - \mathbb{E}[x]\mathbb{E}[y].$$

The random variables x, y are **uncorrelated** if $\text{cov}[x, y] = 0$ or, equivalently, if $\mathbb{E}[xy] = \mathbb{E}[x]\mathbb{E}[y]$. The term "uncorrelated" can be misleading, since two uncorrelated random variables can in fact be (nontrivially) determined by the same random source.

Example B.4.   *Suppose $\Omega = \{-1, 0, 1\}$ and $P(\{\omega\}) = 1/3$ for all $\omega \in \Omega$. The random variable x defined by $x(\omega) = \omega$ satisfies $\mathbb{E}x = \mathbb{E}x^3 = 0$. Therefore, the (nonconstant) random variables x and x^2 are uncorrelated.*

Uncorrelatedness can equivalently be thought of as orthogonality in the space

$$\hat{L} = \{\hat{x} : x \in \mathbb{R}^{\Omega}\} = \{x \in \mathbb{R}^{\Omega} : \mathbb{E}x = 0\}$$

with the covariance inner product $(x \mid y) = \text{cov}[x, y]$. The random variables x and y are uncorrelated if and only if $\hat{x}$ and $\hat{y}$ are orthogonal in $\hat{L}$. Variances, standard deviations, and correlation coefficients are defined in Section 1.4. The norm that is induced by the covariance inner product on $\hat{L}$ corresponds to the standard deviation operator: $\|\hat{x}\| = (\hat{x} \mid \hat{x})^{1/2} = \text{stdev}[x]$. In this context, the Cauchy-Schwarz inequality states that $|\text{corr}[x, y]| \leq 1$ for any random variables x, y, with equality holding if and only if $\hat{x} = \alpha \hat{y}$ or $\hat{y} = \alpha \hat{x}$ for some nonzero scalar α.

On occasion, we are interested in switching from the original strictly positive probability P, with corresponding expectation operator $\mathbb{E}$, to another probability $Q : 2^{\Omega} \to [0, 1]$, whose expectation operator we denote $\mathbb{E}^Q$. The **density** (or **Radon-Nikodym derivative**) of Q with respect to P, denoted dQ/dP, is the random variable

$$\frac{dQ}{dP}(\omega) = \frac{Q(\{\omega\})}{P(\{\omega\})}, \quad \omega \in \Omega.$$

Proposition B.5. *For any random variable* x,

$$\mathbb{E}^Q[x] = \mathbb{E}\left[x \frac{dQ}{dP}\right]. \tag{B.3}$$

Proof. Applying Lemma B.2, we have

$$\mathbb{E}^Q[x] = \sum_{\omega \in \Omega} x(\omega) Q(\{\omega\}) = \sum_{\omega \in \Omega} x(\omega) \frac{Q(\{\omega\})}{P(\{\omega\})} P(\{\omega\}) = \mathbb{E}\left[x \frac{dQ}{dP}\right].$$

∎

Remark B.6. *In the above formulation, we started with the probability* Q *and defined the density* dQ/dP, *which is nonnegative and satisfies* $\mathbb{E}[dQ/dP] = 1$. *Alternatively, one can start with any nonnegative random variable* Z *such that* $\mathbb{E}Z = 1$. *Then* $Q(A) = \mathbb{E}[Z 1_A]$ *defines a probability* $Q : 2^{\Omega} \to [0, 1]$, *and* $Z = dQ/dP$. *The probability* Q *is strictly positive if and only if* Z *is strictly positive.*

B.2 ALGEBRAS AND MEASURABILITY

A set $\mathcal{A} \subseteq 2^{\Omega}$ is an **algebra** if it is nonempty and is closed with respect to the formation of unions and complements: $A, B \in \mathcal{A}$ implies $A \cup B \in \mathcal{A}$ and $A^c \in \mathcal{A}$. A **subalgebra** of the algebra $\mathcal{A}$ is any subset of $\mathcal{A}$ that is also an algebra. From the identities $A \cap B = (A^c \cup B^c)^c$ and $A \setminus B = A \cap B^c$, it follows that an algebra is also closed with respect to the formation of intersections and set differences. Moreover, since Ω is assumed finite, the union or intersection of any collection of elements of an algebra $\mathcal{A}$ is also an element of $\mathcal{A}$. The largest (with respect to inclusion) algebra of subsets of Ω is 2^{Ω}, and the smallest is the **trivial algebra** $\{\emptyset, \Omega\}$. The intersection of any set of algebras is also an algebra. Given any set $\mathcal{S} \subseteq 2^{\Omega}$, the algebra **generated** by $\mathcal{S}$ is the intersection of all algebras that have $\mathcal{S}$ as a subset. Given any $\mathcal{A} \subseteq 2^{\Omega}$, a **minimal** element of $\mathcal{A}$ is any $A \in \mathcal{A}$ such that $B \in \mathcal{A}$ and $B \subseteq A$ implies $B = A$ or $B = \emptyset$.

Example B.7. *Suppose $\Omega = \{1, 2, 3, 4\}$ and consider the partition*

$$\mathcal{A}^0 = \{\{1, 2\}, \{3\}, \{4\}\}.$$

The algebra generated by $\mathcal{A}^0$ is the set

$$\mathcal{A} = \{\emptyset, \{1, 2\}, \{3\}, \{4\}, \{1, 2, 3\}, \{1, 2, 4\}, \{3, 4\}, \Omega\}.$$

Note that the partition $\mathcal{A}^0$ is the set of nonempty minimal elements of $\mathcal{A}$.

Proposition B.8. *(a) Suppose $\mathcal{A}^0$ is a partition of events and let $\mathcal{A}$ be the set consisting of the empty set and any event that can be expressed as a union of elements of $\mathcal{A}^0$. Then $\mathcal{A}$ is the algebra generated by $\mathcal{A}^0$.*

(b) Suppose $\mathcal{A}$ is an algebra of events and let $\mathcal{A}^0$ be the set of all nonempty minimal elements of $\mathcal{A}$. Then $\mathcal{A}^0$ is a partition and $\mathcal{A}$ is the algebra generated by $\mathcal{A}^0$.

Proof. (a) One can easily verify that $\mathcal{A}$ is an algebra. If $\mathcal{B}$ is another algebra containing $\mathcal{A}^0$, then necessarily $\mathcal{B}$ contains every finite union of elements of $\mathcal{A}^0$, and therefore $\mathcal{A} \subseteq \mathcal{B}$. This implies that $\mathcal{A}$ is the algebra generated by $\mathcal{A}^0$.

(b) Let $\mathcal{A}^0 = \{A_1, \ldots, A_n\}$ be the set of minimal nonempty elements of $\mathcal{A}$. Since $A_i \cap A_j \in \mathcal{A}$, minimality of A_i implies that $A_i \cap A_j = \emptyset$ if $i \neq j$. If A is a nonempty element of $\mathcal{A}$, then A is either minimal in $\mathcal{A}$ or contains a nonempty proper subset in $\mathcal{A}$. Since $\mathcal{A}$ is finite, repeating this argument a finite number of times produces some $A_{i_1} \in \mathcal{A}^0$ such that $A_{i_1} \subseteq A$. Similarly, if $A \neq A_{i_1}$, there is some $A_{i_2} \in \mathcal{A}^0$ such that $A_{i_2} \subseteq A \setminus A_{i_1}$; if $A \neq A_{i_1} \cup A_{i_2}$, there is some $A_{i_3} \in \mathcal{A}^0$ such that $A_{i_3} \subseteq A \setminus A_{i_1} \cup A_{i_2}$; and so on. Eventually, A is written as a union of elements of $\mathcal{A}^0$. This argument with $A = \Omega$ proves that $\mathcal{A}^0$ is a partition. By part (a), $\mathcal{A}$ is the algebra generated by $\mathcal{A}^0$. ∎

A partition $\mathcal{A}^0 = \{A_1, \ldots, A_n\}$, or the algebra $\mathcal{A}$ it generates, can be thought of as representing an agent's information. Suppose state $\omega \in \Omega$ is realized, where $\omega \in A_i$. An agent with information $\mathcal{A}$ knows that an event A happened and A^c did not happen if and only if $A_i \subseteq A \in \mathcal{A}$. Inclusion defines a partial order on the set of algebras that has an important interpretation as relative amount of information; the larger the algebra, the more information it carries. Using the definitions and Proposition B.8, we obtain the following related result.

Proposition B.9. *Suppose $\mathcal{A}$ is the algebra generated by the partition $\mathcal{A}^0$, and $\mathcal{B}$ is the algebra generated by the partition $\mathcal{B}^0$. Then $\mathcal{A} \subseteq \mathcal{B}$ if and only if each element of $\mathcal{A}^0$ is a union of elements of $\mathcal{B}^0$.*

On occasion, we are interested in restricting the original state space Ω to some event F, with the interpretation that the event F is known to have occurred. Given any algebra $\mathcal{A}$, generated by the partition $\mathcal{A}^0$, and any event F, we define the notation

$$\mathcal{A} \cap F = \{A \cap F : A \in \mathcal{A}\} \quad \text{and} \quad \mathcal{A}^0 \cap F = \{A \cap F : A \in \mathcal{A}^0\}.$$

$\mathcal{A} \cap F$ is an algebra relative to the restricted state space F and is generated by the partition $\mathcal{A}^0 \cap F$.

Given any algebra $\mathcal{A} \subseteq 2^{\Omega}$, we define measurability of a random variable x with respect to $\mathcal{A}$ to correspond to the intuitive notion that an agent who observes information represented by $\mathcal{A}$ knows the realized value of x. Formally, the random variable x is **measurable** with respect to the algebra $\mathcal{A}$, or is $\mathcal{A}$-**measurable**, if $\{x \leq \alpha\} \in \mathcal{A}$ for every $\alpha \in \mathbb{R}$. The set of $\mathcal{A}$-measurable elements of $\mathbb{R}^\Omega$ is denoted $L(\mathcal{A})$. A random variable is always measurable with respect to 2^Ω and is measurable with respect to the trivial algebra if and only if it is constant. The algebra **generated** by a collection of random variables $\{x_i : i \in I\}$ is the intersection of all algebras relative to which every x_i is measurable, and is denoted $\sigma(x_i : i \in I)$. If the random variable x has canonical representation (B.1), then the algebra $\sigma(x)$ generated by x is the same as the algebra $\mathcal{B}$ generated by the partition $\{B_1, \ldots, B_m\}$. To see why, note that if $\mathcal{A}$ is any algebra such that $x \in L(\mathcal{A})$, then $B_i = \{x \le \beta_i\} \setminus \{x \le \beta_{i-1}\} \in \mathcal{A}$, and therefore $\mathcal{B} \subseteq \mathcal{A}$. Since $x \in L(\mathcal{B})$, $\mathcal{B}$ is the smallest algebra with respect to which x is measurable.

The following equivalent characterizations of measurability follow easily.

Proposition B.10. *Suppose $\mathcal{A}$ is the algebra generated by the partition*

$$\{A_1, \ldots, A_n\}.$$

Then for any random variable x, the following conditions are equivalent:

1. *x is $\mathcal{A}$-measurable.*
2. *$\{x = \alpha\} \in \mathcal{A}$ for every $\alpha \in \mathbb{R}$.*
3. *$\{x \in S\} \in \mathcal{A}$ for any $S \subseteq \mathbb{R}$.*
4. *$\sigma(x) \subseteq \mathcal{A}$.*
5. *$x = \sum_{i=1}^{n} \alpha_i 1_{A_i}$ for some scalars $\alpha_1, \ldots, \alpha_n$.*

It is also straightforward to confirm that the algebra $\sigma(x_1, \ldots, x_n)$ generated by the random variables $x_1, \ldots, x_n$ is generated by the partition consisting of all nonempty events of the form $\{(x_1, \ldots, x_n) = \beta\}$, where $\beta \in \mathbb{R}^n$. We interpret $\sigma(x_1, \ldots, x_n)$ as the information that can be inferred by observing the realization of the random variables $x_1, \ldots, x_n$. For any algebra $\mathcal{A} \subseteq 2^\Omega$, the condition $\sigma(x_1, \ldots, x_n) \subseteq \mathcal{A}$ is equivalent to $x_1, \ldots, x_n \in L(\mathcal{A})$ and can be interpreted as stating that information $\mathcal{A}$ reveals the realization of $x_1, \ldots, x_n$. This interpretation suggests that $\mathcal{A}$ should also reveal the realization of any deterministic function of $x_1, \ldots, x_n$, a claim that is formalized in the following proposition. Given any function $f : \mathbb{R}^n \to \mathbb{R}$, let $f(x_1, \ldots, x_n)$ denote the random variable $f(x_1, \ldots, x_n)(\omega) = f(x_1(\omega), \ldots, x_n(\omega))$, $\omega \in \Omega$.

Proposition B.11. *The following are true for any random variables* $x_1, \ldots, x_n$.

(a) *Given any algebra* $\mathcal{A} \subseteq \mathbb{R}^\Omega$, $x_1, \ldots, x_n \in L(\mathcal{A})$ *if and only if*

$$f(x_1, \ldots, x_n) \in L(\mathcal{A}) \quad \text{for every function } f : \mathbb{R}^n \to \mathbb{R}.$$

(b) *The random variable* y *is* $\sigma(x_1, \ldots, x_n)$-*measurable if and only if there exists a function* $f : \mathbb{R}^n \to \mathbb{R}$ *such that* $y = f(x_1, \ldots, x_n)$.

Proof. Let $\{(x_1(\omega), \ldots, x_n(\omega)) : \omega \in \Omega\} = \{\beta_1, \ldots, \beta_m\} \subseteq \mathbb{R}^n$.

(a) Suppose $x_1, \ldots, x_n \in L(\mathcal{A})$. Given any $\alpha \in \mathbb{R}$, let I_α be the set of indices $i \in \{1, \ldots, m\}$ such that $f(\beta_i) \leq \alpha$. Then

$$\{f(x_1, \ldots, x_n) \leq \alpha\} = \bigcup_{i \in I_\alpha} \bigcap_{j=1}^{n} \{x_j = \beta_{ij}\} \in \mathcal{A}.$$

Therefore, $f(x_1, \ldots, x_n) \in L(\mathcal{A})$. The converse of part (a) is immediate.

(b) Suppose $y = f(x_1, \ldots, x_n)$. Part (a) with $\mathcal{A} = \sigma(x_1, \ldots, x_n)$ implies that y is $\sigma(x_1, \ldots, x_n)$-measurable. Conversely, suppose y is $\sigma(x_1, \ldots, x_n)$-measurable. As noted earlier, $\sigma(x_1, \ldots, x_n)$ is generated by the partition

$$\{B_1, \ldots, B_m\}, \quad \text{where} \quad B_i = \{(x_1, \ldots, x_n) = \beta_i\}.$$

By the last proposition, there exist $\alpha_1, \ldots, \alpha_m \in \mathbb{R}$ such that $y = \sum_{i=1}^{m} \alpha_i 1_{B_i}$. Selecting any function $f : \mathbb{R}^n \to \mathbb{R}$ such that $\alpha_i = f(\beta_i)$, $i = 1, \ldots, m$, results in $y = f(x_1, \ldots, x_n)$. ∎

Corollary B.12. *Suppose* $\mathcal{A}$ *and* $\mathcal{B}$ *are algebras satisfying* $\mathcal{A} \subseteq \mathcal{B} \subseteq 2^\Omega$. *Then* $L(\mathcal{A})$ *is a linear subspace of* $L(\mathcal{B})$, *which is in turn a linear subspace of* $\mathbb{R}^\Omega$.

Corollary B.13. *The linear span of the random variables* $x_1, \ldots, x_n$ *is a linear subspace of the set of all* $\sigma(x_1, \ldots, x_n)$-*measurable random variables.*

B.3 CONDITIONAL EXPECTATION

While probabilities played no role in last section's discussion, the reference strictly positive probability P is key from here on. The conditional expectation of a random variable x given an algebra $\mathcal{B}$ (defined relative to P) is the best estimate of the value of x given information $\mathcal{B}$, in the sense of minimizing the expected squared error.

Definition B.14. *The **conditional expectation** of the random variable x **given the algebra** $\mathcal{B}$, denoted $\mathbb{E}[x \mid \mathcal{B}]$, is the unique random variable y in $L(\mathcal{B})$ such that*

$$\mathbb{E}[(x-y)^2] \le \mathbb{E}[(x-z)^2] \quad \text{for every } z \in L(\mathcal{B}).$$

Remark B.15. *The uniqueness claim in Definition B.14 is a consequence of the assumption that P is strictly positive. In general, any two random variables y, y' that are conditional expectations of x given $\mathcal{B}$ must satisfy $P[y = y'] = 1$ but can take arbitrary values on any event $B \in \mathcal{B}$ such that $P(B) = 0$.*

Geometrically, $\mathbb{E}[x \mid \mathcal{B}]$ is the projection of x onto $L(\mathcal{B})$ in the space $\mathbb{R}^\Omega$ with the inner product $(x \mid y) = \mathbb{E}[xy]$.

Proposition B.16. *Suppose $\mathcal{B} \subseteq 2^\Omega$ is an algebra that is generated by the partition $\mathcal{B}^0$, x is any random variable and y is a $\mathcal{B}$-measurable random variable. Then the following conditions are equivalent:*

1. *$y = \mathbb{E}[x \mid \mathcal{B}]$.*
2. *$\mathbb{E}x = \mathbb{E}y$ and $x - y$ is uncorrelated with every $\mathcal{B}$-measurable random variable.*
3. *$\mathbb{E}[xz] = \mathbb{E}[yz]$ for all $z \in L(\mathcal{B})$.*
4. *$\mathbb{E}[x1_B] = \mathbb{E}[y1_B]$ for all $B \in \mathcal{B}$.*
5. *$\mathbb{E}[x1_B] = \mathbb{E}[y1_B]$ for all $B \in \mathcal{B}^0$.*

Proof. The equivalence $(1 \Longleftrightarrow 3)$ follows from the orthogonal version of the projection theorem, while $(2 \Longleftrightarrow 3)$ is immediate. Letting $z = 1_B$ in condition 3 results in condition 4, which clearly implies condition 5. Finally, suppose condition 5 holds and let $\mathcal{B}^0 = \{B_1, \ldots, B_n\}$. Any $z \in L(\mathcal{B})$ can be expressed as $z = \sum_{i=1}^n \beta_i 1_{B_i}$, for some $\beta_1, \ldots, \beta_n \in \mathbb{R}$. Therefore,

$$\mathbb{E}[xz] = \sum_{i=1}^n \beta_i \mathbb{E}[x1_{B_i}] = \sum_{i=1}^n \beta_i \mathbb{E}[y1_{B_i}] = \mathbb{E}[yz],$$

confirming condition 3. ∎

Proposition B.17.   *For any random variable x and algebras $\mathcal{A}$ and $\mathcal{B}$:*

(a) (law of iterated expectations)

$\mathcal{B} \subseteq \mathcal{A} \implies \mathbb{E}[\mathbb{E}[x \mid \mathcal{A}] \mid \mathcal{B}] = \mathbb{E}[x \mid \mathcal{B}].$

(b) $b \in L(\mathcal{B}) \implies \mathbb{E}[bx \mid \mathcal{B}] = b\mathbb{E}[x \mid \mathcal{B}].$

Proof. (a) Assuming $\mathcal{B} \subseteq \mathcal{A}$, $L(\mathcal{B})$ is a linear subspace of $L(\mathcal{A})$. Projecting x on $L(\mathcal{B})$ is equivalent to first projecting x on $L(\mathcal{A})$ and then further projecting on $L(\mathcal{B})$, which translates to $\mathbb{E}[x \mid \mathcal{B}] = \mathbb{E}[\mathbb{E}[x \mid \mathcal{A}] \mid \mathcal{B}]$.

(b) Given any $b \in L(\mathcal{B})$, let $y = b\mathbb{E}[x \mid \mathcal{B}]$. We apply the equivalence $(1 \iff 3)$ of Proposition B.16 twice, first to justify the middle equality in

$$\mathbb{E}[(bx)z] = \mathbb{E}[x(bz)] = \mathbb{E}[\mathbb{E}[x \mid \mathcal{B}](bz)] = \mathbb{E}[yz] \quad \text{for all } z \in L(\mathcal{B}),$$

and then to conclude that since $y \in L(\mathcal{B})$, the above condition implies $y = \mathbb{E}[bx \mid \mathcal{B}]$. ∎

Corollary B.18. $\mathcal{B} \subseteq \mathcal{A}$ *or* $\mathcal{A} \subseteq \mathcal{B}$ *implies* $\mathbb{E}[\mathbb{E}[x \mid \mathcal{A}] \mid \mathcal{B}] = \mathbb{E}[x \mid \mathcal{A} \cap \mathcal{B}].$

As the term suggests, a conditional expectation can be expressed as an actual expectation relative to a corresponding conditional probability. Recall that the underlying probability P is assumed strictly positive.

Definition B.19.   *For any nonempty event B, the* **conditional probability** *(measure) P* **given** *B is the probability $P(\cdot \mid B) : 2^{\Omega} \to [0, 1]$, where*

$$P(A \mid B) = \frac{P(A \cap B)}{P(B)}, \quad A \subseteq \Omega. \tag{B.4}$$

The expectation operator relative to $P(\cdot \mid B)$ is denoted $\mathbb{E}[\cdot \mid B]$.

Equation (B.4), known as **Bayes rule**, has a simple frequentist interpretation. Suppose the elements of the state space Ω are the possible colors of balls in an urn and $P(\{\omega\})$ is the proportion of balls of color $\omega \in \Omega$. For any $A \subseteq \Omega$, $P(A)$ is the proportion of balls with color in A. Given any $B \subseteq \Omega$, suppose all balls with color not in B are removed from the urn. Then $P(A \mid B)$ is the new proportion of balls with color in A.

Bayes rule extends to expectations.

Proposition B.20.   *For any nonempty event B and random variable x,*

$$\mathbb{E}[x \mid B] = \frac{\mathbb{E}[x 1_B]}{P(B)}.$$

Proof. If $x = \sum_i \alpha_i 1_{A_i}$ for some partition $\{A_1, \ldots, A_n\}$ and scalar α_i, then

$$\mathbb{E}[x \mid B]P(B) = \sum_i \alpha_i P(A_i \mid B)P(B) = \sum_i \alpha_i P(A_i \cap B)$$

$$= \sum_i \alpha_i \mathbb{E}[1_{A_i} 1_B] = \mathbb{E}[x 1_B].$$

■

We can now relate the two notions of conditioning introduced above.

Proposition B.21. *Suppose the algebra $\mathcal{B} \subseteq 2^\Omega$ is generated by the partition $\{B_1, \ldots, B_n\}$. Then for any random variable x,*

$$\mathbb{E}[x \mid \mathcal{B}] = \sum_{i=1}^n \mathbb{E}[x \mid B_i] 1_{B_i}.$$

Proof. Let $y = \sum_{i=1}^n \mathbb{E}[x \mid B_i] 1_{B_i}$. Then, using Proposition B.20,

$$\mathbb{E}[y 1_{B_i}] = \mathbb{E}[\mathbb{E}[x \mid B_i] 1_{B_i}] = \mathbb{E}[x \mid B_i]P(B_i) = \mathbb{E}[x 1_{B_i}], \quad i = 1, \ldots, n.$$

Since $y \in L(\mathcal{B})$, the equivalence $(1 \iff 5)$ of Proposition B.16 implies $y = \mathbb{E}[x \mid \mathcal{B}]$. ■

Conditioning is also defined with respect to random variables.

Definition B.22. *For any random variables $x, y_1, \ldots, y_n$, the conditional expectation of x given $y_1, \ldots, y_n$ is the random variable*

$$\mathbb{E}[x \mid y_1, \ldots, y_n] = \mathbb{E}[x \mid \sigma(y_1, \ldots, y_n)].$$

Let $y : \Omega \to \mathbb{R}^n$ be the **random vector** defined by $y(\omega) = (y_1(\omega), \ldots, y_n(\omega))$, and write $\sigma(y) = \sigma(y_1, \ldots, y_n)$ and $\mathbb{E}[x \mid y] = \mathbb{E}[x \mid y_1, \ldots, y_n]$. Since $\mathbb{E}[x \mid y]$ is $\sigma(y)$-measurable, Proposition B.11 implies that there exists some function $\mu_{x|y} : \mathbb{R}^n \to \mathbb{R}$ such that

$$\mathbb{E}[x \mid y](\omega) = \mu_{x|y}(y(\omega)), \quad \omega \in \Omega. \tag{B.5}$$

The function $\mu_{x|y}$ can be characterized in terms of the **joint probability mass function** of x and y, defined as the function $f_{x,y} : \mathbb{R}^{1+n} \to \mathbb{R}$ such that

$$f_{x,y}(\alpha, \beta) = P[x = \alpha, \ y = \beta], \quad \alpha \in \mathbb{R}, \quad \beta \in \mathbb{R}^n.$$

295

Clearly, $f_{x,y}$ takes nonzero values only over a finite subset of $\mathbb{R}^{1+n}$. An exercise shows the following variant of Bayes rule.

Proposition B.23. *The function* $\mu_{x|y} : \mathbb{R}^n \to \mathbb{R}$ *satisfies* (B.5) *if and only if*

$$\mu_{x|y}(\beta) = \frac{\sum_\alpha \alpha f_{x,y}(\alpha, \beta)}{\sum_\alpha f_{x,y}(\alpha, \beta)},$$

for all $\beta \in \mathbb{R}^n$ *such that* $\sum_\alpha f_{x,y}(\alpha, \beta) > 0$.

Finally, we note the conditional version of Proposition B.5, where $\mathbb{E}^Q[x \mid \mathcal{A}]$ denotes the conditional expectation of x given $\mathcal{A}$ with underlying probability Q, instead of P.

Proposition B.24. *For any strictly positive probability* Q, *random variable* x *and algebra* $\mathcal{A} \subseteq 2^\Omega$,

$$\mathbb{E}^Q[x \mid \mathcal{A}] = \frac{\mathbb{E}[x(dQ/dP) \mid \mathcal{A}]}{\mathbb{E}[dQ/dP \mid \mathcal{A}]}. \tag{B.6}$$

Proof. We use an argument that extends readily to more general spaces. Let

$$\xi = \frac{dQ}{dP} \quad \text{and} \quad y = \frac{\mathbb{E}[x\xi \mid \mathcal{A}]}{\mathbb{E}[\xi \mid \mathcal{A}]}.$$

For any $z \in L(\mathcal{A})$, the conditional expectation properties of Proposition B.17 and the fact that $yz \in L(\mathcal{A})$ imply

$$\mathbb{E}^Q[yz] = \mathbb{E}[yz\xi] = \mathbb{E}[\mathbb{E}[yz\xi \mid \mathcal{A}]] = \mathbb{E}[yz\mathbb{E}[\xi \mid \mathcal{A}]]$$
$$= \mathbb{E}[z\mathbb{E}[x\xi \mid \mathcal{A}]] = \mathbb{E}[\mathbb{E}[xz\xi \mid \mathcal{A}]] = \mathbb{E}[xz\xi] = \mathbb{E}^Q[xz].$$

By the equivalence ($1 \iff 3$) of Proposition B.16, $y = \mathbb{E}^Q[x \mid \mathcal{A}]$. ■

B.4 STOCHASTIC INDEPENDENCE

Two algebras $\mathcal{A}$ and $\mathcal{B}$ are stochastically independent (relative to the given underlying probability P) if for any random variable x whose value is revealed by information $\mathcal{A}$, the best estimate of the value of x given information $\mathcal{B}$ is the same as the best estimate of the value of x given no information. A more precise version of this definition follows.

Definition B.25. *The algebras $\mathcal{A}$ and $\mathcal{B}$ are* **stochastically independent** *if $\mathbb{E}[x \mid \mathcal{B}] = \mathbb{E}[x]$ for every $\mathcal{A}$-measurable random variable x.*

As usual, we regard the set $\hat{L}$ of zero-mean random variables as an inner product space with the covariance inner product. For any algebra $\mathcal{C}$, let

$$\hat{L}(\mathcal{C}) = \hat{L} \cap L(\mathcal{C}),$$

which is the set of zero-mean $\mathcal{C}$-measurable random variables.

Note that the algebras $\mathcal{A}$ and $\mathcal{B}$ are stochastically independent if and only if

$$\mathbb{E}[\hat{x} \mid \mathcal{B}] = 0 \text{ for every } \hat{x} \in \hat{L}(\mathcal{A}).$$

This condition states that the projection of any $\hat{x} \in \hat{L}(\mathcal{A})$ on the linear subspace $\hat{L}(\mathcal{B})$ is zero. Therefore, $\mathcal{A}$ and $\mathcal{B}$ are stochastically independent if and only if $\hat{L}(\mathcal{A})$ and $\hat{L}(\mathcal{B})$ are orthogonal subspaces of $\hat{L}$. Elaborating on this argument, we have the following characterization of stochastic independence.

Proposition B.26. *Suppose that $\mathcal{A}$ and $\mathcal{B}$ are algebras of events, generated by the partitions $\mathcal{A}^0$ and $\mathcal{B}^0$, respectively. Then the following conditions are equivalent:*

1. *$\mathcal{A}$ and $\mathcal{B}$ are stochastically independent.*
2. *Any element of $L(\mathcal{A})$ is uncorrelated with any element of $L(\mathcal{B})$.*
3. *$x \in L(\mathcal{A})$ and $y \in L(\mathcal{B})$ implies $\mathbb{E}[xy] = \mathbb{E}[x]\mathbb{E}[y]$.*
4. *$A \in \mathcal{A}$ and $B \in \mathcal{B}$ implies $P(A \cap B) = P(A)P(B)$.*
5. *$A \in \mathcal{A}^0$ and $B \in \mathcal{B}^0$ implies $P(A \cap B) = P(A)P(B)$.*

Proof. We have already shown the equivalence of the first two conditions, while the equivalence of conditions 2 and 3 is immediate. Letting $x = 1_A$ and $y = 1_B$ in condition 3 gives condition 4, which clearly implies condition 5. Finally, suppose condition 5 holds and let $x = \sum_{i=1}^m x_i 1_{A_i}$ and $y = \sum_{j=1}^n y_j 1_{B_j}$, where $A_1, \ldots, A_m \in \mathcal{A}^0$ and $B_1, \ldots, B_n \in \mathcal{B}^0$. Taking expectations on both sides of the identity

$xy = \sum_{i,j} x_i y_j 1_{A_i \cap B_j}$, and using the assumption $\mathbb{E}1_{A_i \cap B_j} = \mathbb{E}1_{A_i}\mathbb{E}1_{B_j}$, we conclude that $\mathbb{E}[xy] = \mathbb{E}x\mathbb{E}y$, proving condition 3. ∎

As with conditioning, the notion of stochastic independence applies to random variables through the algebras they generate. In particular, the random variables x and y are **stochastically independent** if the algebras $\sigma(x)$ and $\sigma(y)$ are stochastically independent. By Proposition B.11 and the equivalence (1 $\iff$ 2) of Proposition B.26, two random variables x and y are stochastically independent if and only if for any functions $f, g : \mathbb{R} \to \mathbb{R}$, the random variables $f(x)$ and $g(y)$ are uncorrelated. Therefore, any two random variables that are stochastically independent are uncorrelated. The converse is not generally true; the (positive-variance) random variables x and x^2 of Example B.4 are uncorrelated but are not stochastically independent.

The notion of stochastic independence is commonly applied to sets of more than two random variables to mean that each random variable is stochastically independent of the algebra generated by the remaining random variables.

Definition B.27. *The random variables $x_1, \ldots, x_n$ are **stochastically independent** if for every $k \in \{1, \ldots, n\}$, the algebras $\sigma(x_k)$ and $\sigma(x_i : i \neq k)$ are stochastically independent.*

An exercise shows that independence in the above sense is not generally implied by pairwise stochastic independence. Some characterizations of stochastic independence of random variables follow.

Proposition B.28. *For any random variables $x_1, \ldots, x_n$, the following conditions are equivalent:*

1. *$x_1, \ldots, x_n$ are stochastically independent.*
2. *$\mathbb{E}[\prod_{i=1}^n f_i(x_i)] = \prod_{i=1}^n \mathbb{E}[f_i(x_i)]$ for any functions $f_1, \ldots, f_n : \mathbb{R} \to \mathbb{R}$.*
3. *$P[x_1 \in S_1, \ldots, x_n \in S_n] = \prod_{i=1}^n P[x_i \in S_i]$ for all $S_1, \ldots, S_n \subseteq \mathbb{R}$.*
4. *$P[x_1 = \alpha_1, \ldots, x_n = \alpha_n] = \prod_{i=1}^n P[x_i = \alpha_i]$ for all $\alpha_1, \ldots, \alpha_n \in \mathbb{R}$.*

Proof. (1 $\implies$ 2) We argue by induction in n. The claim is trivially true for $n = 1$. Suppose now that we have shown the claim for $n - 1$ variables, and suppose the random variables $x_1, \ldots, x_n$ are stochastically independent. For any functions $f_i : \mathbb{R} \to \mathbb{R}$, the random variables $\prod_{i=1}^{n-1} f_i(x_i) \in L(\sigma(x_1, \ldots, x_{n-1}))$ and $f_n(x_n) \in L(\sigma(x_n))$ are uncorrelated, and therefore, using the inductive hypothesis,

$$\mathbb{E}[\prod_{i=1}^{n} f_i(x_i)] = \mathbb{E}[\prod_{i=1}^{n-1} f_i(x_i)]\mathbb{E}[f_n(x_n)] = \prod_{i=1}^{n} \mathbb{E}[f_i(x_i)].$$

(2 $\implies$ 3)   Let $f_i(x_i) = 1_{\{x_i \in S_i\}}$.

(3 $\implies$ 4)   Let $S_i = \{\alpha_i\}$.

(4 $\implies$ 1)   Suppose condition 4 holds. We verify the last condition of Proposition B.26, with $\mathcal{A} = \sigma(x_1)$ and $\mathcal{B} = \sigma(x_2, \ldots, x_n)$. The partition generating $\mathcal{A}$ consists of elements of the form $A = \{x_1 = \alpha_1\}$ for some $\alpha_1 \in \mathbb{R}$. On the other hand, the partition generating $\mathcal{B}$ consists of elements of the form $B = \{x_2 = \alpha_2, \ldots, x_n = \alpha_n\}$ for some $\alpha_2, \ldots, \alpha_n \in \mathbb{R}$. Picking any A and B of this form, we note that condition 4 implies

$$P(B) = \sum_{\alpha_1 \in \mathbb{R}} P[x_1 = \alpha_1, x_2 = \alpha_2, \ldots, x_n = \alpha_n]$$
$$= \left(\sum_{\alpha_1 \in \mathbb{R}} P[x_1 = \alpha_1]\right) \prod_{i=2}^{n} P[x_i = \alpha_i] = \prod_{i=2}^{n} P[x_i = \alpha_i].$$

Using this fact and condition 4 once more, we find

$$P(A \cap B) = P[x_1 = \alpha_1, \ldots, x_n = \alpha_n] = \prod_{i=1}^{n} P[x_i = \alpha_i] = P[A]P[B].$$

This proves that $\sigma(x_1)$ is stochastically independent of $\sigma(x_2, \ldots, x_n)$. The same argument applies for any permutation of the $x_1, \ldots, x_n$, completing the proof. ∎

B.5 FILTRATION, STOPPING TIMES AND STOCHASTIC PROCESSES

To the basic primitive of an underlying finite state space Ω, we now add $1 + T$ **times**, labeled $0, 1, \ldots, T$. We refer to the intervals between times as **periods**. There are therefore T periods, with period t referring to the interval between times $t - 1$ and t.

A **filtration** is a time-indexed set of algebras $\{\mathcal{F}_t : t = 0, \ldots, T\}$ satisfying

$$\mathcal{F}_{t-1} \subseteq \mathcal{F}_t \subseteq 2^\Omega, \quad t = 1, \ldots, T.$$

The partition generating $\mathcal{F}_t$ is denoted $\mathcal{F}_t^0$. A **spot** (of the filtration) is any pair of the form (F, t), where $t \in \{0, \ldots, T\}$ and $F \in \mathcal{F}_t^0$. A spot is **terminal** if it is of the form (F, T). An **immediate successor** to a nonterminal spot $(F, t - 1)$ is any spot of the form (G, t), where $G \subseteq F$. The set of immediate successors to $(F, t - 1)$ is, therefore,

$$\{(G, t) : G \in \mathcal{F}_t^0 \cap F\}.$$

The spots of the filtration $\{\mathcal{F}_t\}$ can be arranged diagrammatically on an **information tree** (or graph), where each spot is a node that is connected with arcs to its immediate successors. An example is given in Figure 5.1 (of Section 5.1).

We henceforth fix an underlying filtration $\{\mathcal{F}_t : t = 0, \ldots, T\}$ that satisfies

$$\mathcal{F}_0 = \{\emptyset, \Omega\} \quad \text{and} \quad \mathcal{F}_T = 2^\Omega. \tag{B.7}$$

The algebra $\mathcal{F}_t$ represents time-t information. Restriction (B.7), therefore, means that there is no information at time zero and the actual state is revealed at time T.

Example B.29. *A coin is tossed T times. We model the coin uncertainty by letting $\Omega = \{-1, 1\}^T$. A state $\omega \in \Omega$ is therefore a finite sequence $(\omega_1, \ldots, \omega_T)$, where $\omega_t \in \{-1, 1\}$. Time-t information consists of all the coin-toss outcomes up to time t. It is therefore natural to define the partition $\mathcal{F}_t^0$ to represent the 2^t possible values of $(\omega_1, \ldots, \omega_t)$. For every $(\bar{\omega}_1, \ldots, \bar{\omega}_t) \in \{-1, 1\}^t$, the corresponding element of $\mathcal{F}_t^0$ is the event $\{\omega \in \Omega : \omega_1 = \bar{\omega}_1, \ldots, \omega_t = \bar{\omega}_t\}$. Finally, we define the filtration $\{\mathcal{F}_t\}$ by letting $\mathcal{F}_t$ be the algebra generated by $\mathcal{F}_t^0$.*

Given a filtration, we are often interested in defining a time, called a stopping time, that is contingent on available information.

Definition B.30. *A **stopping time** is a function of the form*

$$\tau : \Omega \to \{0, 1, \ldots, T\} \cup \{\infty\}$$

such that $\{\tau \leq t\} \in \mathcal{F}_t$ for every time t.

The identities

$$\{\tau \leq t\} = \bigcup_{u \leq t} \{\tau = u\} \quad \text{and} \quad \{\tau = t\} = \{\tau \leq t\} \setminus \{\tau \leq t - 1\}$$

imply that the function $\tau : \Omega \to \{0, 1, \ldots, T, \infty\}$ is a stopping time if and only if $\{\tau = t\} \in \mathcal{F}_t$ for every time t.

300

Example B.31. *In the context of the last example, let the function $\tau : \Omega \to$ $\{0, 1, \ldots, T, \infty\}$ be defined by $\tau(\omega) = \min\{t : t > 0, \ \omega_t = \omega_{t-1}\}$, with the convention $\min \emptyset = \infty$. Then τ is a stopping time, representing the first time that two consecutive coin-toss outcomes are the same, and taking the value ∞ if there is no such occurrence.*

In the current context of a finite number of states and times, a **stochastic process,** or simply **process,** is any function of the form $x :$ $\Omega \times \{0, 1, \ldots, T\} \to \mathbb{R}$. Given any process x and time t, the random variable $x(\cdot, t) : \Omega \to \mathbb{R}$ is denoted x_t or $x(t)$. For any stopping time τ, the random variable x_τ or $x(\tau)$ is defined by letting $x_\tau(\omega) = x(\omega, \tau(\omega))$, with the convention $x(\omega, \infty) = 0$. Given any state $\omega \in \Omega$, the function $x(\omega, \cdot) :$ $\{0, \ldots, T\} \to \mathbb{R}$ is a **path** of the process x. If α is a scalar, we also write α to denote the process identically equal to α. The notation for adding and multiplying processes is analogous to that for random variables. For example, if x, y and z are processes and α is a scalar, $\alpha x + yz$ is the process that takes the value $\alpha x(\omega, t) + y(\omega, t)z(\omega, t)$ at (ω, t). The notation $x \geq y$ means $x(\omega, t) \geq y(\omega, t)$ for every $(\omega, t) \in \Omega \times \{0, \ldots, T\}$. A process x is **strictly positive** if $x(\omega, t) > 0$ for all (ω, t).

If a process is to represent some observable quantity, then its time-t value should be known by time t. This consideration motivates the important notion of an adapted process. A predictable process is further restricted so that its time-t value is already known at time $t - 1$.

Definition B.32. *The process x is **adapted** if x_t is $\mathcal{F}_t$-measurable, for every time t. A process x is **predictable** if x_t is $\mathcal{F}_{t-1}$-measurable, for every time $t > 0$, and x_0 is constant.*

Since $\mathcal{F}_0 = \{\emptyset, \Omega\}$ and $\mathcal{F}_T = 2^\Omega$, for any adapted process x, x_0 is constant, while x_T can be any random variable. We use the notation

$$\mathcal{L} = \text{set of adapted processes,}$$
$$\mathcal{P} = \text{set of predictable processes,}$$
$$\mathcal{L}_{++} = \text{set of strictly positive adapted processes,}$$
$$\mathcal{P}_0 = \{x \in \mathcal{P} : x_0 = 0\}.$$

Consider any adapted process x. Since x_t is $\mathcal{F}_t$-measurable, for any spot $(F, t), x(\omega, t) = x(\omega', t)$ for all $\omega, \omega' \in F$. We write $x(F, t)$ to denote the value of x at spot (F, t). If $\mathcal{F}_t^0 = \{F_0, \ldots, F_d\}$, then $x_t = \sum_{i=0}^{d} x(F_i, t) 1_{F_i}$. One can therefore regard x as an assignment of a real number to every spot of the information tree, and $\mathcal{L}$ can be identified in this manner with the Euclidean space $\mathbb{R}^{1+K}$, where $1 + K$ is the total number of spots.

An n-**dimensional process** is a column vector $x = (x^1, \ldots, x^n)'$ of processes or, equivalently, any function of the form $x : \Omega \times \{0, 1, \ldots, T\} \to \mathbb{R}^n$. We write $x_t = (x_t^1, \ldots, x_t^n)'$ or $x(t) = (x^1(t), \ldots, x^n(t))'$. An n-dimensional process is **adapted (predictable)** if each one of its components is adapted (predictable). Here, and more generally with any matrix whose elements are stochastic processes, we prefer to use superscripts as indices in order to avoid conflict with subscripts indicating time.

In applications, the underlying filtration is commonly assumed to be **generated** by some given process $B = (B^1, \ldots, B^d)'$, meaning that

$$\mathcal{F}_t = \sigma(B_s^i : s = 1, \ldots, t; \ i = 1, \ldots, d).$$

To be consistent with the filtration restriction (B.7), we assume that the time-zero value $B(0)$ is constant and that Ω consists of all possible realizations of the path of B. In this case, to every spot (F, t), where $t > 0$, there corresponds a sequence $b_1, \ldots, b_t$ of vectors in $\mathbb{R}^d$ such that $F = \{B_s = b_s : s = 1, \ldots, t\}$. Moreover, by Proposition B.11, a process x is adapted if and only if x_0 is constant and for every time $t > 0$, there exists some function $f(t, \cdot) : \mathbb{R}^{d \times t} \to \mathbb{R}$ such that

$$x(\omega, t) = f(t, B(\omega, 1), \ldots, B(\omega, t)), \quad \omega \in \Omega.$$

Example B.33. *Consider again Example B.29. Following each toss, a player receives a dollar if the coin turns up heads and pays out a dollar otherwise. Let B_t be the player's total winnings after t tosses of the coin. The process B is defined by letting $B(\omega, 0) = 0$ and $B(\omega, t) = \sum_{s=1}^{t} \omega_s$ for $t > 0$. One can easily check that the underlying filtration $\{\mathcal{F}_t : t = 0, \ldots, T\}$ is generated by the process B. Suppose the player keeps betting up to the stopping time τ, with the scenario $\{\tau = \infty\}$ corresponding to the player never abandoning the game. Then the player's time-t total winnings are given by the random variable $B_{\tau \wedge t}$, where $\tau \wedge t$ is the stopping time that takes the value $\tau(\omega) \wedge t = \min(\tau(\omega), t)$ at state ω.*

We introduce notation for various useful transformations of stochastic-process paths. For any process x, the **lagged process** x_- is given by

$$x_-(0) = x(0), \quad x_-(t) = x(t-1), \quad t = 1, \ldots, T. \tag{B.8}$$

Clearly, the process x is adapted if and only if x_- is predictable. The **increments process** of x is the process $\Delta x = x - x_-$, given more explicitly as

$$\Delta x_0 = 0, \quad \Delta x_t = x_t - x_{t-1}, \quad t = 1, \ldots, T.$$

The **integral** of the process x with respect to the process y is a process that is denoted $x \bullet y$ and is defined by

$$(x \bullet y)_0 = 0, \quad (x \bullet y)_t = \sum_{s=1}^{t} x_s \Delta y_s, \quad t = 1, \ldots, T.$$

A useful identity that simplifies iterated integrals is

$$x \bullet (y \bullet z) = (xy) \bullet z. \tag{B.9}$$

Example B.34. *Consider the context of the last example. For each time $t > 0$, suppose that a player bets an amount ϕ_t on the outcome of the coin tossed at time t. If the coin comes up heads, the player receives ϕ_t; if the coin comes up tails, the player pays ϕ_t. The size of the bet ϕ_t can be contingent on the coin-toss outcomes up to time $t - 1$, and therefore ϕ_t is $\mathcal{F}_{t-1}$-measurable. Setting $\phi_0 = 0$, the player's betting strategy is the predictable process ϕ. If G_t is the player's net gain (loss if negative) up to time t, then $G = \phi \bullet B$. A specific strategy is to bet one unit of account up to a quitting time represented by the stopping time τ. The scenario $\{\tau = \infty\}$ means the player does not quit and therefore plays up to time T. This strategy corresponds to $\phi_t = 1_{\{t \leq \tau\}}$, in which case $G_t = B_{\tau \wedge t}$. Finally, suppose a second player can bet on coin toss $t \in \{1, \ldots, T\}$ a multiple θ_t of the bet of the first player. That is, if the first player bets ϕ_t, the second player bets $\theta_t \phi_t$. Then the gain process for the second player is $(\theta \phi) \bullet B = \theta \bullet (\phi \bullet B) = \theta \bullet G$.*

We denote $\mathbf{t}$ the process that simply counts time; that is, $\mathbf{t}(t) = t$ for every time t. Therefore, for any process x,

$$(x \bullet \mathbf{t})_0 = 0, \quad (x \bullet \mathbf{t})_t = \sum_{s=1}^{t} x_s, \quad t = 1, \ldots, T.$$

Another useful construction is the **covariation** of two processes x and y, denoted $[x, y]$ and defined as the process

$$[x, y]_0 = 0, \quad [x, y]_t = \sum_{s=1}^{t} (\Delta x_s)(\Delta y_s), \quad t = 1, \ldots, T.$$

Covariation arises naturally in the **integration-by-parts** formula

$$xy = x_0 y_0 + x_- \bullet y + y_- \bullet x + [x, y].$$

We use matrix notation for processes, treating stochastic integration or covariation analogously to multiplication. Given any set of processes $\mathcal{Z}$

303

(for example, $\mathcal{Z} = \mathcal{L}$ or $\mathcal{P}$), $\mathcal{Z}^{n \times m}$ denotes the set of n-by-m matrices whose entries are elements of $\mathcal{Z}$. For any $x \in \mathcal{L}^{n \times m}$ and $y \in \mathcal{L}^{m \times l}$, the processes $x \bullet y$, $[x, y] \in \mathcal{L}^{n \times l}$ are defined by the usual matrix multiplication rules:

$$(x \bullet y)^{ij} = \sum_{k=1}^{m} x^{ik} \bullet y^{kj} \quad \text{and} \quad [x, y]^{ij} = \sum_{k=1}^{m} [x^{ik}, y^{kj}].$$

Finally, vectors of processes are assumed to be column vectors and we write $\mathcal{Z}^{n}$ rather than $\mathcal{Z}^{n \times 1}$.

B.6 MARTINGALES

In this section we combine for the first time the underlying filtration and (strictly positive) probability P, to introduce the essential notion of a martingale. The notation for conditional expectations given time-t information is simplified by writing $\mathbb{E}_t[x]$ instead of $\mathbb{E}[x \mid \mathcal{F}_t]$.

Definition B.35. *A process M is a **martingale** if for all $u, t \in \{0, 1, \ldots, T\}$,*

$$u > t \quad \Longrightarrow \quad M_t = \mathbb{E}_t[M_u].$$

*A **zero-mean martingale** is a martingale M such that $M_0 = 0$ (and therefore $\mathbb{E} M_t = 0$ for all t). $\mathcal{M}$ denotes the set of all martingales, and $\mathcal{M}_0$ denotes the set of all zero-mean martingales.*

Proposition B.36. *For any process M, the following conditions are equivalent:*

1. *M is a martingale.*
2. *M is adapted and $\mathbb{E}_{t-1}[\Delta M_t] = 0$ for all $t > 0$.*
3. *$M_t = \mathbb{E}_t[M_T]$ for all t.*

> **Proof.** $(1 \Longrightarrow 2)$ Apply the definition of a martingale with $u = t + 1$.
>
> $(2 \Longrightarrow 3)$ Noting that $M_t = M_0 + \sum_{s=0}^{t} \Delta M_s$ and $\mathbb{E}_t \Delta M_u = \mathbb{E}_t \mathbb{E}_{u-1} \Delta M_u = 0$ if $u > t$, we compute
>
> $$\mathbb{E}_t M_T = \mathbb{E}_t \left[M_0 + \sum_{s=0}^{T} \Delta M_s \right] = M_0 + \sum_{s=0}^{t} \Delta M_s + \sum_{u=t+1}^{T} \mathbb{E}_t \Delta M_u = M_t.$$
>
> $(3 \Longrightarrow 1)$ If $u > t$, then $\mathbb{E}_t M_u = \mathbb{E}_t \mathbb{E}_u M_T = \mathbb{E}_t M_T = M_t$. ∎

Example B.37. *Continuing with Example B.34, we further assume that the coin is fair, that is,*

$$P(\{\omega\}) = 2^{-T} \quad \text{for all } \omega \in \Omega.$$

An exercise shows that the increments $\Delta B_1, \ldots, \Delta B_T$ are stochastically independent. Since $\mathcal{F}_{t-1}$ is generated by the random variables $\Delta B_1, \ldots, \Delta B_{t-1}$, it follows that $\mathbb{E}_{t-1}[\Delta B_t] = \mathbb{E}[\Delta B_t] = 0$, and therefore $B \in \mathcal{M}_0$. As a consequence, a player who at time t plans to bet a dollar on every coin toss up to a later time u can expect zero net incremental gain: $\mathbb{E}_t[B_u - B_t] = 0$. A natural question is whether the player could beat the odds by following some betting strategy $\phi \in \mathcal{P}$, as formulated in Example B.34. The following proposition shows that this is not possible, since the resulting gain process $\phi \bullet B$ is still a martingale. Moreover, the expected gain is zero no matter what stopping time the player selects to quit betting.

The intuitive claims of the last example are formalized below. The implication (1 $\implies$ 4) is a special case of Doob's optional stopping theorem.

Proposition B.38. *The following conditions are equivalent, for any adapted process M :*

1. *M is a martingale.*
2. *$\phi \bullet M$ is a martingale for every $\phi \in \mathcal{P}$.*
3. *$\mathbb{E}(\phi \bullet M)_T = 0$ for every $\phi \in \mathcal{P}$.*
4. *$M_0 = \mathbb{E}M_{\tau \wedge T}$ for every stopping time τ.*

Proof. (1 $\implies$ 2) Suppose $\phi \in \mathcal{P}$ and M is a martingale. Then

$$\mathbb{E}_{t-1}[\Delta(\phi \bullet M)_t] = \mathbb{E}_{t-1}[\phi_t \Delta M_t] = \phi_t \mathbb{E}_{t-1}[\Delta M_t] = 0, \quad t > 0.$$

Since $\phi \bullet M$ is adapted, it is a martingale (by Proposition B.36).

(2 $\implies$ 3) Immediate.

(3 $\implies$ 4) Given any stopping time τ, the process $\phi_t = 1_{\{t \le \tau \wedge T\}}$ is predictable and satisfies $(\phi \bullet M)_T = M_{\tau \wedge T} - M_0$. If condition 3 holds, then $0 = \mathbb{E}(\phi \bullet M)_T = \mathbb{E}M_{\tau \wedge T} - M_0$.

(4 $\implies$ 1) Suppose condition 4 holds. Given any time $t < T$ and $F \in \mathcal{F}_t$, define the stopping time $\tau = t1_F + T1_{F^c}$. Then

$$M_0 = \mathbb{E}M_\tau = \mathbb{E}[M_t 1_F + M_T 1_{F^c}].$$

Subtracting these equations from

$$M_0 = \mathbb{E}M_T = \mathbb{E}[M_T 1_F + M_T 1_{F^c}],$$

we obtain $\mathbb{E}[M_T 1_F] = \mathbb{E}[M_t 1_F]$, for every $F \in \mathcal{F}_t$. Since M_t is $\mathcal{F}_t$-measurable, it follows (by Proposition B.16) that $M_t = \mathbb{E}_t M_T$. Therefore, M is a martingale. ∎

Remark B.39. *If M is a martingale and ϕ is adapted, then $\phi \bullet M$ is not necessarily a martingale. For example, if $M \in \mathcal{M}_0$ is nonzero and $\phi = \Delta M$, then $\phi \bullet M = [M, M]$, which is clearly not a martingale.*

The compensator of a process is a convenient representation of the conditional mean of the one-period-ahead increment of the process at each spot of the information tree. Formally, the **compensator** of a process x is a process that is denoted x^p and is defined by

$$x_0^p = 0 \quad \text{and} \quad x_t^p = \sum_{s=1}^{t} \mathbb{E}_{s-1}[\Delta x_s], \quad t = 1, \dots, T.$$

Note that x^p is a member of $\mathcal{P}_0$, the set of predictable processes with zero initial value.

A key application of compensators is given in the following decomposition of an adapted processes into a predictable and a martingale part. The result generalizes the observation that any random variable is the sum of its mean and a zero-mean innovation. Equation (B.10) is the **Doob decomposition** of the adapted process x.

Proposition B.40. *Any adapted process x admits a unique decomposition of the form*

$$x = x_0 + A + M, \quad A \in \mathcal{P}_0, \quad M \in \mathcal{M}_0. \tag{B.10}$$

Moreover, in this decomposition, $A = x^p$.

Proof. Suppose x is any adapted process, and let $A = x^p$ and $M = x - x_0 - A$. Recursion $\Delta x_t^p = \mathbb{E}_{t-1}[\Delta x_t]$ implies that $\mathbb{E}_{t-1}[\Delta M_t] = 0$ for all $t > 0$. Since $M_0 = 0$ and M is adapted, it follows that $M \in \mathcal{M}_0$, resulting in the Doob decomposition (B.10).

To show uniqueness, we first argue that $\mathcal{P}_0 \cap \mathcal{M}_0 = \{0\}$. Suppose $x \in \mathcal{P}_0 \cap \mathcal{M}_0$. Then for any time $t > 0$, $\Delta x_t \in L(\mathcal{F}_{t-1})$ and $\mathbb{E}_{t-1}[\Delta x_t] = 0$, which implies that $\Delta x_t = 0$. Since $x_0 = 0$, the whole process x vanishes. Finally, suppose $x \in \mathcal{L}$ has the decomposition (B.10), as well as $x = x_0 + A' + M'$ for some $A' \in \mathcal{P}_0$ and $M' \in \mathcal{M}_0$. Then $A - A' = M' - M \in \mathcal{P}_0 \cap \mathcal{M}_0 = \{0\}$, and therefore $A = A'$ and $M = M'$, confirming the uniqueness of the Doob decomposition. ∎

Corollary B.41. *If M is a predictable martingale, then $M_t = M_0$ for every time t.*

The conditional covariation of two processes is a convenient representation of the conditional covariance of the one-period-ahead increments of the two processes at every spot. For any time t and random variables a, b, we define the **conditional covariance** of a and b given time-t information by

$$\text{cov}_t[a,b] = \mathbb{E}_t[(a - \mathbb{E}_t[a])(b - \mathbb{E}_t[b])] = \mathbb{E}_t[ab] - \mathbb{E}_t[a]\mathbb{E}_t[b].$$

The **conditional covariation** of $x, y \in \mathcal{L}$ is a process in $\mathcal{P}_0$, denoted $\langle x, y \rangle$ and defined by

$$\langle x, y \rangle_0 = 0, \quad \langle x, y \rangle_t = \sum_{s=1}^{t} \text{cov}_{s-1}[\Delta x_s, \Delta y_s], \quad t = 1, \ldots, T.$$

Proposition B.42. *(a) If $M, N \in \mathcal{M}_0$, then*

$$\langle M, N \rangle = (MN)^p = [M, N]^p,$$
$$\mathbb{E}[M_t N_t] = \mathbb{E}\langle M, N \rangle_t = \mathbb{E}[M, N]_t, \quad t = 0, \ldots, T. \tag{B.11}$$

(b) If $x = x_0 + x^p + M$ and $y = y_0 + y^p + N$ (and therefore $M, N \in \mathcal{M}_0$), then $\langle x, y \rangle = \langle M, N \rangle$.

(c) If $x, y \in \mathcal{L}$ and $\alpha, \beta \in \mathcal{P}$, then $(\alpha \bullet x)^p = \alpha \bullet x^p$ and $\langle \alpha \bullet x, \beta \bullet y \rangle = (\alpha\beta) \bullet \langle x, y \rangle$.

Proof. (a) Suppose $M, N \in \mathcal{M}_0$. Using the martingale property, we compute $\Delta\langle M, N \rangle_t = \mathbb{E}_{t-1}[\Delta M_t \Delta N_t] = \mathbb{E}_{t-1}[M_t N_t] - M_{t-1}N_{t-1} = \Delta(MN)_t^p$. This shows that $\langle M, N \rangle = (MN)^p$. Integration by parts implies that $MN - [M, N] = M_- \bullet N + N_- \bullet M \in \mathcal{M}_0$, since M_- and N_- are predictable. Therefore, MN and $[M, N]$ have the same compensator $\langle M, N \rangle$, from which equations (B.11) also follow.

(b) If $\phi \in \mathcal{P}$ and $x \in \mathcal{L}$, then $\Delta \phi_t \in L(\mathcal{F}_{t-1})$ and therefore

$$\text{cov}_{t-1}[\Delta \phi_t, \Delta x_t] = 0, \quad t > 0.$$

Therefore, $\langle \phi, x \rangle = 0$. Using this observation and the bilinearity of the conditional covariation, we find $\langle x, y \rangle = \langle M, N \rangle$.

(c) Suppose $\alpha, \beta \in \mathcal{P}$ and $x, y \in \mathcal{L}$. If $x = x_0 + x^p + M$, then $\alpha \bullet x = \alpha \bullet x^p + \alpha \bullet M$. Since $\alpha \bullet M \in \mathcal{M}_0$, we have $(\alpha \bullet x)^p = \alpha \bullet x^p$. For any time $t > 0$, $\alpha_t, \beta_t \in L(\mathcal{F}_{t-1})$ and therefore

$$\text{cov}_{t-1}[\alpha_t \Delta x_t, \beta_t \Delta y_t] = \alpha_t \beta_t \text{cov}_{t-1}[\Delta x_t, \Delta y_t].$$

Adding up over t gives $\langle \alpha \bullet x, \beta \bullet y \rangle = (\alpha \beta) \bullet \langle x, y \rangle$. ∎

This section's definitions and discussion extend readily to process matrices, using last section's notational conventions. For example, $\mathcal{M}_0^n$ is the set of all n-dimensional column vectors of zero-mean martingales. If $M \in \mathcal{M}_0^n$, then $\phi \bullet M \in \mathcal{M}_0^m$ for every $\phi \in \mathcal{P}^{m \times n}$. The compensator of $x \in \mathcal{L}^{n \times m}$ is the process matrix $x^p \in \mathcal{P}_0^{n \times m}$ defined by $(x^p)^{ij} = (x^{ij})^p$. For any $x \in \mathcal{L}^{n \times m}$ and $y \in \mathcal{L}^{m \times l}$, the conditional covariation process matrix $\langle x, y \rangle \in \mathcal{P}_0^{n \times l}$ is defined by the usual matrix multiplication rule:

$$\langle x, y \rangle^{ij} = \sum_{k=1}^{m} \langle x^{ik}, y^{kj} \rangle.$$

B.7 PREDICTABLE MARTINGALE REPRESENTATION

In this section, we assume that the underlying filtration $\{\mathcal{F}_t\}$ is **uniform**, meaning that there exists a positive integer $1 + d$, called the filtration's **spanning number**, such that every nonterminal spot has $1 + d$ immediate successors. Using this structure, we construct a d-dimensional zero-mean martingale B, relative to which any given martingale M can be uniquely represented as $M = \beta' \bullet B$, where $\beta \in \mathcal{P}_0^d$. A martingale M is entirely determined by its terminal value M_T, since $M_t = \mathbb{E}_t[M_T]$ for all t. There are $(1 + d)^T$ terminal spots, and therefore the dimension of $\mathcal{M}_0$ viewed as a vector space is $(1 + d)^T - 1$. In contrast, this section's representation implies that just d martingales can span $\mathcal{M}_0$, provided we allow linear combinations to be updated dynamically on the information tree.

We begin by constructing an orthonormal basis spanning the single-period uncertainty following a given nonterminal spot. Let us fix any time $t \in \{1, \ldots, T\}$ and event $F \in \mathcal{F}_{t-1}^0$. The assumption of a uniform filtration with spanning number $1 + d$ implies that $\mathcal{F}_t^0 \cap F$ has $1 + d$ elements:

$$\mathcal{F}_t^0 \cap F = \{G_0, G_1, \ldots, G_d\}.$$

On the information tree, $\{(G_i, t) : i = 0, 1, \ldots, d\}$ is the set of immediate successor spots to the nonterminal spot $(F, t-1)$. The set

$$L(F, t) = \left\{ \sum_{i=0}^d \alpha_i 1_{G_i} : \sum_{i=0}^d \alpha_i P(G_i \mid F) = 0, \ \alpha \in \mathbb{R}^{1+d} \right\} \quad (B.12)$$

is a d-dimensional subspace of $L(\mathcal{F}_t)$. Let $\{\Delta^i(F, t) : i = 1, \ldots, d\}$ be a basis of $L(F, t)$ that is orthonormal under the inner product $(a \mid b)_F = \mathbb{E}[ab \mid F]$. The fact that $\Delta^i(F, t) \in L(F, t)$ implies that

$$\mathbb{E}[\Delta^i(F, t) \mid F] = 0. \quad (B.13)$$

The orthonormality of the basis $\{\Delta^i(F, t)\}$ means that

$$\mathbb{E}[\Delta^i(F, t)\Delta^j(F, t) \mid F] = \begin{cases} 1 & \text{if } i = j, \\ 0 & \text{if } i \neq j. \end{cases} \quad (B.14)$$

A concrete example of such a basis follows.

Example B.43. *Let $p_i = P(G_i \mid F)$, $i = 0, \ldots, d$, and consider the linear space $L = \left\{ x \in \mathbb{R}^{1+d} : \sum_{i=0}^d p_i x_i = 0 \right\}$, with the inner product*

$$(x \mid y)_p = \sum_{i=0}^d p_i x_i y_i.$$

An orthogonal basis of L is given by the rows of the matrix

$$e = \begin{bmatrix} p_1 & -p_0 & 0 & 0 & \cdots & 0 \\ p_2 & p_2 & -(p_0+p_1) & 0 & \cdots & 0 \\ p_3 & p_3 & p_3 & -(p_0+p_1+p_2) & \cdots & 0 \\ \vdots & \vdots & \vdots & \vdots & \ddots & \vdots \\ p_d & p_d & p_d & p_d & \cdots & -\sum_{j=0}^{d-1} p_j \end{bmatrix}.$$

309

An orthonormal basis for $L(F, t)$ is defined by

$$\Delta^i(F, t) = (e_i \mid e_i)_p^{-1/2} \sum\nolimits_{j=0}^{i} e_{ij} 1_{G_j}, \quad i = 1, \ldots, d.$$

We use the single-period basis elements to construct d martingales that dynamically span $\mathcal{M}_0$. Let I denote an identity matrix, and recall that $\mathbf{t}$ denotes the process that counts time. The condition $\langle B, B' \rangle = \mathbf{t}I$ below is, therefore, equivalent to $\Delta \langle B^i, B^i \rangle_t = 1$ and $\Delta \langle B^i, B^j \rangle_t = 0$ if $i \neq j$ and $t > 0$.

Theorem B.44. *Suppose the underlying filtration is uniform with spanning number $1 + d$. Then there exists some B in $\mathcal{M}_0^d$ such that $\langle B, B' \rangle = \mathbf{t}I$ and any zero-mean martingale M admits a representation of the form*

$$M = \beta' \bullet B, \quad \beta \in \mathcal{P}_0^d. \tag{B.15}$$

The process β in this representation is unique and can be computed as

$$\beta = \Delta \langle B, M \rangle. \tag{B.16}$$

Finally, any process B in $\mathcal{M}_0^d$ with the above property generates the underlying filtration.

Proof. Given any time $t > 0$, let $\mathcal{F}_{t-1}^0 = \{F_1, \ldots, F_N\}$, where $N = (1 + d)^{t-1}$, and define the $\mathcal{F}_t$-measurable random variables

$$\Delta^i(t) = \sum\nolimits_{n=1}^{N} \Delta^i(F_n, t) 1_{F_n}, \quad i = 1, \ldots, d.$$

Letting $\Delta^i(0) = 0$, this construction defines a d-dimensional adapted process Δ, in terms of which we define the d-dimensional process $B = \Delta \bullet \mathbf{t}$. Conditions (B.13) and (B.14) for every $F \in \mathcal{F}_{t-1}^0$ imply that

$$\mathbb{E}[\Delta^i(t) \mid \mathcal{F}_{t-1}] = 0 \quad \text{and} \quad \mathbb{E}[\Delta^i(t)\Delta^j(t) \mid \mathcal{F}_{t-1}] = \begin{cases} 1 & \text{if } i = j, \\ 0 & \text{if } i \neq j. \end{cases}$$

Therefore, $B \in \mathcal{M}_0$ and $\langle B, B' \rangle = \mathbf{t}I$.

Given any $M \in \mathcal{M}_0$ and $n \in \{1, \ldots, N\}$, the random variable $\Delta M_t 1_{F_n}$ is an element of $L(F_n, t)$, and therefore there exist scalars $\beta^1(F_n, t), \ldots, \beta^d(F_n, t)$ such that

$$\Delta M_t 1_{F_n} = \sum\nolimits_{i=1}^{d} \beta^i(F_n, t) \Delta^i(F_n, t). \tag{B.17}$$

This construction defines predictable processes $\beta^1, \ldots, \beta^d$ in $\mathcal{P}_0$, in terms of which condition (B.17) can be stated as (B.15). Computing the conditional covariation with B' on both sides of equation (B.15) and using the fact that $\langle B, B' \rangle = t I$ results in (B.16), which also confirms the uniqueness of β in representation (B.15).

Showing that B generates the underlying filtration is left as an exercise. ∎

One can draw an analogy between linear combinations of the form $\beta' \cdot B$, where $\beta \in \mathbb{R}^d$ and $\cdot$ represents the Euclidean inner product, and expressions of the form (B.15) in the space $\mathcal{M}_0$. The following terminology, based on this analogy, is not standard but seems natural and is useful for our purposes.

Definition B.45. *A **dynamic basis** of $\mathcal{M}_0$ is an element B of $\mathcal{M}_0^d$ such that every martingale M in $\mathcal{M}_0$ has a unique representation of the form* (B.15). *A **dynamic orthonormal basis** of $\mathcal{M}_0$ is any dynamic basis B of $\mathcal{M}_0^d$ such that* $\langle B, B' \rangle = t I$.

Exercise 14 shows that the above analogy runs deeper, with conditional covariation being a form of dynamic inner product, and with an associated notion of dynamic orthogonality and projection theory. In this sense, the term "dynamic orthonormal basis" is short for "dynamically orthonormal dynamic basis."

The following extension of Theorem B.44 can be shown as an exercise.

Theorem B.46. *$\mathcal{M}_0$ has a d-dimensional dynamic orthonormal basis if and only if the underlying filtration is uniform with spanning number $1 + d$.*

Suppose $B \in \mathcal{M}_0^d$ is a dynamic orthonormal basis of $\mathcal{M}_0$. Proposition B.40 implies that any process $x \in \mathcal{L}$ has a unique decomposition of the form

$$x = x_0 + \alpha \bullet t + \beta' \bullet B, \quad \alpha \in \mathcal{P}_0, \quad \beta \in \mathcal{P}_0^d. \tag{B.18}$$

The coefficients in this representation are computed as

$$\alpha = \Delta x^p \quad \text{and} \quad \beta = \Delta \langle x, B \rangle.$$

311

We refer to (B.18) as the **predictable representation** of x with respect to B. Identity (B.9) implies that

$$\gamma \bullet x = (\gamma \alpha) \bullet t + (\gamma \beta)' \bullet B, \quad \text{for any } \gamma \in \mathcal{P}.$$

Finally, by Proposition B.42, if the process x^i has the predictable representation $x^i = x_0^i + \alpha^i \bullet t + \beta^{i'} \bullet B$, then $\langle x^1, x^2 \rangle = (\beta^{1'} \beta^2) \bullet t$.

B.8 CHANGE OF MEASURE AND MARTINGALES

In this section we study how the martingale property and related concepts are affected by a change of the underlying probability measure. For this purpose, we introduce a new strictly positive probability Q. We use the term "P-martingale" to emphasize the dependence of the martingale property on the underlying probability P. Therefore, M is a Q-martingale if and only if $M_t = \mathbb{E}_t^Q[M_u]$ for $t < u$.

To relate Q-martingales to P-martingales, we define the **conditional density process** of Q with respect to P :

$$\xi_t = \mathbb{E}_t\left[\frac{dQ}{dP}\right], \quad t = 0, 1, \ldots, T. \tag{B.19}$$

Our simplifying assumption $\mathcal{F}_T = 2^\Omega$ implies that $\xi_T = dQ/dP$. The law of iterated expectations and the fact that $\mathbb{E}[dQ/dP] = \mathbb{E}^Q[1] = 1$ imply that

$$\xi \text{ is a strictly positive martingale such that } \mathbb{E}\xi_T = 1. \tag{B.20}$$

Remark B.47. *We defined ξ in terms of Q. Conversely, if we were to start with any process ξ satisfying* (B.20), *the unique probability Q such that $\xi_T = dQ/dP$ is defined by $Q(F) = \mathbb{E}[\xi_T 1_F]$, in which case the martingale property of ξ implies that $\xi_t = \mathbb{E}_t[dQ/dP]$.*

To interpret the value of ξ at any given spot (F, t), note that

$$Q(F) = \mathbb{E}^Q[1_F] = \mathbb{E}\left[\frac{dQ}{dP} 1_F\right] = \mathbb{E}\mathbb{E}_t\left[\frac{dQ}{dP} 1_F\right]$$

$$= \mathbb{E}\left[\mathbb{E}_t\left[\frac{dQ}{dP}\right] 1_F\right] = \xi(F, t) P(F), \quad F \in \mathcal{F}_t^0,$$

where the last equality follows from the fact that ξ_t is constant over F. Therefore, $\xi(F, t) = Q(F)/P(F)$, which can be thought of as the ratio of the likelihood of the path leading to spot (F, t) under Q to the likelihood of the same path under P. This observation makes it clear that inverting the roles of P and Q inverts the conditional density, a fact that can alternatively be shown by applying Proposition B.24 to compute

$$\mathbb{E}_t^Q\left[\frac{dP}{dQ}\right] = \frac{\mathbb{E}_t[(dP/dQ)(dQ/dP)]}{\mathbb{E}_t[dQ/dP]} = \frac{1}{\xi_t}.$$

In relating Q-martingales to P-martingales, the following calculation is key.

Lemma B.48. *For any $x \in \mathcal{L}$,*

$$\mathbb{E}_{t-1}^Q[x_t] = \mathbb{E}_{t-1}\left[\frac{\xi_t}{\xi_{t-1}}x_t\right].$$

Proof. By the law of iterated expectations and Proposition B.24,

$$\xi_{t-1}\mathbb{E}_{t-1}^Q[x_t] = \mathbb{E}_{t-1}\mathbb{E}_t\left[\frac{dQ}{dP}x_t\right] = \mathbb{E}_{t-1}\left[\mathbb{E}_t\left[\frac{dQ}{dP}\right]x_t\right] = \mathbb{E}_{t-1}[\xi_t x_t]. \quad \blacksquare$$

A first connection between Q-martingales and P-martingales is stated in the following result, which is given a pricing interpretation in Section 5.3.2.

Proposition B.49. *Suppose Q is a strictly positive probability and ξ is its conditional density process with respect to P. Then for any $x, y \in \mathcal{L}$,*

$$x + y_- \bullet \mathbf{t} \text{ is a } Q\text{-martingale} \quad \Longleftrightarrow \quad \xi x + (\xi y)_- \bullet \mathbf{t} \text{ is a } P\text{-martingale}.$$

Proof. Using the last lemma, we have

$$\begin{aligned}
\xi_{t-1}\mathbb{E}_{t-1}^Q \Delta(x + y_- \bullet \mathbf{t})_t &= \xi_{t-1}\mathbb{E}_{t-1}^Q[x_t] - \xi_{t-1}x_{t-1} + \xi_{t-1}y_{t-1} \\
&= \mathbb{E}_{t-1}[\xi_t x_t - \xi_{t-1}x_{t-1} + \xi_{t-1}y_{t-1}] \\
&= \mathbb{E}_{t-1}\Delta(\xi x + (\xi y)_- \bullet \mathbf{t})_t.
\end{aligned}$$

The left-hand side vanishes if and only if $x + y_- \bullet \mathbf{t}$ is a Q-martingale, while the right-hand side vanishes if and only if $\xi x + (\xi y)_- \bullet \mathbf{t}$ is a P-martingale. $\blacksquare$

One can think of Proposition B.49 as a generalization of the observation that a random variable x has zero mean under Q if and only if xdQ/dP has zero mean under P. Another way of relating zero-mean random variables under the two probabilities is based on the identity

$$\mathbb{E}x = \mathbb{E}^Q x - \mathrm{cov}\left[x, \frac{dQ}{dP}\right],$$ (B.21)

which implies that x has zero mean under P if and only if $x - \mathrm{cov}[x, dQ/dP]$ has zero mean under Q. The dynamic extension of this idea leads to **Girsanov's theorem**, which is derived below for the case of a finite filtration.

The **stochastic logarithm** of ξ is the process

$$\ell = \frac{1}{\xi_-} \bullet \xi,$$ (B.22)

which is well-defined since ξ is strictly positive. Since ξ_- is predictable, ξ is a martingale, $\ell_0 = 0$ and $1 + \Delta\ell = \xi/\xi_-$, we have

$$\ell \in \mathcal{M}_0 \quad \text{and} \quad 1 + \Delta\ell \in \mathcal{L}_{++}.$$ (B.23)

Proposition B.50. *Suppose Q is a strictly positive probability and ℓ is the stochastic logarithm of the conditional density process of Q with respect to P. Then for any process M,*

$$M \text{ is a P-martingale} \quad \Longleftrightarrow \quad M - \langle M, \ell \rangle \text{ is a Q-martingale.}$$

Proof. Applying Lemma B.48 with $x = \Delta M$, we compute

$$\Delta\langle M, \ell \rangle_t = \mathbb{E}_{t-1}\left[\Delta M_t \frac{\Delta\xi_t}{\xi_{t-1}}\right] = \mathbb{E}^Q_{t-1}[\Delta M_t] - \mathbb{E}_{t-1}[\Delta M_t].$$

Therefore, $\mathbb{E}_{t-1}\Delta M_t = 0$ if and only if $\mathbb{E}^Q_{t-1}\Delta(M - \langle M, \ell \rangle)_t = 0$. ∎

Corollary B.51. *Given any $x \in \mathcal{L}$, if x^p is the compensator of x under the probability P, then $x^p + \langle x, \ell \rangle$ is the compensator of x under the probability Q.*

In the above analysis, we started with the strictly positive probability Q, and we constructed the stochastic logarithm ℓ, which satisfies (B.23). In applications, we often construct Q in terms of ℓ. Suppose we are given a process ℓ satisfying (B.23). The **stochastic exponential** of ℓ is the process ξ defined recursively by

$$\xi = 1 + \xi_- \bullet \ell.$$ (B.24)

One can easily check that ξ is the stochastic exponential of ℓ if and only if ℓ is the stochastic logarithm of ξ. Iterating recursion (B.24) yields the stochastic exponential formula

$$\xi_t = \prod_{s=0}^{t}(1 + \Delta\ell_s), \quad t = 0, 1, \ldots, T. \tag{B.25}$$

The assumed strict positivity of $1 + \Delta\ell$ implies that of ξ. Since ξ_- is predictable and ℓ is assumed to be a martingale, equation (B.24) implies that ξ satisfies (B.20) and therefore defines Q as in Remark B.47.

Introducing last section's theme, in the remainder of this section we assume that $B \in \mathcal{M}_0^d$ is a dynamic orthonormal basis of $\mathcal{M}_0$ under the original probability P, and we compute a dynamic basis and corresponding predictable representations under any other strictly positive probability. We parameterize the set of strictly positive probabilities by the set

$$\mathcal{H} = \{\eta \in \mathcal{P}_0^d : 1 - \eta'\Delta B \in \mathcal{L}_{++}\}.$$

Given any $\eta \in \mathcal{H}$, let $\ell = -\eta' \bullet B$ and define the probability

$$P^\eta(F) = \mathbb{E}[\xi_T 1_F],$$

where ξ is the stochastic exponential of ℓ, given in (B.25) with $1 + \Delta\ell = 1 - \eta'\Delta B$. Every strictly positive probability Q is of the form P^η, where $\eta \in \mathcal{H}$. To see why, let $\ell \in \mathcal{M}_0$ be the stochastic logarithm of the conditional density process ξ of Q with respect to P. By Theorem B.44, $\ell = -\eta' \bullet B$, where $\eta = -\Delta\langle\ell, B\rangle$. A rearrangement of equation (B.22) results in $1 - \eta'\Delta B = \xi/\xi_- \in \mathcal{L}_{++}$, and therefore $\eta \in \mathcal{H}$. Since ξ is the stochastic exponential of ℓ, our earlier discussion implies that $Q = P^\eta$.

Given any $\eta \in \mathcal{H}$, let $\mathbb{E}^\eta$ denote the expectation operator under P^η, and let $\mathcal{M}_0^\eta$ denote the set of every P^η-martingale M such that $M_0 = 0$. Finally, define the process

$$B^\eta = B + \eta \bullet \mathbf{t}.$$

Since $\langle B, -\eta' \bullet B\rangle = -\eta \bullet \mathbf{t}$, Girsanov's theorem in the form of Proposition B.50 implies that B^η is a d-dimensional P^η-martingale. Given any $x \in \mathcal{L}$, the predictable representation (B.18) relative to B is equivalent to the following predictable representation relative to B^η :

$$x = x_0 + (\alpha - \beta'\eta) \bullet \mathbf{t} + \beta' \bullet B^\eta, \quad \alpha \in \mathcal{P}_0, \quad \beta \in \mathcal{P}_0^d. \tag{B.26}$$

315

As a consequence of this equivalence, we have:

Proposition B.52. *For any $\eta \in \mathcal{H}$, B^η is a dynamic basis of $\mathcal{M}_0^\eta$ under P^η.*

Proof. Equation (B.26) with $x = M \in \mathcal{M}_0^\eta$ implies that $M - \beta' \bullet B^\eta = (\alpha - \beta'\eta) \bullet \mathbf{t}$ is in $\mathcal{M}_0^\eta \cap \mathcal{P}$ and therefore vanishes. This shows that $M = \beta' \bullet B^\eta = \beta'\eta \bullet \mathbf{t} + \beta' \bullet B$. Since the predictable representation of M relative to B is unique, the representation $M = \beta' \bullet B^\eta$ for some $\beta \in \mathcal{P}^d$ is also unique. ∎

The dynamic basis B^η of $\mathcal{M}_0^\eta$ is not generally dynamically orthonormal under P^η. For notational convenience, in the remainder of this section we switch from superscript to subscript indexing of processes, for example, writing $B^\eta = (B_1^\eta, \ldots, B_d^\eta)'$. To compute the conditional covariation matrix of B^η under P^η, we introduce, for any $i,j,k \in \{1,\ldots,d\}$, the three-way covariation process $\langle B_i, B_j, B_k \rangle = \langle [B_i, B_j], B_k \rangle$, equivalently defined by

$$\langle B_i, B_j, B_k \rangle_0 = 0 \quad \text{and} \quad \Delta\langle B_i, B_j, B_k \rangle_t = \mathbb{E}_{t-1}[(\Delta B_i)_t(\Delta B_j)_t(\Delta B_k)_t].$$

Proposition B.53. *For any $\eta \in \mathcal{H}$ and $i,j \in \{1,\ldots,d\}$,*

$$\langle B_i^\eta, B_j^\eta \rangle^\eta = I_{ij}\mathbf{t} - (\eta_i\eta_j) \bullet \mathbf{t} - \sum_{k=1}^d \eta_k \bullet \langle B_i, B_j, B_k \rangle, \quad (B.27)$$

where $\langle \cdot, \cdot \rangle^\eta$ denotes conditional covariation under P^η, and I is the $d \times d$ identity matrix.

Proof. The process $\langle B_i^\eta, B_j^\eta \rangle^\eta$ is the compensator of $[B_i^\eta, B_j^\eta]$ under P^η. By Corollary B.51,

$$\langle B_i^\eta, B_j^\eta \rangle^\eta = [B_i^\eta, B_j^\eta]^p - \sum_{k=1}^d \eta_k \bullet \langle B_i^\eta, B_j^\eta, B_k \rangle, \quad (B.28)$$

where the compensator and conditional covariation on the right-hand side are relative to P. Expanding $[B_i + \eta_i \bullet \mathbf{t}, B_j + \eta_j \bullet \mathbf{t}]$, and using the observations

$$[\eta_i \bullet \mathbf{t}, B_j] = \eta_i \bullet B_j \quad \text{and} \quad [\eta_i \bullet \mathbf{t}, \eta_j \bullet \mathbf{t}] = (\eta_i\eta_j) \bullet \mathbf{t},$$

we find that

$$[B_i^\eta, B_j^\eta] = [B_i, B_j] + \eta_i \bullet B_j + \eta_j \bullet B_i + (\eta_i\eta_j) \bullet \mathbf{t}. \quad (B.29)$$

Since $[B_i, B_j]^p = I_{ij}\mathbf{t}$, the first term in (B.28) is computed as

$$[B_i^\eta, B_j^\eta]^p = I_{ij}\mathbf{t} + (\eta_i\eta_j) \bullet \mathbf{t}. \tag{B.30}$$

Decomposition (B.29) and the fact that $\langle B_i, B_k \rangle = \mathbf{t}I_{ik}$ imply

$$\langle B_i^\eta, B_j^\eta, B_k \rangle = \langle B_i, B_j, B_k \rangle + (\eta_i \bullet \mathbf{t})I_{jk} + (\eta_j \bullet \mathbf{t})I_{ik}.$$

Noting that $\sum_k \eta_k \bullet (\eta_i \bullet \mathbf{t})I_{jk} = (\eta_i\eta_j) \bullet \mathbf{t}$, we conclude that

$$\sum_{k=1}^{d} \eta_k \bullet \langle B_i^\eta, B_j^\eta, B_k \rangle = \sum_{k=1}^{d} \eta_k \bullet \langle B_i, B_j, B_k \rangle + 2(\eta_i\eta_j) \bullet \mathbf{t}. \tag{B.31}$$

Substituting (B.30) and (B.31) in the right-hand side of (B.28), we obtain (B.27). ∎

B.9 MARKOV PROCESSES

On a uniform filtration with spanning number $1 + d$, the number of spots is

$$\frac{(1+d)^{T+1} - 1}{d}.$$

Consequently, the time required to sequentially carry out a computation at every single spot of the tree rises exponentially with T, rendering any algorithm based on such an approach impractical for large trees. One way of dealing with this type of complexity is to assume that a model's uncertainty is driven by a relatively low-dimensional Markov process.

Definition B.54. *A k-dimensional adapted process Z is a* **Markov process** *(relative to the filtration $\{\mathcal{F}_t\}$ and the probability P) if for any time $t < T$ and function $f : \mathbb{R}^{k \times (T-t)} \to \mathbb{R}$,*

$$\mathbb{E}[f(Z_{t+1}, \ldots, Z_T) \mid \mathcal{F}_t] = \mathbb{E}[f(Z_{t+1}, \ldots, Z_T) \mid Z_t]. \tag{B.32}$$

Remark B.55. *Since $\sigma(Z_t) \subseteq \mathcal{F}_t$, equation (B.32) is equivalent to the $\sigma(Z_t)$-measurability of $\mathbb{E}[f(Z_{t+1}, \ldots, Z_T) \mid \mathcal{F}_t]$.*

The **Markov property** (B.32) states that the conditional expectation of any random variable that is determined by future values of Z given current information is the same as the conditional expectation of the random variable given only the current value of Z. Suppose $\{z_1, \ldots, z_m\}$ is the set of all possible values Z can take. The expectation on the left-hand side of equation (B.32) is conditional on the entire realized path of a dynamic basis B up to time t. There are $(1 + d)^t$ such paths, and therefore the random variable $\mathbb{E}[f(Z_{t+1}, \ldots, Z_T) \mid \mathcal{F}_t]$ can be thought of as a $(1 + d)^t$-dimensional vector. In contrast, the right-hand side of equation (B.32) is a function of the realization of Z_t, and can be thought of as an m-dimensional vector. The Markov property is tautological if $\{z_1, \ldots, z_m\}$ is the set of all spots. The Markov property becomes useful when coupled with the assumption that m is small relative to the number of all spots, and especially when m does not increase with the number of periods.

The following characterization is useful in verifying the Markov property.

Lemma B.56. *The following conditions are equivalent, for any k-dimensional adapted process Z :*

1. *Z is a Markov process.*
2. *For any time $t > 0$ and function $h : \mathbb{R}^k \to \mathbb{R}$,*

$$\mathbb{E}_{t-1}[h(Z_t)] = \mathbb{E}[h(Z_t) \mid Z_{t-1}].$$

3. *For any spot $(F, t - 1)$ and $z \in \mathbb{R}^k$,*

$$P[Z_t = z \mid F] = P[Z_t = z \mid Z_{t-1} = Z(F, t - 1)].$$

Proof. The implications $1 \implies 2 \iff 3$ are immediate and can be verified as an exercise. We show the less direct implication $2 \implies 1$. Assuming condition 2 holds, we verify the Markov property (B.32) by a backward-in-time induction. For $t = T - 1$, equation (B.32) holds by assumption. For the inductive step, consider any $t \in \{1, \ldots, T - 1\}$, and suppose that condition (B.32) holds for any $f : \mathbb{R}^{k \times (T-t)} \to \mathbb{R}$. We show that the same is true if t is decreased by one. Consider any function $f : \mathbb{R}^{k \times (T-t+1)} \to \mathbb{R}$, and define the function $h : \mathbb{R}^k \to \mathbb{R}$ by $h(z) = \mathbb{E}[f(z, Z_{t+1}, \ldots, Z_T) \mid Z_t = z]$. Using the law of iterated expectations, the inductive hypothesis and condition 2, we compute:

$$\mathbb{E}_{t-1}[f(Z_t,\ldots,Z_T)] = \mathbb{E}_{t-1}\Big[\mathbb{E}_t \sum_{z\in N_t} 1_{\{Z_t=z\}} f(z, Z_{t+1},\ldots,Z_T)\Big]$$

$$= \mathbb{E}_{t-1}\Big[\sum_{z\in N_t} 1_{\{Z_t=z\}}\mathbb{E}_t[f(z, Z_{t+1},\ldots,Z_T)]\Big]$$

$$= \mathbb{E}_{t-1}\Big[\sum_{z\in N_t} 1_{\{Z_t=z\}}\mathbb{E}[f(z, Z_{t+1},\ldots,Z_T) \mid Z_t]\Big]$$

$$= \mathbb{E}_{t-1}[h(Z_t)] = \mathbb{E}[h(Z_t) \mid Z_{t-1}].$$

By Remark B.55, $\mathbb{E}_{t-1}[f(Z_t,\ldots,Z_T)] = \mathbb{E}[f(Z_t,\ldots,Z_T) \mid Z_{t-1}]$, which completes the proof. ∎

We conclude with a useful way of defining a Markov process in terms of a dynamic martingale basis B under the original probability P as well as suitably defined changes of measure. The key new restriction on B is that it has **independent increments**, meaning that the random variables

$$\Delta B_1,\ldots,\Delta B_T \quad \text{are stochastically independent.}$$

Any independent increments process B such that $\mathbb{E}[\Delta B_t] = 0$ for all $t > 0$ is a martingale. Clearly, the converse is not true; an arbitrary martingale need not have independent increments.

Proposition B.57. *Suppose that the underlying filtration is generated by a d-dimensional process B with independent increments (under the strictly positive probability P). Suppose further that the k-dimensional adapted process Z solves*

$$\Delta Z_t = \mu^Z(t, Z_{t-1}) + \sigma^Z(t, Z_{t-1})\Delta B_t,$$

for some functions $\mu^Z : \{1,\ldots,T\} \times \mathbb{R}^k \to \mathbb{R}^k$ and $\sigma^Z : \{1,\ldots,T\} \times \mathbb{R}^k \to \mathbb{R}^{k\times d}$, and that the strictly positive probability Q has a conditional density process $\xi_t = \mathbb{E}_t[dQ/dP]$ that satisfies

$$\frac{\Delta\xi_t}{\xi_{t-1}} = -\eta(t, Z_{t-1})'\Delta B_t, \quad \xi_0 = 1,$$

for some function $\eta : \{1,\ldots,T\} \times \mathbb{R}^k \to \mathbb{R}^d$. Then Z is a Markov process relative to both probabilities, P and Q.

Proof. We show that Z is a Markov process relative to Q. The same argument with $Q = P$ shows that Z is also a Markov process relative to P.

Fixing any time $t > 0$, vector $z \in \mathbb{R}^k$ and function $h : \mathbb{R}^k \to \mathbb{R}$, define $\chi = 1_{\{Z_{t-1}=z\}}$ and compute

$$
\begin{aligned}
\mathbb{E}^Q_{t-1}[h(Z_t)]\chi &= \mathbb{E}_{t-1}\left[\frac{\xi_t}{\xi_{t-1}}h(Z_t)\right]\chi \\
&= \mathbb{E}_{t-1}[(1 - \eta(t, Z_{t-1})'\Delta B_t)h(Z_t)\chi] \\
&= \mathbb{E}_{t-1}[(1 - \eta(t, z)'\Delta B_t)h(z + \mu^Z(t, z) + \sigma^Z(t, z)\Delta B_t)\chi] \\
&= \mathbb{E}_{t-1}[(1 - \eta(t, z)'\Delta B_t)h(z + \mu^Z(t, z) + \sigma^Z(t, z)\Delta B_t)]\chi \\
&= \mathbb{E}[(1 - \eta(t, z)'\Delta B_t)h(z + \mu^Z(t, z) + \sigma^Z(t, z)\Delta B_t)]\chi.
\end{aligned}
$$

The first equation follows from Lemma B.48. The second equation follows from our assumption on ξ and the $\mathcal{F}_{t-1}$-measurability of χ. The third equation follows from our assumption on Z. The fourth equation follows from the $\mathcal{F}_{t-1}$-measurability of χ, and the last equation follows from the stochastic independence of ΔB_t and $\mathcal{F}_{t-1} = \sigma(\Delta B_1, \dots, \Delta B_{t-1})$.

We have shown that $\mathbb{E}^Q_{t-1}[h(Z_t)]$ is constant on the event $\{Z_{t-1} = z\}$, for any z, and therefore it is $\sigma(Z_{t-1})$-measurable. By Remark B.55, $\mathbb{E}^Q_{t-1}[h(Z_t)] = \mathbb{E}^Q[h(Z_t) \mid Z_{t-1}]$, and the claim follows by the last lemma. ∎

B.10 EXERCISES

Note: The instruction "show that" is implied where only a fact is stated.

1. Given any set $\mathcal{S} \subseteq 2^\Omega$ (with Ω finite), show how to construct all elements of the algebra generated by $\mathcal{S}$ by performing Boolean set operations on the elements of $\mathcal{S}$.

2. Prove Proposition B.10.

3. (a) Give an example of two algebras $\mathcal{A}_1$ and $\mathcal{A}_2$ such that $\mathcal{A}_1 \cup \mathcal{A}_2$ is not an algebra.

   (b) For any random variables $x_1, \dots, x_n$, $\sigma(x_1, \dots, x_n)$ is the same as the algebra generated by $\bigcup_{i=1}^n \sigma(x_i)$.

(c) For any algebra of events $\mathcal{A}$, $\sigma(x_1, \ldots, x_n) \subseteq \mathcal{A}$ if and only if $x_1, \ldots, x_n \in L(\mathcal{A})$.

(d) The algebra $\sigma(x_1, \ldots, x_n)$ is generated by the partition of all nonempty events of the form $\{(x_1, \ldots, x_n) = \beta\}$, $\beta \in \mathbb{R}^n$.

4. Let $\hat{L}(\mathcal{B}) = L(\mathcal{B}) \cap \hat{L}$ be the set of all $\mathcal{B}$-measurable innovations. Any $z \in L(\mathcal{B})$ has a unique decomposition $z = \mathbb{E}z + \hat{z}$, where $\hat{z} \in \hat{L}(\mathcal{B})$.

(a) Verify that $\mathbb{E}[(x - z)^2] = (\mathbb{E}x - \mathbb{E}z)^2 + \text{var}[\hat{x} - \hat{z}]$.

(b) Show that $\mathbb{E}[\mathbb{E}[x \mid \mathcal{B}]] = \mathbb{E}[x]$ as a consequence of part (a).

(c) Let $y = \mathbb{E}[x \mid \mathcal{B}]$. Characterize $\hat{y}$ based on the orthogonal projection theorem applied in $\hat{L}(\mathcal{B})$, with the covariance inner product.

(d) Prove the equivalence $1 \iff 2$ of Proposition B.16, using the last two parts.

5. Complete the proof of Proposition B.17 by showing that (in a finite-dimensional inner-product space) if M is a linear subspace of the linear subspace N, then the projection of x on M is the same as the projection on M of the projection of x on N.

6. Construct an example of random variables x_1, x_2, x_3 that are pairwise stochastically independent (meaning that x_i is stochastically independent of x_j if $i \neq j$) but are not stochastically independent.

7. For any random variables $x_1, \ldots, x_n$, the following conditions are equivalent:

- $x_1, \ldots, x_n$ are stochastically independent.
- For every $k \in \{2, \ldots, n\}$, $\sigma(x_k)$ is stochastically independent of $\sigma(x_1, \ldots, x_{k-1})$.
- For any disjoint sets of indices $\{i_1, \ldots, i_k\}$ and $\{j_1, \ldots, j_l\}$, the algebras $\sigma(x_{i_1}, \ldots, x_{i_k})$ and $\sigma(x_{j_1}, \ldots, x_{j_l})$ are stochastically independent.

8. (a) Verify that τ as defined in Example B.31 is a stopping time.

(b) Suppose $\tau_1, \ldots, \tau_n$ are stopping times. Show that $\min\{\tau_1, \ldots, \tau_n\}$ is a stopping time. Is $\max\{\tau_1, \ldots, \tau_n\}$ a stopping time?

(c) For any adapted process x and $S \subseteq \mathbb{R}$, $\tau = \min\{t : x_t \in S\}$ is a stopping time. Assume $\min \emptyset = \infty$.

9. Given the finite stopping time $\tau : \Omega \to \{0, 1, \ldots, T\}$, $\mathcal{F}_\tau$ denotes the set of every event F such that $F \cap \{\tau \leq t\} \in \mathcal{F}_t$ for every time t. We interpret $\mathcal{F}_\tau$ as time-τ information.

(a) $\mathcal{F}_\tau$ is an algebra.

(b) $\mathcal{F}_\tau$ is equal to the set of every event F such that $F \cap \{\tau = t\} \in \mathcal{F}_t$ for every t.

(c) If σ is another stopping time such that $\sigma \le \tau$, then $\mathcal{F}_\sigma \subseteq \mathcal{F}_\tau$.

(d) There exists a unique partition $\{F_1, \dots, F_n\}$ and scalars t_i such that

$$\tau = \sum_{i=1}^{n} t_i 1_{F_i}, \quad F_i \in \mathcal{F}_{t_i}, \quad t_1 < t_2 < \cdots < t_n.$$

In terms of this representation, the algebra $\mathcal{F}_\tau$ is generated by the partition

$$\mathcal{F}_\tau^0 = \bigcup_{i=1}^{n} \mathcal{F}_{t_i}^0 \cap F_i.$$

(e) For any adapted process x, the random variable x_τ is $\mathcal{F}_\tau$-measurable.

(f) If M is a martingale, then $M_\sigma = \mathbb{E}[M_\tau \mid \mathcal{F}_\sigma]$ for any stopping time σ such that $\sigma \le \tau$.

(g) Suppose $\tau_1, \dots, \tau_n$ are finite stopping times, and let $\tau = \min \{\tau_1, \dots, \tau_n\}$. What is the relationship between $\mathcal{F}_\tau$ and the algebras $\mathcal{F}_{\tau_1}, \dots, \mathcal{F}_{\tau_n}$?

10. For any $\phi \in \mathcal{L}$, ϕ is predictable if and only if $\langle \phi, M \rangle = 0$ for every $M \in \mathcal{M}_0$.

11. (a) Prove the last claim of Theorem B.44, that is, that B generates the underlying filtration.

(b) Prove Theorem B.46.

12. $\langle x, y \rangle = [x, y]^p - [x^p, y^p]$.

13. For any $M, N \in \mathcal{M}_0$, let

$$(M \mid N)_{\mathcal{M}} = \mathbb{E}[M_T N_T] = \mathbb{E}\langle M, N \rangle_T = \mathbb{E}[M, N]_T, \qquad \text{(B.33)}$$

where the equalities follow from Proposition B.42.

(a) Verify that $(\cdot \mid \cdot)_{\mathcal{M}}$ is an inner product on $\mathcal{M}_0$.

(b) Consider the bases $\{\Delta^i(F, t) : i = 1, \dots, d\}$, used in the proof of Theorem B.44. For each nonterminal spot $k = (F, t-1)$ and $i \in \{1, \dots, d\}$, let the process $B^{k,i}$ be defined by $B_u^{k,i} = 0$ for $u < t$ and $B_u^{k,i} = \Delta^i(F, t)$ for $u \ge t$. Show that the set of all $B^{k,i}$ constructed this way forms an orthogonal basis of $\mathcal{M}_0$ under the inner product (B.33). How many such basis elements are there? How does this basis compare to the dynamic orthonormal basis in the proof of Theorem B.44? In particular, given any $M \in \mathcal{M}_0$, explain how the coefficients in the representation of M with respect to the two bases relate to each other.

14. (a) Show that the conditional covariation operator is a **dynamic inner product** on $\mathcal{M}_0$, by which we mean a function of the form $\langle \cdot, \cdot \rangle : \mathcal{M}_0 \times \mathcal{M}_0 \to \mathcal{P}_0$ that satisfies, for any $M, N, L \in \mathcal{M}_0$,

- $\langle M, N \rangle = \langle N, M \rangle$.
- $\langle \phi \bullet M + N, L \rangle = \phi \bullet \langle M, L \rangle + \langle N, L \rangle$ for all $\phi \in \mathcal{P}$.
- $\langle M, M \rangle \geq 0$, with equality holding if and only if $M = 0$.

(This definition parallels that of an inner product, substituting predictable processes for scalars and integration for multiplication by scalars.)

(b) Define M and N to be **dynamically orthogonal** if $\langle M, N \rangle = 0$. Note that, by Proposition B.42, M and N are dynamically orthogonal if and only if $MN \in \mathcal{M}_0$, if and only if $[M, N] \in \mathcal{M}_0$. Give an example of two martingales $M, N \in \mathcal{M}_0$ that are orthogonal relative to the inner product (B.33) but are not dynamically orthogonal, that is, $\mathbb{E}[M_T N_T] = 0$ and $\langle M, N \rangle \neq 0$.

(c) For any $M \in \mathcal{M}_0^d$, $\mathcal{S}(M) = \{\phi' \bullet M : \phi \in \mathcal{P}^d\}$ is the linear subspace of $\mathcal{M}_0$ that is **dynamically spanned** by M. Show that the martingales $M, N \in \mathcal{M}_0$ are dynamically orthogonal if and only if $\mathcal{S}(M)$ is orthogonal to N (under the inner product (B.33)), if and only if $\mathcal{S}(M)$ is orthogonal to $\mathcal{S}(N)$. (Therefore, dynamic orthogonality implies orthogonality. For this reason, what we call here dynamic orthogonality is commonly referred to in the literature as strong orthogonality.)

(d) Suppose B is a d-dimensional dynamic orthonormal basis for $\mathcal{M}_0$, and the martingales $M \in \mathcal{M}_0^m$ and $N \in \mathcal{M}_0$ have the predictable representations $M = \beta' \bullet B$ and $N = \gamma' \bullet B$, where $\beta \in \mathcal{P}_0^{d \times m}$ and $\gamma \in \mathcal{P}_0^d$. Show that the following conditions are equivalent:

- $\hat{N}$ is the projection of N onto $\mathcal{S}(M)$ (under the inner product (B.33)).

- $\hat{N} = \theta' \bullet M$ for some $\theta \in \mathcal{P}_0^m$, and $\langle M_i, \hat{N} - N \rangle = 0$ for all $i \in \{1, \ldots, m\}$.

- $\hat{N} = \theta' \bullet M$ for some $\theta \in \mathcal{P}_0^m$ such that for every time t,

$$\mathrm{var}[N_t - (\theta' \bullet M)_t] \le \mathrm{var}[N_t - (\phi' \bullet M)_t] \quad \text{for all } \phi \in \mathcal{P}^m.$$

- $\hat{N} = \theta' \bullet M$ for some $\theta \in \mathcal{P}_0^m$ such that $\beta'(\beta\theta - \gamma) = 0$.

Note that if $m \le d$ and $\beta(\omega, t)$ is full rank for all (ω, t), then $\beta'\beta$ is everywhere invertible, and $\beta'(\beta\theta - \gamma) = 0$ is equivalent to $\theta = (\beta'\beta)^{-1}\beta'\gamma$.

(e) The last part can be viewed as a dynamic version of Proposition A.23. State and prove a dynamic version of Corollary A.24.

15. Suppose P and Q are strictly positive probabilities, and let ξ denote the conditional density process of Q with respect to P. Consider any nonterminal spot $(F, t - 1)$, and let $(G_0, t), \ldots, (G_d, t)$ be its immediate successors. Show that

$$\frac{\xi(G_i, t)}{\xi(F, t - 1)} = \frac{Q(G_i \mid F)}{P(G_i \mid F)}, \quad i = 0, 1, \ldots, d.$$

Using this fact, explain how Proposition B.50 follows by applying identity (B.21) conditionally at each nonterminal spot.

B.11 Notes

This appendix is a stripped down version of a more general theory of probability and stochastic processes. A readable introduction to probability theory, with emphasis on martingales, is Williams (1991). Chow, Robbins and Siegmund (1991) give an elegant quick introduction to martingale theory, as well as the optimal stopping theory behind American option pricing. There are several excellent advanced introductions to probability theory, including Chung (1968) and Billingsley (1995). An efficient overview of a large body of probability theory is given by Kallenberg (2002). The classic reference on discrete-time martingale theory is Doob (1953), who contributed many of the theory's main results. Of particular importance to financial modeling is the application of the ideas introduced in this appendix to settings in which the filtration is generated by Brownian motion continuously in time. Readable introductions to the Brownian theory include Steele (2001) and Øksendal (2003); more advanced standard references include Karatzas and Shreve (1988), Lipster and Shiryaev (2001), and Revuz and Yor (1999). Orthogonal, in a sense, to the Brownian case are point process models, a good introduction to which is Brémaud (1981). Finally, all of the above cases are nested in a general theory of processes, standard references on which are Dellacherie and Meyer (1978–88), Jacod and Shiryaev (2003) and Protter (2004).

Bibliography

ABEL, A. (1990): "Asset Prices under Habit Formation and Catching Up with the Joneses," *American Economic Review, Papers and Proceedings*, 80, 38–42.

ACZÉL, J., AND J. DHOMBRES (1989): *Functional Equations in Several Variables.* Cambridge University Press, New York.

AGNEW, R. A. (1971): "Counter-Examples to an Assertion Concerning the Normal Distribution and a New Stochastic Price Fluctuation Model," *Review of Economic Studies*, 38, 381–383.

ALIPRANTIS, C. D., AND K. C. BORDER (1999): *Infinite Dimensional Analysis: A Hitchhiker's Guide*, 2nd ed. Springer-Verlag, Berlin, Germany.

ALLAIS, M. (1953): "Le Comportement de l'homme rationnel devant de risque: Critique des postulates et axiomes de l'ecole Americaine," *Econometrica*, 21, 503–546.

ANSCOMBE, F. J., AND R. J. AUMANN (1963): "A Definition of Subjective Probability," *Annals of Mathematical Statistics*, 34, 199–205.

ARROW, K. J. (1951): "An Extension of the Basic Theorems of Classical Welfare Economics," in *Proceedings of the Second Berkeley Symposium on Mathematical Statistics*, ed. J. Neyman, pp. 507–532. University of California Press, Berkeley.

—— (1953): "Le Rôle des valeurs boursiéres pour la répartition la meillure des risques," *Econométrie, Colloques Internationaux du Centre National de la Recherche Scientifique*, 40, 41–47.

—— (1963): "The Role of Securities in the Optimal Allocation of Risk Bearing," *Review of Economic Studies*, 31, 91–96.

—— (1965): *Aspects of the Theory of Risk Bearing.* Yrjo Jahnssonin Saatio, Helsinki.

—— (1970): *Essays in the Theory of Risk Bearing.* North Holland, London.

ARROW, K. J., AND G. DEBREU (1954): "Existence of an Equilibrium for a Competitive Economy," *Econometrica*, 22, 265–290.

AUMANN, R. J. (1962): "Utility Theory without the Completeness Axiom," *Econometrica*, 30, 445–462.

—— (1964): "Utility Theory without the Completeness Axiom: A Correction," *Econometrica*, 32, 210–212.

BALASKO, Y. (1988): *Foundations of the Theory of General Equilibrium.* Academic Press, Orlando, FL.

BANSAL, R., AND A. YARON (2004): "Risks for the Long Run: A Potential Resolution of Asset Pricing Puzzles," *Journal of Finance*, 59, 1481–1509.

BENSOUSSAN, A. (1984): "On the Theory of Option Pricing," *Acta Applicandae Mathematicae*, 2, 139–158.

327

BERTSEKAS, D. P. (2003): *Convex Analysis and Optimization*. Athena Scientific, Belmont, MA.

BHAMRA, H. S., L.-A. KÜHN, AND I. A. STREBULAEV (2007): "The Leveraged Equity Risk Premium and Credit Spreads: A Unified Framework," working paper.

BHAMRA, H. S., AND R. UPPAL (2006): "The Role of Risk Aversion and Elasticity of Intertemporal Substitution in Dynamic Consumption-Portfolio Choice with Recursive Utility," *Journal of Economic Dynamics and Control*, 30, 967–991.

BILLINGSLEY, P. (1995): *Probability and Measure*, 3rd ed. John Wiley & Sons, New York.

BLACK, F. (1972): "Capital Market Equilibrium with Restricted Borrowing," *Journal of Business*, 45, 444–454.

BLACK, F., AND M. SCHOLES (1973): "The Pricing of Options and Corporate Liabilities," *Journal of Political Economy*, 3, 637–654.

BLACKWELL, D. (1951): "Comparison of Experiments," in *Proceedings of the Second Berkeley Symposium on Mathematical Statistics and Probability*, ed. J. Neyman. University of California Press, Berkeley.

—— (1953): "Equivalent Comparisons of Experiments," *Annals of Mathematical Statistics*, 24, 265–272.

BOYD, S., AND L. VANDENBERGHE (2004): *Convex Optimization*. Cambridge University Press, Cambridge, United Kingdom.

BREEDEN, D. T. (1979): "An Intertemporal Asset Pricing Model with Stochastic Consumption and Investment Opportunities," *Journal of Financial Economics*, 7, 265–296.

BRÉMAUD, P. (1981): *Point Processes and Queues: Martingale Dynamics*. Springer-Verlag, New York.

BRENNAN, M. J., AND A. KRAUS (1978): "Necessary Conditions for Aggregation in Securities Markets," *Journal of Financial and Quantitative Analysis*, 13, 407–418.

CAMERER, C. F., G. LOEWENSTEIN, AND M. RABIN (eds.) (2004): *Advances in Behavioral Economics*. Princeton University Press, Princeton, NJ.

CAMPBELL, J. Y., AND J. H. COCHRANE (1999): "By Force of Habit: A Consumption-Based Explanation of Aggregate Stock Market Behavior," *Journal of Political Economy*, 107, 205–251.

CANDEAL, J. C., AND E. INDURÁIN (1995): "Homothetic and Weakly Homothetic Preferences," *Journal of Mathematical Economics*, 24, 147–158.

CASS, D., AND J. E. STIGLITZ (1970): "The Structure of Investor Preferences and Asset Returns, and Separability in Portfolio Allocation: A Contribution to the Pure Theory of Mutual Funds," *Journal of Economic Theory*, 2, 122–160.

CHAMBERLAIN, G. (1983a): "A Characterization of the Distributions That Imply Mean-Variance Utility Functions," *Journal of Economic Theory*, 29, 185–201.

—— (1983b): "Funds, Factors, and Diversification in Arbitrage Pricing Models," *Econometrica*, 50, 1305–1324.

CHAMBERLAIN, G., AND M. ROTHSCHILD (1983): "Arbitrage, Factor Structure, and Mean-Variance Analysis on Large Asset Markets," *Econometrica*, 50, 1281–1304.

CHAPMAN, D. A. (1998): "Habit Formation and Aggregate Consumption," *Econometrica*, 66, 1223–1230.

CHEN, H. (2007): "Macroeconomic Conditions and the Puzzles of Credit Spreads and Capital Structure," working paper.

CHEN, Y., T. F. COSIMANO, AND A. A. HIMONAS (2007): "By Force of Habit: An Exploration of Asset Pricing Models Using Analytic Methods," working paper.

CHEW, S. H., AND L. G. EPSTEIN (1989): "The Structure of Preferences and Attitudes toward the Timing of the Resolution of Uncertainty," *International Economic Review*, 30, 103–117.

CHIPMAN, J. S. (1974): "Homothetic Preferences and Aggregation," *Journal of Economic Theory*, 8, 26–38.

CHOW, Y. S., H. ROBBINS, AND D. SIEGMUND (1991): *The Theory of Optimal Stopping*. Dover Publications, Mineola, NY.

CHUNG, K. L. (1968): *A Course in Probability Theory*, 3rd ed. Academic Press, San Diego.

CONNOR, G. (1984): "A Unified Beta Pricing Theory," *Journal of Economic Theory*, 34, 13–31.

CONNOR, G., AND R. A. KORAJCZYK (1989): "An Intertemporal Equilibrium Beta Pricing Model," *Review of Financial Studies*, 2, 373–392.

CONSTANTINIDES, G. M. (1990): "Habit Formation: A Resolution of the Equity Premium Puzzle," *Journal of Political Economy*, 98, 519–543.

—— (2002): "Rational Asset Prices," *Journal of Finance*, 57, 1567–1591.

COX, J., AND C.-F. HUANG (1989): "Optimal Consumption and Portfolio Policies when Asset Prices Follow a Diffusion Process," *Journal of Economic Theory*, 49, 33–83.

COX, J., J. INGERSOLL, AND S. ROSS (1985): "An Intertemporal General Equilibrium Model of Asset Prices," *Econometrica*, 53, 363–384.

COX, J., AND S. ROSS (1976): "The Valuation of Options for Alternative Stochastic Processes," *Journal of Financial Economics*, 3, 145–166.

COX, J., S. ROSS, AND M. RUBINSTEIN (1979): "Option Pricing: A Simplified Approach," *Journal of Financial Economics*, 7, 229–263.

CROUZEIX, J.-P., AND P. O. LINDBERG (1986): "Additively Decomposed Quasiconvex Functions," *Mathematical Programming*, 35, 42–57.

DALANG, R., A. MORTON, AND W. WILLINGER (1990): "Equivalent Martingale Measures and No-Arbitrage in Stochastic Securities Market Models," *Stochastics and Stochastic Reports*, 29, 185–201.

DE FINETTI, B. (1937): "La Prévision: Ses Lois logiques, Ses sources subjectives," *Annales de l'Institute Henri Poincaré*, 7, 1–68.

DEBREU, G. (1952): "A Social Equilibrium Existence Theorem," *Proceedings fo the National Academy of Sciences*, 38, 886–893.

—— (1959): *Theory of Value*. Cowles Foundation Monograph, Yale University Press, New Haven.

—— (1983): *Mathematical Economics: Twenty Papers of Gerard Debreu*. Cambridge University Press, New York.

DEBREU, G., AND T. C. KOOPMANS (1982): "Additively Decomposed Quasiconvex Functions," *Mathematical Programming*, 24, 1–38.

DELBAEN, F., AND W. SCHACHERMAYER (1994): "A General Version of the Fundamental Theorem of Asset Pricing," *Mathematische Annalen*, 300, 463–520.

—— (1998): "The Fundamental Theorem of Asset Pricing for Unbounded Stochastic Processes," *Mathematische Annalen*, 312, 215–250.

—— (2006): *The Mathematics of Arbitrage*. Springer-Verlag, New York.

DELLACHERIE, C., AND P.-A. MEYER (1978–88): *Probabilities and Potential*. 3 vols. North Holland, New York.

DEMARZO, P., AND C. SKIADAS (1998): "Aggregation, Determinacy, and Informational Efficiency for a Class of Economies with Asymmetric Information," *Journal of Economic Theory*, 80, 123–152.

—— (1999): "On the Uniqueness of Fully Informative Rational Expectations Equilibria," *Economic Theory*, 13, 1–24.

DETEMPLE, J., AND F. ZAPATERO (1991): "Asset Prices in an Exchange Economy with Habit Formation," *Econometrica*, 59, 1633–1657.

DIAMOND, P. (1967): "The Role of the Stock Market in a General Equilibrium Model with Technological Uncertainty," *American Economic Review*, 57, 759–776.

DOOB, J. L. (1953): *Stochastic Processes*. John Wiley & Sons, New York.

DRÈZE, J. (1971): "Market Allocation under Uncertainty," *European Economic Review*, 15, 133–165.

DUDLEY, R. M. (2002): *Real Analysis and Probability*. Cambridge University Press, New York.

DUFFIE, D. (1991): "The Theory of Value in Security Markets," in *Handbook of Mathematical Economics*, vol. IV, ed. W. Hildenbrand and H. Sonnenschein, pp. 1615–1682. Elsevier, New York.

—— (2001): *Dynamic Asset Pricing Theory*, 3rd ed. Princeton University Press, Princeton, NJ.

DUFFIE, D., AND L. G. EPSTEIN (1992a): "Asset Pricing with Stochastic Differential Utility," *Review of Financial Studies*, 5, 411–436.

—— (1992b): "Stochastic Differential Utility," *Econometrica*, 60, 353–394.

DUFFIE, D., L. G. EPSTEIN, AND C. SKIADAS (1992): "Infinite Horizon Stochastic Differential Utility," published as an appendix to Duffie and Epstein, 1992b.

DUFFIE, D., P.-Y. GEOFFARD, AND C. SKIADAS (1994): "Efficient and Equilibrium Allocations with Stochastic Differential Utility," *Journal of Mathematical Economics*, 23, 133–146.

DUFFIE, D., AND C.-F. HUANG (1985): "Implementing Arrow-Debreu Equilibria by Continuous Trading of Few Long-Lived Securities," *Econometrica*, 53, 1337–1356.

DUFFIE, D., M. SCHRODER, AND C. SKIADAS (1997): "A Term Structure Model with Preferences for the Timing of Resolution of Uncertainty," *Economic Theory*, 9, 3–23.

DUFFIE, D., AND C. SKIADAS (1994): "Continuous-Time Security Pricing: A Utility Gradient Approach," *Journal of Mathematical Economics*, 23, 107–131.

DUFFIE, D., AND W. ZAME (1989): "The Consumption-Based Capital Asset Pricing Model," *Econometrica*, 57, 1279–1297.

DUMAS, B., R. UPPAL, AND T. WANG (2000): "Efficient Intertemporal Allocations with Recursive Utility," *Journal of Economic Theory*, 93, 240–259.

DYBVIG, P. (1983): "An Explicit Bound on Individual Assets' Deviations from APT Pricing in a Finite Economy," *Journal of Financial Economics*, 12, 483–496.

EKELAND, I., AND R. TÉMAM (1999): *Convex Analysis and Variational Problems*. SIAM, Philadelphia, PA.

EL KAROUI, N., S. PENG, AND M.-C. QUENEZ (2001): "A Dynamic Maximum Principle for the Optimization of Recursive Utilities under Constraints," *Annals of Applied Probability*, 11, 664–693.

ELLICKSON, B. (1993): *Competitive Equilibrium, Theory and Applications*. Cambridge University Press, New York.

ELLSBERG, D. (1961): "Risk, Ambiguity, and the Savage Axioms," *Quarterly Journal of Economics*, 75, 643–669.

EPSTEIN, L. G., AND S. E. ZIN (1989): "Substitution, Risk Aversion, and the Temporal Behavior of Consumption and Asset Returns: A Theoretical Framework," *Econometrica*, 57, 937–969.

—— (1991): "Substitution, Risk Aversion, and the Temporal Behavior of Consumption and Asset Returns: An Empirical Analysis," *Journal of Political Economy*, 99, 263–286.

FLEMING, W. H., AND H. M. SONER (1993): *Controlled Markov Processes and Viscosity Solutions*. Springer, New York.

GALE, D., AND A. MAS-COLELL (1975): "An Equilibrium Existence Theorem for a General Model without Ordered Preferences," *Journal of Mathematical Economics*, 2, 9–15.

GIOVANNINI, A., AND P. WEIL (1989): "Risk Aversion and Intertemporal Substitution in the Capital Asset Pricing Model," NBER working paper No. 2824, Cambridge, MA.

GOLLIER, C. (2001): *The Economics of Risk and Time*. MIT Press, Cambridge, MA.

GORMAN, W. (1953): "Community Preference Fields," *Econometrica*, 21, 63–80.

GRINBLATT, M., AND S. TITMAN (1983): "Factor Pricing in a Finite Economy," *Journal of Financial Economics*, 12, 497–507.

HANSEN, L., AND R. JAGANNATHAN (1991): "Implications of Security Market Data for Models of Dynamic Economies," *Journal of Political Economy*, 99, 225–262.

HARDY, G. H., J. LITTLEWOOD, AND G. PÓLYA (1929): "Some Simple Inequalities Satisfied by Convex Functions," *Messenger of Mathematics*, 58, 145–152.

—— (1934): *Inequalities*. Cambridge University Press, Cambridge, United Kingdom.

HARRISON, M. J., AND D. M. KREPS (1979): "Martingale and Arbitrage in Multiperiod Securities Markets," *Journal of Economic Theory*, 20, 381–408.

HART, O. D. (1974): "On the Existence of Equilibrium in a Securities Model," *Journal of Economic Theory*, 9, 293–311.

—— (1975): "On the Optimality of Equilibrium when the Market Structure Is Incomplete," *Journal of Economic Theory*, 22, 418–443.

HAUGH, M., AND L. KOGAN (2004): "Pricing American Options: A Dual Approach," *Operations Research*, 52, 258–270.

HAYASHI, T. (2005): "Intertemporal Substitution, Risk Aversion and Ambiguity Aversion," *Economic Theory*, 25, 933–956.

HERSTEIN, I. N., AND J. MILNOR (1953): "An Axiomatic Approach to Measurable Utility," *Econometrica*, 21, 291–297.

HILDENBRAND, W., AND A. P. KIRMAN (1988): *Equilibrium Analysis*. Elsevier, New York.

HUBERMAN, G. (1983): "A Simplified Approach to Arbitrage Pricing Theory," *Journal of Economic Theory*, 28, 1983–1991.

INGERSOLL J. E., JR. (1987): *Theory of Financial Decision Making*. Rowman & Littlefield, Totowa, NJ.

—— (1992): "Optimal Consumption and Portfolio Rules with Intertemporally Dependent Utility of Consumption," *Journal of Economic Dynamics and Control*, 16, 681–712.

JACOD, J., AND A. N. SHIRYAEV (2003): *Limit Theorems for Stochastic Processes*, 2nd ed. Springer-Verlag, Berlin.

JAMSHIDIAN, F. (2003): "Minimax Optimality of Bermudan and American Claims and Their Monte-Carlo Upper Bound Approximation," working paper.

JOHNSEN, T. H., AND J. B. DONALDSON (1985): "The Structure of Intertemporal Preferences under Uncertainty and Time Consistent Plans," *Econometrica*, 53, 1451–1458.

JOUINI, E., AND H. KALLAL (1995): "Martingales, Arbitrage, and Equilibrium in Securities Markets with Transaction Costs," *Journal of Economic Theory*, 66, 178–197.

KABANOV, Y. M., AND D. O. KRAMKOV (1994): "No-Arbitrage and Equivalent Martingale Measure: An Elementary Proof of the Harrison-Pliska Theorem," *Theory of Probability and Its Applications*, 39, 523–527.

KAHNEMAN, D., AND A. TVERSKY (1979): "Prospect Theory: An Analysis of Decisions under Risk," *Econometrica*, 47, 263–291.

——— (2000): *Choices, Values, and Frames*. Cambridge University Press, Cambridge, United Kingdom.

KALLENBERG, O. (2002): *Foundations of Modern Probability*. Springer, New York.

KANNAI, Y. (1974): "Approximation of Convex Preferences," *Journal of Mathematical Economics*, 1, 101–106.

——— (1977): "Concavifiability and Constructions of Concave Utility Functions," *Journal of Mathematical Economics*, 4, 1–56.

——— (1981): "Concave Utility Functions — Existence, Constructions, and Cardinality," in *Generalized Concavity and Optimization in Economics*, ed. by S. Shaible and W. T. Ziemba, pp. 543–611. Academic Press, New York.

KARATZAS, I. (1988): "On the Pricing of American Options," *Applied Mathematics and Optimization*, 17, 37–60.

KARATZAS, I., J. LEHOCZKY, AND S. SHREVE (1987): "Optimal Portfolio and Consumption Decisions for a 'Small Investor' on a Finite Horizon," *SIAM Journal of Control and Optimization*, 25, 1557–1586.

KARATZAS, I., AND S. SHREVE (1988): *Brownian Motion and Stochastic Calculus*. Springer Verlag, New York.

KIM, C. (1998): "Stochastic Dominance, Pareto Optimality, and Equilibrium Asset Pricing," *Review of Economic Studies*, 65, 341–356.

KLIBANOFF, P., AND E. OZDENOREN (2007): "Subjective Recursive Expected Utility," *Economic Theory*, 30, 49–87.

KOOPMANS, T. C. (1960): "Stationary Ordinal Utility and Impatience," *Econometrica*, 28, 287–309.

KRANTZ, D. H., R. D. LUCE, P. SUPPES, AND A. TVERSKY (1971): *Foundations of Measurement*, vol. I. Academic Press, San Diego.

KREPS, D., AND E. PORTEUS (1978): "Temporal Resolution of Uncertainty and Dynamic Choice Theory," *Econometrica*, 46, 185–200.

KREPS, D. M. (1981): "Arbitrage and Equilibrium in Economies with Infinitely Many Commodities," *Journal of Mathematical Economics*, 8, 15–35.

——— (1988): *Notes on the Theory of Choice*. Westview Press, Boulder, CO.

LAZRAK, A., AND M. C. QUENEZ (2003): "A Generalized Stochastic Differential Utility," *Mathematics of Operations Research*, 28, 154–180.

LINTNER, J. (1965): "The Valuation of Risk Assets and the Selection of Risky Investments in Stock Portfolios and Capital Budgets," *Review of Economics and Statistics*, 47, 13–37.

——— (1969): "The Aggregation of Investors' Diverse Judgments and Preferences in Purely Competitive Security Markets," *Journal of Financial and Quantitative Analysis*, 4, 347–400.

LIPSTER, R., AND A. SHIRYAEV (2001): *Statistics of Random Variables, I General Theory*, 2nd ed. Springer Verlag, New York.

LUCAS, R.E.B. (1978): "Asset Prices in an Exchange Economy," *Econometrica*, 46, 1429–1446.

LUCE, R. D., AND D. H. KRANTZ (1971): "Conditional Expected Utility," *Econometrica*, 39, 253–271.

LUENBERGER, D. G. (1969): *Optimization by Vector Space Methods*. Wiley, New York.

MACCHERONI, F., M. MARINACCI, AND A. RUSTICHINI (2006): "Ambiguity Aversion, Robustness, and the Variational Representation of Preferences," *Econometrica*, 74, 1447–1498.

MACHINA, M. J. (1982): " 'Expected Utility' Analysis without the Independence Axiom," *Econometrica*, 50, 277–324.

MACHINA, M. J., AND W. S. NEILSON (1987): "The Ross Characterization of Risk Aversion: Strengthening and Extension," *Econometrica*, 55, 1139–1149.

MAGILL, M., AND M. QUINZII (1996): *Theory of Incomplete Markets*. MIT Press, Cambridge, MA.

MAGILL, M., AND W. SHAFER (1991): "Incomplete Markets," in *Handbook of Mathematical Economics*, vol. IV, ed. W. Hildenbrand and H. Sonnenschein, pp. 1523–1614. Elsevier, New York.

MARKOWITZ, H. (1952): "Portfolio Selection," *Journal of Finance*, 7, 77–91.

—— (1959): *Portfolio Selection*. John Wiley & Sons, New York.

MAS-COLELL, A. (1974a): "Continuous and Smooth Consumers: Approximation Theorems," *Journal of Economic Theory*, 8, 305–336.

—— (1974b): "An Equilibrium Existence Theorem without Complete or Transitive Preferences," *Journal of Mathematical Economics*, 1, 237–246.

—— (1985): *The Theory of General Economic Equilibrium*. Cambridge University Press, New York.

MAS-COLELL, A., M. D. WHINSTON, AND J. R. GREEN (1995): *Microeconomic Theory*. Oxford University Press, Oxford.

MCKEAN, H. (1965): "Appendix: Free Boundary Problem for the Heat Equation Arising from a Problem in Mathematical Economics," *Industrial Management Review*, 6, 32–39.

MCKENZIE, L. W. (1954): "On Equilibrium in Graham's Model of World Trade and Other Competitive Systems," *Econometrica*, 22, 147–161.

—— (1955): "Competitive Equilibrium with Dependent Consumer Preferences," in *Proceedings of the Second Symposium in Linear Programming*, ed. H. A. Antosiewicz, pp. 277–294. National Bureau of Standards, Washington, DC.

—— (1959): "On the Existence of General Equilibrium for a Competitive Market," *Econometrica*, 27, 54–71.

MEHRA, R., AND E. C. PRESCOTT (1985): "The Equity Premium: A Puzzle," *Journal of Monetary Economics*, 15, 145–161.

MERTON, R. C. (1969): "Lifetime Portfolio Selection under Uncertainty: The Continuous Time Case," *Review of Economics and Statistics*, 51, 247–257.

—— (1971): "Optimum Consumption and Portfolio Rules in a Continuous-Time Model," *Journal of Economic Theory*, 3, 373–413. Erratum 6 (1973): 213–214.

—— (1972): "An Analytical Derivation of the Efficient Portfolio Frontier," *Journal of Financial and Quantitative Analysis*, 7, 1851–1872.

—— (1973a): "An Intertemporal Capital Asset Pricing Model," *Econometrica*, 41, 867–887.

—— (1973b): "The Theory of Rational Option Pricing," *Bell Journal of Economics and Management Science*, 4, 141–183.

MILNE, F. (1979): "Consumer Preference, Linear Demand Functions and Aggregation in Competitive Asset Markets," *Review of Economic Studies*, 46, 407–417.

—— (1988): "Arbitrage and Diversification in a General Equilibrium Asset Economy," *Econometrica*, 56, 815–840.

MODIGLIANI, F., AND M. MILLER (1958): "The Cost of Capital, Corporate Finance, and the Theory of Investment," *American Economic Review*, 48, 261–297.

MONTEIRO, P. K. (1999): "Quasiconcavity and the Kernel of a Separable Utility," *Economic Theory*, 13, 221–227.

MOSSIN, J. (1966): "Equilibrium in a Capital Asset Market," *Econometrica*, 34, 768–783.

MÜLLER, A., AND D. STOYAN (2002): *Comparison Methods for Stochastic Models and Risks*. Wiley, New York.

NAKAMURA, Y. (1990): "Subjective Expected Utility with Non-Additive Probabilities on Finite State Spaces," *Journal of Economic Theory*, 51, 346–366.

NARENS, L. (1985): *Abstract Measurement Theory*. MIT Press, Cambridge, MA.

NEGISHI, T. (1960): "Welfare Economics and Existence of an Equilibrium for a Competitive Economy," *Metroeconomica*, 12, 92–97.

OBSTFELD, M. (1994): "Risk-Taking, Global Diversification, and Growth," *American Economic Review*, 84, 1310–1329.

ØKSENDAL, B. (2003): *Stochastic Differential Equations*, 6th ed. Springer, New York.

POLLAK, R. A. (1970): "Habit Formation and Dynamic Demand Functions," *Journal of Political Economy*, 78, 745–763.

—— (1971): "Additive Utility Functions and Linear Engel Curves," *Review of Economic Studies*, 38, 401–414.

PRATT, J. W. (1964): "Risk Aversion in the Small and in the Large," *Econometrica*, 32, 122–136.

PROTTER, P. E. (2004): *Stochastic Integration and Differential Equations*, 2nd ed. Springer Verlag, New York.

RABIN, M. (2000): "Risk Aversion and Expected-Utility Theory: A Calibration Theorem," *Econometrica*, 68, 1281–1292.

RAMSEY, F. P. (1926): "Truth and Probability," in *Studies in Subjective Probability (1980)*, ed. H. E. Kyburg Jr. and H. E. Smokler. Robert E. Krieger Publishing Company, New York.

REISMAN, H. (1988): "A General Approach to the Arbitrage Pricing Theory (APT)," *Econometrica*, 56, 473–476.

RENDLEMAN, R. J., Jr., AND B. J. BARTTER (1979): "Two-State Option Pricing," *Journal of Finance*, 34, 1093–1110.

REVUZ, D., AND M. YOR (1999): *Continuous Martingales and Brownian Motion*, 3rd ed. Springer, New York.

ROCKAFELLAR, R. T. (1970): *Convex Analysis*. Princeton University Press, Princeton, NJ.

ROGERS, L.C.G. (2002): "Monte Carlo Valuation of American Options," *Mathematical Finance*, 12, 271–286.

ROLL, R. (1977): "A Critique of the Asset Pricing Theory's Tests; Part I: On Past and Potential Testability of the Theory," *Journal of Financial Economics*, 4, 129–176.

——— (1978): "Ambiguity when Performance Is Measured by the Securities Market Line," *Journal of Finance*, 33, 1051–1069.

ROSS, S. A. (1976a): "The Arbitrage Theory of Capital Asset Pricing," *Journal of Economic Theory*, 13, 341–360.

——— (1976b): "Risk, Return and Arbitrage," in *Risk and Return in Finance*, ed. I. Friend and J. Bicksler. Ballinger, Cambridge, MA.

——— (1978a): "Mutual Fund Separation in Financial Theory: The Separating Distributions," *Journal of Economic Theory*, 17, 254–286.

——— (1978b): "A Simple Approach to the Valuation of Risky Streams," *Journal of Business*, 51, 453–475.

——— (1981): "Some Stronger Measures of Risk Aversion in the Small and the Large with Applications," *Econometrica*, 49, 621–638.

ROTHSCHILD, M., AND J. E. STIGLITZ (1970): "Increasing Risk: I. A Definition," *Journal of Economic Theory*, 2, 225–243.

——— (1971): "Increasing Risk: II. Its Economic Consequences," *Journal of Economic Theory*, 3, 66–84.

——— (1972): "Addendum to 'Increasing Risk: I. A Definition'," *Journal of Economic Theory*, 5, 306.

ROYDEN, H. L. (1988): *Real Analysis*. Macmillan, New York.

ROZEN, K. (2008): "Foundations of Intrinsic Habit Formation," Cowles Foundation Discussion Paper, No. 1642, Yale University.

RUBINSTEIN, M. (1974): "An Aggregation Theorem for Securities Markets," *Journal of Financial Economics*, 1, 225–244.

——— (1976): "The Valuation of Uncertain Income Streams and the Pricing of Options," *Bell Journal of Economics*, 7, 405–425.

RYDER, H. E., AND G. M. HEAL (1973): "Optimum Growth with Intertemporally Dependent Preferences," *Review of Economic Studies*, 40, 1–43.

SAVAGE, L. J. (1954): *The Foundations of Statistics*. Wiley, New York. Reprint Dover Publications, New York, 1972.

SCHACHERMAYER, W. (1992): "A Hilbert-Space Proof of the Fundamental Theorem of Asset Pricing," *Insurance Mathematics and Economics*, 11, 249–257.

SCHRODER, M., AND C. SKIADAS (1999): "Optimal Consumption and Portfolio Selection with Stochastic Differential Utility," *Journal of Economic Theory*, 89, 68–126.

—— (2002): "An Isomorphism between Asset Pricing Models with and without Linear Habit Formation," *Review of Financial Studies*, 15, 1189–1221.

—— (2003): "Optimal Lifetime Consumption-Portfolio Strategies under Trading Constraints and Generalized Recursive Preferences," *Stochastic Processes and Their Applications*, 108, 155–202.

—— (2005): "Lifetime Consumption-Portfolio Choice under Trading Constraints and Nontradeable Income," *Stochastic Processes and Their Applications*, 115, 1–30.

—— (2008): "Optimality and State Pricing in Constrained Financial Markets with Recursive Utility under Continuous and Discontinuous Information," *Mathematical Finance*, 18, 199–238.

SELDEN, L. (1978): "A New Representation of Preferences over 'Certain × Uncertain' Consumption Pairs: The 'Ordinal Certainty Equivalent' Hypothesis," *Econometrica*, 46, 1045–1060.

SHAFER, W., AND H. SONNENSCHEIN (1975): "Equilibrium in Abstract Economies without Ordered Preferences," *Journal of Mathematical Economics*, 2, 345–348.

SHAFER, W. J. (1974): "The Nontransitive Consumer," *Econometrica*, 42, 913–919.

SHARPE, W. F. (1963): "A Simplified Model for Portfolio Analysis," *Management Science*, 9, 277–293.

—— (1964): "Capital Asset Prices: A Theory of Market Equilibrium under Conditions of Risk," *Journal of Finance*, 19, 425–442.

—— (1978): *Investments*. Prentice Hall, Englewood Cliffs, NJ.

SHERMAN, S. (1951): "On a Theorem of Hardy, Littlewood, Polya and Blackwell," *Proceedings of the National Academy of Science*, 37, 826–831.

SINGLETON, K. J. (2006): *Empirical Dynamic Asset Pricing*. Princeton University Press, Princeton, NJ.

SKIADAS, C. (1997): "Subjective Probability under Additive Aggregation of Conditional Preferences," *Journal of Economic Theory*, 76, 242–271.

—— (1998): "Recursive Utility and Preferences for Information," *Economic Theory*, 12, 293–312.

—— (2003): "Robust Control and Recursive Utility," *Finance and Stochastics*, 7, 475–489.

—— (2008a): "Dynamic Portfolio Choice and Risk Aversion," in *Handbooks in OR & MS*, vol. 15, ed. J. R. Birge and V. Linetsky, chap. 19, pp. 789–843. Elsevier, New York.

—— (2008b): "Smooth Ambiguity Aversion Toward Small Risks and Continuous-Time Recursive Utility," working paper, Kellogg School of Management, Northwestern University.

SONNENSCHEIN, H. (1971): "Demand Theory without Transitive Preferences, with Applications to the Theory of Competitive Equilibrium," in *Preferences, Utility and Demand*, ed. J. S. Chipman, L. Hurwicz, M. K. Richter, and H. F. Sonnenschein. Harcourt Brace Jovanovich, New York.

STEELE, J. M. (2001): *Stochastic Calculus and Financial Applications*. Springer-Verlag, New York.

STEIN, C. (1951): *Notes on the Comparison of Experiments*. University of Chicago, Chicago.

STOER, J., AND C. WITZGALL (1970): *Convexity and Optimization in Finite Dimensions*. Springer-Verlag, Berlin, Germany.

STRASSEN, V. (1965): "The Existence of Probability Measures with Given Marginals," *Annals of Mathematical Statistics*, 36, 423–439.

STROTZ, R. H. (1957): "Myopia and Inconsistency in Dynamic Utility Maximization," *Review of Economic Studies*, 23, 165–180.

SUNDARESAN, S. M. (1989): "Intertemporally Dependent Preferences and the Volatility of Consumption and Wealth," *Review of Financial Studies*, 2, 73–89.

SVENSSON, L. (1989): "Portfolio Choice with Non-Expected Utility in Continuous Time," *Economic Letters*, 30, 313–317.

TOBIN, J. (1958): "Liquidity Preference as Behavior Towards Risk," *Review of Economic Studies*, 25, 65–86.

TREYNOR, J. L. (1962): "Toward a Theory of Market Value of Risky Assets," in *Asset Pricing and Portfolio Performance*, ed. R. A. Korajczyk, pp. 15–22. Risk Books, London, 1999.

TVERSKY, A., AND D. KAHNEMAN (1981): "The Framing of Decisions and the Psychology of Choice," *Science*, 211, 453–458.

VOHRA, R. V. (2005): *Advanced Mathematical Economics*. Routledge, London.

VON NEUMANN, J., AND O. MORGENSTERN (1944): *Theory of Games and Economic Behavior*. Princeton University Press, Princeton, NJ.

WAKKER, P. P. (1984): "Cardinal Coordinate Independence for Expected Utility," *Journal of Mathematical Psychology*, 28, 110–117.

—— (1988): "The Algebraic versus the Topological Approach to Additive Representations," *Journal of Mathematical Psychology*, 32, 421–435.

—— (1989): *Additive Representations of Preferences*. Kluwer, Dordrecht, The Netherlands.

WALRAS, L. (1874): *Eléments d'économie pure*. Corbaze, Lausanne. English translation: *Elements of Pure Economics*, R. D. Irwin, Homewood, IL (1954).

WANG, T. (2003): "Conditional Preferences and Updating," *Journal of Economic Theory*, 108, 286–321.

WEIL, P. (1989): "The Equity Premium Puzzle and the Risk-Free Rate Puzzle," *Journal of Monetary Economics*, 24, 401–421.

—— (1990): "Non-Expected Utility in Macroeconomics," *Quarterly Journal of Economics*, 105, 29–42.

WERNER, J. (1997): "Diversification and Equilibrium in Securities Markets," *Journal of Economic Theory*, 75, 89–103.

WILLIAMS, D. (1991): *Probability with Martingales*. Cambridge University Press, Cambridge, United Kingdom.

WILSON, R. (1968): "The Theory of Syndicates," *Econometrica*, 36, 119–132.

YAARI, M. E. (1969): "Some Remarks on Measures of Risk Aversion and Their Uses," *Journal of Economic Theory*, 1, 315–329.

—— (1977): "A Note on Separability and Quasiconcavity," *Econometrica*, 45, 1183–1186.

YAN, J. A. (1980): "Caracterisation d'une class d'ensembles convexes de L^1 ou H^1," *Lecture Notes in Mathematics*, 784, 220–222.

YONG, J., AND X. Y. ZHOU (1999): *Stochastic Controls: Hamiltonian Systems and HJB Equations*. Springer-Verlag, New York.

ZEIDLER, E. (1985): *Nonlinear Functional Analysis and Its Applications III: Variational Methods and Optimization*. Springer-Verlag, New York.

Index

341

state-price process, 137
state-price vector, 7, 137
Stein's lemma, 51
stochastic dominance, 120
stochastic exponential, 314
stochastic logarithm, 314
stochastic process, 301
stochastically independent, 297, 298
stopping time, 300
strict concavity, 212
strictly positive probability, 12, 286
strictly positive process, 301
strongly more risk averse, 128
subalgebra, 289
subgraph, 275
superdifferential, 275, 276
supergradient, 275
supporting hyperplane theorem, 274
supporting vector, 270, 274
synthetic contract, 15, 148

Taylor series, 117
terminal spot, 299
three-way covariation process, 316
TI agent, 69
TI formulation, 240
TI Kreps-Porteus utility, 218
TI preference, 69, 77
TI utility, 217
time, 135, 299
trade, 4, 137
traded cash flow, 4, 137
traded contract, 15, 142
traded payoff, 29
traded return, 17
trading constraints, 19, 191

trading policy, 233
trading strategy, 145
transitive weak preference, 73
translation, 261
translation-invariant preference, 69, 77
translation-invariant utility, 217
trivial algebra, 289
two-fund separation, 34

unbiased, 283
uncorrelated, 287
uniform filtration, 308
union, 285
unit discount bond, 30
unit EIS, 226, 239
unit relative risk aversion, 224, 226, 239
utility, 72
utility gradient, 80
utility gradient density, 208
utility process, 197
utility representation, 72, 73
utility superdifferential, 81

value function, 252
value process, 142
variance, 12
variance-averse preferences, 60
variance-covariance matrix, 31
vector, 259
vector space, 259
vector subspace, 260

weak preference, 73
wealth process, 231, 233

zero-mean martingale, 304